Printed in the United States
By Bookmasters

T0214319

Communications
in Computer and Information Science   1108

Commenced Publication in 2007
Founding and Former Series Editors:
Phoebe Chen, Alfredo Cuzzocrea, Xiaoyong Du, Orhun Kara, Ting Liu,
Krishna M. Sivalingam, Dominik Ślęzak, Takashi Washio, Xiaokang Yang,
and Junsong Yuan

More information about this series at http://www.springer.com/series/7899

Kamel Smaïli (Ed.)

Arabic Language Processing

From Theory to Practice

7th International Conference, ICALP 2019
Nancy, France, October 16–17, 2019
Proceedings

 Springer

Editor
Kamel Smaïli
University of Lorraine
Nancy, France

ISSN 1865-0929 ISSN 1865-0937 (electronic)
Communications in Computer and Information Science
ISBN 978-3-030-32958-7 ISBN 978-3-030-32959-4 (eBook)
https://doi.org/10.1007/978-3-030-32959-4

This Springer imprint is published by the registered company Springer Nature Switzerland AG
The registered company address is: Gewerbestrasse 11, 6330 Cham, Switzerland

Preface

This book constitutes the refereed proceedings of the 7th International Conference on Arabic Language Processing ICALP 2019 (ex-CITALA), held in Nancy, France, in October 2019. The 21 full papers presented were carefully reviewed and selected from about 40 submissions. 60% of the articles have been reviewed by three reviewers and the others by four reviewers using the double-blind review process.

The conference highlighted new approaches related to the Arabic language from basic theories to applications. All the branches of natural language processing (NLP) related to Arabic spoken or text language processing constituted the main kernel of ICALP 2019. The papers covered the following topics: modern standard Arabic, sentiment analysis and opinions mining, code-switching, deep learning, and other aspects of NLP. The volume is organized in four parts: the first is devoted to Arabic dialects and sentiment analysis, an area for which there are several challenges; the second part contains papers focusing on neural techniques for text and speech; the third part comprises papers describing different aspects of modeling modern standard Arabic; and the last one is dedicated to the resources that play an important role in NLP.

October 2019   Kamel Smaïli

Organization

General Chair

Kamel Smaïli   University of Lorraine, France

Program Committee Chair

Kamel Smaïli   University of Lorraine, France

Steering Committee

Karima Abidi	University of Lorraine, France
Karim Bouzoubaa	University of Mohammed V, Morocco
Olivia Brenner	University of Lorraine, France
Joseph Di Martino	University of Lorraine, France
Abdelhamid EL Jihad	University of Mohammed V, Morocco
Abdelfettah Hamdani	University of Mohammed V, Morocco
Abdelmonaime Lachkar	Université Sidi Mohamed Ben Abdellah, Morocco
David Langlois	University of Lorraine, France
Azzedine Lazrek	Université Cadi Ayyad, Morocco
Abdelhak Lekhouaja	Université Mohammed Ier, Morocco
Azzedine Mazroui	Université Mohammed Ier, Morocco
Mohamed-Amine Menacer	University of Lorraine, France

Program Committee

Ahmed Ali	Qatar Computing Research Institute (QCRI), Qatar
Hassina Aliane	Centre de Recherche sur l'Information Scientifique et Technique, Algeria
Frédéric Béchet	University of Aix Marseille Université, France
Almoataz Bellahal-Said	Cairo University, Egypt
Laurent Besacier	University of Grenoble, France
Karim Bouzoubaa	University of Mohammed V, Morocco
Violetta Cavalli-Sforza	Al Akhawayn University, Morocco
Khalid Choukri	European Language Resource Association (ELRA), France
Kareem Darwish	Qatar Computing Research Institute, Qatar
Joseph Di Martino	Loria, University of Lorraine, France
Mona Diab	George Washington University, USA
Abdelhamid El Jihad	University of Mohammed V, Morocco
Mahmoud El-Haj	School of Computing and Communications Lancaster University, UK

Sponsors

Google
University of Lorraine
Loria: Laboratoire lorrain de recherche en informatique et ses applications
ELRA: European Language Resources Association
SIGUL: Special Interest Group: Under-resourced Languages
IDMC: Institut des Sciences Digitales
OLKI: Open Language and Knowledge for Citizens
ALESM: The Arabic Language Engineering Society in Morocco

Contents

Modeling Modern Standard Arabic

Resources: Analysis, Disambiguation and Evaluation

Arabic Dialects and Sentiment Analysis

Generating a Lexicon for the Hijazi Dialect in Arabic

Fatimah Abdullah Alqahtani[1,2(✉)] and Mark Sanderson[1]

[1] Computer Science, School of Science, RMIT University, Melbourne, Australia
{fatimah.alqahtani,mark.sanderson}@rmit.edu.au
[2] College of Computer Science and Information Systems,
Jazan University, Jazan, Kingdom of Saudi Arabia

Abstract. We present a methodology for creating a lexicon for a low-resource Arabic dialect in Saudi Arabia: Hijazi. We show the differences between the Hijazi dialect and Modern Standard Arabic. We annotate articles and tweets using recruited native speakers. We create a lexicon of Hijazi adapted from two resources: Sebawai and Quranic Arabic Corpus. The lexicon is created both manually and automatically by using Hijazi morphology. We detail the methodology to build this lexicon and present results of an evaluation of the corpus formation process.

Keywords: Hijazi dialect · Lexicon generation

1 Introduction

Arabic dialects are a set of linguistic characteristics that belong to a particular environment [1], and are often used in informal daily communication. An increased awareness of the existence and functioning of these dialects has emerged due to the influence of social media, where these dialects are now written.

The Egyptian, Levantine, and Moroccan dialects as well as MSA are considered high-resource; however, others, including the Hijazi Dialect are low-resource [2]. The lack of resources has created an obstacle for researching Hijazi. A dialect of western cities (Makkah, Madinah, Jeddah and Taif) in Saudi Arabia, Hijazi is spoken in the second most populous region[1]. Hijazi has two varieties: urban and rural, and this study focuses on the urban variety. To the best of our knowledge, no one has built resources for Hijazi.

We applied a methodology to create a Hijazi lexicon in which potential Hijazi words were annotated through a comparison with an MSA lexicon. Then, the Hijazi words were analyzed using an approach employed by Darwish, Sajjad and Mubarak [3] for Egyptian dialects to automatically generate an expanded Hijazi word list. We also annotated 3,000 tweets to identify Hijazi content. Our work addresses the following research question: Can a methodology used to create a High-resource Egyptian lexicon be adapted to create a Low-resource Hijazi lexicon?

---

[1] 10,090,256 people in 2015 - http://www.cdsi.gov.sa.

© Springer Nature Switzerland AG 2019
K. Smaïli (Ed.): ICALP 2019, CCIS 1108, pp. 3–17, 2019.
https://doi.org/10.1007/978-3-030-32959-4_1

Section 2 of the research reviews relevant work, Sect. 3 shows the approach use to build Hijazi lexicon. In Sect. 4 Standard and Hijazi Arabic are compared. The approach to generating the Hijazi dialect is presented in Sect. 5. Section 6 describes our evaluation. The paper concludes and gives insight into future work in Sect. 7.

2 Related Work

2.1 Creating Resources in Arabic Dialects

Prior Arabic Dialect corpus building work focused on building monolingual or parallel corpora. Methods vary in the building with most using recruited native speakers.

The COLABA project collected resources from Arabic blogs for four dialects: Egyptian, Iraqi, Levantine, and Moroccan [4]. For harvesting, Diab, Habash, Rambow, Altantawy and Benajiba [4] asked 25 native speakers to generate 40 dialectal queries containing words with multiple orthographies that cover social issues, religion, and politics. The authors asked annotators to translate the queries to MSA and English. The queries were used to extract matching blog data from the web. The researchers created a tool to process and manage the data harvested from the blog.

Harrat, Meftouh and Smaili [5] created a parallel corpus for MSA, Algiers, Annaba, Tunisian, Palestinian, and Syrian. They collected around 2.5K Algiers dialect sentences from transcribed films and TV shows, which were then translated to MSA and Annaba by a native speaker. In the same way, the researchers collected the corpus of Annaba dialect for approximately 3.9K sentences from the transcribed recordings of the daily life of some people of Annaba, which were then translated to MSA and Algiers. Finally, they translated a whole collection of MSA around 6.4K sentences to Tunisian, Palestinian and Syrian by native translators. The Dialect and MSA translation were conducted by twenty-five persons in total for free.

The Gumar Corpus is a large-scale collection of Gulf Arabic consisting of 100 million words from over 1,200 novels published online [6]. The researchers annotated the corpus manually into a sub-dialect of Gulf Arabic, which includes the Saudi, UAE, Bahraini, Qatari, and Omani dialects. Annotations were at the document level. They found that names given to the characters, cities, and event names in the novel helped determine the dialect. The researchers extracted features and rules for these dialects to understand the morphology and to build tools.

Most recently, there is the Curras corpus for the Palestinian dialect [7] that was manually annotated by two annotators for one year. The researchers of this study identified 56,700 tokens in 190 documents compiled from resources such as Facebook, Twitter, blogs, forums, Palestinian stories, Palestinian terms, and scripts from Palestinian TV shows. The researchers used the DIWAN Dialect Word Annotation tool [8] and the MADAMIRA [9] morphological analyzer tool for MSA and Egyptian. A quantitative evaluation was performed for three of the documents, which consist 1,529 tokens by two annotators, who met to review and discuss their annotations. Their agreement was measured by Kappa, and the outcome was almost perfect desirable for different tags (e.g., POS, stem, prefix, etc.).

Darwish, Sajjad and Mubarak [3] employed manual and automatic approaches to collect three lexicons of Egyptian Dialect. In the manual approach, they asked a linguist to extract 1,300 high frequency Egyptian words (MAN) from the Egyptian side of the LDC2012T09 corpus [10] while in the automatic approach, they applied Egyptian morphology rules to generate verbs from Sebawai Arabic roots [11]. The rules added prefixes and suffixes such as pronouns and negation that are compatible with the Egyptian dialect. The rules also substituted letters to change a word to the Egyptian dialect. Filters were applied to the verb and letter substitutions to remove words that were MSA. An MSA word list was drawn from 63 million Arabic tweets and Aljazirah articles.

Mubarak and Darwish [12] presented a multi-dialect corpus from Twitter for Saudi, Egyptian, Iraqi, Lebanese, Syrian, and Algerian. They collected 92 million tweets, which had a user location. The user location of tweets was assigned to one of the Arab countries in GeoNames, which indicate the location in each country. Then, the researchers manually reviewed the location, which they mapped with GeoNames. Also, they manually tried to map locations, which were non-matching with GeoNames. Also, they collected all n-gram words that occurred at least three times in AOC, Aljazeera interview articles, and the GigaWord corpus, which is a text archive of Arabic news sources by Linguistic Data Consortium LDC. These n-gram words were manually labelled by a native Arabic speaker, knowledgeable in different dialects to specify if it was a dialect word and to which dialect it belonged. This resulted in around 2,500 dialect words. The researchers filtered the tweets as dialect tweets by the n-gram dialect words and they got 6.5 million dialect tweets based on the following assumption *"if a sentence contained one of these n-grams, then the sentence is dialectal"*. They used crowdsourcing to evaluate 100 randomly extracted tweets per dialect. They asked crowdsourcing workers, who were from the same countries from which the tweet was issued, to judge whether the tweet dialect coincides in their country. They were not able to get judges for Qatar and Bahrain.

Overall, the reviewed literature shows that many contributions have been made to Egyptian, Levantine and North Africa dialects, also, sub-dialects of Levantine such as Syrian, Palestinian, Jordanian and Lebanese.

2.2 Creating Resources in Low-Resource Languages

Different means of collecting and generating data for low-resource languages have been tried. In 2011, Outahajala, Zenkouar and Rosso [13] manually built a corpus for the Amazighe language: a low-resource language in Morocco, Algeria, Tunisia, Libya, and areas of Egypt. They extracted text from various sources such as the Royal Institute for Amazighe Culture's newsletter and website as well as three primary school textbooks. The corpus was manually annotated by a team of four annotators. It consisted of different POS features to the tokenized Amazighe texts. Three linguists chose random texts and evaluated them. The annotator agreement was 94.89%.

By drawing on the concept of manual tagging, Ramrakhiyani and Majumder [14] provided a corpus of temporal expression recognition in Hindi called ILTIMEX2012. There were three temporal expression classes: data time, a time or duration expression; a frequency, which is a date or time expression; or period, which is a frequency expression. The corpus is composed of 300 documents of a set of articles from the

Hindi newspaper, The FIRE 2011 Hindi corpus [15]. Each document has more than 500 words. ILTIMEX2012 was manually labelled by using the General Architecture for Text Engineering (GATE) tool annotation module. 514 periods, 110 frequency, and 1295 date-time for temporal expressions were included in the corpus. This corpus was used for Hindi temporal expressions identification and classification.

Bird, Gawne, Gelbart and McAlister [16] applied an Android application, which supports recording of speech directly [17]. When finishing a recording, users were asked to add metadata such as name, language, and image. Users could segment the audio and write a transcription and translation. The researchers used the application for collecting audio from Brazil and Nepal. They collected 100k words from 10 h of audio. A challenge with this approach is lack of the participation and scarcity of electricity in the village which is important to charge the device. It was noted in the study that the collection of data for these low-resources languages appeared firstly by collecting speech, which shows that there is no written source for these languages. Also, the crowdsourcing and human approaches consider the conventional method for collecting and building the data for low-resource languages.

For Hijazi, Alahmadi [18] collected more than 30 Hijazi words by asking native Hijazi speakers to give the correct dialect word for an image.

3   Approach

In defining the methodology for our problem of building a Hijazi corpus, we considered our situation. There are no Hijazi language resources available and only a limited amount of edited Hijazi text is available online. However, there is a notable amount of social media content written in Hijazi. Therefore, we examined an approach to building a corpus using a combination of manual and automatic techniques that is adapted from an approach by Darwish, Sajjad and Mubarak [3]. The approach requires access to an initial Hijazi word list, a set of morphological rules, and a list of Arabic word roots. There are two phases of the methodology: corpus creation and evaluation.

Table 1. The 10 most frequent words

Words	Frequency	Source
Ally اللي which	1168	Hijazi
yA يا	597	MSA
All~h الله Allah	435	MSA
E$An عشان because	410	Hijazi
hAdy هادي This	299	Hijazi
hdA هدا This is	258	Hijazi
kdh كده like this	283	Hijazi
Ay$ ايش What	229	Hijazi
wAlly واللي And that	188	Hijazi

We used different resource to build the Hijazi list: articles, dictionaries and building from roots. We found a collection of Hijazi articles in Okaz news[2] which is read in western Saudi Arabia; 156 Hijazi articles were collected manually from February 2011 to September 2014. The set contained 59,225 tokens. An analysis of the most frequent words found most were Hijazi pronouns, as shown in Table 1.

The overview of our process is to pre-process the list of Hijazi words (see Fig. 1 (a)), which involves removing MSA stop words. Next, we check if each remaining word matches to a set of Hijazi verbs rules (Sect. 4.2), if there is a match, the word is considered Hijazi and is added to the MANHijazi list. If there is not a match, the words are compared with three MSA dictionaries: Maajim[3], Alwased,[4] and Alsahah[5], if the word is not found in these dictionaries, then the words is also considered Hijazi and is added to the MANHijazi list.

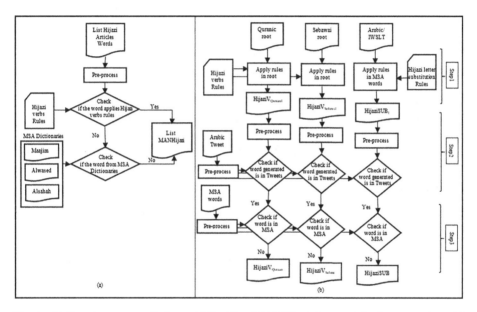

Fig. 1. (a) Creating a manually formed Hijazi list (MANHijazi) from articles by comparing with MSA dictionaries and Hijazi rules, (b) Creating three different list of Hijazi then filter.

Figure 1(b) illustrates the steps of the automatic approach to adding to the list in MANHijazi. First, a set of roots drawn from the two sources: 10,406 from the Sebawai system [11] and 943 verb roots from the Quran. Each root was transformed into multiple verbs by applying a set of Hijazi verbs rules to form two lists of words:

---

[2] http://www.okaz.com.sa.

[3] http://www.maajim.com/dictionary/.

[4] http://shamela.ws/browse.php/book-7028.

[5] http://www.almaany.com.

HijaziV$_{Quraan}$, and HijaziV$_{Sebawai}$. We used the Quran root because it has a real verb root while Sebawai has a large number of roots that are automatically generated. The coverage of this latter set is greater, but it is noisy because of the roots are extracted from different words such as the verbs, nouns and adjectives. In addition, MSA to Hijazi letter substitution rules were applied to a list of MSA words from the Arabic side of the English/Arabic parallel corpus from the International Workshop on Spoken Language Translation (Arabic/IWSLT) 2013 to generate the list Hijazi$_{SUB1}$.

In the next step, the words in the three lists were compared to a list of three million words drawn from Arabic tweets, which were pre-processed using the AraNLP tool [19]. Words that matched were assumed to be some form of Arabic. In the final step, the remaining words in the three lists were compared against a corpus of MSA words OSAC[6] [20], which contains 18,183,511 tokens. Those words that did not match against the corpus were assumed to be Hijazi. We evaluated the lists of words intrinsically by manually investigating a random sample of words drawn from each of the lists.

4   Hijazi Dialect

We describe the basic syntax of the Urban Hijazi Dialect by contrasting it with MSA. We focus on verbs and letter substitutions because these are where the main differences between MSA and Hijazi are found. We examine irregular structures, such as lexical and independent pronouns, and regular structures such as verb and letter substitution.

4.1   Irregular

Lexical. Three past papers – [21–23] – described three differences between the lexicon words in MSA and Hijazi.

1. Lexicon words in Hijazi which have the same meaning in MSA but with different letters. For example, (Bridge, كبري 'kbry' in Hijazi, جسر 'jsr' in MSA), (Maybe, بلكن 'blkn' in Hijazi, احتمال 'AHtmAl' in MSA) and (Good, كويس 'kwys' in Hijazi, طيب 'Tyb' in MSA).
2. Distinguishing dialectal terms in Hijazi which come from the combination of two words, which are called a blend in linguistics. For example, دحين 'dHyn' (now), comes from the words الحين ذا '*A AlHyn'; and كمان 'kmAn' (also), it comes from the words كما إن 'kmA <n'
3. Words in Hijazi and MSA which are written the same word but have different meanings. For example, دول 'dwl', which means 'those' in Hijazi and 'countries' in MSA.

Independent Pronouns. Independent pronouns in Hijazi are distinct from those in MSA. The pronoun for "we" has more than one form. For example, 'AHnA' احنا or

---

[6] https://sites.google.com/site/motazsite/arabic/osac.

'nHnA' نحنا in Hijazi, but it is 'nHn' نحن in MSA. Also, the plural person pronoun is 'AntW' انتو in Hijazi, not antum أنتم as in MSA. The first person 'Anti' انتِ can be written in another form 'Anty' انتي. However, dual pronouns 'ntmA' أنتما and 'hmA' هما and the feminine plural pronouns 'Antn' انتن and 'hn' هن are not used in Hijazi.

The demonstrative pronouns in Hijazi are different from MSA. For the singular, "this" is 'dA' دا for masculine and 'dy' دي for feminine. While in MSA, 'h*A' هذا and 'h*h' هذه are used for masculine and feminine respectively. Also, Hijazi speakers use 'hAdA' هادا for masculine, while 'hAdy' هادي for feminine, feminine plural nouns and for inanimate masculine plural nouns. For plural "these", they used 'hdWl' هدول or 'hdWlA' هدولا or 'dWl' دول or 'dWlA' دولا instead of 'h&lA'' هؤلاء in MSA.

4.2 Regular

We present the main features of the Hijazi in negation, verb, and letter substitution.

Negation. The 'mA-' ما prefix is the only particle used for negation in all tenses of Hijazi verbs. However, in MSA, 'lA' لا, 'lm' لم, 'ln' لن, 'lys' ليس are used to negate a verb in addition to 'mA-' ما. Also, the 'mA' ما prefix is used for the negative pronouns in Hijazi instead of 'lys' ليس in MSA. In negating adjectives and nouns, the word 'mw' مو can be used while in MSA 'lA' لا, and 'lys' ليس are used [21].

The Verb. We consider verbs from two points: tense and structure. There are three main tenses in MSA: past, present, and future. However, [21–23]showed that some verb forms differ between MSA and Hijazi:

- Hijazi adds a verbal particle as a prefix / bi-/ب + verb (e.g. /bi-yiktub/ بيكتب 'byktb' he writes) in the expression of present tense, but MSA does not have this verbal particle.
- Hijazi adds a verbal particle as a prefix /in-/إن or ان + verb (e.g. /inktub/انكتب 'Anktb' was written), although some speakers add the prefix /At/اتـ 'At' + verb (e.g. /Atktab/ اتكتب 'Atktb' was written) in the expression of passive past tense, but MSA does not have this verbal particle.
- Hijazi adds a verbal particle as a prefix /ħa-/ح 'H' +verb (e.g. /ħa-yiguul/حيقول 'Hyqwl' he'll say) in the expression of future tense. Or Add the word/raħ/راح 'rAH' + verb (e.g./raħ-yiguul/ راح يقول 'rAH yqwl' he'll say). Instead of the word سوف 'swf' 'will', which is add before the verb in MSA, or the letter س 's', which is add in prefix of verb in MSA.

There are two types of verbs across MSA and Hijazi: sound (صحيح SHyH) or weak (معتل mEtI):

- **Sound verbs** are those verbs that do not include (w) و or (y) ي in the root letters. In the past verb of singular feminine, Hijazi adds the letter 'ي' 'y' to the end of a word such as the word كتبت 'ktbti' (she wrote) to be كتبتي 'ktbty' in Hijazi. Furthermore, there are double-sound verbs (الفعل المضعف AlmuDEf), where the second and third letter of the root are the same, such as دقَ daqqa -يدقَ yadiqqu (to knock). In the past verb of singular, Hijazi removes the third letter to be دقيت 'dqyt' (knocked) and add the suffix يت 'yt' in You (masculine), while دققت 'dqqtu' in MSA with adding suffix ت't'.

Also, there are (المهموز الفعل mahmuuz) Hamzated verbs, where ء is one of the consonants, such as أكل '>kal' - يأكل 'y>kl' (to eat). In general, there is no difference between masculine and feminine in Hijazi for all tenses of verbs. In Hijazi, the formulas for the masculine and feminine are the same in the plural form.

- **Weak verbs** are those verbs that contain و (w) or ي (y), as one or two of the root letters. There are three types of weak verbs, Hijazi weak verbs have different patterns among themselves and with MSA:
  - Assimilated verbs (المثال الفعل), which begin with و 'w' or ي 'y' such as وقف 'wqf' يقف 'yqf', 'to stand up'. In the present form, MSA removes the letter و 'w' and replaces it with ا 'A' like اقف 'Aqf', while Hijazi keeps the letter و 'w' and adds the prefix ب 'b' like باوقف 'bAwqf' (will stand).
  - Hollow verbs (الأجوف الفعل), which are the second letter in the root is ا 'A', و 'w' or ي 'y', such as قام 'qAm' يقوم 'yqwm', 'to get up'. ا 'A' is replaced with و 'w' in the present tense. Also, ا 'A' is replaced with ي 'y' in the present tense, such as باع 'bAE' يبيع 'ybyE', 'to sell'.
  - Defective verbs (الناقص الفعل), which end the root of the verb with و 'w' or ي 'y' such as رمى 'rmY' يرمي 'yrmy', 'to throw'. 'Y' is replaced by 'y' or ا 'A' is replaced by 'w', as in the example نما 'nmA' ينمو 'ynmw' 'to grow'.

Letter Substitution. Hijazi people write in a way that reflects their pronunciation. This leads to some letter substitutions between MSA and Hijazi [21–23]. Example substitutions as shown in Table 2.

Table 2. The letter substitutions between MSA and Hijazi

Letter in MSA	Letter substitution in Hijazi	Example in MSA	Example in Hijazi
'ذ' '*'	'ز' z / 'د' d	'*kryAt' (memories)/ 'k*Ab' (liar)	'zkryAt'/ 'kdab'
'ث' 'v'	'ت' t / 'س' s	'vqyl' (heavy)/ 'mvAl' (example)	'tqyl'/ 'msAl'
'ض' 'D'	'ز' z	'bAlDbT' (exactly)	'bAlzbT'
'أ' '>'	'ي' y	'bd>t' (I started)	'bdyt'
'ئ' '}'	'ي' y	'EwA}l' (families)	'EwAyl'
'ه' 'h'	'و' w	'klh' (All of)	'klw'

5 Experiment

This section firstly presents the process used to collect our Hijazi dialect corpus. We collected data from two different domains: articles and tweets. Each domain required different approaches to annotation, as described below. Also, this section shows the method used to generate the lexicon of Hijazi dialect verbs automatically.

5.1   Articles

To obtain a word list, we split the gathered articles into tokens by using whitespace and other punctuation characters (".,?!") as delimiters. In informal text, words are not always split by whitespace, so the letter و "w" "and", was also used as a delimiter. Next, we remove Arabic stop-words by using a list from the Ranks NL [24]. The remaining words were confirmed as Hijazi by:

1. Checking manually if the word is a verb, then checking if it fits the Hijazi verb structure described in Sect. 4. If yes, then it is a Hijazi verb.
2. If the word is not a verb or the name of a person or a place, then a search for the word in three extensive MSA lexicons was conducted: Maajim, Alwased and Alsahah. If the word was in one of the three, then it was considered an MSA word, otherwise, it was considered a Hijazi word.

This leaves us with 1,363 MANHijazi words. A manual examination of the words revealed that the distribution of POS were 904 verbs (simple present - passive past - future), which common use the verb form 'فعل' and 'انفعل', 62 pronouns, prepositions, 56 adverbs, 82 adjectives, 18 question, 12 interjections, 6 phrases and 202 nouns. The highest number of verbs demonstrates that the main difference between Hijazi and MSA is in verbs.

5.2   Tweets

To label tweets, we used Hijazi native speakers. Three thousand tweets, which were geo-located in the western cities of Saudi Arabia, Jeddah, Makkah, Taif, Medina and Yanbu were collected from March to May 2014. The tweets were pre-processed through manual inspection. All URLs, embedded images and user-related information (i.e. display name, avatar/display image and user mention) were removed from the tweets and their content was checked to ensure none were offensive.

Native Speakers. We obtained 3000 tweets from Mourad, Scholer and Sanderson [25] that had locations in the western cities of Saudi Arabia: Jeddah, Makkah, Taif, Medina, and Yanbu. Three native Hijazi speakers were recruited to annotate the 3000 tweets. We used a questionnaire, which had the list of tweets, to ask the speakers to label the tweets. The speakers were asked to record the tweet's dialect type (Hijazi or non-Hijazi) and details of which Hijazi words indicated that the tweet belonged to the dialect. The speakers were given one week for the task.

Fleiss' Kappa measured an annotator agreement of 0.89. From the annotation, we found that there were 372 Hijazi tweets from the original 3000, Table 3 shows the number of tweets from each city. There were 666 words in the Hijazi tweets and 311 unique word forms. Statistical comparisons between the Hijazi articles and tweets are shown in Table 4. We can see that this approach to labeling Hijazi tweets generated a limited lexicon, and therefore an automatic approach is also needed to extend the lexicon Hijazi.

Table 3. Identifying Hijazi and non-Hijazi dialect tweets by cities

City	Hijazi	Non-Hijazi	Total
Jeddah	200	1277	1477
Makkah	69	520	589
Taif	45	331	376
Medina	42	377	419
Yanbu	16	123	139
Total	372	2628	3000

Table 4. Description of Hijazi articles and tweets

Features	Articles	Tweets
Number of	156	372
words	59223	4672
Unique words	16270	2872
Average sentence length	96.3	10
Short words (<=3 characters)	17537	1555
Long words (>=7 characters))	9602	424
Unique Hijazi words	1367	35

5.3   Automatic Generation of Hijazi Dialect Words

The methodology used to expand the Hijazi lexicon verbs, follows a two-stage approach from Darwish, Sajjad and Mubarak [3]:

3. Generating a lexicon by using morphological rules of the dialect combined with roots (Quranic verbs root and Sebawai roots). The rules will generate multiple verbs from a single root.
4. Filtering the lexicon.

Automatic Generating Word. To generate Hijazi verbs from each root, prefixes were added to the root to set a tense (present, future, present/future passive). In Hijazi, object pronouns are attached to the verb as suffixes. A suffix set of Hijazi dialect are shown in Table 5. Also, there are ten subject pronouns: I "انا", you "أنتَ", you "أنتِ", you "أنتم", you "أنتنّ", we "نحن", they "هم", they "هنّ", he "هو", she "هي", and each pronoun has associate suffixes from the suffixes set.

Table 5. Suffixes set in Hijazi Dialect

Suffix in Hijazi	Example
Suffix length 1	ت, ه, ي, ك, و
Suffix length 2	وك, كي, ها, هم, كم, وا, وه, ني, نا
Suffix length 3	وكي, وكم, وها, وهم, وني, ولي, ونا

The rules have the following form: Sign, Root_Length, Condition, Prefix, Suffix

- Sign: contains (= ,>) to compare with the root length.
- Root_Length: the length of the root in the rule to apply the rule condition. Note that the first letter begins with index 0.
- Condition(s): it has three main sections:
  - index: contains the index number to verify, it can provide a specific index, a range of index or all indexes in the root.
  - verify: contains a letter or collection of letters to check if the letter is in the given index.
  - action: if the condition of verifying achieved then apply the action, which can be R to remove a specific letter in the index or change to a letter or collection of letters, which leads to generate multi-root.
- Prefix: the prefixes are added at the beginning of the root. If multiple prefixes are listed, then from single root multi verbs will be generated.
- Suffix: the suffixes are added at the end of the verb, which generated from the Prefix stage, by attaching appropriate suffixes as appropriate for the pronouns to generate Hijazi, (HijaziV$_{Quraan}$) and (HijaziV$_{Sebawai}$).

After applying the rules, the total number of Hijazi words generated from the two roots sets, Sebawai and Quraan, are 1,585,461 and 184,227 respectively. Example of the generation process are shown in Table 6.

For letter substitution, we used an MSA list of words from an English/Arabic parallel corpus[7], which consists of a dataset of around 150 k sentences. We apply substitution rules (from Sect. 4.2) if there is a letter in any word of MSA list match in Hijazi letter substitution then changed it to the appropriate letter in the Hijazi. We have obtained in 3,800 letter substitutions in Hijazi Arabic (Hijazi$_{SUB}$).

Filtering the Generating Word. The lists of Hijazi words, (HijaziV$_{Quraan}$, HijaziV$_{Sebawai}$, and Hijazi$_{SUB}$) were filtered by using steps 2 and 3 as shown in Fig. 1(b). The purpose of step 2 was to remove ambiguous or error words produced by one of the automatic generation methods. Also, this technique had a disadvantage; there might have been deletions of unused Hijazi words in tweets. We obtained 30,389, 25,599 and 1,630 words for HijaziV$_{Sebawai}$, HijaziV$_{Quraan}$, and Hijazi$_{SUB}$ respectively from this step. Then, we applied the step 3 to ensure there were no MSA words in the lists. In the end, the total number of HijaziV$_{Sebawai}$, HijaziV$_{Quraan}$, and Hijazi$_{SUB}$ from step 3 were 24,413, 12,428 and 1,074 respectively. The verbs intersection in HijaziV$_{Sebawai}$ and HijaziV$_{Quraan}$ are around 10,595 verb words, while there is no intersection between the list of verbs (HijaziV$_{Sebawai}$ and HijaziV$_{Quraan}$) and Hijazi$_{SUB}$.

---

[7] From the International Workshop on Arabic Language Translation.

Table 6. An example illustrating the automatic generating Hijazi word

Phase 1						
Context	=, 3, (1,ا , (ا, ي, و)), (كم,- ,كي, ك,هم, ها, ه) , (با, ب),					
	Sign	Root_Length	Condition		Prefix	Suffix
	=	3	(1,ا , (ا, ي, و))		با, ب	ه, ها, هم, ك, كي, كم
			Index	verify	action	
			1	ا	و, ي ,ا	
Phase 2						
Root	نام "nAm" sleep , length of root (نام)= 3					
Changing the root by using action	Check if the index 1 in the root نام "nAm" has a letter "ا", then apply the action by changing the letter "ا" to "ا", "ي", "و". word1: نام					
	word1: نام		word2:نيم		word3:نوم	
Add prefix	word11: بنام, word12: بانام		word21:بنيم , word22: بانيم		word31: بنوم , word32	
Add suffix	word111: بنام, word112: بنامه, word113:بنامها , word114: بنامهم, word115: بنامك, word116: بنامكي, word117: بنامكم word121: بانام, word122: بانامه, word123:بانامها , word124: بانامهم, word125: بانامك, word126: بانامكي, word127: بانامكم		word211: بنيم, word212: بنيمه, word213:بنيمها , word214: بنيمهم, word215: بنيمك, word216:بنيمكي , word217: بنيمكم word221: بانيم, word222: بانيمه, word223:بانيمها , word224: بانيمهم, word225: بانيمك, word226:بانيمكي word227:بانيمكم		word311: بنوم, word312: بنومه, word313:بنومها , word314: بنومهم, word315: بنومك, word316: بنومكي, word317: بنومكم word321: بانوم, word322: بانومه, word323: بانومها , word324: بانومهم, word325: بانومك, word326:بانومكي , word327:بانومكم	

6   Evaluation

Comparative evaluation with past work is not available since to the best of our knowledge this is the first study to generate a Hijazi lexicon. Instead, we used intrinsic evaluation to show the accuracies of the three Hijazi lexicons. We manually investigated randomly sampling a 2% from HijaziV$_{Sebawai}$, HijaziV$_{Quraan}$, and Hijazi$_{SUB}$: 490, 250, and 22 words, respectively, to estimate the coverage of the accuracy of lists. The error rate (ER) was calculated from the proportion of error words. As shown in the Table 7, HijaziV$_{Quraan}$ has the highest number of Hijazi dialect words (227) with an error rate of 0.09. In contrast, Hijazi$_{SUB}$ has the highest error rate of 0.27 in 22 words while the HijaziV$_{Sebawai}$ was 0.16. An analysis of errors was conducted, see Table 7. Three error types were found:

- Alternative root: the generated verb looks like a Hijazi word, but a Hijazi speaker would use a different root.
  - In HijaziV$_{Sebawai}$, alternative Hijazi root has the highest error rate of 69 error words. For example, the word اتعمش 'AtEm$', 'weak eyesight' from the word 'Em$', is used as the adjective and it is اعمى 'AEmY', 'blind', ضعف نظره 'DEf nZrh' as an adjective in Hijazi, or انعمى 'AnEmY' 'to blind' as the verb.
  - In HijaziV$_{Quraan}$, the highest number of such errors was 14. Examples include: حيميد 'Hymyd', "to shake from the root" ميد where 'myd' is replaced with هز 'hz' to be حيهز 'Hyhz'.
- Incorrect root: the generated verb looks like a Hijazi word, but the root is not an MSA verb root. The incorrect root was due to errors in the automatically created Sebawai list. An example of this is in Sebawai [11], ملم 'mlm', 'has knowledge', the root is a noun according to the dictionary Maajim not a verb root, has been applied the Hijazi rule to become حتملم 'Atmlm' in HijaziV$_{Sebawai}$, which is not Hijazi verb.
- Error a rule: the rule should not have been applied to all words. In HijaziSUB, the errors are due to the mistaken assignment for rules in word or root. For example, in the word الرضا 'AlrDa' "satisfaction", the letter ض "D" changed to ز 'z' to become 'Alrza', which is not Hijazi words.

Table 7. The Distribution of Hijazi and non-Hijazi words in the evaluation

Type of list	No. words	Sample words 2%	Hijazi words in 2%	Non-Hijazi words in 2%	Error rate	Distribution error rate		
						Alternative Hijazi root	Incorrect root	Error rule
HijaziV$_{Sebawai}$	24,413	490	409	81	0.16	69	6	6
HijaziV$_{Quraan}$	12,428	250	227	23	0.09	14	0	8
HijaziSUB	1,074	22	16	6	0.27	0	0	6

This technique of using the morphological rule of Hijazi is considered a good starting point to generate the Hijazi automatically, where we started from 1,363 and now we have 24,413, 12,428 and 1,074 for HijaziV$_{Sebawai}$, HijaziV$_{Quraan}$, and Hijazi$_{SUB}$ respectively. The intrinsic manual evaluation for HijaziV$_{Sebawai}$ and HijaziV$_{Quraan}$ give a different type of answer: once has more words with high error rate while the other has few words with low error rate.

7 Conclusion

In this paper we asked the following research question: can a methodology, used to create a High-resource Egyptian, lexicon be adapted to create a Low-resource Hijazi lexicon?

We explained a method for building a lexicon of a low-resource Arabic dialect in Saudi Arabia: Hijazi, using human experts. We expanded a lexicon of Hijazi words by covering different Hijazi morphologies rules in a manual and in automatic approaches that can be used in this research and the future as a benchmark. Morphological rules were applied to two different root sets: Quranic and Sebawai roots. The Hijazi lexicon generated can be used for computational linguistic research and NLP tools. This lexicon would help in some applications such as electronic translation.

We evaluated Hijazi lexicon manually. Based on the result of our experiments, we found that the methodology can be applied to create a Hijazi lexicon. Also, we found that the linguistic phenomena in the Hijazi are the first step that allows us to build a Hijazi lexicon. For future work, we plan to expand the size of our corpus to maximize the coverage of the domain of the Hijazi dialect lexicon and mapping with MSA. We also plan to develop a morphological analyzer for the Hijazi dialect, and then build an automatic classification to annotate the Hijazi dialect.

References

1. Anis, I.: On The Arabic Dialects. Maktabat al-Anglo al-Misriyya, Cairo (1952)
2. Biadsy, F., Hirschberg, J., Habash, N.: Spoken Arabic dialect identification using phonotactic modeling. In: Proceedings of the EACL 2009 Workshop on Computational Approaches to Semitic Languages 2009, pp. 53–61. Association for Computational Linguistics (2009)
3. Darwish, K., Sajjad, H., Mubarak, H.: Verifiably effective Arabic dialect identification. In Proceedings of the 2014 Conference on Empirical Methods in Natural Language Processing (EMNLP), pp. 1465–1468 (2014)
4. Diab, M., Habash, N., Rambow, O., Altantawy, M., Benajiba, Y.: COLABA: Arabic dialect annotation and processing. In: LREC Workshop on Semitic Language Processing, pp. 66–74 (2010)
5. Harrat, S., Meftouh, K., Smaili, K.: Creating parallel Arabic dialect corpus: pitfalls to avoid. In: 18th International Conference on Computational Linguistics and Intelligent Text Processing (CICLING) (2017)
6. Khalifa, S., Habash, N., Abdulrahim, D., and Hassan, S.: A large scale corpus of Gulf Arabic. arXiv preprint arXiv:1609.02960 (2016)
7. Jarrar, M., Habash, N., Alrimawi, F., Akra, D., Zalmout, N.: Curras: an annotated corpus for the Palestinian Arabic dialect. Lang. Resour. Eval. 51(3), 745–775 (2017)
8. Al-Shargi, F., Rambow, O.: DIWAN: a dialectal word annotation tool for Arabic. In: Proceedings of the Second Workshop on Arabic Natural Language Processing, pp. 49–58 (2015)
9. Pasha, A., et al.: MADAMIRA: a fast, comprehensive tool for morphological analysis and disambiguation of Arabic. In: LREC, vol. 14, pp. 1094–1101 (2014)
10. Zbib, R.,et al.: Machine translation of Arabic dialects
11. Darwish, K.: Building a shallow Arabic morphological analyzer in one day. In: Proceedings of the ACL-02 Workshop on Computational Approaches to Semitic Languages (2002)
12. Mubarak, H., Darwish, K.: Using Twitter to collect a multi-dialectal corpus of Arabic. In: Proceedings of the EMNLP 2014 Workshop on Arabic Natural Language Processing (ANLP), pp. 1–7 (2014)
13. Outahajala, M., Zenkouar, L., Rosso, P.: Building an annotated corpus for Amazighe. In: Will appear In: Proceedings of 4th International Conference on Amazigh and ICT (2011)

14. Ramrakhiyani, N., Majumder, P.: Approaches to temporal expression recognition in Hindi. ACM Trans. Asian Low-Resour. Lang. Inf. Process. **14**(1), 2 (2015)
15. Palchowdhury, S., Majumder, P., Pal, D., Bandyopadhyay, A., Mitra, M.: Overview of FIRE 2011. In: Majumder, P., Mitra, M., Bhattacharyya, P., Subramaniam, L.Venkata, Contractor, D., Rosso, P. (eds.) FIRE 2010-2011. LNCS, vol. 7536, pp. 1–12. Springer, Heidelberg (2013). https://doi.org/10.1007/978-3-642-40087-2_1
16. Bird, S., Gawne, L., Gelbart, K., McAlister, I.: Collecting bilingual audio in remote indigenous communities. In: Proceedings of COLING 2014, the 25th International Conference on Computational Linguistics: Technical Papers, pp. 1015–1024 (2014)
17. Hanke, F.R., Bird, S.: Large-scale text collection for unwritten languages. In: Proceedings of the Sixth International Joint Conference on Natural Language Processing, pp. 1134–1138 (2013)
18. Alahmadi, S.D.: Loanwords in the urban Meccan Hijazi dialect: an analysis of lexical variation according to speakers' sex, age and education. Int. J. Engl. Linguist. **5**(6), 34 (2015)
19. Althobaiti, M., Kruschwitz, U., Poesio, M.: AraNLP: a Java-based library for the processing of Arabic text. In: Proceedings of the 9th Language Resources and Evaluation Conference (LREC), Reykjavik, pp. 4134–4138 (2014)
20. Saad, M.K., Ashour, W.: OSAC: open source arabic corpora. In: Proceedings of the EEECS 2010 the 6th International Symposium on Electrical and Electronics Engineering and Computer Science, pp. 118–123. European University of Lefke, Cyprus (2010)
21. Sieny, M.E.: The Syntax of Urban Hijazi Arabic. Librairie du Liban, Beirut (1973)
22. Omar, M.K.: Saudi Arabic, Urban Hijazi Dialect: Basic Course. Foreign Service Institute, Washington, D.C. (1975)
23. Arabic Variant Identification Aid. http://terpconnect.umd.edu:80/~nlynn/AVIA/Level3/index.htm. Accessed 06 May 2015
24. RANKS NL - Arabic stopword list. https://www.ranks.nl/stopwords/arabic. Accessed 02 Feb 2015
25. Mourad, A., Scholer, F., Sanderson, M.: Language influences on Tweeter geolocation. In: Jose, Joemon M., Hauff, C., Altıngovde, I.S., Song, D., Albakour, D., Watt, S., Tait, J. (eds.) ECIR 2017. LNCS, vol. 10193, pp. 331–342. Springer, Cham (2017). https://doi.org/10.1007/978-3-319-56608-5_26

Natural Arabic Language Resources for Emotion Recognition in Algerian Dialect

Habiba Dahmani[1(✉)], Hussein Hussein[2], Burkhard Meyer-Sickendiek[2], and Oliver Jokisch[3]

[1] Department of Electrical Engineering,
University of Mohamed Boudiaf, M'Sila, Algeria
habiba.dahmani@univ-msila.dz
[2] Department of Literary Studies, Free University of Berlin, Berlin, Germany
{hussein,bumesi}@zedat.fu-berlin.de
[3] Institute of Communications Engineering,
Leipzig University of Telecommunications (HfTL), Leipzig, Germany
jokisch@hft-leipzig.de

Abstract. In this paper, we present and describe our first work to design and build a natural Arabic visual-audio database for the computational processing of emotions and affect in speech and language which will be made available to the research community. It is high time to have spontaneous data representative of the Modern Standard Arabic (MSA) and its dialects. The database consists of audio-visual recordings of some Arabic TV talk shows. Our choice comes down on the different dialects with the MSA. As a first step, we present a sample data of Algerian dialect. It contains two hours of audio-visual recordings of the Algerian TV talk show "Red line". The data consists of 14 speakers with $1,443$ utterances which are complete sentences. 15 emotions investigated with five that are dominants: enthusiasm, admiration, disapproval, neutral, and joy. The emotion corpus serves in classification experiments using a variety of acoustic features extracted by *openSMILE*. Some algorithms of classification are implemented with the *WEKA* toolkit. Low-level audio features and the corresponding delta features are utilized. Statistical functionals are applied to each of the features and delta features. The best classification results - measured by a weighted average of f-measure - is 0.48 for the five emotions.

Keywords: Emotion recognition · Arabic language resources · Algerian dialect

1 Introduction

Emotions are omnipresent whether we speak or not. It is a continuous state of mind. Emotions are the mind of our verbal and non-verbal reactions. Without emotions, our reactions are incomprehensible. Without even partial or minimal presence of emotions, we are somehow sick or less intelligent as we should

© Springer Nature Switzerland AG 2019
K. Smaïli (Ed.): ICALP 2019, CCIS 1108, pp. 18–33, 2019.
https://doi.org/10.1007/978-3-030-32959-4_2

be normally. Therefore, the importance of emotions in our daily lives is self-evident. Studying emotions to improve the quality of our interactions between humans or between humans and machines is essential.

The progress in automatic processing includes the understanding of natural language. This make emotions detection and classification within the speech signal possible. Speech includes all linguistic features such as the phonological, lexical, semantic information, prosodic information. The information expressed through speech can be divided into three categories: linguistic (such as accent, phrase and sentence type), paralinguistic (for example: intention, attitude and speaking style), and nonlinguistic information (such as age, gender, physical and emotional states of speakers). The acoustic parameters correlating with prosodic properties are fundamental frequency, duration, and intensity. Nonlinguistic information is concerned with information about age, gender, physical and emotional states of speakers [19]. In human interactions, the listener interprets and responds to the emotive state of the speaker and adjusts the reaction depending on the emotions that the speaker communicates. Consequently, it is extensively argued that artificial intelligence needs to recognize human emotions and understand them in order to achieve natural Human-Machine communication. Recognizing human emotions mainly from the speech signal is a challenging process for many reasons. In general, studies mention two principal difficulties: audio-video databases and recognition algorithms [45].

Indeed developing a database is a requirement for building emotion recognition. Emotional speech recognition, based on recorded and annotated databases, has received much attention from many researchers [10, 11, 13, 24, 25, 31, 33, 47, 49, 52]. However, there is a growing need for real-time and offline emotion recognition systems that are based on an analysis of the speech signal or both visual and speech signal. A significant emotion recognition obstacle is the quality of the recorded speech samples; more specifically: the quality, the size and the type of the database. The speech corpora are either acted, induced or natural. Acted or simulated corpora are collected from professional television or radio actors who are widely used in research work. Natural databases can be used for real-world emotion modelling. These databases are created by collecting the real world conversations such as Call center conversation, a conversation between patient and doctors, or TV show programs, etc. [12, 20].

Arabic language and its dialects are still considered a relatively resource-poor language when compared to other languages such as English [53]. In its dialectal forms, Arabic is the mother tongue of more than 250 million speakers. The Arabic language has three forms: classical Arabic or literary Arabic language, Modern Standard Arabic (MSA), and Colloquial Arabic. Classical Arabic is essentially the form of the language found in the Quran, the MSA is a modern form of Arabic used in news media and formal speech, and by definition dialects are spoken. These Dialects have no written standards.

In recent years, concerning Arabic affective computing, there has been a considerable amount of works on the collection of emotional speech. However, most databases built up to now are induced, small, and just constructed for particular purposes. The corpora are mostly recorded by unprofessional actors, which affect the quality of the generated speech. Another problem is the lack of enough recorded multimodal data of emotions. Most of the developed databases are not available for public use. Thus, the ultimate consequence of this domain is the absence of coordination and collaboration among researchers in this field. Hence the need to think and proceed to build a large database for this language and its dialects.

This paper reports progress in constructing an Arabic natural database that presents speech in the context of natural interactions where emotion is conveyed via multiple modalities. This database will be available online for sharing with the scientific community. Algerian dialect data is used as a sample data segmented and annotated to 15 emotions. There are five dominant emotions that are: enthusiasm, admiration, disapproval neutral, and joy. We classify these emotions with several machine learning algorithms to experiment variety of acoustic features.

The remainder of this paper is organized as follows: The state-of-the-art for emotion recognition in Arabic is presented in Sect. 2. Section 3 provides an overview about the database (spontaneous Algerian data) as well as collection and annotation steps. Section 4 illustrates the experiment by feature extraction and classification of emotions. The results are described in Sect. 5 and finally, conclusions and future works are presented in Sect. 6.

2   Emotion Recognition in Arabic

The need and the motivation for such a work for the Arabic natural language processing (NLP) are imperative. Then, our primary goal is to show the scarcity of the Arabic linguistic resources and to confirm too that little work has been devoted for the analysis of emotional speech in Arabic by presenting a state-of-the-art overview of Arabic studies that have been carried out in this domain.

Going through the literature of Arabic speech emotion processing, we find some studies and a few more or less significant emotional databases. Between 2005 and 2006, we find three Syrian works about the introduction of the emotion parameters for Arabic text-to-speech synthesis [2,4]. Al-Dakkak et al. tried to improve the Arabic synthetic speech (MSA Arabic) in order to sound as natural. They incorporated different prosodic features with five emotions: anger, joy, sadness, fear, and surprise in an educational Arabic text-to-speech system. The authors elected three sentences for each emotion. Each sentence is recorded twice, one emotionless and the other with the intended emotion. They did not specify the number of speakers or any further details about their database. To generate prosody automatically, they considered the most crucial acoustic parameters: pitch, duration, and intensity. In 2011, Khalil reported in [27,28] that he constructed a well-annotated corpus for anger and neutral emotion states from real-world Arabic speech dialogues for his experiments. It consists of a set of recorded episodes of a live Arabic political debate show: The Opposite Direction program of Al-Jazeera Satellite Channel. The number of samples extracted from the selected episodes are more than 400 samples for anger emotion state, varied from one second to 9 s with different speaker gender in different Arabic cultures. The second source of his data is an angry customer's call: This is a phone call published on YouTube that features a customer who was very angry while speaking with the agent. The call duration was four minutes long. He was able to extract 45 samples of data which reflect anger states from this clip. He used prosodic and spectral features and several classifiers are evaluated: Support Vector Machine (SVM), Probabilistic Neural Networks (PNN), simple decision tree, and decision tree forest.

Azmy et al. in [6,7] built an Arabic unit selection voice that could carry emotional information. Three emotional states are covered: normal, sad, and questions. They used the text-to-speech from RDI 'the Engineering Company for the Development of Digital Systems' (RDITTS) for Saudi speaker database. This database consists of 10 h of recording with neutral emotion and one hour of recordings with four different emotions that are: sadness, happiness, surprise, and enquiring. However, they did not give any reference or either further details about this database. The authors used an automatic emotion classification system: Emovoice. The system comes with a predefined two classification models; probabilistic Naïve Bayesian (NB) and SVM classifiers [51]. Meddeb et al. in [34] propose the architecture of Automatic Emotion Recognition from Speech in order to recommend a system for TV programs based on human behavior. The emotional recognition for the remote control includes unimodal and multimodal approach and shows the hierarchical recognition steps of emotions. They used the six following databases: two publicly available ones, the Danish Emotional Speech corpus (DES) and Berlin Emotional Database (EMO-DB), and four databases from the interface project with Spanish, Slovenian, French, and English emotional speech. In 2014, they created their own Tunisian dialect sound database for automatic emotion speech recognition always to achieve intelligent remote control. They called it the Tunisian Emotional Speech database (TUES). The database composed primarily of sound passages and isolated word recorded by actors where the ages, sex, and region are different. The sentences are designed to use for recording the seven emotions: neutral, anger, surprise, disgust, fear, happiness, and sadness. This database contains 720 speech samples. The length of speech samples is up to five seconds [36]. Hammami reported in [22] that his search resulted in finding a single emotional speech database called Emotional speech database of Research Groups on Intelligent Machines (REGIM_TES). The database is from the National Engineering School of Sfax in Tunisia and developed by Meddeb et al. in [35,37–39]. Due to undisclosed reasons, the database has been made private. The REGIM_TES database is composed primarily of isolated words and very short, semantically neutral phrases made of few collocate words not exceeding four. The research used 12 actors, six of each gender to generate five emotion categories that include: anger, fear, happiness, sadness, and neutral. The selected descriptors in the study are the pitch of voice, energy, Mel Frequency Cepstral Coefficients MFCCs, Formant, Linear Predictive Coding (LPC) and the spectrogram. They experienced a different type of classifiers and they opted for the SVM multiclass classifier.

Meftah et al. [40] describe an emotional speech corpus recorded for MSA (KSUEmotions: the King Saud University Emotions). The KSUEmotions corpus recordings contain five hours of emotional MSA speech for five emotions: neutral, sadness, happiness, surprised, and angry as well as 16 sentences, and 20 speakers from three countries: Saudi Arabia, Yemen, and Syria. From Damascus University, Al-Faham and Ghneim [5] built an Arabic emotional speech corpus, covering five emotions: happiness, anger, sadness, surprise, and neutrality to recognize the Arabic user's emotional state by analyzing the speech signal. The speech data used in the experiment contains 24 emotional Arabic sentences recorded by six performers (3 male and three female) and every sentence recorded twice for every emotion. The classification results in these works are carried out using the *WEKA* software [21] and by using neural network classifier based on Multilayer Perceptron (MLP) with rhythm metrics as new descriptors.

Another research about the spontaneous emotional Arabic database is from Klaylat's et al. in [29,30]. They confirmed that no natural emotional Arabic corpus was found to date. A realistic speech corpus from Arabic TV shows is collected. The videos are labeled by their perceived emotions, i.e. happy, angry, or surprised. The corpus composed of 1,384 records with 505 happy, 137 surprised and 741 angry units. The unit is one second of speech. Low-Level Descriptors (LLDs) are extracted using the open source *openSMILE* feature extractor [14] that is developed at the Technische Universität München (TUM). Thirty-five classification models are applied to the Sequential Minimal Optimization (SMO) classifier. Finally, Abdo et al. [1] built an MSA audio-visual corpus. The corpus is annotated both phonetically and visually and dedicated to emotional speech processing studies. 500 sentences are critically selected based on their phonemic distribution with six emotions (happiness, sadness, fear, anger, inquiry, and neutral). The recorded audio-visual corpus is contributing to the field of speech processing specifically Text-to-Speech (TTS) applications. The authors intend to let the corpus publically available for general research purposes.

It becomes clear from this short overview of the Arabic emotion processing studies and achievements that textcolorredthe Arabic language and its dialects initially require the construction of important databases to be shared freely online for the scientific community. The availability of these resources will strengthen and encourage useful research in the automatic processing of the Arabic language in general and coordination between researchers in this field. This overview is condensed in Table 1. The Table gives the most important databases for the recognition of emotions. It is ordered by publication date.

3   Database

The collection of new emotional speech databases that tries to overcome the limitations of the existing corpora is a crucial necessity. These efforts lead to widespread knowledge of language technology.

Table 1. List of Arabic speech emotion databases.

Name	Type	MSA or dialect	Speakers	Linguistic material (Nr. of sentences)	Emotions	References
KSUEmotions	Simulated	MSA	20	16	5 emotions: neutral, sadness, happiness, surprised, questioning	[40,41]
Egypt	Acted	MSA	07	500	6 emotions: happiness, sadness, fear, anger, inquiry, neutral	[1]
REGIM_TES	Acted	Tunisian	-	-	-	[39]
Arabic-Natural-Audio-Dataset	Natural	Dialectal (Egyptian, Jordan, Gulf, Lebanese)	06	-	3 emotions: happiness, anger, surprised	[29,30]

3.1   Data Acquisition

The undergoing database consists of a collected data of spontaneous emotional speech in Arabic language, including MSA and colloquial Algerian, Tunisian, Lebanese, Jordanian, Syrian, and Egyptian which will be made available to the research community. The database consists of audio-visual recordings of some Arabic TV talk shows, segmented into broadcasts. The corpus contains spontaneous and very emotional speech recorded from discussions between the guests of the talk shows. We decided to select some TV talk shows for this data collection because the spontaneous discussions between the talk show guests are often somewhat affective. Such interpersonal communication leads to a wide variety of emotional states, depending on the topics discussed. These topics were mainly personal issues such as friendship crises, questions about paternity or romantic affairs: emotionally intense and discussing hot social phenomena. So far, We collected about 50 broadcasts of the talk show for Arabic (including MSA, and Algerian, Tunisian, Lebanese, Jordanian, Syrian, and Egyptian dialects). In the present work, only the Algerian data is processed. The number of programs and dialects can be expanded further to balance the database concerning the number and gender of speakers and also the categories of emotions.

3.2   Case Study: Algerian Emotional Speech

"Red Line", a weekly social program on Al-Shorouk Algerian channel. A talk show where guests are invited to talk. The show is presented by three permanent hosts; anchorwomen who appear on each program, introduces and interacts with the guests. Religious and psychological opinions are present. Social program sometimes deals with sensitive subjects that are difficult to discuss. The program begins in a studio on a red background, with shapes and lines that reflect the orientation of the program [50].

Both MSA and dialects are used for communication. Dialectal Arabic is a term that covers Arabic dialects, resulting from linguistic interference between the Arabic language and local or neighboring languages as a result of the process of Arabization or any cultural influence due mainly to colonization, migration, trade, and more recently the media. Algerian dialect is generally described as an Arabic idiom attached to the Maghrebian Arabic group (Algerian, Moroccan, Tunisian and Libyan). However, its morphology, syntax, pronunciation, and vocabulary are quite different from other Arabic dialects. Algerian Arabic is established on a substrate that was initially Berber, Latin (African Romance Language), and to a lesser extent Punic. It has also been enriched by the languages of the powers that influenced this region including Ottoman Turkish, Spanish, and French. This dialect is characterized by the multitude including sub-dialects that are clearly variants of Arabic, and other sub-dialects that are non-Arabic which we call the Amazigh dialect. Therefore, the Algerian and the other North African dialects are considered a little distant from the MSA. While the Arabic dialects of the East: Egypt, Sudan, Levantine, Gulf countries are dialects closer to the MSA. We focus in this study on the Algerian dialect which is classified by the Algerians themselves as a mixture of three languages: Arabic, Berber, and French.

3.3 Segmentation and Emotional Labelling

The corpus contains spontaneous and very emotional speech recorded from unscripted, authentic discussions between the guests of the talk show. These first records consist of two hours which are segmented in the first step into smaller units or clips containing the whole dialogue between a limited number of talk show guests. In general, such discussions are extracted as videos containing the audio and video signals. In a second step, the dialogues are segmented into turns: the turn is when the one partner finishes speaking, and the other partner takes over. The third step is to segment these turns to utterances. These utterances were mainly complete sentences, but sometimes also grammatically incomplete sentences which were due to the spontaneous nature of the interactions. Many utterances had to be discarded because of background music, applause from the audience, and overlaps between speakers or other interruptions. The audio signal was stored separately for each sentence. An identification is given to each speaker and each utterance. We have four categories of speakers and each category is designed by four characters. The anchor women appointed by Mode (moderator), for the other speakers, we used these letters G, H, P, S to indicate respectively, Guest, Host, Principal, Speaker. GH is for the permanent speakers with the moderator in the talk show. GP is for the principal Guest in each episode. Guest Speaker (GS) is a guest among several or among the spectators of the show. Concerning the two digits: the first number concerns the episode number and the second number is for the speaker's order in the show (for example GS11 is the first guest speaker in episode one).

The collected data contains 1,443 utterances from 14 different speakers among them 5 females (two little girls and 3 adult females). But it should be noted that there are actually three dominant speakers (see Fig. 1): moderator of the show (Mode), the psychologist (GH01), and the religious expert (GH02).

The next step should be to define the emotions and their data segments or emotional analysis units. Indeed, the most crucial problem for the analysis of emotional data is to determine what an emotional utterance is, where it starts and where it ends [8]. The data were evaluated by three human listeners. Each listener assessed the emotional content for the whole of utterances in terms of the emotion categories. Categorical rating involved applying labels from a list of terms (a total of 28 emotions until now). However, only 15 emotions were detected in the collected database and rated for the present data: Anger, Joy, Happiness, Sadness, Disapproval, Admiration, Surprise, Enthusiasm, Adoration, Calm, Gratitude, Reproach, Neutral, Sympathy, and Satisfaction. The raters watch the videos and the corresponding audio files and then they try to follow the emotion and define exactly the audio part related to the emotion. However, we insist on the fact that our method will be significantly reduced for the rest of the data and we will use a higher number of raters to be able to complete the evaluation of the whole database. There are about five emotions that are more present than others (Enthusiasm, Admiration, Disapproval, Neutral, and Joy) as shown in Fig. 2.

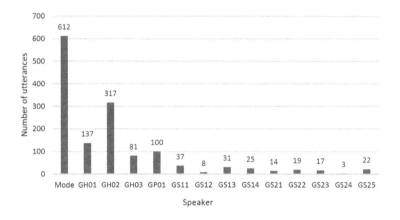

Fig. 1. The distribution of utterances per speaker.

3.4   Recording Quality

The video files are MPEG-coded image sequences of 352×288 pixels with a frame rate of 25 fps. A constant code rate of 1.15 Mbit/s was used. Recordings were taken with a sampling frequency of 48 kHz and later downsampled to 16 kHz (16 bit). These criteria are commonly used for speech databases.

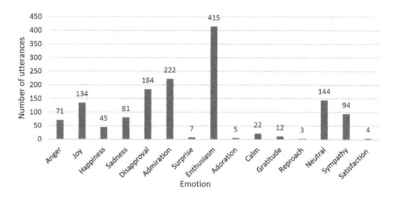

Fig. 2. The distribution of utterances per emotion.

4   Experiment

The performance of a variety of audio features and several classifiers is investigated to determine the best-suited features and classifiers for the classification of emotions.

4.1   Features

Feature extraction can be split into two categories according to the processing domain: the time-domain features and frequency-domain features. The time-domain features are Zero-Crossing Rate (ZCR) and short-time average energy. The frequency-domain features are pitch or fundamental frequency (F_0), spectral features (band energy, spectral roll-off, spectral flux, and spectral centroid), cepstral features (MFCCs), and linear prediction features (LPC).

We perform feature extraction for emotions by using the *openSMILE* feature extraction tool [14]. The feature set contains features which result from LLDs with the corresponding delta coefficients (ΔLLD) and statistical functionals applied to each of the LLD and ΔLLD. The main LLD used in the experiment are the features described above. The features are energy, pitch, ZCR, spectral features, MFCCs, and Line Spectral Frequencies (LSP) which are computed from LPC coefficients. The default values of coefficients in *openSMILE* are used (12 cepstral coefficients for MFCCs and 8 linear predictive coding coefficients for LPC). The following statistical functionals are used for every feature: min, max, range, standard deviation and mean.

Many feature vector sets are used:

* A (120 features): MFCCs
* B (50 features): Energy, pitch, ZCR
* C (230 features): Energy, pitch, ZCR, spectral features
* D (350 features): Energy, pitch, ZCR, spectral features, MFCCs
* E (430 features): Energy, pitch, ZCR, spectral features, MFCCs, LSP

* F (384 features): Baseline feature set of the Emotion Challenge in the Interspeech 2009 [46]
* G (6373 features): Baseline feature set of the Computational Paralinguistics Challenge (ComParE) in the Interspeech 2013 [44]
* H (6552 features): The large *openSMILE* emotion feature set with more functionals and more LLD [15].

We used the feature sets A-E in a previous experiment of acoustic event classification for the utilization in the sector of healthcare.

4.2 Classification

A series of classifiers are selected in order to determine the best-suited classifier for the evaluation. The following machine learning algorithms with default values using the *WEKA* data mining toolkit [21] are applied for the recognition of emotions:

* **IBk**: the Instance-Based (IB) classifier with a number of (k) neighbors is the K-Nearest Neighbours (KNN) classifier using the euclidean distance and 1-nearest neighbour [3].
* **AdaBoostM1**: the boosting algorithm uses the Adaboost M1 method [17].
* **LogitBoost**: The classifier performs additive logistic regression [18].
* **SimpleLogistic**: a classifier for building linear logistic regression models [32, 48].
* **RandomTree**: Random trees is a collection of decision trees that considers K randomly chosen attributes at each node [16].
* **RandomForest**: The classifier of random forest consists of several uncorrelated decision trees [9].
* **SMO**: The Sequential Minimal Optimisation (SMO) for training a Support Vector Machines (SVM) classifier [23, 26, 42].
* **J48**: The J48 algorithm used to generate a pruned or unpruned decision tree [43].

We implement our experiment for the recognition of emotions only on the five emotions that are more present than others: Enthusiasm, Admiration, Disapproval, Neutral, and Joy.

5 Results

The performance is measured using the f-measure which is the harmonic mean between precision and recall. Table 2 shows the classification results by applying eight kinds of feature sets and eight classifiers. We used the extracted features and classifiers to classify the five emotions: Enthusiasm, Admiration, Disapproval, Neutral, and Joy. The Table shows that the SMO classifier yielded better results (0.48) than other classifiers for different feature sets. The best results according to the features are for the feature sets D and E (with the SMO classifier) (0.47 and 0.48, respectively). Increasing the number of feature engineering from feature set (B) to (E) leads to a slight improvement in the results.

Adding MFCCs to the feature set C yielded better improvement of results (see the columns C and D). The results by using baseline features (feature sets F and G) and large *openSMILE* emotion feature set (H) are in general not better than feature engineering sets (A till E).

Table 2. Experimental results (weighted average of f-measure) obtained with the 10 fold cross-validation by applying different feature sets on several classification algorithms.

	A	B	C	D	E	F	G	H
SimpleLogistic	0.42	0.33	0.39	0.46	0.46	0.42	0.42	0.42
SMO	0.42	0.20	0.39	0.47	0.48	0.40	0.42	0.44
IBk	0.42	0.33	0.36	0.42	0.42	0.41	0.34	0.46
AdaBoostM1	0.20	0.23	0.20	0.20	0.25	0.20	0.23	0.20
LogitBoost	0.38	0.35	0.39	0.44	0.44	0.40	0.42	0.40
J48	0.33	0.30	0.34	0.34	0.37	0.32	0.34	0.40
RandomForest	0.40	0.34	0.40	0.40	0.44	0.35	0.32	0.45
RandomTree	0.30	0.32	0.34	0.35	0.34	0.29	0.28	0.34

Analyzing the confusion matrix in the Table 3 for the five emotions by using the SMO classifier and the feature set E, we find that the most misclassifications are between "Admiration" and "Enthusiasm", "Disapproval" and "Enthusiasm", and "Joy" and "Enthusiasm". This means that the recognition of Enthusiasm between the among five emotions is the most difficult task. We think it is understandable because enthusiasm is a little bit of all these emotions. thanks to this example, we realized the importance of the annotation phase and also the use of a more precise method: dimensional labeling approach.

Table 3. The confusion matrix for the five emotions with the SMO classifier and the feature set E.

	Admiration	Disapproval	Enthusiasm	Joy	Neutral	Sum
Admiration	**96**	17	83	12	14	222
Disapproval	14	**99**	60	2	9	184
Enthusiasm	82	44	**219**	38	32	415
Joy	7	8	50	**64**	5	134
Neutral	21	19	49	3	**52**	144

6   Conclusion and Future Works

In this paper, we presented the first steps of our work whose objective is to design and build a new Natural Arabic multimodal spontaneous emotion database for the research community in order to facilitate the research in the field. We have tried to highlight some points concerning the importance of the Arabic language and the fact that, there is insufficient interest in this language regarding the recognition of emotions or regarding all disciplines of artificial intelligence in overall. Arabic is one of the oldest languages in the world. It is one of the first widely used languages nowadays. So it is really vital to give a lot of importance to further study this language and its variants which are its dialects. Basically, high quality and large speech corpora are required for the emotion recognition task. However, the existing MSA and dialectal Arabic speech corpora are very sparse and are of low quality. For some Arabic dialects, speech resources do not exist at all. That is why it is difficult to initiate research and studies in this field. With our research, we mainly pursued two goals. The first one is to collect a high-quality MSA and dialectal speech corpus. The second goal is to rapidly develop phonetic transcriptions for dialectal speech data. We have started with an overview of the Arabic language from an emotion recognition point of view. This overview shows that it is not easy to access extensive and up-to-date freely available Arabic corpora. it should be noted that the use of corpora has been a major factor in the recent advance in artificial intelligence in general and in the natural language processing development and evaluation particularly.

We measured the performance of emotion classification by using a variety of audio features and several classifiers for five emotions in the Algerian dialect.

However, our current work has certain limitations, which give rise to our future work as follows: (1) Considering the Arabic language and its dialects (besides the different varieties of the natural language in its self) is a problem for speech recognition before being a problem for the recognition of emotions. Simply, these varieties cannot be modelled in an appropriate way. Firstly, for the transliteration of what has been said, we propose to use Romanization method for transcription of the speech corpus. (2) Continuing to perform different annotations like prosodic, Part-of-Speech tags, and syntactic labels and segmentation in word and chunk levels. (3) We will investigate both methods: the dimensional and the category labels for the emotional annotation and use the two classic criteria for assessing the quality of such labels: validity and reliability. (4) For naturalistic data, both acoustic and linguistic features should be employed, both for a deeper understanding and a better classification performance. We will establish different measures of impact and discuss the mutual influence of acoustics and linguistics. (5) The classification will be experimented using different levels, word, chunk, and utterances. Classification performance relies on deep learning and pattern recognition techniques. One defies to address in emotion classification is how to prune into this depth of methods and find a good one for this specific task. And of course, we have to deal with the curse of dimensionality and class skewness or the sparse data problem in the output space. As a result, the multimodal spontaneous corpus will be designed for general analysis of human behavior of emotional as well as for automatic emotion classification purposes.

References

1. Abdo, O., Abdou, S.M., Fashal, M.: Building audio-visual phonetically annotated Arabic corpus for expressive text to speech. In: INTERSPEECH, pp. 3767–3771 (2017)
2. Abou Zliekha, M., Al Moubayed, S., Al Dakkak, O., Ghneim, N.: Emotional audio-visual Arabic text to speech. In: The XIV European Signal Processing Conference (EUSIPCO) (2006)
3. Aha, D., Kibler, D., Albert, M.: Instance-based learning algorithms. Mach. Learn. 6, 37–66 (1991)
4. Al-Dakkak, O., Ghneim, N., Zliekha, M.A., Al-Moubayed, S.: Emotion inclusion in an Arabic text-to-speech. In: 2005 13th European Signal Processing Conference, pp. 1–4. IEEE (2005)
5. Al-Faham, A., Ghneim, N.: Towards enhanced arabic speech emotion recognition: comparison between three methodologies. Asian J. Sci. Technol. 07(03), 2665–2669 (2016)
6. Azmy, W.M., Abdou, S., Shoman, M.: The creation of emotional effects for an Arabic speech synthesis system. In: The Egyptian Society of Language Engineering, International Workshop, ESOLE (2013)
7. Azmy, W.M., Abdou, S., Shoman, M.: Arabic unit selection emotional speech synthesis using blending data approach. Int. J. Comput. Appl. 81(8), 22–28 (2013)
8. Batliner, A., Fischer, K., Huber, R., Spilker, J., Nöth, E.: How to find trouble in communication. Speech Commun. 40(1–2), 117–143 (2003)
9. Breiman, L.: Random forests. Mach. Learn. 45(1), 5–32 (2001)
10. Burkhardt, F., Paeschke, A., Rolfes, M., Sendlmeier, W.F., Weiss, B.: A database of German emotional speech. In: Ninth European Conference on Speech Communication and Technology (2005)
11. Calix, R.A., Khazaeli, M.A., Javadpour, L., Knapp, G.M.: Dimensionality reduction and classification analysis on the audio section of the SEMAINE database. In: D'Mello, S., Graesser, A., Schuller, B., Martin, J.-C. (eds.) ACII 2011. LNCS, vol. 6975, pp. 323–331. Springer, Heidelberg (2011). https://doi.org/10.1007/978-3-642-24571-8_43
12. Douglas-Cowie, E., et al.: The HUMAINE database: addressing the collection and annotation of naturalistic and induced emotional data. In: Paiva, A.C.R., Prada, R., Picard, R.W. (eds.) ACII 2007. LNCS, vol. 4738, pp. 488–500. Springer, Heidelberg (2007). https://doi.org/10.1007/978-3-540-74889-2_43
13. Engberg, I.S., Hansen, A.V., Andersen, O., Dalsgaard, P.: Design, recording and verification of a Danish emotional speech database. In: Fifth European Conference on Speech Communication and Technology (1997)
14. Eyben, F., Weninger, F., Gross, F., Schuller, B.: Recent developments in openSMILE, the Munich open-source multimedia feature extractor. In: Proceedings of the 21st ACM International Conference on Multimedia, MM 2013, Barcelona, Spain, pp. 835–838 (2013). https://doi.org/10.1145/2502081.2502224
15. Eyben, F., Weninger, F., Wöllmer, M., Schuller, B.: openSMILE: open-Source Media Interpretation by Large feature-space Extraction. audEERING GmbH (2016)

16. Frank, E., Kirkby, R.: Weka Classifiers Trees: Random Tree. http://weka.
sourceforge.net/doc.dev/weka/classifiers/trees/RandomTree.html   (2018).
Accessed 22 Feb 2018

17. Freund, Y., Schapire, R.E.: Experiments with a new boosting algorithm. In: Thirteenth International Conference on Machine Learning, pp. 148–156. Morgan Kaufmann, San Francisco (1996)

18. Friedman, J., Hastie, T., Tibshirani, R.: Additive Logistic Regression: a Statistical
View of Boosting. Stanford University, Technical report (1998)

19. Fujisaki, H.: The Interplay Between Physiology, Physics and Phonetics in the Production of Tonal Features of Speech of Various Languages. In: Proceedings of the
10th International Workshop Speech and Computer (SPECOM), Patras, Greece,
pp. 39–48, October 2005

20. Grimm, M., Kroschel, K., Narayanan, S.: The vera am mittag German audio-visual
emotional speech database. In: 2008 IEEE International Conference on Multimedia
and Expo, pp. 865–868. IEEE (2008)

21. Hall, M., Frank, E., Holmes, G., Pfahringer, B., Reutemann, P., Witten, I.H.: The
WEKA data mining software: an update. SIGKDD Explor. 11(1), 10–18 (2009).
https://doi.org/10.1145/1656274.1656278

22. Hammami, A.: Towards developing a speech emotion database for Tunisian Arabic
(2018)

23. Hastie, T., Tibshirani, R.: Classification by pairwise coupling. In: Jordan, M.I.,
Kearns, M.J., Solla, S.A. (eds.) Advances in Neural Information Processing Systems, vol. 10. MIT Press, Cambridge (1998)

24. Hozjan, V., Kacic, Z., Moreno, A., Bonafonte, A., Nogueiras, A.: Interface
databases: design and collection of a multilingual emotional speech database. In:
LREC (2002)

25. Jovicic, S.T., Kasic, Z., Dordevic, M., Rajkovic, M.: Serbian emotional speech
database: design, processing and evaluation. In: 9th Conference Speech and Computer (2004)

26. Keerthi, S., Shevade, S., Bhattacharyya, C., Murthy, K.: Improvements to platt's
SMO algorithm for SVM classifier design. Neural Comput. 13(3), 637–649 (2001)

27. Khalil, A., Al-Khatib, W., El-Alfy, E.S., Cheded, L.: Anger detection in Arabic
speech dialogs. In: 2018 International Conference on Computing Sciences and Engineering (ICCSE), pp. 1–6. IEEE (2018)

28. Khalil, A.A.A.S.: Real-Time Anger Detection In Arabic Speech Dialogs. Ph.D.
thesis, King Fahd University of Petroleum and Minerals (Saudi Arabia) (2011)

29. Klaylat, S., Osman, Z., Hamandi, L., Zantout, R.: Emotion recognition in Arabic
speech. Analog. Integr. Circuits Signal Process. 96(2), 337–351 (2018)

30. Klaylat, S., Osman, Z., Hamandi, L., Zantout, R.: Enhancement of an Arabic
speech emotion recognition system. Int. J. Appl. Eng. Res. 13(5), 2380–2389 (2018)

31. Kostoulas, T., Ganchev, T., Mporas, I., Fakotakis, N.: A real-world emotional
speech corpus for modern Greek. In: LREC (2008)

32. Landwehr, N., Hall, M., Frank, E.: Logist. Model Trees 95(1–2), 161–205 (2005)

33. Liberman, M.: Emotional prosody speech and transcripts (2002). http://www.ldc.
upenn.edu/Catalog/CatalogEntry.jsp?catalogId=LDC2002S28

34. Meddeb, M., BenAmmar, M., Alimi, A.: Towards a recommendation system for TV
programs based on human behavior. In: The International Conference on Control,
Engineering Information Technology, CEIT, pp. 180–182 (2013)

35. Meddeb, M., Hichem, K., Alimi, A.: Automated extraction of features from Arabic
emotional speech corpus. Int. J. Comput. Inf. Syst. Ind. Manag. Appl. IJCISIM 8,
184–194 (2016)

36. Meddeb, M., Karray, H., Alimi, A.M.: Intelligent remote control for TV program based on emotion in Arabic speech. arXiv preprint arXiv:1404.5248 (2014)
37. Meddeb, M., Karray, H., Alimi, A.M.: Speech emotion recognition based on Arabic features. In: 2015 15th International Conference on Intelligent Systems Design and Applications (ISDA), pp. 46–51. IEEE (2015)
38. Meddeb, M., Karray, H., Alimi, A.M.: Content-based arabic speech similarity search and emotion detection. In: Hassanien, A.E., Shaalan, K., Gaber, T., Azar, A.T., Tolba, M.F. (eds.) AISI 2016. AISC, vol. 533, pp. 530–539. Springer, Cham (2017). https://doi.org/10.1007/978-3-319-48308-5_51
39. Meddeb, M., Karray, H., Alimi, A.M.: Building and analysing emotion corpus of the Arabic speech. In: 2017 1st International Workshop on Arabic Script Analysis and Recognition (ASAR), pp. 134–139. IEEE (2017)
40. Meftah, A., Alotaibi, Y., Selouani, S.A.: Designing, building, and analyzing an Arabic speech emotional corpus. In: Workshop on Free/Open-Source Arabic Corpora and Corpora Processing Tools Workshop Programme, p. 22 (2014)
41. Meftah, A.H., Alotaibi, Y.A., Selouani, S.A.: Evaluation of an Arabic speech corpus of emotions: a perceptual and statistical analysis. IEEE Access 6, 72845–72861 (2018)
42. Platt, J.: Fast training of support vector machines using sequential minimal optimization. In: Schoelkopf, B., Burges, C., Smola, A. (eds.) Advances in Kernel Methods - Support Vector Learning. MIT Press, Cambridge (1998). http://research.microsoft.com/ jplatt/smo.html
43. Quinlan, R.: C4.5: Programs for Machine Learning. Morgan Kaufmann Publishers, San Mateo (1993)
44. Schuller, B.,et al.: The INTERSPEECH 2013 computational paralinguistics challenge: social signals, conflict, emotion, autism. In: Proceedings of Interspeech, Lyon, France, pp. 148–152 (2013)
45. Schuller, B., Batliner, A., Steidl, S., Seppi, D.: Recognising realistic emotions and affect in speech: state of the art and lessons learnt from the first challenge. Speech Commun. 53(9–10), 1062–1087 (2011). https://doi.org/10.1016/j.specom.2011.01.011
46. Schuller, B.W., Steidl, S., Batliner, A.: The INTERSPEECH 2009 emotion challenge. In: Proceedings of Interspeech, Brighton UK, pp. 312–315 (2009)
47. Staroniewicz, P., Majewski, W.: Polish emotional speech database – recording and preliminary validation. In: Esposito, A., Vích, R. (eds.) Cross-Modal Analysis of Speech, Gestures, Gaze and Facial Expressions. LNCS (LNAI), vol. 5641, pp. 42–49. Springer, Heidelberg (2009). https://doi.org/10.1007/978-3-642-03320-9_5
48. Sumner, M., Frank, E., Hall, M.: Speeding up logistic model tree induction. In: Jorge, A.M., Torgo, L., Brazdil, P., Camacho, R., Gama, J. (eds.) PKDD 2005. LNCS (LNAI), vol. 3721, pp. 675–683. Springer, Heidelberg (2005). https://doi.org/10.1007/11564126_72
49. Sun, X., Lichtenauer, J., Valstar, M., Nijholt, A., Pantic, M.: A multimodal database for mimicry analysis. In: D'Mello, S., Graesser, A., Schuller, B., Martin, J.-C. (eds.) ACII 2011. LNCS, vol. 6974, pp. 367–376. Springer, Heidelberg (2011). https://doi.org/10.1007/978-3-642-24600-5_40
50. TV, E.: RED line (in Arabic: Khat Ahmar - social talk show (2019). https://tv.echoroukonline.com
51. Vogt, T., André, E., Bee, N.: EmoVoice—a framework for online recognition of emotions from voice. In: André, E., Dybkjær, L., Minker, W., Neumann, H., Pieraccini, R., Weber, M. (eds.) PIT 2008. LNCS (LNAI), vol. 5078, pp. 188–199. Springer, Heidelberg (2008). https://doi.org/10.1007/978-3-540-69369-7_21

52. Yilmazyildiz, S., Henderickx, D., Vanderborght, B., Verhelst, W., Soetens, E., Lefeber, D.: EMOGIB: emotional gibberish speech database for affective human-robot interaction. In: D'Mello, S., Graesser, A., Schuller, B., Martin, J.-C. (eds.) ACII 2011. LNCS, vol. 6975, pp. 163–172. Springer, Heidelberg (2011). https://doi.org/10.1007/978-3-642-24571-8_17
53. Zaghouani, W.: Critical survey of the freely available Arabic corpora. arXiv preprint arXiv:1702.07835 (2017)

An Empirical Evaluation
of Arabic-Specific Embeddings
for Sentiment Analysis

Amira Barhoumi[1,2(✉)], Nathalie Camelin[1], Chafik Aloulou[2], Yannick Estève[1],
and Lamia Hadrich Belguith[2]

[1] LIUM, Le Mans University, Le Mans, France
{amira.barhoumi.etu,nathalie.camelin,yannick.esteve}@univ-lemans.fr
[2] MIRACL, Sfax University, Sfax, Tunisia
amirabarhoumi29@gmail.com, {chafik.aloulou,l.belguith}@fsegs.rnu.tn

Abstract. In this paper, we propose several specific embeddings in Arabic sentiment analysis (SA) framework. Indeed, Arabic is characterized by its agglutination and morphological richness contributing to great sparsity that could affect embedding quality. This work presents a rigorous study that compares different types of Arabic-specific embeddings. We evaluate them with 2 neural architectures: one based on convolutional neural network (CNN) and the other one based on Bidirectional Long Short-Term Memory Bi-LSTM. Experiments are done on the *Large Arabic-Book Reviews* corpus LABR. Our best results boost previous published accuracy by 1.9%. Moreover, we experiment combination of our individual systems defining very confident decision, reaching an accuracy of 92.2% on 98.25% of LABR test dataset.

Keywords: Sentiment analysis · Arabic language · Embeddings · Deep learning · Convolutional neural network · Recurrent neural network

1 Introduction

With the widespread of Internet and the revolution of social networks, every one could express his feelings and emotions regarding various topics, entities, products, persons, *etc.* Many academic and industrial efforts are focusing on analyzing opinions and sentiments by investigating automatic techniques to extract convenient information.

Sentiment analysis (SA) task [34] refers to identifying the subjectivity and the polarity of a given textual statement [35]. Generally, the subjectivity distinguishes objective statements (*facts*) from subjective ones (*opinions*). The polarity consists in associating positive/negative classes to statements (sometimes extended to three or more by adding neutral class or more fine-grained categories). SA and its applications have spread many languages and the most of works deal with Indo-European ones. Indeed, several researches have been carried out for English language. However, there has been less progress for Arabic.

© Springer Nature Switzerland AG 2019
K. Smaïli (Ed.): ICALP 2019, CCIS 1108, pp. 34–48, 2019.
https://doi.org/10.1007/978-3-030-32959-4_3

The majority of recent works on Arabic SA requires word embeddings as inputs. These embeddings deal mainly with words as *space separator units* in order to capture semantic and syntactic similarities. Their quality needs large corpora so that each word in the vocabulary appears multiple times in different contexts. Arabic is characterized by its agglutination and morphological richness that contribute to sparsity. For that, we should not ignore Arabic word complexity. In this work, we target the complex structure of Arabic words in SA task. To that end, we start by describing different ways of dealing with agglutinate and morphological rich specificity of Arabic. We investigate 6 ways to build Arabic-specific embeddings: one set by lexical unit (word, token, token\clitics, lemma, light stem and stem). Then, we integrate these embeddings into 2 neural architectures: the first one is based on Convolutional Neural Network (CNN); and the second one is based on Bidirectional Long Short-Term Memory (BiLSTM). We choose networks with different nature: CNN offers advantages in selecting relevant local features and BiLSTM has proven its ability in learning sequential information.

The rest of the paper is structured as follows. The related work is introduced in Sect. 2. We detail, in Sect. 3, Arabic specificity and propose in Sect. 4 our Arabic-specific embeddings. In Sect. 5, we present our neural architectures for Arabic SA task. We report, in Sect. 6, the experimental framework and discuss obtained results in Sect. 7. Finally, we conclude in Sect. 8 and give some outlooks to future works.

2 Related Works

The research field on Arabic is characterized by a lack of sentiment resources: annotated corpora and lexicons[1]. For an overview of Arabic SA field, [1,2,9] build a complete survey. Most of the existing methods in SA can be divided into three approaches: knowledge based, machine learning based and hybrid. The first is symbolic, it uses lexicon and linguistic rules. The second is a statistical approach that relies on machine learning methods. As the third is hybrid, it combines the two previous ones: it uses both lexicons and machine learning algorithms.

Research in sentiment analysis has benefited from scientific advances in deep learning techniques, and several recent works have been done with this type of learning for Arabic. [5] tests different deep networks. [11,18] use a convolutional neural network (CNN) architecture. [6,23,24] use recurrent neural network (RNN) and its variants.

The majority of neural networks takes as input continuous vector representations of words (*word embeddings*). Contextualized word embeddings *Elmo* [37] recently appears to handle both linguistic contexts and word syntax/semantic. Word2vec [32] and Glove [36] are the most common algorithms for learning pretrained embeddings. There are some embedding resources that are freely available for Arabic language. [18,44] built word embedding sets obtained by training *skip-gram* and *CBOW* versions of word2vec. [11] presents a relevant comparison

---

[1] [3,13] and [9] summarize all freely available corpora for Arabic SA task.

of these embedding resources and shows that their systems suffer from a low coverage of pre-trained embeddings at word level. Up to our knowledge, [40] is the only work dealing with Arabic specificity. They studied the effect of incorporating morphological information to word embedding in 2 ways: (i) including POS tags with words before embedding and, (ii) performing lemma abstraction of morphological embeddings obtained in (i). In this work, we present a rigorous comparison of different ways dealing with agglutination and morphology.

3   Specificity of Arabic Language

Arabic is a Semitic language. It is characterized by its agglutination and morphological richness. It is also difficult due to diacritization problem. For example, the word جمل can be interpreted in 3 ways: جَمَل /jamalun/ (camel), جُمَل /joumalun/ (sentenses) and جَمَّل /jammala/ (beautify). Each interpretation is made by different diacritization and reflects well-defined polarity: neutral polarity for the 2 first ones and positive polarity for the last one.

Moreover, Arabic word structure is very complex. In fact, if we consider a word as a sequence of characters delimited by two separators (blank or any punctuation mark), this word structure is very complex. It is composed of inflected form and (zero or several) clitics. It can be decomposed into proclitic(s) at its beginning, inflected form and enclitic(s) at its end. For example, the word أسيعجبه /AsyEjbh/ (will he like it?) consists of interrogation ا /A/ and future س /s/ particles, inflected form يعجب /yEjb/ and relative pronoun ه /h/, which are all agglutinated. Moreover, the words فسيعجبك /fsyEjbk/ (and you will like), فيعجبهم /fyEjbhm/ (and they like) and يعجبني /yEjbny/ (I like) share the same base unit يعجب /yEjb/ (like). Popular techniques of word embeddings (word2vec and Glove) will consider these three words as different units and build an embedding for each one of them. This limits embedding quality. For SA, it is important to consider the relation between such words. For that, we should not ignore Arabic word structure in embedding construction. We detail, in Sect. 4, our Arabic-specific embeddings.

4   Arabic-Specific Embeddings

In this section, we propose Arabic-specific embeddings corresponding to various lexical units. First, we describe different possible units in Arabic. Then, we present three techniques to build embeddings: word2vec based, character n-gram based and character-based.

Dealing with Arabic morphology, [40] studies the effect of incorporating morphological information to word embedding. They incorporate morphological knowledge with word embedding in 2 ways: (i) including POS tags with words before embedding and, (ii) performing lemma abstraction of morphological embeddings obtained in (i). In this work, we proceed differently.

We conduct a thorough study of embeddings of multiple lexical units. These units are obtained by applying NLP tools like tokenization[2], lemmatization (See Footnote 2), light stemming[3] and stemming[4]. This processing seems necessary to reduce the sparsity and increase shared semantics. Arabic sentences are composed of words separated by space. Tokenization is the process of word splitting into parts known as morphological segments or tokens: a set of clitics and base *token*. Lemmatization refers to the process of relating a given textual item to the actual lexical or grammatical morpheme corresponding to dictionary input. Stemming consists in reducing each word to its root (stem). However, light stemming refers to the process of stripping off a small set of prefixes and/or suffixes, without dealing with infixes [29]. Therefore, we investigate 6 different lexical units: word, token, token\clitics, lemma, light stem and stem. For the token\clitics, we decompose words at the morphological level.

Then, we delete all possible proclitics (و, ف, ب, ل, س, أ, ك, ال) and enclitics (وَا, ات, ان, ون, ة, نَا, تن, تم, تمَا, كن, كم, كمَا, هن, هم, همَا, هَا, ه, ك, ي) in order to keep only inflected form that we define as *token\clitics*. Unlike affixes, clitics [8] do not change or affect the word form or meaning and they do not usually contribute to sentiment analysis. Thus, their deletion could enhance the embedding quality in SA task.

We think that granularity level of word representation could impact embedding quality. And, it is better to test possible granularity levels[5]. For relevant study of lexical embedding quality, we detail, in the following, 3 techniques of embedding construction: word2vec based, character n-gram based and character-based.

4.1 Word2vec Model

Word2vec model [32] is a three-layer neural network that is trained to reconstruct linguistic contexts of words. It produces word embeddings, such that words sharing common contexts are closely located in the embedding space. Word2vec can utilize either of two model architectures to produce a distributed representation of words: continuous bag-of-words (CBOW) or skip-gram (SG). Skip-gram architecture is generally more powerful than CBOW [11,18,32]. So, we use skip-gram for embedding construction.

4.2 Character N-Gram Model

FastText is another method [12] that attempts to capture morphological information of words. It is an extension of word2vec (skip-gram version) [32], that

---

[2] http://qatsdemo.cloudapp.net/farasa/.
[3] https://github.com/motazsaad/arabic-light-stemming-py.
[4] https://pypi.org/project/Tashaphyne/.
[5] We expect stem embeddings give bad results as words lose semantics by stemming.

takes into account sub-words[6] information. FastText associates embeddings to character n-grams, and words are then represented by the summation of these vectors. So, fastText is able to extract more semantic relations between words sharing common character n-grams. It allows also obtaining embeddings for unseen rare words by summing its known character n-gram vectors. Various studies [16, 27, 38, 42] show that computing word embeddings on character n-grams using fastText performs better than using word2vec at the word-level. Moreover, fastText shows comparable results but significantly less training time.

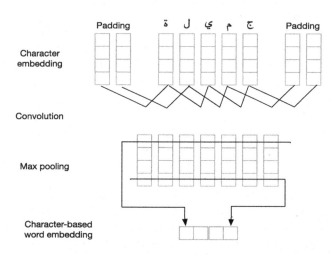

Fig. 1. The process of extracting character-based word embedding via CNN.

4.3   Character-Based Embeddings

Morphological information extraction needs to take into consideration all characters of a word. In Arabic, informative features may appear at the beginning (like the proclitic *interrogation particle* " أ " in " أيستحق " often used in irony), in the middle (like the *affirmative particle* " ل " in " فليقرأه "), or at the end.

Previous studies [15, 41] have shown that CNN is effective to extract morphological information from characters of words. They used CNN to represent the words with character-based embeddings. This type of embeddings has been very useful for Named Entity Recognition NER task [31]. Figure 1 shows the CNN we use to extract character representation of a given word. The CNN is similar to the one in [31]. In fact, words are initially padded on both sides. For each word, convolution operation and max pooling are applied to extract new feature vector that represents character-based embedding of the word. Dropout layer is also applied on character embeddings (CNN inputs). The dropout technique is powerful for regularization in order to reduce overfitting in neural networks.

---

[6] Each word is represented as a bag of n-grams of characters.

5   Description of Our Arabic SA Architectures

We present, in this section, two neural architectures. The first is based on convolutional neural network (CNN) and the second is based on a CNN-BiLSTM network.

5.1   CNN Based System

CNN architecture gives good performance in sentiment analysis for both English [28] and Arabic [11,18] languages. As a consequence, we consider a CNN architecture similar to the one described in [18] with adaptation of pre-trained embeddings for SA task. Each document Doc[7] is represented by a fixed-size matrix of embeddings $M(n, k)$ with n the length of the document and k the dimension of the embedding. CNN applies a *convolution* via filters whose window size is in $\{3, 4, 5\}$, in order to extract new features from the embedding matrix $M(n, k)$. Then, *max_pooling* is applied to the output of the convolution layer in order to only preserve the most relevant features that are concatenated at a fully connected layer with *dropout*[8]. Finally, the CNN applies the *sigmoid* function to the output layer to generate the polarity of the input document. Two polarities are possible: positive or negative. The architecture is illustrated in Fig. 2. Many hyper-parameters could be fine-tuned in CNN architecture: size of filters, rate of the dropout, pooling way, *etc.* We detail in the following the choices of two parameters: document length and padding/truncating type.

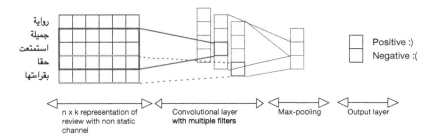

Fig. 2. CNN architecture for an example review

Document Length. As mentioned above, the CNN input is a fixed-size matrix. In our case, the matrix represents a review: each word occurrence of the review is represented by an embedding. In order to choose the fixed-size n of documents (*i.e.* the number of words to take into account), we use the formula (1) with the hypothesis of Gaussian length's distribution (with m the mean of word number in the documents and SD the standard deviation.)

$$n = m + 2 \times SD \tag{1}$$

---

[7] Each word w_i in Doc is represented by x_i: a k dimension vector ($x_i \in \mathbb{R}^k$).

[8] The rate of the dropout is 0.5.

Padding/Truncating. We define here how to represent documents in case the number of words is not n. When the length of any review is greater than n, it is necessary to cut additional words: it is the *truncating*. And when the review is shorter, then it is necessary to fill the representation of the review with zeros: it is the *padding*. But there are three ways to proceed: cut/fill at the beginning of the document (pre), or at the end of the document (post), or equally on both extremities. To choose the most appropriate protocol, we propose to conduct an analysis of polar words contained in the documents to determine which segment contains the most relevant information for the classification. In the context of sentiment analysis, this information mainly includes the sentiment words and negation terms that are often used in opinion expression. To determine the polarity of a word, a lexicon of polar words has been built. It is the fusion of 15 existing sentiment lexicons [4, 7, 10, 22, 39] (Arabic ones and others translated from English to Arabic). The resulting lexicon contains 51968 positive words and 45638 negative words. This lexicon will be available soon. For negation terms, we define a list of the following Arabic negation terms: { مَا, ليس, لن, لم, لا, غير}.

Statistics have to be computed on the experiment corpus to measure segment informativeness with regards to the presence of polarized words and negation terms. Document are divided into three equal parts and the percentage of sentiment words or negation terms contained in each of the three segments is calculated. If the most informative segment is the first one, post-padding/truncating will be applied. However, if the third segment is the most informative, pre-padding/truncating will be applied. The equal-padding/truncating on both extremities is applied in the third case.

5.2 CNN-BiLSTM Based System

The Long Short Term Memory LSTM [25] is a variant of recurrent neural network that captures long-distance dependencies. It is composed of appropriate neural units that allow *forgetting* or *memorizing*: some observations from the past will have more weight than others if they are considered more relevant for classification during training. LSTM is very effective for capturing sequence information which can help to analyze sentiments [23]. For SA task, it is beneficial to have access to both past and future contexts. BiLSTM [43] uses two LSTMs to learn each word of the sequence based on both its past and future context. BiLSTM is very useful for works like sentiment classification [14, 17, 26, 30]. In this work, we choose to reinforce the BiLSTM with CNN (see Fig. 1), obtaining *CNN-BiLSTM* architecture.

The role of the CNN is to compute the character-based embeddings (see Sect. 4.3). Character-based embeddings are useful for NER and POS tagging tasks [31]. So, we decide to evaluate *CNN-BiLSTM* system[9] for SA purpose. Figure 3 illustrates the architecture of our *CNN-BiLSTM* system based on *NeuroNLP*[10] toolkit. For each word in the review, the character-based embedding

---

[9] We kept the same parameters as in [31].
[10] https://github.com/XuezheMax/NeuroNLP2

is obtained by the CNN (as illustrated in Fig. 1). Then, it is concatenated with pre-trained unit embeddings to feed the BiLSTM. Our system predicts a class (positive or negative) for each review's word. The class referring to maximum number of word labels is assigned as the global polarity of the review.

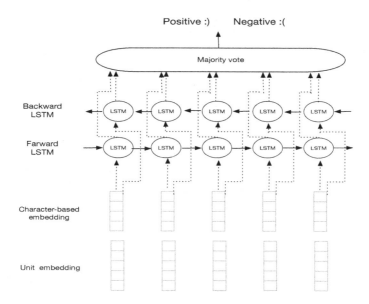

Fig. 3. CNN-BiLSTM architecture for SA task.

6 Experimental Framework

6.1 LABR Corpus

In this work, we used the corpus LABR [33] to evaluate our systems. It contains 63k book reviews: a note (number of stars from 1 to 5) is associated to each review. In a binary classification framework, we regrouped the reviews as proposed in [33]: the reviews associated with one or two stars compose the *negative* class and those with four or five stars represent the *positive* class. Thus the neutral reviews are not considered. The official corpus used, in this work, is composed of 33234 reviews (84% positive) for the training set and 8366 for the test set (85% positive). This is the official train/test split. Note that 10% of the training set is used as a validation set.

6.2 Choice of CNN Parameters

Document Length: Applying the formula (1) to LABR training dataset, we obtain an average review's length of 64 words and a standard deviation of 117.71

words. So, we get a threshold n of 300 words, and each document will be represented by 300 words. In LABR training corpus, more than 96% of the reviews contains less than 300 words.

Padding/Truncating: The protocol proposed in Subsect. 5.1 is applied to LABR training corpus. Statistics are reported in Table 1. It shows the informativeness of the first segment of documents that includes the largest percentage of polar words and negation terms. The other two-thirds are not as informative as the first one. We could therefore suppose that Internet users explicitly express their opinions at the beginning of the review and then justify themselves in a more factual way. The first third of each document therefore seems to contain relevant information to polarity classification.

Table 1. Informativity of different segments in LABR training set.

		1st segment	2nd segment	3rd segment
Train	% positive words	16,33	0,73	0,82
	% negative words	7,29	0,34	0,63
	% negation terms	0,74	0,03	0,002

As results, the post-padding/truncating seems to be the most appropriate to SA of LABR dataset. If the document contains more than 300 words, its end will be cut off. If it is smaller, it will be filled by 0 as necessary.

6.3 Corpora for Embedding Training

For embedding construction, we consider a dataset *Global* that represents the fusion of existing Arabic SA and newspaper datasets. The three sentiment corpus are: BRAD [20] gathering $510k$ book reviews, HARD [21] composed of $373k$ hotel reviews and the train set of LABR [33] formed by $23k$ book reviews. The news corpus AbuElKhair [19] is composed of $5222k$ news.

A pre-processing is applied to clean and normalize *Global*. Then, we apply six processing with NLP tools on *Global* and obtain six datasets: each one corresponds to lexical unit $\in$ {word, token, token\clitics,lemma, light stem, stem}. Our Arabic-specific embeddings are obtained by training word2vec and fastText on the six datasets. As results, we obtain 12 embedding sets. The latter will be freely available soon.

6.4 Evaluation Measures

In this work, the mainly measures in classification problems are used: accuracy, precision, recall and F1 measure. The accuracy (A) computes the ratio of true predicted labels. The macro-precision (P) is the mean of precision of all classes. The precision of class C_i computes the ratio of the number of documents that were correctly predicted C_i among the total number of documents that are C_i predicted. The macro-recall (R) is the mean of recall of all classes. The recall of a class C_i computes the ratio of the number of documents that were correctly predicted C_i among the number of documents originally associated to C_i. F1 measure is the harmonic mean of P and R.

7   Results and Discussion

In this paper, we investigate two neural architectures: CNN and CNN-BiLSTM. We evaluate them considering 12 embedding sets: *unit_Emb*, where *unit* $\in$ {word, token, token\clitics,lemma, light stem, stem} and *Emb* $\in$ {w2v, char-n}. As mentioned above, character-based embeddings are part of the CNN-BiLSTM architecture (see Sect. 5.2) and so, they are not considered as input. These *unit_Emb* are used as input to our architectures. As a result, we evaluate 24 systems: 12 are CNN based *CNN+unit_Emb*, and 12 based on CNN-BiLSTM *CNN-BiLSTM+unit_Emb*.

Table 2. Evaluation of CNN and CNN-BiLSTM with different lexical embeddings.

Unit	Emb.	CNN				CNN-BiLSTM			
		A	P	R	F1	A	P	R	F1
word	w2v	91.1	85.7	76.3	80.7	<u>90.9</u>	83.5	78.3	<u>80.8</u>
	char_n	91.2	85.2	<u>77.2</u>	81	<u>90.9</u>	83.1	**79**	**81**
token	w2v	91.2	85.8	76.7	81	90.8	83.8	77.3	80.4
	char_n	91.2	85.8	76.7	81	90.7	83.8	76.7	80.1
token\clitics	w2v	91.2	<u>86.4</u>	76.0	80.9	90.8	83.8	77.2	80.4
	char_n	91.2	85.7	76.7	80.9	<u>90.9</u>	**84.6**	76.7	80.4
Lemma	w2v	**91.5**	85.8	**78**	**81.7**	**91**	<u>84.3</u>	76.9	80.4
	char_n	<u>91.4</u>	**87**	76.4	<u>81.4</u>	**91**	83.6	<u>78.5</u>	**81**
light stem	w2v	91.2	85.6	76.8	81	90.8	83	78	80.4
	char_n	<u>91.4</u>	86.3	76.8	81.3	90.7	83.3	77.4	80.3
stem	w2v	89	81.2	69.8	75.1	89.3	80.2	73.9	76.9
	char_n	88.8	81.3	69	74.6	89.1	79.9	73.4	76.5

Table 2 shows the performances of both CNN and CNN-BiLSTM on test dataset. The best performance is mentioned in bold and the second best one is underlined. We note that CNN outperforms CNN-BiLSTM, whatever the lexical unit. The best performance[11] (91.5%) is obtained with *CNN+lemma_w2v*: CNN with lemma embeddings (trained with w2v model). Our best system *CNN+lemma_w2v* outperforms the existing systems tested on LABR dataset.

---

[11] We compare firstly accuracy, if equality then F1 measure.

[18] obtained an accuracy of 89.6% and [11] obtained 89.34% of accuracy. That means a gain of 1.9% compared to [18] and 2.16% compared to [11]. It is important to mention that [18] and [11] use the same CNN architecture. The only difference with our CNN architecture is the 2 parameters: document length and padding/truncating type described in Sect. 5.1. To measure the impact of parameter adjustment on CNN performance, we test the system of [18] and [11] with our new parameters, and obtain an accuracy of 90% and 90.3% respectively. So, we conclude that the profit of parameter adjustment that brings at least 0.4% on gain.

The best CNN system has 91.5% accuracy and is obtained with lemma_w2v embedding, and the second best one is obtained with lemma_char-n vectors. However, the best two CNN-BiLSTM gives 91% of accuracy with lemma_char-n and lemma_w2v embeddings. We could deduct that lemma represent the best Arabic unit for sentiment analysis.

Also, we note that CNN and CNN-BiLSTM get pretty much the same performances with token and token\clitics embeddings. This could explain clitics removal process and justify non-necessity of clitics for SA task. Moreover, we note that stem embeddings give as expected the worst results.

Besides, we measure the effect of our truncating process applied on reviews before classification. The length of truncated reviews vary from 2 to 2988 units[12]. The number of truncated documents is 233 (203 positive and 30 negative) in LABR test set. It looks that long reviews are rather positive than negative. Reviews truncating process does not seem affect the performance. In fact, we trained the systems by taking into consideration all reviews contents without truncating, and we obtained closed performances.

Furthermore, we investigate combination outputs of the different neural systems. In fact, these lexical embeddings behave differently as they were built for possible Arabic lexical units and with different techniques. We think that combining them could enhance performances. The worst performances are obtained with stem embeddings. So, we exclude them from the combination framework.

Two combination protocols are tested: *Oracle* and *Consensus*. The *Oracle* protocol allows to know the maximum border performance that could be obtained with the ideal combination way. It considers the correct label if it is predicted by at least one system. However, the *consensus* protocol only considers documents which are associated with same labels by all systems. It measures their agreement degree. As a result, the coverage is no longer 100% but the confidence in the prediction is very high. Results are reported in Table 3. In this work, we test 2 combination frames. The first one *All\stem* consists in combining all CNN_unit_Emb systems and CNN-BiLSTM_unit_Emb ones. We consider all units except stem. The second frame *2 Best* consists in combining the best 2 CNN systems and the best 2 CNN-BiLSTM ones. In *All\stem*, we obtain an oracle with 100% of accuracy for both CNN and CNN-BiLSTM. This means that correct label is predicted by at least one system. We note also system agreement

---

[12] The maximum length of reviews is equal to 3300 units.

on correctly classified reviews, with 86.75% of coverage with CNN and 81.7% with CNN-BiLSTM.

In the frame *2 Best*, CNN systems and CNN-BiLSTM ones achieve the same accuracy 92.2%. However, CNN cover more than CNN-BiLSTM. The best coverage is 98.25%. So, we conclude that *2 Best* combination frame with CNN define larger *strong decision*. The decisions outside this consensus indicate the reviews that must be carefully analyzed. The decisions outside this consensus determines the reviews that must be carefully analyzed. To go further, we analyze disagreement of CNN systems, focusing on the 146 (1.75% of test set) *no-agreement* reviews of the test set. They are composed of 68 positive reviews and 78 negative ones. More precisely, regarding the corresponding ranking stars, they are composed of 39.72% of 2 star reviews and 13.69% of 1 star reviews, corresponding to the negative class for our systems. Concerning the positive class, the *no agreement* reviews contain 33.56% of 4 star reviews and only 13.01% of 5 star ones.

Table 3. Evaluation of different combination setups.

	Protocol	CNN		CNN-BiLSTM	
		Coverage	Accuracy	Coverage	Accuracy
All\stem	*Oracle*	100%	100%	100%	100%
	Consensus	86.57%	100%	81.70%	100%
2 Best	*Oracle*	100%	92.3%	100%	92.5%
	Consensus	**98.25%**	**92.2%**	96.96%	92.2%

8   Conclusion and Future Works

In this paper, we investigated the specificity of Arabic language in Sentiment Analysis framework. We take into consideration its agglutination and morphological richness. We implemented 12 Arabic-specific embedding sets: *unit_Emb*, where *unit* $\in$ {word, token, token\clitics,lemma, light stem, stem} and *Emb* $\in$ {w2v, char-n}. We investigated two neural architectures with our different embeddings: the first one is based on CNN and the second one is based on BiLSTM. Results show that CNN outperforms CNN-BiLSTM. The best system *CNN+lemma_w2v* achieves 91.5% of accuracy. We show also that lemma are the best lexical unit for sentiment analysis.

As future work, we want to investigate contextualized embeddings *ELMO* in Arabic sentiment analysis. These embeddings are known by their ability to handle both linguistic contexts and syntax/semantic of words.

Moreover, one other perspective is to explore the track of *sentiment embeddings* as proposed by [45] that proves their role for performance improvement in sentiment analysis task. Finally, we would evaluate the different existing types of embeddings in several natural language processing *NLP* tasks like POS tagging, NER, syntactic and semantic analogies.

References

1. Al-Ayyoub, M., Khamaiseh, A.A., Jararweh, Y., Al-Kabi, M.N.: A comprehensive survey of Arabic sentiment analysis. Inf. Process. Manag. (2018)
2. Al-Ayyoub, M., Khamaiseh, A.A., Jararweh, Y., Al-Kabi, M.N.: A comprehensive survey of Arabic sentiment analysis. Inf. Process. Manag. **56**(2), 320–342 (2019)
3. Al-Kabi, M., Al-Ayyoub, M., Alsmadi, I., Wahsheh, H.: A prototype for a standard Arabic sentiment analysis corpus. Int. Arab J. Inf. Technol. **13**(1A), 163–170 (2016)
4. Al-Moslmi, T., Albared, M., Al-Shabi, A., Omar, N., Abdullah, S.: Arabic sentilexicon: constructing publicly available language resources for Arabic sentiment analysis. J. Inf. Sci. **44**(3), 345–362 (2018)
5. Al Sallab, A., Hajj, H., Badaro, G., Baly, R., El Hajj, W., Shaban, K.B.: Deep learning models for sentiment analysis in Arabic. In: Proceedings of the Second Workshop on Arabic Natural Language Processing, pp. 9–17 (2015)
6. Al-Smadi, M., Talafha, B., Al-Ayyoub, M., Jararweh, Y.: Using long short-term memory deep neural networks for aspect-based sentiment analysis of Arabic reviews. Int. J. Mach. Learn. Cybern., 1–13 (2018)
7. Al-Twairesh, N., Al-Khalifa, H., Al-Salman, A., Al-Ohali, Y.: Arasenti-tweet: a corpus for arabic sentiment analysis of saudi tweets. Procedia Comput. Sci. **117**, 63–72 (2017)
8. Alotaiby, F., Foda, S., Alkharashi, I.: Clitics in Arabic language: a statistical study. In: Proceedings of the 24th Pacific Asia Conference on Language, Information and Computation, pp. 595–601 (2010)
9. Badaro, G., et al.: A survey of opinion mining in Arabic: a comprehensive system perspective covering challenges and advances in tools, resources, models, applications, and visualizations. ACM Trans. Asian Low-Resour. Lang. Inf. Process. (TALLIP) **18**(3), 27 (2019)
10. Badaro, G., Baly, R., Hajj, H., Habash, N., El-Hajj, W.: A large scale Arabic sentiment lexicon for Arabic opinion mining. In: Proceedings of the EMNLP 2014 Workshop on Arabic Natural Language Processing (ANLP), pp. 165–173 (2014)
11. Barhoumi, A., Camelin, N., Estève, Y.: Des représentations continues de mots pour l'analyse d'opinions en arabe: une étude qualitative. In: 25e conférence sur le Traitement Automatique des Langues Naturelles (TALN 2018). Rennes, France, May 2018. https://hal.archives-ouvertes.fr/hal-01757776
12. Bojanowski, P., Grave, E., Joulin, A., Mikolov, T.: Enriching word vectors with subword information. arXiv preprint arXiv:1607.04606 (2016)
13. Boudad, N., Faizi, R., Oulad Haj Thami, R., Chiheb, R.: Sentiment analysis in Arabic: a review of the literature. Ain Shams Eng. J. (2017). https://doi.org/10.1016/j.asej.2017.04.007
14. Chen, T., Xu, R., He, Y., Wang, X.: Improving sentiment analysis via sentence type classification using BiLSTM-CRF and CNN. Expert. Syst. Appl. **72**, 221–230 (2017)
15. Chiu, J.P., Nichols, E.: Named entity recognition with bidirectional LSTM-CNNs. Trans. Assoc. Comput. Linguist. **4**, 357–370 (2016)
16. Cliche, M.: Bb_twtr at semeval-2017 task 4: Twitter sentiment analysis with CNNs and LSTMS. arXiv preprint arXiv:1704.06125 (2017)
17. Cong, D., Yuan, J., Zhao, Y., Qin, B.: A joint model for sentiment classification and opinion words extraction. In: Sun, M., Liu, T., Wang, X., Liu, Z., Liu, Y. (eds.) CCL/NLP-NABD -2018. LNCS (LNAI), vol. 11221, pp. 337–347. Springer, Cham (2018). https://doi.org/10.1007/978-3-030-01716-3_28

18. Dahou, A., Xiong, S., Zhou, J., Haddoud, M.H., Duan, P.: Word embeddings and convolutional neural network for Arabic sentiment classification. In: Proceedings of COLING 2016, the 26th International Conference on Computational Linguistics: Technical Papers, pp. 2418–2427 (2016)
19. El-Khair, I.A.: 1.5 billion words Arabic corpus. arXiv preprint arXiv:1611.04033 (2016)
20. Elnagar, A., Einea, O.: Brad 1.0: book reviews in Arabic dataset. In: 2016 IEEE/ACS 13th International Conference of Computer Systems and Applications (AICCSA), pp. 1–8. IEEE (2016)
21. Elnagar, A., Khalifa, Y.S., Einea, A.: Hotel Arabic-reviews dataset construction for sentiment analysis applications. In: Shaalan, K., Hassanien, A.E., Tolba, F. (eds.) Intelligent Natural Language Processing: Trends and Applications. SCI, vol. 740, pp. 35–52. Springer, Cham (2018). https://doi.org/10.1007/978-3-319-67056-0_3
22. ElSahar, H., El-Beltagy, S.R.: Building large Arabic multi-domain resources for sentiment analysis. In: Gelbukh, A. (ed.) CICLing 2015. LNCS, vol. 9042, pp. 23–34. Springer, Cham (2015). https://doi.org/10.1007/978-3-319-18117-2_2
23. Hassan, A.: Sentiment analysis with recurrent neural network and unsupervised neural language model (2017)
24. Heikal, M., Torki, M., El-Makky, N.: Sentiment analysis of Arabic tweets using deep learning. Procedia Comput. Sci. **142**, 114–122 (2018)
25. Hochreiter, S., Schmidhuber, J.: Long short-term memory. Neural Comput. **9**(8), 1735–1780 (1997)
26. Hyun, D., et al.: Target-aware convolutional neural network for target-level sentiment analysis. Inf. Sci. **491**, 166–178 (2019)
27. Joulin, A., Grave, E., Mikolov, P.B.T.: Bag of tricks for efficient text classification. EACL **2017**, 427 (2017)
28. Kim, Y.: Convolutional neural networks for sentence classification. arXiv preprint arXiv:1408.5882 (2014)
29. Larkey, L.S., Ballesteros, L., Connell, M.E.: Light stemming for Arabic information retrieval. In: Soudi, A., Bosch, A., Neumann, G. (eds.) Arabic Computational Morphology. Text, Speech and Language Technology, vol. 38, pp. 221–243. Springer, Dordrecht (2007). https://doi.org/10.1007/978-1-4020-6046-5_12
30. Ma, S., Sun, X., Lin, J., Ren, X.: A hierarchical end-to-end model for jointly improving text summarization and sentiment classification. arXiv preprint arXiv:1805.01089 (2018)
31. Ma, X., Hovy, E.: End-to-end sequence labeling via bi-directional LSTM-CNNs-CRF. In: Proceedings of the 54th Annual Meeting of the Association for Computational Linguistics (Volume 1: Long Papers), vol. 1, pp. 1064–1074 (2016)
32. Mikolov, T., Sutskever, I., Chen, K., Corrado, G.S., Dean, J.: Distributed representations of words and phrases and their compositionality. In: Advances in Neural Information Processing Systems, pp. 3111–3119 (2013)
33. Nabil, M., Aly, M., Atiya, A.: Labr: A large scale Arabic sentiment analysis benchmark. arXiv preprint arXiv:1411.6718 (2014)
34. Nasukawa, T., Yi, J.: Sentiment analysis: capturing favorability using natural language processing. In: Proceedings of the 2nd International Conference on Knowledge Capture, pp. 70–77. ACM (2003)
35. Pang, B., Lee, L., et al.: Opinion mining and sentiment analysis. Found. Trends® Inf. Retr. **2**(1–2), 1–135 (2008)

36. Pennington, J., Socher, R., Manning, C.: Glove: global vectors for word represen-
    tation. In: Proceedings of the 2014 Conference on Empirical Methods in Natural
    Language Processing (EMNLP), pp. 1532–1543 (2014)
37. Peters, M.E., et al.: Deep contextualized word representations. In: Proceedings of
    NAACL (2018)
38. Pylieva, H., Chernodub, A., Grabar, N., Hamon, T.: Improving automatic catego-
    rization of technical vs. Laymen medical words using FastText word embeddings.
    In: 1st International Workshop on Informatics & Data-Driven Medicine (IDDM
    2018), Lviv, Ukraine, November 2018. https://halshs.archives-ouvertes.fr/halshs-
    01968357
39. Saif, M. Mohammad, M.S., Kiritchenko, S.: Sentiment lexicons for Arabic social
    media. In: Proceedings of 10th Edition of the Language Resources and Evaluation
    Conference (LREC), Portorož, Slovenia (2016)
40. Salama, R.A., Youssef, A., Fahmy, A.: Morphological word embedding for Arabic.
    Procedia Comput. Sci. **142**, 83–93 (2018)
41. Santos, C.D., Zadrozny, B.: Learning character-level representations for part-of-
    speech tagging. In: Proceedings of the 31st International Conference on Machine
    Learning (ICML-14), pp. 1818–1826 (2014)
42. Schmitt, M., Steinheber, S., Schreiber, K., Roth, B.: Joint aspect and polarity
    classification for aspect-based sentiment analysis with end-to-end neural networks.
    In: Proceedings of the 2018 Conference on Empirical Methods in Natural Language
    Processing, pp. 1109–1114 (2018)
43. Schuster, M., Paliwal, K.K.: Bidirectional recurrent neural networks. IEEE Trans.
    Signal Process. **45**(11), 2673–2681 (1997)
44. Soliman, A.B., Eissa, K., El-Beltagy, S.R.: AraVec: a set of Arabic word embedding
    models for use in Arabic NLP. Procedia Comput. Sci. **117**, 256–265 (2017)
45. Yu, L.C., Wang, J., Lai, K.R., Zhang, X.: Refining word embeddings for sentiment
    analysis. In: Proceedings of the 2017 Conference on Empirical Methods in Natural
    Language Processing, pp. 534–539 (2017)

A Fine-Grained Multilingual Analysis Based on the Appraisal Theory: Application to Arabic and English Videos

Karima Abidi[✉], Dominique Fohr, Denis Jouvet, David Langlois, Odile Mella, and Kamel Smaïli

Loria University of Lorraine, Nancy, France
{abidi,fohr,jouvet,langlois,mella,smaili}@loria.fr

Abstract. The objective of this paper is to compare the opinions of two videos in two different languages. To do so, a fine-grained approach inspired from the appraisal theory is used to analyze the content of the videos that concern the same topic. In general, the methods devoted to sentiment analysis concern the study of the polarity of a text or an utterance. The appraisal approach goes further than the basic polarity sentiments and consider more detailed sentiments by covering additional attributes of opinions such as: Attitude, Graduation and Engagement.

In order to achieve such a comparison, in AMIS (Chist-Era project), we collected a corpus of 1503 Arabic and 1874 English videos. These videos need to be aligned in order to compare their contents, that is why we propose several methods to make them comparable. Then the best one is selected to align them and to constitute the data-set necessary for the fine-grained sentiment analysis.

Keywords: Video analysis · Sentiment analysis · Appraisal theory · Word embedding

1 Introduction

The explosive growth of the communication tools such as the television and the Internet has facilitated the rapid broadcasting of the information. Consequently, several television programs and news are available in different languages. However, the access to the information expressed in a foreign language is inaccessible to many users. To tackle this problem, the AMIS (*Access to Multilingual Information and Opinions*) project proposes to develop a multilingual information comprehension help system without human intervention. AMIS is a Chist-Era project, the principal objective is to develop a system, helping people to understand the content of a source video by presenting its main ideas in a target understandable language. This system is based on several components such as: video summarization, audio summarization, text summarization, automatic speech recognition system, machine translation and sentiment analysis

© Springer Nature Switzerland AG 2019
K. Smaïli (Ed.): ICALP 2019, CCIS 1108, pp. 49–61, 2019.
https://doi.org/10.1007/978-3-030-32959-4_4

Fig. 1. Scenario 1 - the most basic approach to newscast summarization

[5,23] and [4]. Four architectures have been proposed, one of these scenarios is given in Fig. 1, which corresponds to a pipeline assembly of some of the mentioned components.

This architecture is the one that has been used in this article for our experiments.

Another aspect of AMIS is to compare two videos in two languages about the same topic and to produce a grain-fined sentiment analysis of their contents. In this article, we will focus only on this aspect of AMIS project. The rest of this paper is organised as follows. Section 2 presents the used video database. Then, we present an overview of the global model proposed to align and analyse the AMIS videos that deal with the same object in terms of opinions in Sect. 3. In Sect. 4, we describe the proposed method to identify the comparable AMIS videos. A fine-grained multilingual sentiment analysis approach is proposed in Sect. 5 and finally, we conclude.

2   Video Database of AMIS

In order to develop the AMIS system, a large corpus of newscasts and reports from different channels (see Table 1) were crawled by using a list of controversial Hashtags (see Table 2). More details on the crawling method is given in [14]. In Table 3, we give the number of the harvested videos for each monolingual corpora.

Table 1. The channels used for harvesting.

English channels	BBC news, France 24, RT, Euronews
Arabic channels	النهار ,الشروق ,العربية ,القدس ,الاولى Nessma, i24news, France 24, RT, Euronews, BBC news
French channels	France 24, RT, Euronews

Table 2. The used controversial Hashtags.

#Syria	#RealMadrid-FCBarcelona	#Animal-rights
#Trump	#Women's-rights	#Homosexual-marriage
#Drug-liberalization	#Death-sentence	#Occupied-territories

Table 3. The number of videos per language

Language	Number of videos
English	1874
Arabic	1503
French	2046

3 An Overview of the Global Approach

Our objective is to make comparable the videos produced by the AMIS system. We have to mention that the comparability does not concern two well-written documents in the same language. In fact, we have two challenges to overcome in our case, the comparability is about the transcriptions of two speech recognition systems, one is in Arabic and the second is in English. That means that texts to make comparable include several errors. The second challenge concerns the multilingual aspect of the produced documents. In other words, we have to align two texts one is in Arabic and the second is in English. Several works, on multilingual comparability, have been proposed by the international community [3,9,10,13,22]. Overall, they concern documents harvested from social networks, Wikipedia, etc. But, in our knowledge there is very little work on the aspect of comparability on multilingual videos.

To achieve this goal, it is necessary to align the collected videos [12] and to take into account the qualitative aspect of the comparison material produced by the ASR systems. Once the comparable pairs are identified, the next step is to compare them in terms of opinions. In Fig. 2, we present a global overview of the model we propose and that will be explained further.

Our approach is based on the use of two Automatic Speech Recognition systems (ASR), one in Arabic [18] and one in English [8]. It is also based on a module of videos alignment and an elaborated procedure of fine-grained sentiment analysis.

4 Identifying Comparable Videos

In this article, we will present two methods of comparability: one which is well widespread, it is based on a dictionary method, and a new one based on the word embedding (Word2vec) [19]. These methods are explained in detail in the following sections.

4.1 Dictionary-Based Method

The method consists in looking-up into a dictionary if the translation of the words of the source video V_s exist in the target one V_t and vice versa. The idea is to align all the pairs of videos that share as many words as possible between the source and the target videos. To do so, we need to measure the comparability

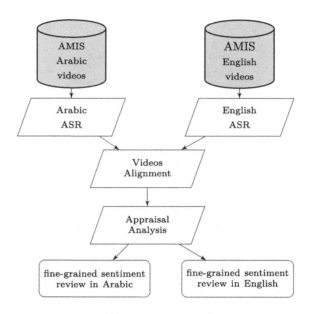

Fig. 2. An overview of the multilingual fine-grained sentiment analysis

between the videos pairs. The pair of videos that gets the best score is considered as the best comparable videos. For that, we used the well-known measure proposed by Li and Gaussier [15]. This comparability measure can be defined as the expectation of finding, for each English word w_e (respectively w_a) of the source video V_s (respectively of the target video V_t), its translation in the video V_t (respectively in the source video V_s).

The comparability measure is estimated as follows:

$$LG(V_s, V_t) = \frac{\sum\limits_{w \in \{l_s \cap D_s\}} \sigma(w, l_t) + \sum\limits_{w \in \{l_t \cap D_t\}} \sigma(w, l_s)}{\mid l_s \cap D_s \mid + \mid l_t \cap D_t \mid} \qquad (1)$$

Where D_s is the source part (English) of the bilingual dictionary, D_t is the target part (Arabic) of the dictionary. l_s and l_t are respectively the list of words of the source and the target video.

σ is a function using two parameters: a word w and a list of words (l_s). This function indicates whether potential translations of the word w represented by the list $T(w)$ include at least one word in the list l_s.

$$\sigma(w, l_s) = \begin{cases} 1 \; if \; T(w) \cap l_s \neq \emptyset \\ 0 \; else \end{cases} \qquad (2)$$

For this experimentation, we used the bilingual dictionary OMWN (Open Multilingual WordNet)[1] that contains 17,785 Arabic and English pairs.

---

[1] http://compling.hss.ntu.edu.sg/omw/.

The initial results of this approach led to bad performance. In fact, the drawback of this approach is its dependency of a bilingual dictionary. Whatever the size of this dictionary, the coverage issue arises especially for rich morphological language such as Arabic. In this language the word is composed, in the majority of cases, of the concatenation of a root and affixes. A root in Arabic is considered as a producer of words, that is why from a single root, several words can be produced. For example: the root كتب (*write*) with particular affixes produce different words with different meanings: يكتب (*he writes*), مكتبة (*library*), مكتب (*office*), etc. Consequently, in order to improve the coverage of the dictionary, we used the Buckwalter Arabic Morphological Analyzer to segment the words. Even if English does not have the same morphological constraints as Arabic, we also used a morphological analyzer (TreeTagger tool)[2] in order to reduce the missing inflected forms of words in the processed videos. In our experiments, the dictionary-based method includes in addition to the bilingual dictionary OMWN, all the inflectional form of its words.

As described above, the method necessitates a large bilingual dictionary, we replaced in another experiment the previous dictionary, by a translation table built on a parallel corpus of 9 million parallel sentences that led to a translation table of 297,176 pairs of Arabic and English entries [17].

4.2 Word Embedding Approach

The idea of this method is to investigate to what extent the semantic information encoded by words embedding approach can be used to retrieve the words semantically close to each other in two documents in which each of them is written in a different language. To do so, we used the CBOW method of Word2Vec model proposed by [19] to extract the bilingual vector representation of words. The CBOW method is trained over a large parallel corpus (9 million sentences in English and Arabic) with the objective to capture strong semantic relationships between the Arabic and English words. Each Arabic word is assigned a list of correlated English words which is calculated by a method proposed by the authors of [1].

To estimate the comparability between an Arabic and English videos, we used the same formula as in the previous Sect. 4.1 except that σ is a function that returns 1 if a word in the target video exist in the correlated words list of a word of the source video.

4.3 Experimentation

The methods presented previously are evaluated on a test corpus composed of 123 pairs of comparable videos extracted from the Euronews web site [8]. All the videos have been transcribed by our Arabic and English ASR systems depending on the language of the videos. The performance is given in terms of

---

[2] https://www.cis.uni-muenchen.de/~schmid/tools/TreeTagger/.

one of the classical measures in information retrieval topic: Recall ($R@1$, $R@5$ and $R@10$). In Table 4, we report the results of the three methods: the one based on a dictionary with the use of the morphological analyzers ($DicMA$), the one based on a translation table ($DicTT$) and finally the one based on a bilingual vector representation of words ($CBOW$). This table shows that $DicTT$ achieves the best results in comparison to the two others. The recall at rank 1 is 70% and grows up to 92% at rank 10. This result is encouraging, it allows, in almost cases to retrieve in the Top10 the right pair of comparable videos. The $CBOW$ method achieves similar result as the $DicMA$. This result is very interesting, since without external resources (a bilingual dictionary and a morphological analyzer), we can get almost the same performance. Consequently, this method could be used in under-resourced languages such as Arabic dialects.

Table 4. The performance of different comparability methods in terms of $R@1$, $R@5$, and $R@10$ on a test corpus.

Rappel	$R@1$	$R@5$	$R@10$
$DicMA$	43	65	76
$DicTT$	**70**	90	92
$CBOW$	39	62	75

By using the best method presented in this table, we retrieved all the pairs of comparable videos from the database of AMIS that led to 360 Arabic-English comparable videos. We recall that the total number of Arabic videos is 1,542, they concern several topics. Although videos were collected in different language using corresponding hashtags, that does not mean that each video in a given language has a matching comparable video in another language (in the collected video corpus). Furthermore, we selected only the pairs of videos for which the scores of comparability are high.

5   Multilingual Fine-Granularity Sentiment Analysis

In general, the methods devoted to sentiment analysis concern the study of the polarity of a text or an utterance. The sentiments in this case are reduced to the three classical opinions: positive, negative or neutral. In some other studies, fine-grained categories are added to have a more detailed analysis by using emotions such as (anger, disgust, fear, joy, sadness, and surprise) [24] or by adopting a linguistic theory such as appraisal [25],[20],[11] and [2].

The appraisal approach has been developed by White and Martin [16] within the theory Systemic Functional Linguistics [6]. The idea is to go further than the basic polarity sentiments and consider more detailed sentiments by covering additional attributes of opinions such as: Attitude, Graduation and Engagement.

The theory is supported by a graph, which represents the different sentiment categories expressed by a speaker (Fig. 3).

- **Attitude.** The category *Attitude* gives the type of appraisal being expressed as either *affect*, *appreciation*, or *judgment*.
  - *Affect.* This sub-category of *Attitude* describes the emotional reactions (happy, miserable, angry, etc.).
  - *Appreciation.* It concerns the opinion that a person has about the inner or outer qualities of an object (beautiful, innovative, amazing, etc.).
  - *Judgment.* This sub-category describes the behaviour of somebody in a social context (lucky, brave, famous, etc.).
- **Engagement.** Sentiment can be expressed directly or indirectly, it reflects the possibility of the production of an event (perhaps, seems, etc.)
- **Graduation.** This category refers to the strength or the force of emotion and attitude in each appraisal category. The graduation is globally expressed via modifiers, for example the combination of the 'modifier' "very" with an adjective intensifies the meaning of the utterance. There is another sub-category of Graduation, named *Focus*. It makes the meaning of something either more precise or less precise. For example: *a true challenge* or *it is a challenge*. In the first example, the challenge seems to be harder than in the second example.

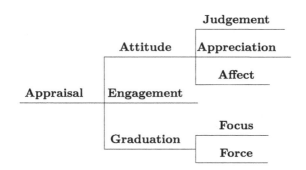

Fig. 3. Appraisal taxonomy

5.1   Building Appraisal Lexicon

In the following, for commodity reasons we will use only the categories: *Attitude* and *Graduation*. To build the appraisal lexicon, we started from an English opinion lexicon composed of 4,913 negative words and 2,718 positive words developed by Minqing Hu and Bing Liu [7]. Besides, we created a list of 363 words with their appraisal categories inspired from the examples of Martin and White's book [16] that we named *MW363*. This led to a list of words with their polarities and appraisal categories, some examples are given in Table 5. Then the idea is to use a lexicon with appraisal categories larger than the one we created (*MW363*). That is why, we decided to assign for each entry of the Bing Liu's lexicon the corresponding appraisal *Attitude* category by using a method combining Word2Vec and the *MW363*. The method consists in representing each word of respectively the Bing Liu's and *MW363* lexicons by a word embedding approach by using

Table 5. Few examples of words with appraisal and polarity opinions

Word	Attitude sub-category	Polarity
Lucky	Judgment	Positive
Obscure	Judgment	Negative
Confident	Affect	Positive
Love	Affect	Positive
Helpful	Appreciation	Positive

the vectors trained on 100 billion words calculated from various news articles of Google[3]. To do so, for each word X from Bing Liu's lexicon, we find its top-n closest words to $MW363$. Each word of this list is labeled by a sub-category of *Attitude*. Then, we assign to X the sub-category which is predominant in this latter list.

Since the words of Bing Liu's lexicon have already polarity signs, when we assign them an appraisal sub-category, we get new sub-category with a polarity. That means, for example, a word may have an *Affect* sub-category but this one will be signed by the initial polarity. Each word of the Bing Liu's lexicon will be assigned an appraisal positive or negative score (S_{app}) calculated as in the formula 3. A positive or negative score respectively indicates how positive or negative is the word in terms of the Attitude sub-category. The achieved lexicon that corresponds to the initial lexicon of Bing Liu is henceforth increased by the *Attitude* appraisal category. It will be referred in the following as BingApp.

$$S_{App}(X) = \frac{1}{d_n} \sum_{i=1}^{d_n} cosine(X, W_i) * P_{W_i} \qquad (3)$$

Where:

- d_n: The number of words in the predominant sub-category in the list of the n closest words with X.
- W_i: A word belonging to the list of the predominant attitude sub-category.
- X: A word of Bing Liu's sentiment lexicon.
- $P_{W_i} = \begin{cases} +1 \text{ if } W_i \text{ is positive} \\ -1 \text{ otherwise.} \end{cases}$

We recall that our objective is to compare two videos one in English and the other in Arabic in terms of fine-grained opinions. In order to work with the same material in Arabic and in English, we translated BingApp into Arabic and we kept for each Arabic word the same sub-category and the same score as the English word. In Table 6 we give few examples of the achieved lexicon.

---

[3] https://code.google.com/archive/p/word2vec/.

Table 6. Few examples of BingApp.

English word	Arabic translation	Appraisal categories /Sub-category	S_{App}	Polarity
Criminal	مجرم	Attitude/Judgment	-0.45	N
Attentive	منتبه	Attitude/Judgment	0.41	P
Worried	قلق	Attitude/Affect	-0.45	N
Satisfied	راض	Attitude/Affect	0.24	P
Harmonious	متناغم	Attitude/Appreciation	0.63	P

5.2   Fine-Granularity Sentiment Predicting Model

To be able to make an efficient fine-grained sentiment analysis, we need to enrich BingApp by adding other categories. To do so, we have to take into account, at least, two linguistic phenomena. To illustrate our purpose, let study the following example: *This cake is not very good*. We can remark that this sentence contains a negation form that precedes the phrase (*very good*). Consequently, the underlying opinion of this sentence can be completely inverted.

In this example, the adverb (*very*) is used to emphasis the adjective *good*. In other words, it modifies its intensity by adding force to this adjective. This phenomenon must be considered, especially knowing that the *Force* is an existing sub-category of the *Graduation* category.

– *Dealing with the Negation*. We added a new category to the appraisal taxonomy that we called *Inversion*, with its sub-category *Negation*. Then, we added to BingApp, the negation words (*Not, No, Neither, Nor, etc.*) and assigned them to the *Inversion* category. During the analysis step, if the *Inversion* category is identified in an utterance, then the polarity of the word following the negation item is inverted.
– *Dealing with the Force*. To consider the *Force* in the analysis, we added to the dictionary BingApp several modifier words that we assigned to the subcategory *Force* of the category *Graduation*. We shared these modifiers through 4 classes. Each class indicates the intensity of the modifier and it is assigned a score proportional to its capacity to intensify a word. These weights have been set by hand. In Table 7, we give some examples of the new *Force* classes and their corresponding words that have been inserted into BingApp.

Table 7. The four classes of the intensity modifiers.

Force classes	Modifiers
Extreme	hardly, scarcely, barely, very, greatly, etc.
High	large, less, distant, more, etc.
Moderate	somewhat, relatively, rather, reasonably, many, etc.
Low	slightly, least, small, etc

In Fig. 4, we illustrate the new taxonomy of the appraisal theory.

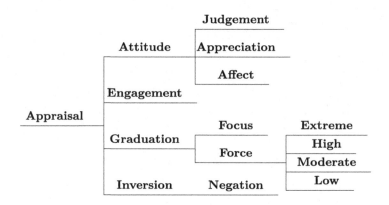

Fig. 4. Appraisal taxonomy

In order to evaluate the quality of our lexicon, we decided to use it in the assessment of the publicly available collection of movie reviews constructed by [21]. This standard test consists of 1,000 positive and 1,000 negative reviews. In order to study the impact of the use of the Inversion category that we added to the appraisal theory, we selected only the reviews that are concerned by this category. This led to a test corpus of 992 reviews including 538 positive reviews. In Table 8 we reported the recall and the precision values obtained by using the standard Bing Liu's lexicon and by the lexicon we created BingApp.

Table 8. Comparison of Bing Liu's lexicon and BingApp on a test Review corpus

Method	Recall	Precision
Bing Liu's	69.0	68.8
BingApp	**70.9**	**71.0**

In this experiment BingApp yields to better performance even if the difference is not very important. This test is not the main result of this work. It has been done only in order to know whether we use Bing Liu's or BingApp lexicon for evaluating the opinions underlying the videos. In conclusion, we consider that the appraisal approach led to better results, thanks to the dictionary we created, in comparison to the classical method based on the polarity supported by Bing Liu's lexicon.

5.3 Evaluation on AMIS Videos

In the following, we propose to assess finely the opinions within the videos by using BingApp, the appraisal lexicon we created. A quantitative and qualitative evaluation is proposed. Each video is evaluated by a score we propose in formula 4.

$$S = \sum_{i=1}^{N} \alpha(w_{i-k}^{i-1}) * S_{App}(w_i) \qquad (4)$$

Where N is the size of the video in terms of number of words. α is a weight depending on the *Inverted* or the *Force* sub-category of the k words preceding the word w_i (k is set to 2). It is the size of the cache in which the *Force* or the *Negation* are looked for.

The second assessment focuses on a qualitative evaluation in which we summarize the expressed opinion in the video. The idea is to facilitate the interpretation of the underlying opinion within a video and not just give an overall assessment score. A template of the opinion review is proposed in Fig. 5.

The sentiment of the video is positive with a score $[X_p]$ and negative with a score $[X_n]$. X_{aff}% of the video concerns emotional reactions. X_{Jug}% of the video concerns the human behaviour according to social norms and $1 - (X_{aff} + X_{Jug})$% of the video is about the appreciation of no human being entities. The force of the subject: ([target word]) is [augmented/reduced] thanks to the word [Modifier]

Fig. 5. The template used to generate the qualitative evaluation

This template corresponding to the review presented to the user indicates how much the video is negative or positive? What is the percentage of each subcategory of the category *Attitude*? Which word has been augmented or reduced? And which word participated to the augmentation or the reduction of the *Force*. An example is given in Fig. 6.

Example: *well, to coin a phrase, the reports of "babe: pig in the city" 's death at the hands of a dark, scary, Felliniesque interpretation have been greatly exaggerated.*
Evaluation
The sentiment of the video is positive with a score **0.45** and negative with a score-**2.28**. **22.22**% of the video concerns emotional reactions. **44.44**% of the video concerns the human behaviour according to social norms and **33.34**% of the video is about the appreciation of no human being entities. The force of the subject: (**interpretation**) is **augmented** thanks to the word **greatly**

Fig. 6. An example of qualitative evaluation.

6 Conclusion

In this article the objective was twofold. The first one consisted in aligning the videos of AMIS project by making comparable the Arabic and the English videos describing the same subject. We tested three methods and compared them. The best one has been used to align the whole database of AMIS. Then we used a new method based on the appraisal approach allowing to have a fine-grained opinion analysis. For that, we created a new lexicon including more than 7,000 entries, each of them is assigned to the appraisal category. This dictionary served to evaluate quantitatively and qualitatively the content of videos. A review template has been proposed to summarize the opinions inside the video.

Acknowledgements. We would like to acknowledge the support of Chist-Era for funding this work through the AMIS (Access Multilingual Information opinionS) project.

References

1. Abidi, K., Menacer, M.A., Smaïli, K.: CALYOU: a comparable spoken ALgerian corpus extracted from YOUTube. In: 18th Annual Conference of the International Speech Communication Association, Stockholm Sweden, Interspeech (2017)
2. Alamsyah, A., Rahmah, W., Irawan, H.: Sentiment analysis based on appraisal theory for marketing intelligence in Indonesia's mobile phone market (2015)
3. Barrón-Cedeño, A., España-Bonet, C., Boldoba, J., Màrquez, L.: A factory of comparable corpora from Wikipedia. In: Proceedings of the Eighth Workshop on Building and Using Comparable Corpora, Beijing, China, 30 July 2015, pp. 3–13 (2015)
4. Garcia-Zapirain, B., et al.: A proposed methodology for subjective evaluation of video and text summarization. In: Choroś, K., Kopel, M., Kukla, E., Siemiński, A. (eds.) MISSI 2018. AISC, vol. 833, pp. 396–404. Springer, Cham (2019). https://doi.org/10.1007/978-3-319-98678-4_40
5. Grega, M., et al.: An integrated AMIS prototype for automated summarization and translation of newscasts and reports. In: Choroś, K., Kopel, M., Kukla, E., Siemiński, A. (eds.) MISSI 2018. AISC, vol. 833, pp. 415–423. Springer, Cham (2019). https://doi.org/10.1007/978-3-319-98678-4_42
6. Halliday, M.A.K.: An Introduction to Functional Grammar, 3rd edn. Hodder Arnold, London (1994)
7. Hu, M., Liu, B.: Mining and summarizing customer reviews. In: Proceedings of the Tenth ACM SIGKDD International Conference on Knowledge Discovery and Data Mining, KDD 2004 (2004)
8. Jouvet, D., Langlois, D., Menacer, M.A., Fohr, D., Mella, O., Smaïli, K.: About vocabulary adaptation for automatic speech recognition of video data. In: ICNLSSP 2017 - International Conference on Natural Language, Signal and Speech Processing, Casablanca, Morocco, pp. 1–5. (2017)
9. Karima, A., Smaïli, K.: Measuring the comparability of multilingual corpora extracted from Twitter and others. In: Series, S.L. (ed.) The Tenth International Conference on Natural Language Processing (HrTAL2016), Dubrovnik, Croatia, September 2016
10. Kim, J., Li, J.J., Lee, J.H.: Evaluating multilanguage-comparability of subjectivity analysis systems. In: Proceedings of the 48th Annual Meeting of the Association for Computational Linguistics, ACL 2010, Stroudsburg, PA, USA, pp. 595–603. Association for Computational Linguistics (2010)
11. Korenek, P., Simko, M.: Sentiment analysis on microblog utilizing appraisal theory. World Wide Web **17**(4), 847–867 (2014)

12. Koźbiał, A., Leszczuk, M.: Collection, analysis and summarization of video content. In: Choroś, K., Kopel, M., Kukla, E., Siemiński, A. (eds.) MISSI 2018. AISC, vol. 833, pp. 405–414. Springer, Cham (2019). https://doi.org/10.1007/978-3-319-98678-4_41
13. Langlois, D., Saad, M., Smaïli, K.: Alignment of comparable documents: comparison of similarity measures on French-English-Arabic data. Nat. Lang. Eng. (2018). https://doi.org/10.1017/S1351324918000232
14. Leszczuk, M., Grega, M., Koźbiał, A., Gliwski, J., Wasieczko, K., Smaïli, K.: Video summarization framework for newscasts and reports - work in progress. In: Dziech, A., Czyżewski, A. (eds.) Multimedia Communications, Services and Security (2017)
15. Li, B., Gaussier, É.: Improving corpus comparability for bilingual lexicon extraction from comparable corpora. In: COLING 2010, 23rd International Conference on Computational Linguistics, Proceedings of the Conference, Beijing, China, 23–27 August 2010, pp. 644–652 (2010)
16. Martin, J., White, P.: The Language of Evaluation Appraisal in English. Palgrave Macmillan, London (2005)
17. Menacer, M.A., Langlois, D., Mella, O., Fohr, D., Jouvet, D., Smaïli, K.: Is statistical machine translation approach dead? In: ICNLSSP 2017 - International Conference on Natural Language, Signal and Speech Processing, Casablanca, Morocco, pp. 1–5. ISGA (2017)
18. Menacer, M.A., Mella, O., Fohr, D., Jouvet, D., Langlois, D., Smaili, K.: An enhanced automatic speech recognition system for Arabic. In: Proceedings of the Third Arabic Natural Language Processing Workshop, pp. 157–165 (2017)
19. Mikolov, T., Chen, K., Corrado, G., Dean, J.: Efficient estimation of word representations in vector space. In: ICLR (Workshop) (2013)
20. Momtazi, S.: Fine-grained German sentiment analysis on social media. In: LREC (2012)
21. Pang, B., Lee, L.: A sentimental education: sentiment analysis using subjectivity summarization based on minimum cuts. In: Proceedings of the ACL (2004)
22. Saad, M., Langlois, D., Smaïli, K.: Extracting comparable articles from wikipedia and measuring their comparabilities. Procedia - Soc. Behav. Sci. **95**, 40–47 (2013)
23. Smaïli, K., et al.: A first summarization system of a video in a target language. In: Choroś, K., Kopel, M., Kukla, E., Siemiński, A. (eds.) MISSI 2018. AISC, vol. 833, pp. 77–88. Springer, Cham (2019). https://doi.org/10.1007/978-3-319-98678-4_10
24. Strapparava, C., Mihalcea, R.: SemEval-2007 task 14: affective text. In: Proceedings of the 4th International Workshop on Semantic Evaluations, SemEval 2007, Stroudsburg, PA, USA, pp. 70–74. Association for Computational Linguistics (2007)
25. Whitelaw, C., Garg, N., Argamon, S.: Using appraisal groups for sentiment analysis. In: Proceedings of the 14th ACM International Conference on Information and Knowledge Management, CIKM 2005 (2005)

Neural Techniques for Text and Speech

Extractive Text-Based Summarization of Arabic Videos: Issues, Approaches and Evaluations

Mohamed Amine Menacer[1(✉)], Carlos-Emiliano González-Gallardo[2],
Karima Abidi[1], Dominique Fohr[1], Denis Jouvet[1], David Langlois[1],
Odile Mella[1], Fatiha Sadat[3], Juan-Manuel Torres-Moreno[2,4],
and Kamel Smaïli[1]

[1] Loria, University of Lorraine, Nancy, France
{mohamed-amine.menacer,karima.abidi,fohr,jouvet,langlois,
mella,smaili}@loria.fr
[2] LIA, Avignon Université, Avignon, France
{carlos-emiliano.gonzalez-gallardo,juan-manuel.torres}@univ-avignon.fr
[3] UQAM, Montreal, QC, Canada
sadat.fatiha@uqam.ca
[4] Poliyechnique Montréal, Montreal, QC, Canada

Abstract. In this paper, we present and evaluate a method for extractive text-based summarization of Arabic videos. The algorithm is proposed in the scope of the AMIS project that aims at helping a user to understand videos given in a foreign language (Arabic). For that, the project proposes several strategies to translate and summarize the videos. One of them consists in transcribing the Arabic videos, summarizing the transcriptions, and translating the summary. In this paper we describe the video corpus that was collected from YouTube and present and evaluate the transcription-summarization part of this strategy. Moreover, we present the Automatic Speech Recognition (ASR) system used to transcribe the videos, and show how we adapted this system to the Algerian dialect. Then, we describe how we automatically segment into sentences the sequence of words provided by the ASR system, and how we summarize the obtained sequence of sentences. We evaluate objectively and subjectively our approach. Results show that the ASR system performs well in terms of Word Error Rate on MSA, but needs to be adapted for dealing with Algerian dialect data. The subjective evaluation shows the same behaviour than ASR: transcriptions for videos containing dialectal data were better scored than videos containing only MSA data. However, summaries based on transcriptions are not as well rated, even when transcriptions are better rated. Last, the study shows that features, such as the lengths of transcriptions and summaries, and the subjective score of transcriptions, explain only 31% of the subjective score of summaries.

Keywords: Text summarization · Video summarization · Automatic
speech recognition · Segmentation

© Springer Nature Switzerland AG 2019
K. Smaïli (Ed.): ICALP 2019, CCIS 1108, pp. 65–78, 2019.
https://doi.org/10.1007/978-3-030-32959-4_5

1   Introduction

Understanding the content of a video in a foreign language could be considered as a dream. However, research in video analysis, automatic speech recognition and machine translation has evolved significantly and the results today can be considered encouraging. In this article, part of the Chist-Era founded AMIS[1] (Access Multilingual Information opinionS) project, we address the problem of understanding a video in a foreign language.

In the scope of this project, we consider that we understand the content of a video if we can summarize it correctly. Therefore, this project uses several research disciplines related to natural language processing, namely video analysis, automatic speech recognition, segmentation of speech transcriptions and automatic summarization. Moreover, it is essential to evaluate the performance of such a system, either to make it public or to highlight the new research challenges related to this problem. It is indeed very difficult to find an objective measure allowing to assess the whole system, since this one is the result of several technologies and models.

As part of this project we considered that the foreign language is the Arabic language, so we developed a speech recognition system for Arabic that we named ALASR [17] (Arabic Loria Automatic Speech Recognition system). We have also developed a machine translation system that translates the results of the Arabic transcript into English. We worked on real data that we crawled from TV channels broadcasting in Arabic, such as: Euronews, AlArabiya, Skynews, etc. We also collected videos from Algerian channels broadcasting in Arabic, but necessarily using sometimes the Algerian dialect.

When testing ALASR on Algerian channels data, the performance collapsed. This drove us to adapt ALASR to dialectal data, which led to better results. Regarding the global assessment, we conducted a subjective evaluation that allowed us to test not only the result of speech recognition, but also the automatic summarizing system.

The rest of this paper is organized as follows. Section 2 presents our video corpus. The Arabic ASR system is presented in Sect. 3, and its adaptation on Algerian dialect in Sect. 4. An automatic sentences segmentation module is shown in Sect. 5; Sect. 6 shows the automatic text summarizer employed in this work. Section 7 presents our results, and finally, Sect. 8 concludes this paper.

2   Video Corpus

A project such as AMIS requires to collect videos in order to estimate the parameters of our models and to evaluate our approach. For that, French, English and Arabic videos have been collected. Videos have been selected according to a set of controversial Twitter hash-tags such as #womenrights or #syria given that one goal of the AMIS project is to compare opinions on videos in different languages that deal with the same topic; more details on the collection process can be

---

[1] http://deustotechlife.deusto.es/amis/.

found in [11]. The overall video corpus corresponds to more than 300 h of video, that is about 100 h in each of the three languages (French, English and Arabic). The video data come from various channels such as Euronews, France24, BBC and AlArabiya.

With respect to the Arabic videos, more than 1,500 videos have been collected. They come from channels such as AlArabiya, France24, SkynewsArabia, Euronews, EchoroukTV, EnnaharTV, BBC, etc. The duration of the videos vary from one minute up to more than one hour.

3   Arabic Automatic Speech Recognition

The training of the acoustic models and the recognition experiments were carried out with the ALASR system developed at LORIA laboratory. ALASR is based on the Kaldi toolkit [20]. For the acoustic parameters, 13-dimensional Mel-Frequency Cepstral Coefficients (MFCC) augmented with their first and second order derivatives were computed. 37 acoustic models were trained: 34 phone models, one model for silence, one for respiration and one for noise. A Deep Neural Network (DNN) was used to produce posterior probabilities for the context dependent phone densities of the Hidden Markov Models (DNN-HMM models). The DNN consists of 6 layers with 2,048 hidden neurons each. For the input layer, 11 frames were concatenated, and the output layer has 4,264 output neurons, corresponding to the 4,264 senones (contextual phone densities). A total of 30 millions parameters were estimated using 54 h of Arabic Broadcast News Speech Corpus. 5 h of spoken data were used for tuning (Dev) and 5 other hours for evaluating the performance of ALASR system (Test).

Linguistic knowledge is required to capture the properties of the language. For this reason, we trained two 4-gram language models one on the Gigaword corpus and the other on the train transcripts of the acoustic data. Since these two corpora are unbalanced, the two language models were combined linearly by optimizing the weights of the linear interpolation on the transcripts of the acoustic Dev set. Due to memory constraints, we decided to prune the full 4-gram language model by minimizing the relative entropy between the full and the pruned model [22]. This led to a total number of 4M n-grams in the pruned language model compared to 983M n-grams in the full language model. This later model will be used for rescoring the lattice produced by the system.

The pronunciation lexicon makes the link between the language model and the acoustic model. The absence of the short vowels (diacritics) in written texts brings issues in the pronunciation modelling. In fact, for each Arabic grapheme-based form, the ASR system has to consider all the pronunciation possibilities. There are two approaches to deal with this issue:

Grapheme-based approach. This approach considers for Arabic that the pronunciation of each word is simply its grapheme decomposition, and therefore, graphemes represent the basic units for the acoustic model. While this approach is the simplest way to build a lexicon, it will not provide an explicit representation of short vowels, which might lead to recognition errors.

Phoneme-based approach. Unlike the previous approach where short vowels are implicitly modeled with the surrounding consonants in the acoustic modelling, this approach provides an explicit representation of short vowels in the pronunciation modelling. This approach is adopted in this work.

In order to create the phoneme-based model, we selected the 109k most frequent words from the Gigaword corpus (1 billion word occurrences) plus the words that appear more than 3 times in the transcripts of the acoustic Train set. Afterwards, only words for which pronunciation variants exist in an external lexicon [2] were kept. This process produces a lexicon having 95k unique grapheme-based words and 485k pronunciation variants, that is an average of 5.07 pronunciations per word. This lexicon is referred in the following as MSA_{lex}. Table 1 illustrates the evaluation of ALASR system on the Test corpus.

Table 1. Performance of ALASR before and after rescoring the lattice (WER: Word Error Rate, OOV: Out-Of-Vocabulary.).

System	WER (%)	OOV (%)
ALASR	15.32	2.5
ALASR+Rescoring	14.02	

Using a pruned language model accelerates the decoding process but it affects the performance of the system. By rescoring the produced lattice, new hypotheses are generated based on the probabilities of the full 4-gram language model, which leads to an absolute improvement of 1.3%.

4   Adaptation of the Automatic Speech Recognition System to the Algerian Dialect

Most of Arab people do not use MSA in their daily conversations, since their mother tongue is an Arabic dialect that is mainly derived from MSA. The Arabic dialect varies from one country to another and sometimes more than one dialect can be found within a country. These variants are mainly influenced by the history of the region itself [15].

The Algerian dialect is one of the Maghrebi dialects spoken in the western Arab countries. It is one of the hardest dialect to be recognized by an ASR system. This is due to the fact that this variant of Arabic language uses many borrowed words (mainly French) and alters the pronunciation of many words of MSA [9,10]. Furthermore, the borrowed words could be used such as in the original language, or they could be altered in order to respect the morphological structure of the Arabic language.

Building a robust speech recognition system requires feeding the training models with spoken and written data of the targeted language. Unfortunately, these kinds of data does not exist for the Algerian dialect since it is mainly spoken and there is no standards nor rules to write it. Our approach to recognize the Algerian dialect is to explore data sharing between the languages that impact the dialect, namely MSA and French. The main idea is to extend a small spoken corpus of the Algerian dialect with speech data from the MSA and the French languages, for training the acoustic models.

The aligned dialectal spoken corpus was created by having native Algerian people reading 4.6k sentences extracted from PADIC [14,16] and CALYOU [1] corpora. Statistics about the resulted corpus, named ADIA (Algerian Dialect) in the following, are presented in Table 2. It should be noted that the speakers of the test data are different from those of the training and development data.

Table 2. Some figures of ADIA corpus.

Subset	Duration	Number of speakers		
		Female	Male	Total
Train	240 min	1	3	4
Dev	40 min	1	1	2
Test	75 min	1	2	3

The same architecture used to build the ALASR system is used to train an initial acoustic model for the Algerian dialect based on the Train part of the ADIA corpus. This Train corpus was increased, afterwards, gradually by using acoustic data extracted from those used in ALASR system (MSA corpora) and with data extracted from ESTER (a French corpus) [5]. The optimal amount of acoustic data of each language to include in the training data was determined by minimizing the WER on the ADIA Dev corpus. We found that using a too large amount of MSA and French spoken data has a negative impact on the system performance. The optimal WER was obtained by adding 12 h of MSA data and 12 h of French data to the ADIA Train corpus.

The language model we propose, is a linear combination of four bigram models. Two of them were trained on MSA textual data: Gigaword and transcripts of the MSA acoustic Train set. The two others were trained on dialectal data: PADIC and CALYOU. The weights of the linear interpolation are estimated on a development corpus composed by a mixture of MSA and dialect data.

The initial MSA lexicon (MSA_{lex}) was extended by the most frequent words extracted from dialectal textual data (PADIC and CALYOU), which led to a lexicon of size of 125k words. The pronunciation variants of these dialectal words were produced by adapting the G2P approach proposed in [8].

In the first experimental phase, we want to evaluate how ALASR system performs on dialectal spoken data. Afterwards, we report the system performance by combining data from the three languages (dialect, MSA and French) to recognise the ADIA Test corpus. Table 3 summarizes the obtained results.

Table 3. Performance of the ASR systems on ADIA Test corpus.

System	Training acoustic data	WER (%)	OOV (%)
ALASR	MSA	78.5	33.6
S_1	ADIA	40.0	6.8
S_2	ADIA+MSA+Fr	**37.7**	

Since the Algerian dialect does not share many words with MSA (this is indicated by the high percentage of the OOV rate), ALASR system collapses completely when it was applied on the Test ADIA corpus. On the other side, with only 4 h of dialectal training data (S_1 system), a WER of 40% was obtained. Moreover, by increasing this limited training corpus with data that come from MSA and French corpora, an absolute improvement of 2.3% is achieved. This shows the possibility to use data covering several languages to improve the recognition of a specific language.

5   Sentence Boundary Detection

Automatic speech recognition (ASR) systems aim to transform spoken data into a textual representation which may be used on further NLP tasks including POS tagging, semantic parsing, question answering, machine translation and automatic text summarization, [4,12]. The vast majority of ASR systems focus on generating the correct sequence of transcribed words without taking into account the structure of the transcribed document, thus producing transcripts that lack of syntactic information like sentence boundaries [7,26]. However, optimal sentence boundary segmentation over ASR transcripts has shown to be crucial over further NLP tasks like entity and relation extraction, topic detection and automatic summarization [13,18,21].

Sentence Boundary Detection (SBD) aims to automatically split into sentences an unpunctuated text; nevertheless in spoken language the notion of sentence is not as well defined as in formal written sources. Separating into speaker utterances is a straightforward solution in spoken language, but in a standard conversation, utterances may be very long thus producing very long segments. In addition, disfluencies like repetitions, restarts, revisions, hesitations and interruptions make the definition of a sentence unclear. The concept of Semantic Unit (SU), introduced by the Linguistic Data Consortium on the SimpleMDE V5.0 guideline, is considered to be an atomic element of the transcript that achieves to express a complete idea [23]. A SU may correspond to the equivalent of a sentence in written text, a phrase or a single word. It seems to be an inclusive conception of a segment and is flexible enough to deal with the majority of spoken language troubles.

We implemented the SBD system based on character embeddings and Convolutional Neural Networks (CNN) described in [6] to segment the automatic transcripts into SUs. In·this architecture, the CNN classifies the middle word of a 5-word window into *boundary* or *not boundary*. Character embeddings are word embedding representations where each word is expressed as the sum of their n-gram character vectors. This type of embedding representation is very useful for morphology rich languages like Arabic. To conduct our experiments we opted for the FastText character embedding [3] pre-trained vectors[2], which consist of 300 dimensions 610,977 vectors. The input layer of the CNN architecture proposed in [6] is represented by a 5×300 matrix representing the relation between a window of 5 words and their 300 dimension FastText vectors. The hidden architecture of the CNN consist of an arrange of convolutional, pooling and fully connected layers blocks followed by three fully connected layers. Finally, the output layer is composed of two neurons corresponding to two the possible output classes.

We performed the CNN training with a 70M words subset (Asharq Al-Awsat news wire) from the Arabic Gigaword[3] dataset. Table 4 shows the performance of the system in terms of the F1-score[4] for both classes over an evaluation set of 10.5M samples Detailed explanation of the CNN architecture and extended performance evaluation are available in [6].

Table 4. Performance of the CNN based SBD system for the classes *boundary* and *no boundary*.

Class	F1-score
Boundary	0.684
No boundary	0.980

6 Automatic Text Summarization

An automatic summary is a text generated by a software, that is coherent and contains a significant amount of relevant information from the source text. Usually, the compression rate ρ of the summary is less than a third of the length of the original document [25]. Automatic Text Summarization (ATS) systems aim to produce summaries from a source document. In general, the ATS algorithms work well if the source contains well-written documents like news, books, chapters, etc. In these kinds of documents, the sentences are reasonably well

---

[2] https://fasttext.cc/docs/en/crawl-vectors.html.
[3] https://catalog.ldc.upenn.edu/LDC2011T11.
[4] Harmonic mean combining Precision and Recall.

delimited: the borders of sentences are the final point, and the markers ? and
!. In our case, where source documents correspond to transcripts from an ASR
system, the deal is very different. Punctuation marks are non-existent and no
phrase delimitation are available, thus the SBD system described in Sect. 5 is
applied before any summarization process is performed and segments salience is
computed.

An extract is the assembly of fragments that have been extracted from a
source text. The aim of an extract is to give a quick overview of the original
document content. Extraction is an efficient topic and genre independent ATS
method [25]. Surface-level methods do not delve into the linguistic depths of
a document; rather they use some linguistic elements in order to identify the
relevant segments of a document. Used in several studies on summarization,
surface-level techniques use the occurrences of words to weight sentences.

In order to produce extractive text-based summaries, we opted for the Artex
algorithm [24,25]. This method is very simple, fast and efficient. The main idea
is to map the source document (P sentences, n types terms, in a suitable space
representation of a matrix $S_{[P \times n]}$. Each term is weighted by a classical $TF.IDF$,
without stop-words and punctuation. All terms are stemmed using a Porter
algorithm [19]. The original Artex version is able to process English, French
and Spanish [24], but we adapted the prepossessing modules in order to process
Arabic language. In the matrix space, Artex searches to compute a weight for
each sentence i, using a scalar product between the main topic, the sentence i
and the main type "word". The main topic is computed as the sum of P vector
sentences. The main type "word" is computed as the sum of n vector words. The
sentences close to the main topic and using several terms ad hoc the topic, are
retained to generate the summary following a ρ ratio.

7   Experiments

To evaluate the results of the automatic summarization system, we decided
to conduct a subjective evaluation. The evaluators are asked to give a score
between 1 and 5 for both ALASR system and the automatic summarization system according to the ranking assessment of Tables 5 and 6. It is necessary to
evaluate the automatic speech recognition system because the automatic summarization system depends on it. In Table 7, we give some details about the
evaluation of 27 videos. Each of them was summarized 3 times depending on
several percentage (ρ ratio) of the original video. The Arabic videos concerned
by the evaluation are those extracted in the framework of the project AMIS
and concern the following channels: Euronews, AlArabiya and Skynews. Three
native Arabic speakers evaluated the videos. The smallest transcribed video is
composed of 52 words and the longest one of 394 words.

Table 5. Rating scale for the ALASR system assessment.

1	Incomprehensible transcription
2	Only certain segments of the video are understandable
3	A substantial proportion of the transcription is understandable
4	The transcription is very understandable
5	The transcription is not only understandable, but it is fluid and does not seem to involve linguistic errors (syntactic or semantic)

Table 6. Rating scale for the automatic summarization system assessment.

1	Incomprehensible summary
2	Only some events of the original video are found in the summary and overall the text is incomprehensible
3	A substantial proportion of the events in the original video are in the summary and overall the text is understandable
4	Very good summary and the text is very correct
5	Excellent summary

Table 7. Some figures concerning the subjective evaluation.

Count	Value
Videos	27
Summary per Video	3
Channel TV	3
Evaluators	3
Size of the shortest summary (in words)	52
Size of the longest summary (in words)	394

In Fig. 1, we draw the Box plot of the results of the subjective evaluation of the ALASR system and of the automatic summary system. The latter system depends obviously on the result of the ASR system. That is why we report them in the same diagram. Half of the population of the ASR evaluation received an evaluation between 3 and 4 and the upper Quartile is equal to 4 which means that 25% of the transcriptions have received the highest score. These results indicate that the developed ALASR system performs very well.

In Fig. 2, we analyse the lengths, in terms of words, of the transcriptions and the summaries in order to attempt to find a relationship between the size of the summary, and the performance of the automatic summarization system. The Quartile Q_1 is equal to 81, that means that 25% of the summaries have a length smaller than 81 words knowing that the longest transcription is composed of 394 words. Also, 25% of the population has a length greater than 140 words, which correspond to 35% of the longest video.

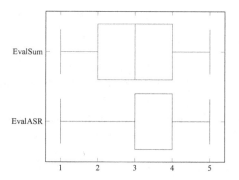

Fig. 1. The Box plot corresponding to the subjective evaluation of the Arabic ASR and the automatic summarization systems on MSA data.

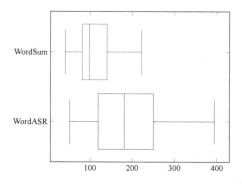

Fig. 2. The Box plot corresponding to the number of words of the Arabic ASR and the automatic summarization systems.

The same evaluators conducted another assessment, it concerns the evaluation of the Arabic ASR and the automatic summarization systems in which some video sequences are in Algerian dialect. To do so, 6 videos from Algerian TV, namely Echorouk and Ennahar were recognized by ALASR and by the system we adapted to better recognize the Algerian dialect. Figure 3 shows the number of the examples that receive scores between 1 and 5. We can remark that no video received a rating of 5 and consequently no more summary received this score. Only 6 videos have been ranked 4, but unfortunately no summary was ranked 4. 12 evaluations on the Arabic ASR are considered as not understandable and 15 among the population have a bad summary (score = 1). These bad results were expected with an Arabic ASR not adapted to the Algerian dialect.

By transcribing the videos with the adapted Arabic ASR system (Fig. 4) for Algerian dialect, no improvement on high score ratings and especially for score 5 was found, on the other hand 12 examples of the population were ranked 4 and this led to 2 summaries with a score 4.

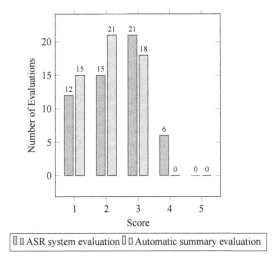

Fig. 3. The number of responses for each score of the subjective assessment of dialectal data with ALASR system.

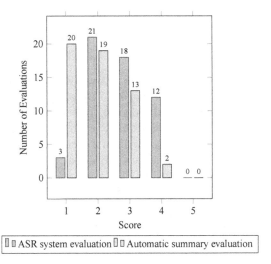

Fig. 4. The number of responses for each score of the subjective assessment of dialectal data with the adapted ASR system.

In order to study the relationship between the scores of the summary and the other parameters such as: the number of words ($ASRWord$) of the original video, the score of the ASR system ($ASRScore$) and the number of words of the summary ($SumWord$), we decided to use the multiple linear regression that has the objective to model the linear relationship between the explanatory independent variables mentioned above and the dependent response variable ($EvalSum$).

We use the statistical metric (R^2), named coefficient of determination to measure how much of the variation in outcome can be explained by the variation in the independent variables. It measures the adequacy between a model resulting from a multiple linear regression and the observed data which made it possible to establish the relationship. On our dataset of 243 examples, $R^2 = 0.310$, this indicates that 31% of the dispersion is explained by the regression model. This is not high value, but it is not completely null. If we consider the null hypothesis as $H_0 : a_1 = a_2 = a_3 = 0$ and the alternative hypothesis as at least one of the a_i is different from 0. The model F depending on R^2 is calculated as follows:

$$ F = \frac{\frac{R^2}{p}}{\frac{1-R^2}{n-p-1}} \tag{1} $$

Where n is the size of the sample and p is the number of degrees of freedom. The calculated value of F is equal to 35.899. F follows a Fisher law at $(p, n-p-1)$ degrees of freedom. The theoretical $F(2, 240)$ is equal to 3.239. In conclusion, the critical region of the test is therefore: rejection of H_0 because $F > F_{0.95}(2, 240)$. The hypothesis that there is a relationship between the explanatory variables and the score of the automatic summarization system can not be ruled out.

8   Conclusion

In this paper, we present and evaluate an extractive text-based summarization method for Arabic videos, which is proposed in the scope of AMIS project. AMIS aims at helping a user to understand videos given in a foreign language (Arabic in this study and research), by translating and summarizing the videos through several strategies. One strategy consists in transcribing the Arabic videos and summarizing the transcriptions. The evaluations of summaries were objective and also subjective.

The objective evaluation of the ASR system showed the necessity to include dialectal material in the training data when the Algerian dialect is used in the videos. This result was confirmed by the subjective evaluation of ASR outputs: when dialectal data is used for training, transcriptions of Algerian dialect videos are better evaluated. However, the automatic summaries obtained from the transcriptions do not lead to the same conclusion: with dialectal data in training, the summaries are judged less good. In order to better understand these contrasting results, we tried to measure which features of summaries influence the judgement. This study showed that original lengths of videos, lengths of summaries and ASR performance explain only 31% of the subjective scores. Furthermore, a statistical analysis shows that a relationship between these features and the scores given to summaries can not be ruled out.

This research shows the difficulty to evaluate results for complex projects such as AMIS as the summarization task requires a high degree of cognitive effort during the evaluation. So the question is how to automatically predict the quality of summaries? To answer to this question, in future work, we would like to more deeply explore which features influence the quality of summaries. For that, it will be necessary to increase the number of evaluated videos.

Acknowledgment. We acknowledge the support of Chist-Era for funding this research through the AMIS (Access Multilingual Information opinionS) project.

References

1. Abidi, K., Menacer, M.A., Smaili, K.: CALYOU: a comparable spoken algerian corpus harvested from Youtube. In: 18th Annual Conference of the International Communication Association (Interspeech) (2017)
2. Ali, A., Zhang, Y., Cardinal, P., Dahak, N., Vogel, S., Glass, J.: A complete Kaldi recipe for building Arabic speech recognition systems. In: 2014 IEEE Spoken Language Technology Workshop (SLT), December 2014, pp. 525–529 (2014). https://doi.org/10.1109/SLT.2014.7078629
3. Bojanowski, P., Grave, E., Joulin, A., Mikolov, T.: Enriching word vectors with subword information. Trans. Assoc. Comput. Linguist. **5**, 135–146 (2017)
4. Che, X., Wang, C., Yang, H., Meinel, C.: Punctuation prediction for unsegmented transcript based on word vector. In: LREC (2016)
5. Galliano, S., Geoffrois, E., Mostefa, D., Choukri, K., Bonastre, J.F., Gravier, G.: The ESTER phase II evaluation campaign for the rich transcription of French broadcast news. In: Ninth European Conference on Speech Communication and Technology (2005)
6. González-Gallardo, C.E., Pontes, E.L., Sadat, F., Torres-Moreno, J.M.: Automated sentence boundary detection in modern standard Arabic transcripts using deep neural networks. Procedia Comput. Sci. **142**, 339–346 (2018)
7. Gotoh, Y., Renals, S.: Sentence boundary detection in broadcast speech transcripts. In: ASR 2000-Automatic Speech Recognition: Challenges for the New Millenium ISCA Tutorial and Research Workshop (ITRW) (2000)
8. Harrat, S., Meftouh, K., Abbas, M., Smaïli, K.: Grapheme to phoneme conversion - an Arabic dialect case. In: Spoken Language Technologies for Under-resourced Languages (2014)
9. Harrat, S., Meftouh, K., Smaïli, K.: Creating parallel Arabic dialect corpus: pitfalls to avoid. In: 18th International Conference on Computational Linguistics and Intelligent Text Processing (CICLING), Budapest, Hungary, April 2017. https://hal.archives-ouvertes.fr/hal-01557405
10. Harrat, S., Meftouh, K., Smaïli, K.: Maghrebi Arabic dialect processing: an overview. J. Int. Sci. Gen. Appl. **1** (2018). https://hal.archives-ouvertes.fr/hal-01873779
11. Leszczuk, M., Grega, M., Koźbiał, A., Gliwski, J., Wasieczko, K., Smaïli, K.: Video summarization framework for newscasts and reports – work in progress. In: Dziech, A., Czyżewski, A. (eds.) MCSS 2017. CCIS, vol. 785, pp. 86–97. Springer, Cham (2017). https://doi.org/10.1007/978-3-319-69911-0_7
12. Linhares Pontes, E., González-Gallardo, C.-E., Torres-Moreno, J.-M., Huet, S.: Cross-lingual speech-to-text summarization. In: Choroś, K., Kopel, M., Kukla, E., Siemiński, A. (eds.) MISSI 2018. AISC, vol. 833, pp. 385–395. Springer, Cham (2019). https://doi.org/10.1007/978-3-319-98678-4_39
13. Makhoul, J., et al.: The effects of speech recognition and punctuation on information extraction performance. In: Ninth European Conference on Speech Communication and Technology (2005)

14. Meftouh, K., Harrat, S., Smaïli, K.: PADIC: extension and new experiments. In: 7th International Conference on Advanced Technologies ICAT. Antalya, Turkey, April 2018. https://hal.archives-ouvertes.fr/hal-01718858
15. Meftouh, K., Bouchemal, N., Smaïli, K.: A study of a non-resourced language: the case of one of the algerian dialects. In: The Third International Workshop on Spoken Languages Technologies for Under-Resourced Languages - SLTU 2012, Cape-town, South Africa, May 2012, pp. 1–7 (2012). https://hal.archives-ouvertes.fr/hal-00727042
16. Meftouh, K., Harrat, S., Jamoussi, S., Abbas, M., Smaili, K.: Machine translation experiments on PADIC: a parallel Arabic dialect corpus. In: Proceedings of the 29th Pacific Asia Conference on Language, Information and Computation, pp. 26–34 (2015)
17. Menacer, M.A., Mella, O., Fohr, D., Jouvet, D., Langlois, D., Smaïli, K.: Development of the Arabic Loria Automatic Speech Recognition system (ALASR) and its evaluation for Algerian dialect. In: ACLing 2017–3rd International Conference on Arabic Computational Linguistics, Dubai, United Arab Emirates, November 2017, pp. 1–8 (2017). https://hal.archives-ouvertes.fr/hal-01583842
18. Mrozinski, J., Whittaker, E.W., Chatain, P., Furui, S.: Automatic sentence segmentation of speech for automatic summarization. In: 2006 IEEE International Conference on Acoustics Speech and Signal Processing Proceedings, vol. 1, p. I. IEEE (2006)
19. Porter, M.F.: An algorithm for suffix stripping. Program **14**(3), 130–137 (1980)
20. Povey, D., et al.: The Kaldi speech recognition toolkit. In: IEEE 2011 Workshop on Automatic Speech Recognition and Understanding. In: IEEE Signal Processing Society (2011). iEEE Catalog No.: CFP11SRW-USB
21. Shriberg, E., Stolcke, A., Hakkani-Tür, D., Tür, G.: Prosody-based automatic segmentation of speech into sentences and topics. Speech Commun. **32**(1–2), 127–154 (2000)
22. Stolcke, A.: Entropy-based pruning of backoff language models. arXiv preprint cs/0006025 (2000)
23. Strassel, S.: Simple metadata annotation specification V5, January 2003. http://www.ldc.upenn.edu/Projects/MDE/Guidelines/SimpleMDE
24. Torres-Moreno, J.M.: Artex is anotheR TEXt summarizer. arXiv preprint arXiv:1210.3312 (2012)
25. Torres-Moreno, J.M.: Automatic Text Summarization. Wiley, London (2014)
26. Yu, D., Deng, L.: Automatic Speech Recognition. Springer, London (2016). https://doi.org/10.1007/978-1-4471-5779-3

Automatic Identification Methods on a Corpus of Twenty Five Fine-Grained Arabic Dialects

Salima Harrat[1(✉)], Karima Meftouh[2], Karima Abidi[3], and Kamel Smaïli[3]

[1] École Normale Supérieure de Bouzaréah, Algiers, Algeria
slmhrrt@gmail.com
[2] Badji Mokhtar University, Annaba, Algeria
karima.meftouh@univ-annaba.dz
[3] Loria - University Lorraine, Nancy, France
{karima.abidi,kamel.smaili}@loria.fr

Abstract. This research deals with Arabic dialect identification, a challenging issue related to Arabic NLP. Indeed, the increasing use of Arabic dialects in a written form especially in social media generates new needs in the area of Arabic dialect processing. For discriminating between dialects in a multi-dialect context, we use different approaches based on machine learning techniques. To this end, we explored several methods. We used a classification method based on symmetric Kullback-Leibler, and we experimented classical classification methods such as Naive Bayes Classifiers and more sophisticated methods like Word2Vec and Long Short-Term Memory neural network. We tested our approaches on a large database of 25 Arabic dialects in addition to MSA.

Keywords: Arabic dialects · Automatic dialect identification · Dialect resources · Parallel dialectal corpora

1 Introduction

Standard Arabic is the official language of Arab countries, it is used in formal speech, education, and newspapers. In contrast people, all over the Arab world use Arabic dialects in their everyday conversations. Indeed, Arabic dialects are a variant of the Arabic language (besides Modern Standard Arabic and classical Arabic). Most research classifies Arabic dialects according to East-west dichotomy [8]: Maghrebi dialects (Algeria, Morocco, Tunisia, Lybia, and Mauritania) and middle-east dialects (Egypt, Sudan, Gulf countries and Levantine countries). Another research [25] classifies them according to the ethnic and social diversity of Arab speakers as rural and Bedouin variants.

Arabic dialects differ widely between and within Arab countries. Arabic dialects share a lot of features with standard Arabic which makes them close to each other but also have specific characteristics related to each one. Social media and mobile telephony have contributed to the increased use of Arabic

© Springer Nature Switzerland AG 2019
K. Smaïli (Ed.): ICALP 2019, CCIS 1108, pp. 79–92, 2019.
https://doi.org/10.1007/978-3-030-32959-4_6

dialects in a written form. In this context, discriminating between dialects in a multi-dialectal corpus of texts is a challenging issue, especially when dialects belong to regions from the same Arabic country. In this case, it is fine-grained identification where we have to distinguish between very close dialects.

In this paper, we deal with the dialect identification at the sentence level. We used several approaches and experimented different features. The features are those parameters that are supposed to characterize specifically each language. Consequently, they are crucial and not easy to determine.

The remainder of this article is organized as follows: in Sect. 2 we highlight the most challenges issues related to Arabic dialects identification, we present the most important points that make this task a hard one. Section 3 summarizes relevant research efforts in dialect identification, while Sect. 4 presents our contribution in this area by describing the four approaches we explored. In Sect. 5 we give a brief description of the dialectal corpus we used for training our classifiers and Sect. 6 is allocated to the results of our experiments. Section 7 concludes this paper.

2   Arabic Dialects Identification Challenges

In their oral form, Arabic dialects are relatively easy to distinguish. In fact, prosody and tone bring important information about them. But, in their written form, and compared to other languages, Arabic dialects are difficult to identify. They are similar languages that share a lot of features and words although they may differ from one Arab country to another and from one city to another within the same country. In the following, we enumerate the reasons that make difficult the issue of the identification of Arabic dialects.

- They share a lot of lexical units with modern standard Arabic. Consequently, distinguishing between Arabic dialects is a hard task.
- Some words are shared among Arabic dialects but with different meanings. For example, the Egyptian word which means *why* exists in other dialects like Algerian but with another meaning: *for him.*
- In the conversation, Arab people tend to switch to standard Arabic especially when discussing matters relating to religion. Thus, the use of standard Arabic makes the identification task confusing.
- The lack of dialectal resources such as monolingual and multilingual corpora makes the identification task a challenging issue. Indeed, the identification data-driven approaches require important amounts of data to reach acceptable accuracy rates, such resources are not available for most Arabic dialects.

3   Related Work

Several studies in the area of Arabic NLP attempted to deal with the dialect identification issue. Different approaches have been adopted. Early work in this area [26] used language modeling (LM) based approach to identify the dialect at the sentence level. The authors created for the purpose of this research the Arabic Online Commentary Dataset (OAC) (a collection of 52M-word monolingual dataset rich in dialectal content and annotated thanks to the crowdsourcing principle). Each dialect of this corpus was modeled by a 3-gram LM, then the sentence perplexity was computed to score each sentence of the test corpus.

The same authors in [27] used the previously created Arabic Online Commentary Dataset (with the annotated data) to train classifiers using word and character language models. They use 1-gram, 2-gram of words and 1-gram, 3-gram and 5-gram of letters. They conducted two-way classification: MSA vs. Dialect, and multi-way classification: (MSA, multiple dialects). They explored two identification approaches, by creating: a first system where they use MSA-only data and attempt to determine how MSA-like a sentence is. They extracted a vocabulary of 2.9M of words from the Arabic Gigaword Corpus. Then each sentence is given an OOV percentage of dialectal words, when this percentage reached a fixed threshold, the sentence is considered as being dialectal. The second system used perplexity to classify sentences, a language model using only MSA data was trained on 43M words extracted from the article bodies of the AOC. When exceeding a perplexity threshold the sentence is classified as being dialectal. The authors conclude that classifiers trained with dialectal data (with word 1-gram LM) significantly outperform classifiers which use MSA data only.

Later supervised approach was used to address dialect identification. The authors in [6] proposed a supervised approach to predict whether the sentence is MSA-like or Egyptian. To this end, they trained a Naive Bayes Classifier (NBC) using token based features and perplexity based features, in addition to other features like (percentage of punctuation, numbers, special-characters, number of words & average word-length, etc.). They evaluated their system on the Egyptian part of the OAC described above. In [19], The authors used Markov character-based n-grams language models and NBC trained on social media data for Arabic dialect identification task. They first experimented with 1-gram, 2-gram and 3-gram character-based LMs. Then, they trained NB classifiers using the three LMs as features. The identification task covered 18 Arabic dialects. They also conducted experiments on 6 groups of dialects defined regards to geographical repartition. The achieved results show that NB classifier outperforms the character-based n-gram Markov model for most Arabic dialects. In the same vein, the best accuracy rates are got with NBC with 2-gram LM features.

The authors of [20] dealt with fine-grained dialect identification. They attempted to identify 25 dialects of different Arabic cities in addition to MSA. They also perform dialect identification within 6 geographical regions. They used a Multinomial Naive Bayes (MNB) classifier for the learning task. The classifiers are trained by word and character n-gram LMs. They conduct a set of experiments by varying the use of features from character/word 1-gram to 5-grams and by combining them. The best accuracy was reached with features from word 1-gram LM, 1-gram to 3-gram character LM and Character/Word 5-gram LM probability scores.

Other research used SVM approach to address the dialect identification issue. In [3], the authors presented a multi-dialect, multi-genre, human annotated corpus of dialectal Arabic (Egyptian, Gulf, Levantine, Maghrebi, and Iraqi) extracted from online newspaper commentary and Twitter. They used crowd-sourcing via mechanical Turk to annotate the data. In terms of size, the corpus contains 27239 newspaper comments including 583K words and 40229 tweets including 666K words. With these data, they dealt with dialect identification by combining LMs and machine learning. They use two classifiers: SVM with a linear kernel and NB classifiers both trained on word n-gram LM features. The results show that the 1-gram based model performs better than 2-gram/3-gram based models for both SVM and NBC. Moreover, the NB classifier gives better results.

A similar method was used in [12] where the authors used the Multidialectal Parallel Corpus of Arabic [2] to perform dialect identification. They used a SVM classifier with word 1-gram/2-gram LMs and character 1-gram to 4-gnam LMs features (without any preprocessing step). The authors used SVM to perform multi-class classification. They also used a meta-classifier (SVM based) trained by the class probability outputs of lower classifiers (described above). Each lower (SVM) classifier is learned from one feature type. The authors reported an accuracy of 74% on the 6-way identification task. For 2-way identification, the accuracy reached 94% and The best features are those related to 3 gram.

The authors of [4] used lexical, phonological, morphological, and syntactic features to distinguish between dialectal Egyptian and MSA. They used Random Forest (RF) classification for two-way dialect-MSA identification. The RF classifier was trained on the Egyptian side of OAC [26] and 150K MSA sentences from an English-MSA parallel corpus. It used word 1-gra/2-gram/3-gram LMs and character 1-gram to 5-gram LMs as features. The authors show that the RF classifier performs better when it uses features extracted from segmented data in addition to lexical features.

Another interesting work is that described in [5]. It presents Aida2, a token and sentence level dialect identification system that distinguishes between MSA and Egyptian dialect. It uses a set of classifiers to deal with the identification task on the two levels. At token level, the identification is considered as sequence labeling task. The authors used Conditional Random Field (CRF) classifier which is trained by using decisions from several underlying components: MADAMIRA morphological analyzer [17], a tokenized 5-gram Language Model, a compiled lexicon of Arabic modality triggers, and a Named Entity Recognizer. The output of this first module is then given to the sentence level identification module which relies on two independent underlying classifiers. The first one uses tokenized-level LMs, thus it yields detailed and specific information about the tokens. The second one is based on surface forms MSA and Egyptian dialect 5-gram LMs. Each of the two classifiers gives a class label and a confidence score to the input sentence. Given this information, a Decision Tree classifier provides the final class of the sentence.

In the same vein, the authors of [21] dealt with the identification of code-switching between MSA and Moroccan dialect in discussion boards and blog text. The identification task is considered as a sequence labeling problem which the authors treat by using CRF. Regards to the data, the authors created their annotated corpus from scratch by downloading discussion boards and blogs and proceeded to the annotation for the purpose of identification. To train the CRF classifier, they used 5 types of features like the words and their surrounding words with their affixes, structural properties such as if the word contains numbers, character language models and lexical knowledge from an external source such as word lists. The authors combined these features in order to identify the best combination which gives the best accuracy.

4 Identification Approaches

In the following, we present the different approaches we tested and evaluated.

4.1 Long Short-Term Memory Neural Network Approach

A recurrent neural network (RNN) in which the connections are made between units which form a directed cycle, which allows it to exhibit a dynamic temporal behavior for the model. Long Short Term Memory Networks (LSTM) [9] are a special class of neural networks able to learn long-term dependencies. They are designed especially to avoid the long-term dependency problem. Their main characteristic is that they remember information for long periods of time. This class of neural network has been efficient for many NLP tasks such as language modeling [24], sentiment analysis [16], word embedding learning [11], as well as in other area like automatic speech recognition [7] and image captioning [13].

We consider the dialect identification task as a multi-class classification problem that we attempt to solve with Long Short-Term Memory (LSTM) networks: given a sentence s_j, dialect features vectors V_i with their corresponding labels l_i, we have to predict l_j by using V and s_j. We designed a recurrent network classifier that takes as input a vector of characters/words n-grams (for characters n varies from 1 to 5 and for words it varies between 1 and 2). It goes through a LSTM layer, then to a drop out layer to prevent over-fitting. The last layer of the network is a softmax that gives a probability distribution over the different dialect labels.

After several setup configurations, we retained the following parameters for our neural network architecture:

- Input vector dimension is variable, it depends on the vectorization parameters. We used character and word level vectorization with different orders.
- LSTM layer units: 128
- Droupout rate: 0.2

4.2   Word Embedding Based Approach

The idea is to investigate to what extent the semantic information encoded by word embedding can be used to identify the varieties of Arabic dialects. For this reason, we used the CBOW method of Word2Vec model [15] to extract the vector representation of the words. Given the limited size of the dialectal corpora and knowing that neuronal network methods necessitate an important amount material for training, we decided to increase the data by using the infra-lexical information of the provided corpus. That is why each sentence of each dialect of the multi-dialect corpus is segmented into 2, 3, 4 and 5 grams of characters. In addition, the original sentence is kept in the corpus necessary for the training. After this step, only the vectors representing the typical words of each dialect are kept for the test. The typical words are those words or infra-lexical units that are characteristic of a dialect. To identify these units, we kept for a dialect only the units that do not occur in other dialects.

To label a sentence s with its appropriate tag t from the $|D|$ dialects, we calculate the similarity between the units of s and the list of typical words of each dialect as follows.

$$d_k = \frac{1}{|s|} \sum_{i=1}^{|s|} \min_{1 \leq j \leq |L_k|} E(s_i, w_j^k) \tag{1}$$

$$i_l = \underset{1 \leq k \leq |D|}{argmin}(d_k) \tag{2}$$

where:

- $|s|$ is the number of words of s,
- L_k is the list of typical words of the dialect k,
- E is the Euclidean distance,
- w_j^k is the word j belonging to the list of typical words of the dialect k,
- and $|D|$ is the number of dialects/language (distinct labels).

Then we assign the label l corresponding to the dialect that gives the smallest distance.

4.3   Symmetric Kullback-Leibler for Classification

In this approach, we constitute a General Vocabulary (GV) from the different training corpora. The vocabulary is composed of all the words, the bi-grams and with all the infra-lexical units from one to five. Then, the distribution of each dialect is calculated in accordance to GV. Each dialect d_i is then represented by a vector where each dimension is given by $P(u_k|d_i)$. Where u_k indicates a unit of GV and d_i corresponds to the dialect i. All the probabilities are smoothed to avoid zero probabilities for unknown words of the test corpus.

For the test, each sentence is segmented similarly to what has been done for the training. Then we calculate the symmetric Kullback-Leibler measure [10] (see Eq. 3), we used several years ago to identify emails [1], between the distribution of the test sentence and the distribution of each dialect. We assign then the sentence to the dialect that provides the smallest score.

$$D(P||Q) = \sum_x ((P(x) - Q(x)) Log \frac{P(x)}{Q(x)} \tag{3}$$

4.4 Multinomial Naïve Bayes (MNB) approach

Naïve Bayes classifiers are widely used in different applications in natural language processing and particularly in text classification [14,18,23] due to their efficiency and their acceptable predictive performance. That is why we consider them to deal with the dialect identification issue. MNB estimates the conditional probability of a particular term given a class as the relative frequency of the term t in all documents belonging to the class C.

In order to train our MNB classifier, we used 1-gram, 2-gram and 3-gram as features supported by a TF-IDF vector We also used a special character to mark the start of the sentences. We note that we utilized Term Frequency-Inverse Document Frequency (TF-IDF) scores [22].

5 Data Description

For training and testing our classifiers, we used the MADAR shared task data [20]. It consists of two parallel multi-dialect corpora:

- The first corpus (MADAR-Corpus26) is composed of parallel sentences translated to 25 dialects of several cities from the Arab countries (see Table 1), in addition to modern standard Arabic. Each dialect/language includes 1600 sentences for training and 200 sentences for test purpose.

Table 1. MADAR-Corpus26 countries and cities.

Country	City		Country	City	
Algeria	Algiers	ALG	Palestine	Jerusalem	JER
Morocco	Rabat	RAB	Syria	Beirut	BEI
	Fes	FES		Damascus	DAM
Tunisia	Tunis	TUN		Aleppo	ALE
	Sfax	SFX	Iraq	Mosul	MOS
Libya	Tripoli	TRI		Baghdad	BAG
	Benghazi	BEN		Basra	BAS
Egypt	Cairo	CAI	Saudi Arabia	Riyadh	RIY
	Alexandria	ALX		Jeddah	JED
	Aswan	ASW	Oman	Muscat	MUS
Sudan	Khartoum	KHA	Qatar	Doha	DOHA
Jordan	Amman	AMM	Yemen	Sana'a	SAN
	Salt	SAL			

– The second corpus (MADAR-Corpus6) is a collection of 10K additional sentences translated to the dialects of five selected cities: Beirut, Cairo, Doha, Tunis, and Rabat.

In Table 2, we give an example of parallel sentences from MADAR-Corpus26 (the first corpus).

6   Experiments

We built a set of classifiers based on the approaches described above by using the two MADAR corpora (MADAR-Corpus26 and MADAR-corpus6). For each classifier, we tested several combinations of features to identify the ones that increase the accuracy values. We report in Table 3 the best-achieved results and in Table 7 the features that yield the best accuracy rate for each approach.

The best achieved results are those got with the multinomial NB approach, followed by the LSTM, then Kullback-Leibler, while the word embedding values come last. Sophisticated approaches did not give the intended results. We expected to have better or at least equivalent results with the neural network approach. But the experiments show that MNB performs better. This is due in our opinion to the size of the training data; Indeed neural networks require an important amount of data to perform best.

In addition, 6-way identification classifiers perform better than 26-way identification. This is a natural and expected result since the confusion is reduced when using fewer dialects and more data. It is worth noting 6-way identification results follows the same scale of values as 26-way identification, MNB results remain the best followed by LSTM, Kullback-Leibler and W2Vec values. But we can mention that the results of the LSTM and the symmetric Kullback-Leibler are close to each other.

For the MNB classifiers (for convenience we refer to them by MNB-MADAR-Corpus26 & MNB-MADAR-Corpus6) which achieved the best scores, we computed respectively, Precision, Recall, and F1-score at class level (see Tables 4 and 5). We also generated the confusion matrix of these classifiers in order to have an idea about the dialects they recognize better than others and the errors they make. For presentational reasons, we report in Table 6 a summary of MNB-MADAR-Corpus26 confusion matrix, while in Fig. 1 we show the confusion matrix of MNB-MADAR-Corpus6.

For 26-way classification, the dialects with low confusion rates were better identified than others. The Mosul dialect (MOS) achieved the best scores. Although it is an Iraqi dialect, it is well distinguished compared to the other Iraqi dialects (BAG and BAS). These two last are confused by a rate of 18.5%. Similarly, the classifier tends to confuse the dialects belonging to the same countries. The most confused dialect pairs are RAB & FES, SFX & TUN, CAI & ASW, ALX & ASW and BEN & TRI, in addition to MUS which is the most confused dialect with MSA. Furthermore, the Levantine dialects because of their

Table 2. Example of parallel sentences from MADAR-Corpus26.

City	Dialect or language	Sentence
	MSA	هناك ، أمام بيانات السائح تماما .
Beirut	BEI	صار هونيك ، بالظبط قدام مكتب استعلامات السياح .
Cairo	CAI	ده قدامك هناك ، يادوبك قدام مكتب استعلامات السياحة .
Doha	DOH	هو ذاك الصوب ، بالضبط جدام استعلامات السياح بالضبط .
Rabat	RAB	راه تما ، مقابل مكتب استعلامات السياح بالضبط .
Tunis	TUN	اهوكا غادي ، بالضبط قدام البيرو متاع الارشادات السياحية .
Alexandria	ALX	هو هناك ، قدام الاستعلامات السياحية على طول .
Algiers	ALG	راهو لهيك ، بالضبط قدام المكتب تع معلومات السياح .
Aswan	ASW	هناك ، قدام مكتب ارشادات السياح على طول .
Damascus	DAM	موجود هنيك ، قدام مكتب معلومات السياح بالزبط .
Jeddah	JED	شوفه هناك ، قدام مكتب المعلومات السياحية بالضبط .
Ryadh	RIY	هناك ، بالضبط مقابل مكتب معلومات السياح .
Sfax	SFX	أوكي غادي ، قدام مكتب الإرشادات السياحية بالضبط .
Baghdad	BAG	موجود هناك ، بالضبط مقابيل مكتب المعلومات السياحية .
Meaning	There, just in front of tourist information	

Table 3. Dialect identification results using different approaches.

Training corpus	MADAR-Corpus 26			MADAR-Corpus 6		
Approach	Precision	Recall	F1-score	Precision	Recall	F1-score
Word Embedding	50.11	49.90	49.74	83.96	83.90	83.83
Symmetric Kullback-Leibler	53.21	68.27	53.79	89.05	89.48	89.03
Multinomial Naïve Bayes	69.80	69.15	**69.09**	92.54	92.50	**92.50**
LSTM networks	58.04	61.54	58.33	89.23	89.17	89.18

closeness are also confused with each other (AMM & JER and DAM & AMM). The recall values of all these dialects are lower compared to other values recorded for dialects such as ALG and SAN that are the only ones belonging to Algeria and Yemen in this order.

For 6-way classification, the scores are better. The most confused dialects are RAB & TUN followed by CAI & DOH, then BEI & DOH and BEI & CAI (with the same confusion rate), while the most confused dialects with MSA are DOH and CAI.

Table 4. MNB-MADAR-Corpus26 dialect identification results by dialect/language.

Dial./Lang.	Precision	Recall	F1-score	Dial./Lang.	Precision	Recall	F1-score
MOS	83.41	85.50	84.44	ALE	78.12	62.50	69.44
ALG	78.08	85.50	81.62	DOH	72.04	67.00	69.43
SAN	87.79	75.50	81.18	KHA	63.29	75.00	68.65
MSA	71.49	89.00	79.29	BAS	67.15	69.50	68.30
ALX	76.17	81.50	78.74	JED	68.45	64.00	66.15
TRI	69.26	80.00	74.25	CAI	73.97	54.00	62.43
RAB	78.98	69.50	73.94	ASW	59.55	65.50	62.38
FES	72.25	75.50	73.84	RIY	57.14	64.00	60.38
SFX	67.52	79.00	72.81	SAL	61.90	58.50	60.15
BEI	78.70	66.50	72.09	DAM	56.02	60.50	58.17
BEN	70.87	73.00	71.92	JER	54.63	62.00	58.08
TUN	75.14	65.00	69.71	MUS	65.52	47.50	55.07
BAG	76.97	63.50	69.59	AMM	50.43	59.00	54.38

Table 5. MNB-MADAR-Corpus6 dialect identification results by dialect/language.

Dialect/language	Precision	Recall	F1-score
MSA	95.09	96.80	95.94
RAB	94.04	93.10	93.57
TUN	94.25	91.80	93.01
BEI	93.03	90.70	91.85
DOH	88.21	92.80	90.45
CAI	90.72	89.90	90.31

In terms of features, we confirm that using n-grams features helps to increase accuracy. All the classifiers perform better when they are fit with such information. Character n-grams order varies from 1 to 5, while for word n-grams lower order (1 and 2) achieve the best results. It should be noted that for the MNB classifier, we used sentence likelihood computed from the 26 word uni-gram language models.

Table 6. MNB-MADAR-Corpus26 confusion matrix summary.

Dial./lang	Recal	Most confused	Confusion %	Less confused[a]
ALE	62.5	DAM/JER	7.5	ALG BAG FES MOS RAB
ALG	85.5	MSA	2.5	ASW BEI BEN CAI JED
ALX	81.5	ASW	9.0	TRI
AMM	59.0	JER	12.5	ALG ALX BEN FES MSA MUS RAB SFX
ASW	65.5	ALX	12.5	DOH JED JER KHA SFX TUN
BAG	63.5	BAS	18.5	ALX ASW BEN CAI DAM JED JER KHA SFX TUN
BAS	69.5	BAG	10.5	ALG ASW BEI DAM JER KHA MUS RAB SAL SAN
BEI	66.5	DAM	6.5	BAS ALX ASW KHA MSA SAN TRI
BEN	73.0	TRI	6.5	ALX JED MOS RAB
CAI	54.0	ASW	17.5	BAS ALE MOS RAB
DAM	60.5	AMM	11.5	ALX ASW BAG BAS MUS SFX TUN
DOH	67.0	RIY	6.0	ALE JER MSA TRI
FES	75.5	RAB	11.5	ALE AMM ASW BEN KHA MUS RIY TUN
JED	64.0	RIY	6.5	ALX MSA
JER	62.0	AMM	9.5	ASW BAG CAI MUS RIY SAN
KHA	75.0	MSA	2.5	ALE BAS DOH SAN SFX TUN
MOS	85.5	BAS	4.0	ALG BEN DAM FES KHA MSA MUS RIY SAL TUN
MSA	89.00	MUS	2.5	ALE BAG BAS BEN JED MOS MOS SFX TRI
MUS	47.5	MSA	15.0	ALX ALE BEI JER RAB SAL SAN TRI RAB SAL SAN TRI
RAB	69.5	FES	18.5	BEN DOH JER MUS TUN
RIY	64.0	MUS	5.5	AMM CAI JER TRI
SAL	58.5	AMM /JER	9.0	BAG DOH FES MOS MUS SAN SFX
SAN	75.5	RIY	4.0	ALE ALG ASW JER MSA RAB
SFX	79.0	TUN	10.5	ASW BAG BEI JED JER KHA MSA MUS RAB SAL SAN
TRI	80.0	BEN	8.0	ALG AMM BAG BAS CAI DAM MOS RAB SAN
TUN	65.0	SFX	19.0	ALE ASW FES JED JER

[a] Confusion rate is equal to 0.5 for all these classes.

Table 7. The dialect features used in the different approaches.

Approach	Word n-grams features	Character n-grams features
Word Embedding		2-gram to 5-gram
Symmetric Kullback-Leibler	1-gram and 2-gram	1-gram to 5-gram
Multinomial Naïve Bayes	1-gram to 2-gram	1-gram to 5-gram +LMs Prob
LSTM networks	1-gram	4-gram

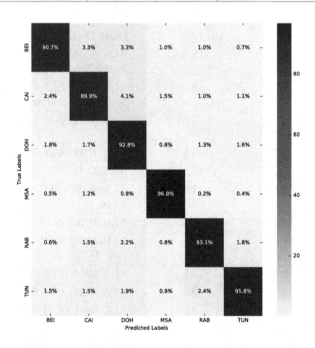

Fig. 1. MNB-MADAR-Corpus6 confusion matrix.

7   Conclusion

In this paper, we explored several approaches to tackle the issue of dialect identification with a set of 25 dialects belonging to some cities from the Arab countries in addition to MSA. We considered neural network approaches by using words embedding and LSTM networks. Unfortunately, the achieved results were not as what we expected, the size of the available training data was not sufficient to learn such classifiers. For W2Vec approach, we get the worst results (F1-score of 49.90 vs 61.54 from LSTM method). In the same vein, we experimented with the symmetric Kullback-Leibler distance. The obtained results did not exceed F1-score of 53.79 but with a recall of 68,27. The best results were achieved by the Multinomial Naïve Bayes classifier. It performs better than all other classifiers with an F1-score of 69.09. All the described classifiers were trained by using different features combinations. The character and word n-grams remain the best features for text classification, especially of Arabic dialects.

References

1. Bigi, B., Brun, A., Haton, J.P., Smaïli, K., Zitouni, I.: A comparative study of topic identification on newspaper and e-mail. In: Proceedings of the 8th International Symposium on String Processing and Information Retrieval - SPIRE 2001, pp. 238–241. Laguna de San Rafael, Chili (2001)
2. Bouamor, H., Habash, N., Oflazer, K.: A multidialectal parallel corpus of Arabic. In: Proceedings of the Language Resources and Evaluation Conference, LREC-2014, pp. 1240–1245 (2014)
3. Cotterell, R., Callison-Burch, C.: A multi-dialect, multi-genre corpus of informal written Arabic. In: LREC, pp. 241–245 (2014)
4. Darwish, K., Sajjad, H., Mubarak, H.: Verifiably effective Arabic dialect identification. In: EMNLP, pp. 1465–1468 (2014)
5. Elfardy, H., Al-Badrashiny, M., Diab, M.: AIDA: identifying code switching in informal Arabic text. In: EMNLP, p. 94 (2014)
6. Elfardy, H., Diab, M.: Sentence level dialect identification in Arabic. In: ACL, vol. 2, pp. 456–461 (2013)
7. Graves, A., Mohamed, A.R., Hinton, G.: Speech recognition with deep recurrent neural networks. In: 2013 IEEE International Conference on Acoustics, Speech and Signal Processing, pp. 6645–6649. IEEE (2013)
8. Hetzron, R.: The Semitic Languages. Routledge language family descriptions, Routledge (1997). https://books.google.dz/books?id=nbUOAAAAQAAJ
9. Hochreiter, S., Schmidhuber, J.: Long short-term memory. Neural Comput. 9(8), 1735–1780 (1997)
10. Kullback, S., Leibler, R.A.: On information and sufficiency. Ann. Math. Stat. 22(1), 79–86 (1951)
11. Li, J., Lin, X., Rui, X., Rui, Y., Tao, D.: A distributed approach toward discriminative distance metric learning. IEEE Trans. Neural Netw. Learn. Syst. 26(9), 2111–2122 (2014)
12. Malmasi, S., Refaee, E., Dras, M.: Arabic dialect identification using a parallel multidialectal corpus. In: Hasida, K., Purwarianti, A. (eds.) Computational Linguistics. CCIS, vol. 593, pp. 35–53. Springer, Singapore (2016). https://doi.org/10.1007/978-981-10-0515-2_3
13. Mao, J., Xu, W., Yang, Y., Wang, J., Huang, Z., Yuille, A.: Deep captioning with multimodal recurrent neural networks (M-RNN). arXiv preprint arXiv:1412.6632 (2014)
14. McCallum, A., Nigam, K., et al.: A comparison of event models for naive bayes text classification. In: AAAI-98 Workshop on Learning for Text Categorization, vol. 752, pp. 41–48. Citeseer (1998)
15. Mikolov, T., Chen, K., Corrado, G., Dean, J.: Efficient estimation of word representations in vector space. In: ICLR (Workshop) (2013). http://arxiv.org/abs/1301.3781
16. Pal, S., Ghosh, S., Nag, A.: Sentiment analysis in the light of LSTM recurrent neural networks. Int. J. Synth. Emot. 9(1), 33–39 (2018). https://doi.org/10.4018/IJSE.2018010103

17. Pasha, A., et al.: Madamira: a fast, comprehensive tool for morphological analysis and disambiguation of Arabic. In: Proceedings of the Language Resources and Evaluation Conference (LREC), Reykjavik, Iceland (2014)
18. Rish, I., et al.: An empirical study of the naive bayes classifier. In: IJCAI 2001 Workshop on Empirical Methods in Artificial Intelligence, vol. 3, pp. 41–46 (2001)
19. Sadat, F., Kazemi, F., Farzindar, A.: Automatic identification of Arabic dialects in social media. In: Proceedings of the First International Workshop on Social Media Retrieval and Analysis, pp. 35–40. ACM (2014)
20. Salameh, M., Bouamor, H.: Fine-grained Arabic dialect identification. In: Proceedings of the 27th International Conference on Computational Linguistics, pp. 1332–1344. Association for Computational Linguistics (2018). http://aclweb.org/anthology/C18-1113
21. Samih, Y., Maier, W.: Detecting code-switching in moroccan Arabic social media. SocialNLP@ IJCAI-2016, New York (2016)
22. Spärck Jones, K.: A statistical interpretation of term specificity and its application in retrieval. J. Documentation **28**, 11–21 (1972)
23. Su, J., Shirab, J.S., Matwin, S.: Large scale text classification using semi-supervised multinomial naive bayes. In: Proceedings of the 28th International Conference on Machine Learning (ICML-11), pp. 97–104. Citeseer (2011)
24. Sundermeyer, M., Schlüter, R., Ney, H.: LSTM neural networks for language modeling. In: Thirteenth Annual Conference of the International Speech Communication Association (2012)
25. Watson, J.C.: Phonology and Morphology of Arabic. Phonology of the World's Languages. Oxford University Press, New York (2007)
26. Zaidan, O.F., Callison-Burch, C.: The Arabic online commentary dataset: an annotated dataset of informal Arabic with high dialectal content. In: Proceedings of the 49th Annual Meeting of the Association for Computational Linguistics: Human Language Technologies: short papers-Volume 2, pp. 37–41. Association for Computational Linguistics (2011)
27. Zaidan, O.F., Callison-Burch, C.: Arabic dialect identification. Comput. Linguist. **1**(1), 171–202 (2012)

Aggregation of Word Embedding and Q-learning for Arabic Anaphora Resolution

Saoussen Mathlouthi Bouzid[(⊠)] and Chiraz Ben Othmane Zribi

National School of Computer Science, RIADI Lab,
University of Manouba, Manouba, Tunisia
Mathlouthi.saw@gmail.com, Chiraz.zribi@ensi-uma.tn

Abstract. In many linguistic situations, the repetitions of objects and entities are reduced to the pronoun. The correct interpretation of pronouns plays an important role in the construction of meaning. Thus, the resolution of the pronominal anaphors remains a very important task for most natural language processing applications. This paper presents a novel approach to resolve pronominal anaphora in Arabic texts. At first, we identify non-referential pronouns by using an iterative self-training SVM method. After, we resolve the antecedents by combining a Q-learning method with a Word2Vec based method. The Q-learning method seeks to optimize, for each anaphoric pronoun, a sequence of criteria choice to evaluate the antecedents and look for the best. It uses syntactic criteria as preference factors to favor candidate antecedents over others. The Word2Vec method uses the word embedding model AraVec 3.0. It provides the semantic similarity measures between antecedent word vectors and pronoun context vectors. To combine Q-learning and Word2Vec results, we use a ranking aggregation method. The resolution system is evaluated on literary, journalistic and technical manual texts. Its precision rate reaches until 80.82%.

Keywords: Word2vec · Q-learning · Syntactic · Semantic · Self-training · SVM · Ranking aggregation · Pronominal anaphora · Arabic

1 Introduction

Anaphora is a linguistic phenomenon that plays an important role in the construction of meaning. It implements the different possibilities of resumption of an element in a text. Each anaphoric pronoun depends on another expression, called reference or antecedent, that must be found in the previous (or sometimes the following) part of the text. The pronominal anaphora resolution aims at finding the reference, usually a noun phrase (NP), of an anaphoric pronoun. The implementation of anaphora resolution system can reveal the ambiguity of the text, understand sentences and check the consistency of context. So, such a resolution system has become necessary in many applications of Natural Language Processing (NLP) mainly the applications of information extraction and topics detection.

© Springer Nature Switzerland AG 2019
K. Smaïli (Ed.): ICALP 2019, CCIS 1108, pp. 93–107, 2019.
https://doi.org/10.1007/978-3-030-32959-4_7

Several anaphor resolution works were done for English and other languages, but few works have focused on the Arabic. The lack of NLP resources for Arabic and the specificities of the language can influence the anaphor resolution and make the task more difficult.

The pronominal anaphora resolution that we propose task in this paper includes two main steps: a preliminary step for the identification of non-referential pronouns and a second step for the resolution. The non-referential pronouns identification uses an iterative self-training SVM method. It exploits a set of patterns-based and linguistic-based information as classification features. The resolution step is a combination between a Q-learning based method and word embedding model. For Q-learning method, we considered a set of morpho-syntactic criteria that favor some candidate antecedents over others. The Q-learning algorithm gives the optimal combination of criteria, in order to evaluate the antecedents and choose the best of them. For word embedding method, we used the pre-trained model AraVec 3.0[1]. The word vectors provided by this model allow to calculate the semantic affinity between the pronoun and these candidate antecedents. The combination of the two methods exploits both syntactic and semantic information gives better results.

This article consists of six sections. In Sect. 2 we give the specificities of the Arabic language that influence the task of resolution. In Sect. 3, we conduct a comparative study of the state of the art between the different existing works. In Sect. 3, we describe the method of identifying non-referential pronouns. We explain the steps of our approach, in Sect. 4, and we detail both of the Q-learning and the Word2Vec method. Finally, we present our test corpus, the results of the experiments and their comparisons to the other Arabic works.

2   Impact of Arabic Specificities on Anaphora Resolution

There are several types of anaphora in Arabic. Pronominal anaphora includes personal (subjects and objects), demonstrative and relative pronouns. Personal pronouns can be isolated or suffixed (1). They are generally anaphoric and referential. But they can be non-referential like in the sentence (1). Demonstrative pronouns are generally cataphoric[2] (2). They can also be anaphoric, but in some cases they are non-referential. Relative pronouns are always anaphoric. They refer to the NP (Noun Phrase) that immediately precedes them (3).

(1)   إنــها تمطر (It's raining)
(2)   فكه عينيك بتلك البسط الخضراء (Enjoy your eyes from these green valleys)
(3)   البسط التي نسجتها يد الطبيعة (The valleys that have been created by nature).

Arabic is a morphologically rich language marked by several distinctive characteristics mainly: the agglutination of clitics[3] to words, the diacritical[4] marks in the

---

[1] https://github.com/bakrianoo/aravec.

[2] The cataphor is the case where the anaphora precedes its antecedent.

[3] Clitics are elements of grammar attached to the root of a word.

[4] Short vowels in Arabic are replaced by symbols called diacritics.

Arabic texts, and the exceptional case of gender and number agreement. These characteristics influence the anaphora resolution problem. Firstly, the agglutination of clitics to words can induce a problem of ambiguity to determine whether the word contains a pronoun or not. For example, in the word كتابـه (his book) the letter ـه is an enclitic pronoun attached to the root while in the word منتبه (attentive) the letter ـه is a part of the word. Secondly, the lack of diacritical marks in several Arabic texts can produce a morphological ambiguity and even grammatical ambiguity, like the non-vowelized word فهم that can be interpreted like a verb فَهِمَ (understanding) or like a personal pronoun هم attached to coordinating conjunction ف giving the agglutinative form فَهُمْ (so they). In addition, the gender and number agreement in Arabic language poses an exceptional case; this is the case where the anaphoric pronoun in singular feminine form can refer a non-human plural noun, like in the example (4). Moreover, the sentences' length, the frequency of anaphoric expressions and the lack of punctuation make more difficult the segmentation of text. So the range of possible candidates of each anaphora grows wider. The example (5) illustrates the frequency and the diversity of anaphora in one sentence.

(4) ملّت عجول الفلاح ضيق المرابض فجاء وحلـها من معالفـها (The farmer's calves had disliked the tightness of the stable then he came and dissolved them from their mangers)

(5) فكه عينيك بتلك البسط الخضراء التي نسجتـها يد الطبيعة نفسـها فتلك هي السعادة بعينـها (enjoy your eyes to these green valleys that have been created by nature itself, that's all happiness)

3 Previous Work

The anaphor resolution task was the research topic of several NLP works. We can distinguish four types of approaches: rule-based approaches, statistical approaches, learning-based approaches and hybrid approaches. Language-based approaches operates on several sources of knowledge such as Lappin and Leass [1], Mitkov [2], Schmolz et al. [3] for English. Gelain and Sedogbo [4], Bittar [5], Nouioua [6] for the French, Fallahi and Shamsfard [7] for Persian, Ashima and Mohana [8] for India. The work of Mitkov [2] was adapted to the Arabic language in Mitkov et al. [9]. However, linguistic knowledge remains insufficient especially for morphologically rich languages such as Arabic. In fact, linguistic rules alone are unable to resolve semantic ambiguities.

Some works have been based on statistical methods such as the works Seminck and Amsili [10] for English, Elghamry et al. [11] for the Arabic. The work of Elghamry presents a statistical dynamic algorithm. It uses collocational evidence, recency and bands as related features. The bands are used to divide iteratively the search space in order to reduce the number of candidate antecedents. Other works have used machine learning methods to cover the shortcomings of language rules. Most of them considered the resolution as a classification problem and they exploited the characteristic vectors of the pronoun-antecedent pairs, such as the work Aone and Bennett [12] for Japanese, Li et al. [13] for English and Aktas et al. [14] for the German language. However, supervised learning requires large labeled data sources, which is sometimes expensive and difficult for some languages. Approaches based on unsupervised learning, such as the work Charniak and Elsner [15], are fewer.

For hybrid approaches, the authors have combined language rules and learning techniques into a single representation to take advantage of both and to cover one another's shortcomings. Among the works that have opted for this type of approach, we can cite: Weissenbacher and Nazarenko [16], Kamune and Agrawal [17] for English, Dakwale et al. [18], Mujadia et al. [19] for Hindi, Abolohom and Omar [20], Hammami [21] for Arabic. The work of Abolohom and Omar [20] combines 16 rules and a k-Nearest Neighbor classifier. Hammami [21] classifies the pairs (pronoun-antecedent) using a learning algorithm (RIPPER) and a set of morphological features.

4   Identification of Non-referential Pronouns

The main goal of our resolution system is to look for the best antecedent of the anaphoric pronoun in the list of candidate antecedents. Pronouns are identified using their part-of-speech values that are generated by the morphological analyzer of Ben Othman [22]. Then they are filtered to eliminate non-referential pronouns and to avoid the loss of time in the search for non-existent antecedents. To identify the non-referential pronouns, we used a semi-supervised self-training learning method. It exploits an SVM classifier and operates on a set of patterns-based and linguistic-based features. The non-referential pronouns identification is a quite difficult task and needs enough information to have a good result. We achieved a linguistic study in Arabic texts to identify the effective features and the most important constructions of non-referential pronouns.

4.1   Classification Features

The classification features include linguistic-based and pattern-based features. The linguistic-based features are grammatical and syntactical features. Grammatical features indicate the grammatical value, the gender and the number of the current pronoun and of the words surrounding it. Syntactical features concern important syntactical characteristics like the existence of a discriminating delimiter that immediately follows the pronoun, the existence of a specific particle or an impersonal verb after the pronoun.

The pattern-based features test the verification of the non-referential patterns. Non-referential patterns can be grouped into confirmation patterns, time and climate patterns, proverbs and sayings and other constructions of patterns.

Examples of confirmation patterns:

- إنّه مِنَ [غير] (it is [not]) + defined adjective
- إنّه (it is) + Specific delimiter + مِنْ أنْ + verb
- إنّه مَنْ (Whoever) + verb/أنّه مَنْ (qui) + verb/لعلّه مَنْ (maybe who) + verb

The most used time and climate patterns:

- إنّها/إنّه (it is) + specific climate or atmosphere verb
- إنّها (it is) + number [hour/time] + specific words

The other non-referential patterns:

- ما (what) + verb + attached pronoun
- لا يزال/مازال (still) + هناك (There is) + nom

4.2 An Iterative Self-training SVM Method

SVM is a binary classification method based on the use of the functions, called kernel, that allow optimal data separation [23]. In the self-training SVM algorithm, the SVM classifier is first trained on a small set of labeled data (the initial training corpus). Next, it is used to predict labels of unlabeled examples. A subset of unlabeled examples, with their predicted tags, is selected to increase the initial labeled training set. Then, the classifier is newly trained on the recent training data and used to classify other unlabeled examples. This process is repeated several times until all unlabeled data are processed or a maximum number of iterations is reached. At each iteration, the system selects only the most accurate and the most informative instances and then adds them to the set of labeled data. The self-training SVM process includes the flowing steps:

- Training step: the SVM classifier is trained on the labeled data.
- Prediction step: the trained classifier is used to classify the unlabeled data and to predict their labels. Each newly-labeled data has an estimation probability used as a confidence measure.
- Selection step: From the obtained predictions, the system selects only the most accurate and the most informative instances and then adds them to the labeled data. Therefore, we applied two stages of selection:
  - The first stage of selection retains only the instances for which the prediction probability of the class is high.
  - The second stage of selection keeps the most informative data by using similarity measures as Euclidean distance or similarity cosine measures. These methods of measure give more information about the nearest class to each point data.

Selection step handles instance by instance and chooses only instances that check both conditions and verify the two filter stages. For each iteration, the SVM classifier is re-trained on newly-labeled data.

5 Resolution Approach Combining Q-learning and Word2Vec

Our resolution system looks for the best antecedent of each pronoun using syntactic and semantic knowledge in order to favor candidates over others. Syntactic knowledge are preference criteria capable to evaluate and disambiguate candidate antecedents. Semantic knowledge offers the semantic similarity of words. The semantic affinity between the candidate antecedents and the context of the pronoun makes it possible to judge the best antecedent. The syntactic knowledge is used as preference criteria in a

Q-learning method. The semantic knowledge, given by a pre-trained word2Vec model, is used to select the most semantically similar antecedents regarding the context.

The input of our system is the set of pronouns and the candidate antecedents. Our resolution approach combines two methods: a Q-learning method and a word2Vec method. The Q-learning algorithm uses a set of syntactic criteria and interacts with its environment to choose the best combination of criteria, then to evaluate antecedents. The word embedding model uses word vectors, of the pre-trained model AraVec 3.0, to compute similarity measures between the antecedent vector and the mean vector of the pronoun context. Each method provides, for each pronoun, a ranking list of antecedents. To choose the final order of rank, we used a ranking aggregation method. Figure 1 shows the resolution approach process.

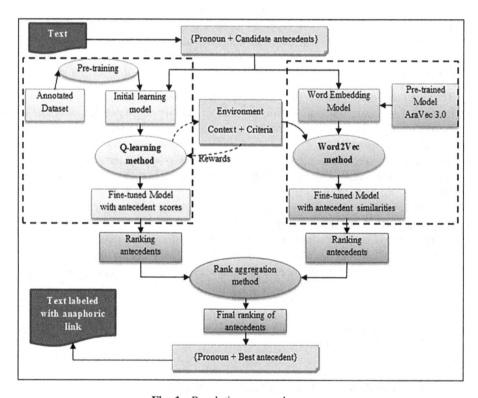

Fig. 1. Resolution approach process

5.1 Q-learning Method

The preference criteria combination for judging the best candidate for each pronoun is unknown in advance and changes according to the context of the pronoun. We have opted for a reinforcement learning approach because it is an effective method for learning in an uncertain and dynamic environment. The environment of our system includes the pronoun, its morpho-syntactic information and the list of linguistic criteria. The choice of reinforcement learning is justified by the following reasons:

- In Arabic, the lack of large data and labeled with anaphoric links makes the use of fully supervised learning quite difficult.
- The environment of the resolution system is dynamic, because on the one hand the list of antecedents is limited to a window of words, and on the other hand, the linguistic criteria and their relevance can change according to the pronoun and the style of the treated text.
- The resolution system seeks to optimize a sequence of decisions (choice of criteria) in order to find the best candidate antecedent.

The anaphora resolution system learns by itself while interacting with its environment. It reinforces the actions that prove to be the best, and this, in order to maximize the rewards obtained at the end. The Q-learning algorithm is one of the most used reinforcement learning techniques. It balances exploration and exploitation processes. The Q-learning algorithm uses a reward matrix R and interacts with its environment containing the context of the pronoun and a list of criteria. This matrix R is initialized during a pre-learning phase that uses some labeled texts.

Syntactic Criteria. The criteria for evaluating antecedents are more or less effective. They represent preferences and not absolute factors. Their relevance depends on the context of the anaphoric pronoun and even on the style of the text, and they are estimates of counts made on some texts tagged with anaphoric link. The set of syntactic criteria is summarized in the Table 1.

Table 1. Syntactic criteria used by Q-learning method

Syntactic criteria	Description
Definiteness	Defined NPs are preferred to those undefined
Topic	The subjects of the current and/or precedent sentences are more favored
Recency	The closest antecedents are the most salient
Paragraph header	The entity ahead of the paragraph is a preferred candidate
Proper noun	The proper noun are important elements of speech and are preferred to others
Repetition	Candidate antecedents whose lemmas are repeated several times in the text are more favored
Precedent pronoun antecedent	The candidate who has already been chosen as antecedent for the preceding pronoun is privileged

Q-learning Process. Our reinforcement learning system is modeled by a Markov Decision Process (MDP). The set of states includes the initial state S_{-I}, the intermediate states representing all possible combinations of criteria and the final state S_{-F}. The initial state S_{-I} of the PDM contains information about the pronoun Pr. The combination of the criteria (CC) is unknown. The possible actions, from state to other, are the choice of criteria. Each transition from one state S_i to another S_{-j} has an associated reward value r_{ij}. The final state S_{-F} contains the optimal sequence of actions that represents the best combination of criteria. Each state S_i can go directly to the final state S_{-F} with a reward r_{iF}. The reward r_{ij} is the participation frequency of the criteria combination of the state S_{-j}, in the resolution of pronoun with similar context. Figure 2 shows an example of the MDP representation for 2 criteria.

The Q-learning [24] algorithm uses two matrices Q and R. The matrix R is a two-dimensional matrix; the lines represent the set of states and the columns are the actions. The actions are the criteria c_x and the final action Φ which makes it possible to go directly to the final state. The contexts of the states contain all combinations of criteria. From each state, there are possible actions (their rewards are r_{ij}) and others not allowed actions (their rewards are equal to -1).

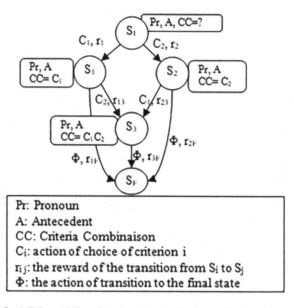

Fig. 2. MDP modeling for choosing the best combination of criteria

The matrix Q is initialized to 0, and it is updated using the reward matrix R. With this matrix Q, the traces are updated according decisions taken in the past. The system learns from experience and explores from one state to another until reaching the goal. In the final matrix Q, the set of optimal actions corresponds to the best combination of criteria capable to evaluate the antecedents of the treated pronoun. The formula (1) is used to update the matrix Q.

$$Q(S_i, a) \leftarrow Q(S_i, a) + \alpha * [R(S_i, a) + \gamma * \text{Max}[Q(\text{next state, all actions})]] \qquad (1)$$

The formula (1) allows to update $Q(S_i, a)$. At each selection of a criterion c, the agent observes the reward $R(S_i, \text{action})$ and the new state S_{-i+1} and updates the matrix Q. The parameters alpha (α) and gamma (γ) have a range of 0 to 1; alpha is a learning factor, it controls the update rate, gamma is a discount factor to moderate the impact of future rewards. The Q-learning algorithm goes as follows:

```
1.  Set the alpha (α) and gamma (γ) parameters, set the
    environment rewards in matrix R, initialize matrix Q
    to zero.
2.  For each episode:
        Select a random initial state S_i.
        While final state is not reached Do
        a.  Select a possible action a from S_i
        b.  Consider going to the next state
        c.  Get maximum Q value for this next state
        d.  Compute Q(S_i, a) using formula (1)
        e.  Update matrix Q
        f.  Set the next state as the current state.
        End Do
    End For
```

The Q-learning algorithm allows to select the best combination of criteria for each pronoun Pr. Our goal is to give a score to each antecedent in order to evaluate it. The score of an antecedent depends on the relevance of the combination criteria CC. But the criteria of combination CC are not all checked by the antecedent. So, if the antecedent A checks the criterion c (Verif (A, c) = 1) then its score increases by adding the relevance otherwise its score decreases (Verif (A, c) = -1). The evaluation scores allow to judge the best antecedent. The evaluation score calculated for each antecedent is described by the formula (2).

$$score_{Eval} = \sum_{\forall c \in CC} Verif(A, c) * relevance(c) \qquad (2)$$

5.2 Word2Vec Method

In the last few years, the word embedding model have been illustrated and highlighted in many different NLP tasks. AraVec 3.0 is a distributed word representation open source project which aims to provide the Arabic NLP research community with free to use, powerful word embedding models. The models are built carefully using multiple different Arabic text resources to provide wide domain coverage [25]. The model, that we used, is built using web pages collected from Wikipedia articles in Arabic language.

We exploited the word vectors of the AraVec 3.0 model to extract the semantic affinity between the pronoun and each of these antecedents; we proceeded by calculating the cosine value of these two vectors:

- Vector of antecedent word
- Average vector of the context: it is the average of the word-vectors around the pronoun.

The context of the pronoun contains a number (empirically fixed) of words sur-rounding the pronouns without considering the particles. For the case of an attached pronoun, the word attached to the pronoun is considered in the context.

The cosine similarity measures of each pair pronoun-antecedent allow to show the most similar antecedents to the pronoun context. We found (experimentally) that the best antecedents must have a cosine value greater than a threshold of 0.2. The ante-cedent with the best cosine value is considered the first. So, antecedents are ordered by decreasing cosine value except for the case of attached pronouns; for this case of pronouns, we have discarded the antecedents having a cosine value very close to 1 (about 0.9), since the word attached must not be a synonym of the pronoun.

5.3   Combination of Q-learning and Word2Vec

Each of the Q-learning and Word2Vec methods gives an ordered list of antecedents. The values of scores and similarities given by Q-learning and Word2Vec respectively are not compatible and we cannot combine them. In this case, we can only work on the ranking of each method. Several methods have been proposed for this rank aggregation problem.

We tested the kemeny Optimal Aggregation method (using Integer-Programming with Python) and we proposed our own simple but effective method. Our method calculates, for each antecedent, the sum of the votes given by the two methods. It ranks the antecedents in ascending order of the sum of votes. In the case of conflict, ie two antecedents have the same sum of votes; we decide the best based on scores and similarities values, and we choose the antecedent having the highest score (or simi-larity). Our ranking method favors the antecedent having discriminant values of scores or similarities. The thresholds, that are used to judge the discriminant values, are determined experimentally.

6   Experiments and Results

To measure the efficiency of the proposed approach, we achieved different experiments. Firstly, we evaluated the self-training approach for the identification of non-referential pronouns. Secondly, we conducted experiments for the main resolution approach combining Q-learning and Word2Vec.

6.1   Corpus

To evaluate the identification of non-referential approach, we used a corpus of literary texts extracted from children's stories and a Tunisian basic education textbook. The experimental data set includes the training data and the test data. The training data includes 10877 words and 1525 pronouns. It consists of a small set of labeled data using 68 pronouns (4.5%) and a big set of unlabeled data using 1457 pronouns (95.5%). Usually, the number of referential pronouns is much larger than the number of non-referential pronouns. For labeled data, we tried to use a data set balanced in number of referential and non-referential pronouns; this to provide a better classification of unlabeled instances. For unlabeled data, the size of data set is quite large, and it is difficult to provide a balanced number referential and non-referential pronouns. Then, we proceed to apply the Weka SMOTE[5] filter to create new instances of non-referential data. The test data contains about 440 words and 67 pronouns.

To evaluate the performance of the main resolution approach, we conducted several experiments on a variety of texts. The corpus includes, firstly, literary texts extracted from a Tunisian basic education textbook, and secondly technical manuals and journalistic texts extracted from the web. This corpus contains 4201 words and 436 pronouns of which 409 are referential. The pre-training stage uses training texts containing 5196 words and 638 pronouns. Note that for the Q-learning method, we used training texts just to initialize the model but not for the reinforcement learning process.

6.2   Evaluation of Results

Our system has been able to detect all the anaphoric pronouns and to identify them according to their types. It covers all the anaphors considered in the resolution and generates, for most pronouns, a non-empty list of candidate antecedents.

Evaluation of Non-referential Identification Approach. We performed several tests to show the effectiveness of the semi-supervised self-training SVM approach. Table 2 shows the performance of the proposed approach using the first and the second stage of selection. The first stage retains the most accurate data; the second stage keeps the most informative data based on Euclidean distance or cosine similarity method. The use of the two selection stages keeps the most accurate and most informative data. The following evaluations were performing on the test data.

Table 2. Results of the self-training SVM approach

Selection step		Precision	Precision of non-referential class	Precision of referential class
First selection stage		83.75%	87.5%	80%
Two selection stages	Euclidean distance	**90%**	**96.7%**	83.3%
	Cosine similarity	**90%**	80.6%	**97.2%**

The experiment results showed that the use of the two stages of selection improves the SVM classifier learning and produces better classification model. So, select both the most accurate and the most informative instances filters newly-labeled data and holds the most confident. This approach allowed as to increase the set of labeled training data and to improve classification. It could correctly classified 96.7% of pronouns.

---

[5] The filter resamples a dataset by applying the Synthetic Minority Oversampling TEchnique (SMOTE). The amount of SMOTE and the number of nearest neighbors may be specified as needed in order to balance the two-class instances size.

Evaluation of Resolution Approach. To show the effectiveness of the proposed approach that combines the Q-learning and Word2Vec methods, we present in Table 3 the precision rate of each method and the final precision of their combination. From this table, we can first deduce that the combination approach outperforms the other methods for all types of texts.

Table 3. Evaluation of the proposed methods

Texts methods	Technical manuals texts	Journalistic texts	Literary texts
Q-learning	72.73%	77.21%	65.43%
Word2Vec	68.53%	75.50%	60.11%
Combination	**80.82%**	**79.77%**	**66.49%**

The proposed approach combines both reinforcement learning method and word embedding method. It benefits from their advantages and exploits the syntactic and semantic knowledge sources. Thus, some occurrences of pronouns, which were not correctly resolved by the first method, have been corrected by the second.

For the evaluation of combination using the rank aggregation methods, we tested the Kemeny Optimal Aggregation method and our discriminant value ranking method. As shown by Fig. 3 the discriminant value method is the best.

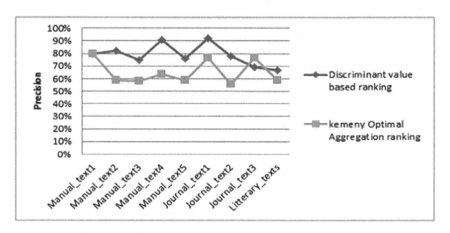

Fig. 3. Results of the combination approach for two aggregation methods

We have noticed that the results of literary texts are worse than those of other types of texts. This can be explained by the complexities of literary texts, where the sentences are much longer and the size of the candidate antecedents list increases and can reach up to 20 candidates. The failed resolutions in literary texts can be explained too, by the presence of a candidate whose identification requires the use of a pragmatic level, ie deduced from the comprehension of the general context of the text. Like in the example

(6), the pronoun **هما** refers to the two distant names ابن عرس et الصبي. Also, by studying this low precision rate, we noticed that a lot of errors came from a reference to proper names. Several pronouns refer to proper names, not all of them are recognized by the pre-trained model AraVec 3.0. By eliminating the resolution of pronouns that refer to a proper name, we could have better results for literary texts. Without considering proper name cases, the Q-learning, the Word2Vec and the combination methods give respectively a precision rate equals to 71.93%, 66.08% and 73.10%, that's why we intend to improve the reference to proper name in the future.

وأغلق **عليهما** البيت فتركه الناسك عند الصبي ولم يجد من يخلفه عند ابنه غير ابن عرس داجن عنده (6)

(and he did not find anyone to keep his son except the weasel who lives with him, he left it with the boy and he closed the house on them).

6.3   Comparison to Arabic Works

As mentioned before, several works have treated the pronominal anaphora resolution in the English language but very few researchers were interested in the Arabic. To have a meaningful comparison, we compared our approach to similar work for Arabic language. To our knowledge the previous Arabic works are: Mitkov et al. [9], Elghamry et al. [11], Abolohom and Omar [20], Hammami [21]. Mitkov et al. [9] proposed a rule-based method. The tests are made on 63 examples of a technical manuals. Their evaluation reached a rate of success equal to 95.2%. The work of Elghamry [11] presented a statistical dynamic algorithm based on "bootstrapping". The evaluation used a corpus including web documents and reached 78% precision. Abolohom et al. [20] proposed a hybrid approach that combines rule-based method and the K-NN supervised learning method. They tested their approach using a corpus extracted from the Holy Quran. They obtained a rate of precision equal to 71.7%. Hammami [21] used a rule-based learner method (RIPPER). It reached 69.2% precision on manual technical texts containing 419 pronouns. Compared to those works, our approach gives encouraging results since it was tested for different types of texts.

7   Conclusion

This article presents a new hybrid method combining Q-learning and Word2Vec for the resolution of pronominal anaphors in Arabic texts. The Q-learning method exploits a set of syntactic criteria. It looks for the optimal combination of criteria with the highest reward values. This combination of criteria is used to evaluate the possible antecedents and calculate their scores. The output of the Q-learning method is an ordered list of antecedents. The Word2Vec based method uses the pre-trained model AraVec 3.0. It exploits the word vectors of this model and calculates the semantic similarity between the antecedent and the pronoun context. The output of the Word2vec method is, also, another ordered list of antecedents. The combination of the two methods exploits the votes of each ordered list and uses a rank aggregation method to select the best antecedent.

As future work, we aim to expand our corpus and perform more experiments. We also plan to improve the semantic representation of words and apply other word embedding models. Finally, we suggest to test our methods for other languages.

References

1. Lappin, S., Leass, H.J.: An algorithm for pronominal anaphora resolution. Computat. Linguist. **20**(4), 535–561 (1994)
2. Mitkov, R.: Robust pronoun resolution with limited knowledge. In: Proceedings of the 18th International Conference on Computational Linguistics (COLING 1998)/ACL 1998, Montreal, Canada (1998)
3. Schmolz, H., Coquil, D., Döller, M.: In-depth analysis of anaphora resolution requirements. In: 2012 23rd International Workshop on Database and Expert Systems Applications, Vienna, Austria (2012)
4. Gelain, B., Sedogbo, C.: La résolution d'anaphore à partir d'un lexique-grammaire des verbes anaphoriques. In: COLING 1992 Proceedings of the 14th Conference on Computational Linguistics, France, vol. 3, pp. 901–905 (1992)
5. Bittar, A.: Un algorithme pour la résolution d'anaphores événementielles. Université Paris 7 Denis Diderot, UFR de Linguistique (2006)
6. Nouioua, F.: Heuristique pour la résolution d'anaphores dans les textes d'accidents de la route. Villetaneuse, Institut Galilée, Université Paris 13, F-93430 (2007)
7. Fallahi, F., Shamsfard, M.: Recognizing anaphora reference in Persian sentences. Int. J. Comput. Sci. **8**, 324–329 (2011)
8. Ashima, A., Mohana, B.: Improving anaphora resolution by resolving gender and number agreement in Hindi language using rule based approach. Indian J. Sci. Technol. **9**(32) (2016)
9. Mitkov, R., Belguith, L., Stys, M.: Multilingual robust anaphora resolution. In: Proceedings of the Third International Conference on Empirical Methods in Natural Language Processing (EMNLP-3), Granada, Spain, pp. 7–16 (1998)
10. Seminck, O., Amsili, P.: A computational model of human preferences for pronoun resolution. In: Proceedings of the Student Research Workshop at the 15th Conference of the European Chapter of the Association for Computational Linguistics, Valencia, Spain, pp. 53–63 (2017)
11. Elghamry, K., Al-Sabbagh, R., El-Zeiny, N.: Arabic anaphora resolution using Web as corpus. In: Proceedings of the Seventh Conference on Language Engineering, Cairo, Egypt, pp. 1–18 (2007)
12. Aone, C., Bennett, S.W.: Applying machine learning to anaphora resolution. In: Wermter, S., Riloff, E., Scheler, G. (eds.) IJCAI 1995. LNCS, vol. 1040, pp. 302–314. Springer, Heidelberg (1996). https://doi.org/10.1007/3-540-60925-3_55
13. Li, D., Miller, T., Schuler, W.: A pronoun anaphora resolution system based on factorial hidden Markov models. In: Proceedings of the 49th Annual Meeting of the Association for Computational Linguistics, Portland, Oregon, 19–24 June 2011, pp. 1169–1178 (2011)
14. Aktas, B., Scheffler, T., Stede, M.: Anaphora resolution for Twitter conversations: an exploratory study. In: Proceedings of the Workshop on Computational Models of Reference, Anaphora and Coreference, New Orleans, Louisiana, 6 June 2018, pp. 1–10 (2018)
15. Charniak, E., Elsner, M.: EM works for pronoun anaphora resolution. In: Proceedings of EACL, pp. 48–156 (2009)

16. Weissenbacher, D., Nazarenko, A.: Identifier les pronoms anaphoriques et trouver leurs antécédents: l'intérêt de la classification bayésienne. In: Proceeding of TALN, pp. 145–155 (2007)
17. Kamune, K., Agrawal, A.: Hybrid approach to pronominal anaphora resolution in English newspaper text. Int. J. Intell. Syst. Appl. **02**, 56–64 (2015). https://doi.org/10.5815/ijisa. 2015.02.08. Published Online January 2015 in MECS
18. Dakwale, P., Mujadia, V., Sharma, D.M.: A hybrid approach for anaphora resolution in Hindi. In: International Joint Conference on Natural Language Processing, Nagoya, Japan, pp. 977–981 (2013)
19. Mujadia, V., Gupta, P., Sharma, D.M.: Pronominal reference type identification and event anaphora resolution for Hindi. Int. J. Comput. Linguist. Appl. **7**(2), 45–63 (2016)
20. Abolohom, A., Omar, N.: A hybrid approach to pronominal anaphora resolution in Arabic. J. Comput. Sci. **11**(5), 764–771 (2015). https://doi.org/10.3844/jcssp.2015.764.771
21. Hammami, S.: La résolution automatique des anaphores pronominales pour la langue arabe. Thèse de doctorat. Université de Sfax, Faculté des Sciences Economiques et de Gestion, Sfax, Tunisie (2016)
22. Ben-Othmane, C.: De la synthèse lexicographique à la détection et à la correction des graphies fautives arabes. Ph.D. thesis. Université de Paris XI, Orsay (1998)
23. Mohamadally, H., Fomani, B.: SVM: Machines à Vecteurs de Support ou Séparateurs à Vastes Marges. BD Web, ISTY3 Versailles St Quentin, France (2006)
24. Sigaud, O., Garcia, F.: Apprentissage par renforcement Processus décisionnels de Markov en IA. Groupe PDMIA, 27 février 2008
25. Abu Bakr, S., Kareem, E., El-Beltagy, S.R.: AraVec: a set of Arabic word embedding models for use in Arabic NLP. In: 3rd International Conference on Arabic Computational Linguistics, ACLing 2017, Dubai, United Arab Emirates, 5–6 November 2017

LSTM-CNN Deep Learning Model
for Sentiment Analysis of Dialectal Arabic

Kathrein Abu Kwaik[1]([✉]), Motaz Saad[2], Stergios Chatzikyriakidis[1],
and Simon Dobnik[1]

[1] CLASP, Department of Philosophy, Linguistics and Theory of Science,
Box 200, 405 30 Gothenburg, Sweden
{kathrein.abu.kwaik,stergios.chatzikyriakidis,simon.dobnik}@gu.se
[2] The Islamic University of Gaza, Gaza, Palestine
motaz.saad@gmail.com

Abstract. In this paper we investigate the use of Deep Learning (DL) methods for Dialectal Arabic Sentiment Analysis. We propose a DL model that combines long-short term memory (LSTM) with convolutional neural networks (CNN). The proposed model performs better than the two baselines. More specifically, the model achieves an accuracy between 81% and 93% for binary classification and 66% to 76% accuracy for three-way classification. The model is currently the state of the art in applying DL methods to Sentiment Analysis in dialectal Arabic.

Keywords: Sentiment Analysis · Arabic dialects · Deep Learning · LSTM · CNN

1 Introduction

With the emergence of social media, large amounts of valuable data become available online and easy to access. Social media users discuss everything they care about through blog posts or tweets, share their opinions and show interest freely; while they do not actually do it in person. We read about political debates, social problems, questions about a particular product, etc. Companies also use social networks to promote their products and services, and explore people's opinions to improve their products and services, thereby generating a huge amount of data. In this context, the need for an analytical tool that can process the users data and classify them in terms of sentiment polarities is increased and become a necessity.

Sentiment analysis (SA) or Opinion Mining (OM) is the task of determining and detecting the polarity/opinion in a given piece of text and classifying it into positive, negative or neutral and in some fine grained cases also a mixed class. English and other European languages have been explored in the majority SA tools and research; recent efforts extend the focus to other low-resources languages such as Arabic and dialectal Arabic.

© Springer Nature Switzerland AG 2019
K. Smaïli (Ed.): ICALP 2019, CCIS 1108, pp. 108–121, 2019.
https://doi.org/10.1007/978-3-030-32959-4_8

Arabic is one of the five most spoken languages in the world, spoken by more than 422 million native speakers[1]. The situation in Arabic is a classic case of diglossia, whereby the written formal language differs substantially from the spoken vernacular [1,2]. Modern standard Arabic (MSA) is heavily based on Classical Arabic and constitutes the official written language used in government affairs, news, broadcast media, books and education. MSA acts as the lingua franca amongst Arabic native speakers [3]. However, the spoken language (collectively referred to as Dialectal Arabic) widely varies across the Arab world. Moreover, there is neither standard written orthography nor formal grammar for these dialects.

To predict the sentiment of an Arabic piece of text, the majority of the works rely on Machine Learning (ML) algorithms like Linear Support Vector Classification (LinearSVC), Multinomial Naive Bayes (MNB) and others [4–9]. Even though these classifiers are very easy to implement and achieve good results, they require a lot of feature engineering before applying the data to the classifiers. Therefore, work in Arabic sentiment analysis still depends heavily on the morphological and syntactic aspects of the language, such as POS tagging, word stemming, the sentiment lexicons and other hand-crafted features. It was in these areas that there have been several improvements in detecting sentiment.

After the remarkable improvement brought about by Deep Learning (DL) over the traditional ML approaches, researchers tend to investigate and explore the performance of the deep neural networks in analysing different kinds of Arabic texts and extract features for some NLP tasks such as: Language Identification, Text Summarising, Sentiment Analysis and so on [10–12].

In this paper we introduce a deep neural network which combines Bi-directional Long-Short Term Memory Networks (Bi-LSTM) with Convolutional Neural Networks (CNN) to predict the polarity of a text and classify it as either having positive or negative polarity. We exploit some available Arabic sentiment datasets: LABR [13], ASTD [14] and Shami-Senti [15] with different sizes and different dialects. Our system outperforms the state-of-the-art deep learning models for particular datasets like ASTD [16] with improvements on smaller datasets.

The paper is organised as follows: Sect. 2 gives a brief review of existing work that uses deep learning for Arabic Sentiment Analysis. In Sect. 3 we briefly discuss the deep learning architectures and we experiment two baselines: a simple LSTM model and the Kaggle model which uses a combination of LSTM and CNN layers, In Sect. 4, we propose our model and show that it outperforms both baselines, and achieves state-of-the-art results for DL models. Finally, In Sect. 5 we conclude and discuss directions for future work.

---

[1] http://www.unesco.org/new/en/unesco/events/prizes-and-celebrations/celebrations/international-days/world-arabic-language-day-2013/.

2   Related Work

Sentiment Analysis is usually considered a supervised classification task, where the texts are classified into two or more sentiments classes by providing a dataset with the text and the sentiment label. The common approach in SA is the use of ML through language modelling and feature engineering.

Most of the SA techniques in Arabic use words and character n-gram features with different representation settings and different classifiers [13,17–19]. In some cases, ensemble classifiers are used [20,21]. Moreover, sentiment lexicons are additional and valuable sources of features that have been used to enrich features for SA [22–25].

In [26], the authors introduce a subjectivity and sentiment analysis system for Arabic tweets by extracting different sets of features such as the form of the words (Stem, Lemma), POS tagging, the presence of the sentiment adjective and the Arabic form of the tweet (MSA or DA), in addition to other Twitter-specific features such as the userID (person, organization) and the gender of the user. In [8] a language model is built and different machine learning classifiers are used to handle tweets in MSA and Jordanian.

An early deep learning framework for Sentiment Analysis for Arabic is proposed in [27]. The authors explore several network architectures based on Deep Belief networks, Deep Auto Encoder and the Recursive Auto Encoder. The authors there do not mention the range of labels of the polarity classification. They use The Linguistic Data Consortium Arabic Tree Bank (LDC ATB) dataset and show that the model outperforms the state of the art models on the same dataset by around 9% in terms of F-score. They get an accuracy of 74.5%.

Baly et al. [28] build a deep learning model to detect the polarities of tweets in a 5-scale classification that ranges from very negative to very positive. They retrieve tweets from 12 Arab countries in 4 regions (the Arab Gulf, the Levant, Egypt and North Africa). They collect 470 K tweets. Their deep learning model consists of an embedding layer followed by an LSTM layer. Pre-trained word embeddings are applied using the skip-gram model from Word2Vec. The authors investigate the performance of their model on different morphological forms (lemma and stem). They achieve an accuracy of 70% for the Egyptian tweets and lemma embeddings while for UAE tweets they get 63.7% accuracy.

Soumeur et al. [29] investigate the Sentiment Analysis in the Algerian users' comments on various Facebook brand pages of companies in Algeria. They collect 100 K comments written in Algerian, but they only annotate 25 K comments as positive, negative or neutral. They apply a CNN as a feature extractor and transformation network. Their model consists of three type of layers, three CNN layers each with 50 filters and 3 kernel size, followed by pooling layers and the fully connected layers to predict the sentiment of the comment. Their model achieves an 89.5% accuracy.

SEDAT, a sentiment and emotion analyser model, was built in [30] using Arabic tweets. Word and document embeddings in addition to a set of semantic features are used. All the extracted features into CNN-LSTM networks followed by a fully connected layer are applied. The data has been obtained from the public datasets for SemEval2018 (Task 1: Affect in Tweets), which has a size of nearly 7 K tweets. The authors further calculate Spearman's correlation coefficient over the baseline models which they outperform with 0.01–0.02 points of difference.

Recently, an ensemble deep learning model was proposed in [16]. There, the authors combine CNN and LSTM models to predict the sentiment of Arabic tweets exploiting Arabic Sentiment Tweets Dataset (ASTD). The model outperforms the state-of-the-art deep learning models F1-score of 53.6%, as they achieve an accuracy of 65% and an F1-score of 64.46%.

3   Deep Learning Baselines for Sentiment Analysis

In this section we present two baseline DL systems for dialectal sentiment analysis. But first, we will talk about the word representation and Deep learning network architectures briefly, in the following subsections.

3.1   Word Representation

Although word embedding vectors are easy to train, there are many pre-trained word vectors that were trained on a large amount of textual data. In this work we use Aravec, which is Arabic pre-trained word embeddings [31]. The Aravec are pre-trained using large data from multiple source like Twitter and Wikipedia and implemented by Word2Vec [32]. Each sample/sentence is replaced by a 2D vector representation of dimension $n \times d$, where n is the number of words in the sentence and d is the length of the embedding vector. After many trials we decided to apply the Aravec-CBOW model of dimension $d = 300$.

3.2   LSTM Network

The traditional Continuous Bag of Word model (CBOW) allows to encode arbitrary length of sequence inputs as fixed-size vectors, but this disregards the order of the features in the sequence [32]. In contrast, Recurrent Neural networks (RNN) represent arbitrary-sized sequences in a fixed-size vector as CBOW, while they pay attention to the structure of the input sequence. Special RNNs with gated architecture such as LSTMs have proven very powerful in capturing statistical regularities in sequential inputs [33].

LSTM is the first network that introduces the gating mechanism and is designed to capture the long-distance dependencies and solve the problem of vanishing gradients [34]. While the LSTM is a feed-forward network that reads the sequence from left to right, the Bidirectional LSTM (Bi-LSTM) connects two layers from opposite directions (forward and backward) over the same output. The output layer receives information from both the preceding sequence (backwards) and following sequence (forward) states simultaneously. It is thus very useful when the context of the input is needed, for example when the negation term appears after a positive term [35].

3.3 Convolutional Neural Networks

Convolutional Neural Networks (CNN) are feature extractor networks that are able to detect indicative local predictors in a large structure [36]. They are designed to combine these predictors to produce a fixed sized vector representation that captures and extracts the most informative local aspects for the prediction task.

For text classification, we use a 1D-CNN, a well known CNN architecture for dealing with sequences. It uses a convolution layer with a window size k that is able to identify the indicative k-grams in the input text, and then act as an n-gram detector [33]. Every CNN applies a nonlinear function called a filter, which transforms a window of size k into scalar values. After applying a multi-filter, the CNN produces m vectors, where each vector corresponds to a filter. Thus, a pooling task is required to combine all of the m vectors into a single m dimension vector. Generally, CNNs focus more on the informative features and disregard their locations in the input text [35,37].

3.4 Datasets

We use the following corpora in our experiments (the characteristics of these corpora are presented in Table 1):

– LABR [13]: it is one of the largest SA datasets to date for Arabic. The data are extracted from a book review website and consist of over 63 k book reviews written mostly in MSA with some dialectal phrases. We use the binary balanced and unbalanced subsets of LABR, in addition to the three-way classification subsets. In LABR, user ratings are used in order to classify sentences. Ratings of 4 and 5 stars are taken by the authors as positive, ratings of 1 and 2 stars are taken as negative and 3 star ratings are taken as neutral. In the binary classification case, 3 star ratings are removed, keeping only the positive and negative labels.
– ASTD [14]: it is an Arabic SA corpus collected from Twitter and focusing on the Egyptian dialect. It consists of approximately 10 k tweets which are classified as objective, subjective positive, subjective negative, and subjective mixed.
– Shami-Senti [15]: a Levantine SA corpus. It contains approximately 2 k posts from social media sites in general topics, classified as Positive, Negative and Neutral from the four main countries where Levantine is spoken: Palestine, Syria, Lebanon and Jordan.

Data Preparation. We apply the following pre-processing steps on all corpora:

1. Remove special characters, punctuation marks and all diacritics;
2. Remove all digits including dates;
3. Remove all repeated characters and keep only two repeated characters, using the algorithm from [15];
4. Remove any non-Arabic characters.

Table 1. The number of instances per category in the corpora used in our experiments

Corpus	NEG	POS	Neutral
Shami-Senti	935	1,064	243
LABR 3 balanced	6,580	6,578	6,580
LABR 2 balanced	6,578	6,580	
LABR 2 Un-Balanced	8,222	42,832	
ASTD	1,496	665	738

We replace every instance sentence with its corresponding word embedding vector from a pre-trained AraVec model [31]. In case of words that occur in the text but do not have an embedding in the pre-trained model, we look for the most similar words, and use them in order to get the corresponding word embeddings vector. More specifically, we look that the distance between the input word and the word in the Aravec model does not exceed two characters either from the beginning or the end of the word. The maximum length of every sentence is fixed to 70 words, thus we apply post-padding with zeros to ensure that all input sentences have the same length.

3.5   LSTM Baseline

This section describes our LSTM baseline. The Keras library has been used for the implementation of all experiments [38]. After many trials we used the Keras checkpoint function to save the best weight model. The checkpoint function automatically stops training when the validation loss starts increasing. After several experiments we decide to use the Adam optimiser with categorical cross entropy loss function for the multi-classification task, and RMSprop[2] for binary classification. The parameters we used in the baseline model are selected after running a number of experiments playing around with the different parameters as shown in Table 2. After many experiments, the parameters that lead to the best result for the baseline are highlighted in bold in the Table 2.

The first experiment we conduct uses a simple LSTM network which consists of an Embedding Layer with pre-trained word embedding followed by two LSTM layer with 128 and 64 output units respectively, followed by a fully connected Relu activation layer with 100 output units and a 0.5 dropout layer. Finally, a dense Sigmoid layer to predict the labels is used.

Table 3 shows the results for various LSTM-BiLSTM models with different combinations. The LSTM → LSTM experiment is the baseline model described above, while in the BiLSTM → LSTM experiment, we change the first layer with a BiLSTM layer. Finally, we try both BiLSTM on the data (BiLSTM → BiLSTM). The model seems to be overfitting the data with the accuracy being very low (less than the 50%). When we apply the baseline model (LSTM → LSTM) on ASTD and ShamiSenti corpora we get a 53% accuracy for both.

---

[2] https://keras.io/optimizers/.

Table 2. General parameters of deep learning models

Parameter	Value
Dataset split	80% train, 10% development, 10% test
Max number of features	[7K, 10K, **15K**, 25 K, 40K]
Embedding size	[100, **300**]
Embedding model	**CBOW**, Skip-gram
Embedding trainable	**True**, False
Max sample length	[50, **70**, 100]
Filter	[23, 64, 128]
Kernel size	[1, 2, 3, 4, 5, 6]
Pool size	[1, 2, 3, 4, 5]
Batch size	[32, **50**, 100, 128, 256]
Max epoch	10, 50, **100**, 1000
Dropout	0.2, **0.5**, 0.7
Optimiser	**Adam, RMSprop**, SGD
Activation function	Softmax, **Sigmoid, Relu**
LABR split (train/validation/test)	[70, 10, 20]
ASTD and Shami-Senti split (train/validation/test)	[80, 10, 10]

Table 3. Accuracy of networks with two sequential LSTM/BiLSTM layers for three-way classification

Dataset	Experiment name	Accuracy
LABR 3	LSTM → LSTM (baseline model)	41.9%
LABR 3	BiLSTM → LSTM	42.3%
LABR 3	BiLSTM → BiLSTM	40.6%
ASTD	LSTM → LSTM	53%
Shami-Senti	LSTM → LSTM	53%

Given the low accuracy on the three class task, we investigate the task of binary sentiment classification using BiLSTM → LSTM model from the second experiment on all of datasets (LABR, ASTD, Shami-Senti) as it produces the highest accuracy among all the previous experiments. In the binary task, we employ RMSprop as an optimiser with binary cross entropy loss function. Table 4 shows the results.

Table 4. Accuracy of the BiLSTM → LSTM model with binary classification task on our corpora

Corpus	Test
LABR 2 balanced	55.34%
LABR 2 un-balanced	**81**%
ASTD	**68.5**%
Shami-Senti	54.5 %

The system achieves an unexpected result on the ASTD and LABR 2 unbalanced datasets of 68.5% and 81% accuracy respectively. Table 5 shows the confusion matrix for both of these datasets. Since in the ASTD corpus the negative samples are approximately two-thirds the positive ones, the model tends to predict the negative class as an output label more often than the positive label. Similarly, in the LABR 2 unbalanced the model is biased towards the majority class, i.e. the positive class.

Table 5. Confusion matrix for the BiLSTM → LSTM model for ASTD and LABR 2 unbalanced corpora.

ASTD corpus			LABR 2 unbalanced		
	Predicted			Predicted	
	Positive	Negative		Positive	Negative
Actual Positive	11	**45**	Actual Positive	**8036**	505
Negative	23	**136**	Negative	**1555**	114

3.6 Kaggle Baseline

As a next step, we implement the winner model from the Kaggle sentiment analysis competition which was build for English sentiment analysis and has achieved an accuracy of 96%.[3] They used the Amazon Fine Food Reviews dataset, which includes 568,454 reviews, each review has a score from 1 to 5. The model is illustrated in Fig. 1 and consists of a CNN layer with max pooling of size 2 and a dropout layer to exclude some features, followed by one LSTM layer, and at the end, a fully connected layer to predict one output class among 3 sentiment classes (Positive, Negative and Neutral).

Fig. 1. Kaggle winner model

We train the model using LABR, ASTD and Shami-Senti and apply both three-way and binary classification. The results are shown in Table 6. We get a high accuracy for the LABR 2 unbalanced corpus and the ASTD corpus, 80.6% and 70.7% respectively. Taking a look at the confusion matrix in Table 7, we see that the model does not learn well. Being biased towards the majority class every time, it is clear that the model is over-fitting the training data.

---

[3] https://www.kaggle.com/monsterspy/conv-lstm-sentiment-analysis-keras-acc-0-96.

Table 6. Accuracy of the Kaggle model on three-way and binary sentiment classification

Corpus	Three-way classification	Binary classification
Shami-Senti	49%	52.3%
LABR 2 unbalanced		**80.6%**
LABR 2 balanced		53.1%
LABR 3	60%	
ASTD	59.3%	**70.7%**

Table 7. Confusion matrix for the Kaggle model on the ASTD and LABR 2 unbalanced corpora.

ASTD corpus				LABR 2 unbalanced		
		Predicted				Predicted
		Positive	Negative			Positive Negative
Actual	Positive	5	**51**	Actual	Positive	**8153** 387
	Negative	12	**147**		Negative	**1591** 78

4   Our Model

In the previous section we have seen that using a combination of LSTM with a CNN enhances the accuracy of the model. Given these results, we propose a more sophisticated model than the one used in the Kaggle experiments that uses several CNN layers employing different filters and kernels to extract as many features as possible. In addition, we use a BiLSTM to extract the features from both directions and keep track of their effects. In contrast to the Kaggle model, in our model the BiLSTM precedes the CNN layers. We assumed that this configuration would provide a more informative representation of the sequential structure of sentences. The results, we get as shown in Table 8, seem to justify this assumption as our model performs better than Kaggle in all datasets. Figure 2 shows the best performing configuration which consists of an Embedding layer initialised with pre-trained word embedding vectors of size 300 and a max features of 15K, followed by two BiLSTM layers of 128 and 64 output units respectively and 0.5 dropout. The second BiLSTM layer is fed into parallel CNN layers with 5 region sizes (kernels) [2, 3, 4, 5, 6] and 3 filters [32, 64, 128] where we employ *Keras* functional API to build them. Each CNN layer is followed by Global MaxPooling layer. At the end of the CNN network we have a concatenated layer to merger all the outputs into one dimensions vector. This vector feeds into a fully connected Relu layer with 10 output units. Finally, Sigmoid layer with 3 output units for three-way classification and one binary unit for binary classification is used.

Our model achieves high accuracy results for binary sentiment classification in LABR, ASTD and Shami-Senti. The LABR 2 unbalanced dataset again has a high accuracy of 80.2%, when we look to the confusion matrix it is nearly the

Table 8. Accuracy of the proposed model In addition to the comparing results from the two baselines on the three-way and binary sentiment classification

Corpus	Three-way classification			Binary classification		
	Our model	Kaggle	LSTM	Our model	Kaggle	LSTM
Shami-Senti	76.4%	49%	53%	93.5%	25.3%	54.5%
LABR 2 unbalanced				80.2%	80.6%	55.34%
LABR 2 balanced				81.14%	53.1%	81%
LABR 3	66.42%	60%	41.9%			
ASTD	68.62%	59.3%	53%	85.58%	70.7%	68.5%

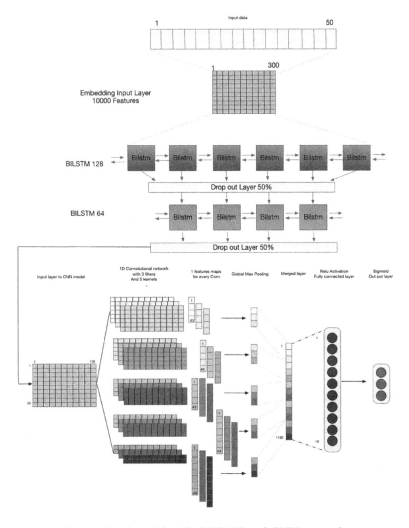

Fig. 2. Final model with BiLSTM and CNN networks

same like the one that has shown in Table 7. It is very clear that the LABR 2 unbalanced dataset does not learn well due to the data imbalance problem, which misleads the performance of the DL network although it has a reasonable size of training data.

Table 9 shows the confusion matrix for the three corpora. Even though the multi-classification results are not very high, our model outperforms the state-of-the-art deep learning models for some corpora like ASTD, where they achieve accuracy of 65% and F-score 64.5% [16]. In our proposed model we get an accuracy of 68.62% and an F-score equal to 69%. Both LABR 3 and ASTD are still suffering from the inaccurate annotation for the third neutral class. They assign the 3 star rating to neutral sentiment which complicates things, given that a 3 star rating might be quite positive or quite negative depending on a number of contextual parameters. This problem makes it hard to achieve very high accuracy when building a multi classification system using these corpora.

Table 9. Confusion matrix for the proposed model in the ASTD, Shami-Senti and the LABR 2 balanced corpora.

ASTD corpus			Shami-Senti			LABR2 Balanced		
		Predicted			Predicted			Predicted
		Pos Neg			Pos Neg			Pos Neg
Actual	Pos	46 | 18	Actual	Pos	94 | 4	Actual	Pos	561 | 80
	Neg	13 | 138		Neg	9 | 93		Neg	168 | 506

5   Conclusion and Future Work

In this paper we have investigated the use of Deep Learning architectures for dialectal SA. We first started by experimenting with a simple LSTM architecture on three dialectal SA datasets with poor results. We then took an off-the-shelf SA model that uses a combination of an LSTM and a CNN, i.e. Kaggle, and observed a better performance. Finally, we proposed our own model, which is a more elaborate BiLSTM $\rightarrow$ CNN with more convolutional layers, and obtained state-of-the-art results on the datasets that DL approaches have been previously applied to (i.e. the ASTD). In general, the results are promising but there is definitely room for improvement, especially on the threeway classification task.

One of the things that we would like to try in the future is the use of word embeddings specifically trained for the SA task, as well as even more complex DL architectures, for example those that use an attention mechanism. Another thing we want to do is to increase ShamiSenti's size, so that it is size-wise comparable to LABR3. It will then be possible to check whether the quality of the data will help the model obtain better accuracy scores, and furthermore check the effect of data size on the model's performance.

Acknowledgements. Kathrein Abu Kwaik, Stergios Chatzikyriakidis and Simon Dobnik are supported by grant 2014-39 from the Swedish Research Council, which funds the Centre for Linguistic Theory and Studies in Probability (CLASP) in the Department of Philosophy, Linguistics, and Theory of Science at the University of Gothenburg.

References

1. Versteegh, K.: The Arabic Language. Edinburgh University Press, Edinburgh (2014)
2. Ferguson, C.A.: Diglossia. Word **15**(2), 325–340 (1959)
3. Mustafa, S.: The Arabic Language. Routledge, London (2008)
4. Gamal, D., Alfonse, M., El-Horbaty, E.-S.M., Salem, A.-B.M.: Opinion mining for Arabic dialects on twitter. Egypt. Comput. Sci. J. **42**(4), 52–61 (2018)
5. Oussous, A., Lahcen, A.A., Belfkih, S.: Improving sentiment analysis of Moroccan tweets using ensemble learning. In: Tabii, Y., Lazaar, M., Al Achhab, M., Enneya, N. (eds.) BDCA 2018. CCIS, vol. 872, pp. 91–104. Springer, Cham (2018). https://doi.org/10.1007/978-3-319-96292-4_8
6. Farra, N., Challita, E., Assi, R.A., Hajj, H.: Sentence-level and document-level sentiment mining for Arabic texts. In: 2010 IEEE International Conference on Data Mining Workshops, pp. 1114–1119. IEEE (2010)
7. Duwairi, R.M.: Sentiment analysis for dialectical Arabic. In: 2015 6th International Conference on Information and Communication Systems (ICICS), pp. 166–170. IEEE (2015)
8. Duwairi, R.M., Marji, R., Sha'ban, N., Rushaidat, S.: Sentiment analysis in Arabic tweets. In: 2014 5th International Conference on Information and Communication Systems (ICICS), pp. 1–6. IEEE (2014)
9. Elarnaoty, M., AbdelRahman, S., Fahmy, A.: A machine learning approach for opinion holder extraction in Arabic language. arXiv preprint arXiv:1206.1011 (2012)
10. Abandah, G.A., Graves, A., Al-Shagoor, B., Arabiyat, A., Jamour, F., Al-Taee, M.: Automatic diacritization of Arabic text using recurrent neural networks. Int. J. Doc. Anal. Recogn. (IJDAR) **18**(2), 183–197 (2015)
11. Lulu, L., Elnagar, A.: Automatic Arabic dialect classification using deep learning models. Procedia Comput. Sci. **142**, 262–269 (2018)
12. Elaraby, M., Abdul-Mageed, M.: Deep models for Arabic dialect identification on benchmarked data. In: Proceedings of the Fifth Workshop on NLP for Similar Languages, Varieties and Dialects (VarDial 2018), pp. 263–274 (2018)
13. Aly, M., Atiya, A.: LABR: a large scale Arabic book reviews dataset. In: Proceedings of the 51st Annual Meeting of the Association for Computational Linguistics (Volume 2: Short Papers), vol. 2, pp. 494–498 (2013)
14. Nabil, M., Aly, M., Atiya, A.: ASTD: Arabic sentiment tweets dataset. In: Proceedings of the 2015 Conference on Empirical Methods in Natural Language Processing, pp. 2515–2519 (2015)
15. Qwaider, C., Saad, M., Chatzikyriakidis, S., Dobnik, S.: Shami: a corpus of Levantine Arabic dialects. In: Proceedings of the Eleventh International Conference on Language Resources and Evaluation (LREC-2018) (2018)
16. Heikal, M., Torki, M., El-Makky, N.: Sentiment analysis of Arabic tweets using deep learning. Procedia Comput. Sci. **142**, 114–122 (2018)

17. Mountassir, A., Benbrahim, H., Berrada, I.: An empirical study to address the problem of unbalanced data sets in sentiment classification. In: 2012 IEEE International Conference on Systems, Man, and Cybernetics (SMC), pp. 3298–3303. IEEE (2012)

18. Shoukry, A., Rafea, A.: Sentence-level Arabic sentiment analysis. In: 2012 International Conference on Collaboration Technologies and Systems (CTS), pp. 546–550. IEEE (2012)

19. Elawady, R.M., Barakat, S., Elrashidy, N.M.: Different feature selection for sentiment classification. Int. J. Inf. Sci. Intell. Syst. **3**(1), 137–150 (2014)

20. Omar, N., Albared, M., Al-Shabi, A.Q., Al-Moslmi, T.: Ensemble of classification algorithms for subjectivity and sentiment analysis of Arabic customers' reviews. Int. J. Adv. Comput. Technol. **5**(14), 77 (2013)

21. Al-Saqqa, S., Obeid, N., Awajan, A.: Sentiment analysis for Arabic text using ensemble learning. In: 2018 IEEE/ACS 15th International Conference on Computer Systems and Applications (AICCSA), pp. 1–7. IEEE (2018)

22. Al-Ayyoub, M., Khamaiseh, A.A., Jararweh, Y., Al-Kabi, M.N.: A comprehensive survey of Arabic sentiment analysis. Inf. Process. Manag. **56**(2), 320–342 (2019)

23. Abdul-Mageed, M., Diab, M.T., Korayem, M.: Subjectivity and sentiment analysis of modern standard Arabic. In: Proceedings of the 49th Annual Meeting of the Association for Computational Linguistics: Human Language Technologies: short papers-Volume 2, pp. 587–591. Association for Computational Linguistics (2011)

24. Badaro, G., et al.: A light lexicon-based mobile application for sentiment mining of Arabic tweets. In: Proceedings of the Second Workshop on Arabic Natural Language Processing, pp. 18–25 (2015)

25. Badaro, G., Baly, R., Hajj, H., Habash, N., El-Hajj, W.: A large scale Arabic sentiment lexicon for Arabic opinion mining. In: Proceedings of the EMNLP 2014 Workshop on Arabic Natural Language Processing (ANLP), pp. 165–173 (2014)

26. Abdul-Mageed, M., Diab, M., Kübler, S.: SAMAR: subjectivity and sentiment analysis for Arabic social media. Comput. Speech Lang. **28**(1), 20–37 (2014)

27. Al Sallab, A., Hajj, H., Badaro, G., Baly, R., El Hajj, W., Shaban, K.B.: Deep learning models for sentiment analysis in Arabic. In: Proceedings of the Second Workshop on Arabic Natural Language Processing, pp. 9–17 (2015)

28. Baly, R., et al.: Comparative evaluation of sentiment analysis methods across Arabic dialects. Procedia Comput. Sci. **117**, 266–273 (2017)

29. Soumeur, A., Mokdadi, M., Guessoum, A., Daoud, A.: Sentiment analysis of users on social networks: overcoming the challenge of the loose usages of the Algerian dialect. Procedia Comput. Sci. **142**, 26–37 (2018)

30. Abdullah, M., Hadzikadicy, M., Shaikhz, S.: SEDAT: sentiment and emotion detection in Arabic text using CNN-LSTM deep learning. In: 2018 17th IEEE International Conference on Machine Learning and Applications (ICMLA), pp. 835–840. IEEE (2018)

31. Soliman, A.B., Eissa, K., El-Beltagy, S.R.: AraVec: a set of Arabic word embedding models for use in Arabic NLP. Procedia Comput. Sci. **117**, 256–265 (2017)

32. Mikolov, T., Sutskever, I., Chen, K., Corrado, G.S., Dean, J.: Distributed representations of words and phrases and their compositionality. In: Advances in Neural Information Processing Systems, pp. 3111–3119 (2013)

33. Goldberg, Y.: Neural network methods for natural language processing. Synth. Lect. Hum. Lang. Technol. **10**(1), 1–309 (2017)

34. Pascanu, R., Mikolov, T., Bengio, Y.: On the difficulty of training recurrent neural networks. In: International Conference on Machine Learning, pp. 1310–1318 (2013)

35. Schmidhuber, J.: Deep learning in neural networks: an overview. Neural Netw. **61**, 85–117 (2015)
36. Goodfellow, I., Bengio, Y., Courville, A.: Deep Learning. MIT press, Cambridge (2016)
37. LeCun, Y., Bengio, Y., Hinton, G.: Deep learning. Nature **521**(7553), 436 (2015)
38. Gulli, A., Pal, S.: Deep Learning with Keras. Packt Publishing Ltd., Birmingham (2017)

Sentiment Analysis of Code-Switched Tunisian Dialect: Exploring RNN-Based Techniques

Mohamed Amine Jerbi[1(✉)], Hadhemi Achour[1], and Emna Souissi[2]

[1] Université de Tunis, ISGT, LR99ES04 BESTMOD, 2000 Le Bardo, Tunisia
mohamedaminejerbil@gmail.com, Hadhemi_Achour@yahoo.fr
[2] Université de Tunis, ENSIT, 1008 Montfleury, Tunisia
emna.souissi@ensit.rnu.tn

Abstract. With the increasing use of social networks and the multilingualism that characterizes the Internet in general and the social media in particular, an increasing number of recent research works on Sentiment Analysis and Opinion Mining are tackling the analysis of informal textual content, which includes language alternation, known as code-switching. To date, very little work has addressed in particular, the analysis social media of the Tunisian dialect, which is characterized both by a frequent occurring of code-switching and by a double script (Arabic and Latin) when written on the social media. Our study aims to explore and compare various classification models based on RNNs (Recurrent Neural Networks), precisely on LSTM (Long Short-Term Memory) neural networks.

Keywords: Sentiment analysis · Code-switching · Tunisian dialect · Social media · Deep learning · RNN · LSTM · Bi-LSTM · Deep-LSTM

1 Introduction

Code-switching (CS) is the alternation of at least two linguistic codes in a single conversation. It is defined in [1] as «*the mixing, by bilinguals (or multilinguals), of two or more languages in discourse, often with no change of interlocutor or topic.*». CS may occur at any level of linguistic structure such as a clause, a single sentence, a constituent or even a word.

This phenomenon is very common on social networks, blogs and forums, especially within multilingual communities. In terms of NLP tasks, code-switching data reveals a number of problems requiring dedicated tools handling the mixed data specificities [2]. In particular, when it comes to sentiment analysis within this kind of textual content, emotions and opinions can be expressed in several different ways in different languages, which can complicate the automatic sentiment detection and opinion mining tasks [3].

In this work, we focus on sentiment analysis (SA) in Tunisian dialect textual productions that are generated on the social media and which are characterized by a very frequent use of code-switching. The automatic processing of the Tunisian dialect on social networks is a challenging task and is still in its infancy, especially when

© Springer Nature Switzerland AG 2019
K. Smaïli (Ed.): ICALP 2019, CCIS 1108, pp. 122–131, 2019.
https://doi.org/10.1007/978-3-030-32959-4_9

considering the very low availability of linguistic resources and dedicated NLP tools, despite the growing interest it arouses among many researchers in the last few years [4].

The Tunisian dialect (TD), known as the "*Darija*" or "*Tounsi*", the TD is a variant of the Arabic language, quite different from the MSA, because it derives from different substrates and a mixture of several languages: Punic, Berber, Arabic, Turkish, French, Spanish and Italian [4]. When used on the social media, TD is characterized by an unformal writing style, enclosing emoticons, elongated specific words and a simplified syntax with misspellings. In addition, Tunisian social media users produce a content using a mixture of many languages (French, English, standard Arabic and Tunisian dialect) and they are able to easily switch between them. TD can be written using the Arabic or the Latin script with the use of numeric digits replacing some Arabic letters. The phenomenon of code-switching is mainly a result of multilingualism. In Tunisia, CS is frequent and represents a feature of the local way of speech. In text, CS generally occurs between MSA and TD when it is written in Arabic script and between French/English and TD when it is written with Latin alphabet. Furthermore, some texts (especially in the social media and advertising spots) mix both Arabic and Latin scripts.

Till today, very little work has been done on TD sentiment analysis. Moreover, CS and multiscript writing phenomenon have not always been taken into account in previous works on TD SA. As for the adopted approaches, they were mainly based on classical machine learning classifiers.

In this work, we propose an approach based on deep learning techniques for the SA of code-switched TD data, collected from the social media. Given the lack of available NLP tools for the TD, we propose as a first exploratory study of this problem, to evaluate the performance of a sentiment classification (Positive/Negative), based on Recurrent Neural Networks (RNNs) and word embeddings, and using the freely available corpus TSAC[1] (Tunisian Sentient Analysis Corpus) [5]. TSAC includes a set of opinions extracted from social networks, written in both Latin and Arabic scripts and containing code switching. This will allow us to compare our results with those obtained by Mdhaffar et al. [5] who have experienced Naïve Base (NB), Support Vector Machine (SVM) and Multi-Layer Perceptron (MLP) classifiers using TSAC corpus. For our part, we propose to experiment and compare the classifiers LSTM, bi-LSTM, deep-LSTM and deep-bi-LSTM, which, to our knowledge, have not yet been explored in the case of Tunisian Dialect SA.

The next section of this paper is dedicated to a brief review of previous work carried out on the SA of code-switched texts and a review of work on the Tunisian dialect SA. In Sect. 3, we present our approach for classifying code-switched Tunisian dialect comments. We present in particular, the principle of each proposed classifier. The experiments and results obtained are presented in Sect. 4 and Sect. 5 is dedicated to the conclusion and future perspectives.

---

[1] TSAC Corpus is available at: https://github.com/fbougares/TSAC.

2 Related Work

This section presents a brief literature review on SA in code switched text. It then, focuses on a comprehensive review of works related to SA of Tunisian dialect textual content, in order to study how the code-switching phenomena, widely present in dialectical writings, have been treated so far.

2.1 Code-Switched Text SA

Several works have tackled SA in code-switched data using a variety of approaches. Mataoui et al. [6] proposed a lexicon-based SA approach for the Algerian Vernacular Arabic. They used three lexicons: Keywords lexicon, negation words lexicon and intensification word Lexicon. Their process is divided into four models: common phrases similarity computation module, pre-processing module, language detection & stemming module, and Polarity computation module. The experimental results showed that their system obtains an accuracy of 79.13%.

Other works have adopted a machine learning-based approach, such as Vilares et al. [7] who compared in their study, different machine learning algorithms to perform multilingual polarity classification in three different environments. Their goal was to compare the performance of supervised models. They trained all their classifiers using a L2 regularized logistic regression. They proposed an English monolingual model, a Spanish monolingual model (using language identification tools), and a multilingual model trained on a mixed dataset that does not need any language recognition step. The latter seems to outperform the monolingual models. In this category of approaches that are based on machine learning methods, we can also cite Barman et al. [8], Supraja and Rao [9], and Vilares et al. [10].

Sentiment analysis of code-switched text has also been tackled using deep learning approaches. Indeed, Wang et al. [3] collected at first their dataset based on Chinese and English mixed code-switching text from Chinese social media. They then explored the challenges of emotions in code-switching text, more precisely, the monolingual and bilingual information in each post. They worked on capturing the informative words from the code-switching context. They dealt with these challenges by proposing a Bilingual Attention Network model to integrate the attention vectors in order to predict the emotion. They first used an LSTM network to build a document representation for each post. Secondly, the document representation is projected into three vectors by collecting the representation of informative words from monolingual and bilingual context. And thirdly a full-connected layer is used to integrate the three attention vectors, and predict the emotion using the Softmax function. Joshi et al. [11], worked on a Hindi-English code-mixed annotated dataset for sentiment analysis, extracted from Facebook popular pages in India. They introduced how to learn sub-word level representations in LSTM (Subword-LSTM) deep neural network architecture instead of word-level and character-level representations. Their Subword-LSTM system using character embeddings as a first layer provides a higher F-score than Char-LSTM and captures more sentiments in Code Mixed and other varieties of noisy data from the social media.

Moreover, it should be noted that, some research works have used both machine learning and deep learning methods. Baly et al. [12], for example used as a corpus, the Arabic Sentiment Twitter Data (ASTD) [13]. They explored the performance of the feature engineering approach using SVM with Word n-grams and Character n-grams and a deep learning approach using Recursive Neural Tensor Network (RNTN) with the sentiment treebank, on Arabic Twitter. The results showed that the RNTN achieves best performance, and confirms the advantage of recursive deep learning, over models that apply feature engineering.

2.2   Tunisian Dialect SA

Ameur et al. [14] highlighted the social network influence on the events of the Tunisian revolution and focused on their work on emotion analysis of Tunisian Facebook pages. They collected comments from Facebook pages in order to analyze sentiments written in Tunisian dialect, and proposed a method for dynamic emotional dictionaries construction based on the use of a language identification tool and the use of emotion symbols (emoticons) as indicators of sentiment polarity, without using external linguistic resources and they considered nine classes: *surprised*, *satisfied*, *happy*, *gleeful*, *romantic*, *disappointed*, *sad*, *angry* and *disgusted*.

Sayadi et al. [15] used a manually annotated dataset extracted from Twitter and compared five different classifiers: Naive Bayes (NB), Support Vector Machines (SVM), k-Nearest Neighbor (NN), Decision Trees (DT) and Random Forest (RF) using the information Gain feature selection method applied to Sentiment Analysis. They tested the trained classifiers on their dataset composed of Tunisian Dialect and Modern Standard Arabic. The dataset was a collection of 10 k tweets written in Arabic letters. SVM classifiers trained with 1-gram, 2-grams and 3-grams as features, gave the best results.

Mdhaffar et al. [5] proposed a freely available and annotated Tunisian Dialect corpus of 17 k comments, extracted from Facebook, called TSAC (Tunisian Sentiment Analysis Corpus). They focused on SA of the Tunisian dialect applying Machine Learning techniques to determine the polarity of comments, such as Support Vector Machines (SVM), Naive Bayes (NB), and Multi-Layer Perceptron (MLP). They trained the Tunisian dialect SA system and obtained an accuracy of 77% with SVM, 78% with MLP and 58% with NB.

For their part, Mulki et al. [16] have proposed to study the impact of several preprocessing techniques on TD SA. They experimented two SA models: a supervised machine learning based model (SVM and NB) and a lexicon-based model. They showed the importance of the stemming, emoji and negation tagging preprocessing tasks for the TD SA. They also showed that adding name entities tagging to these tasks leads to best results.

2.3   Discussion

From this brief state of the art, we can notice that several approaches have been proposed to deal with the sentiment analysis of code-switched text, ranging from linguistic approaches, machine learning, deep learning and hybrid approaches. It seems that approaches integrating deep learning methods are leading to the best performance. We can also deduct that, the preferred approach in several studies, which seems to be the most effective, is that which considers the multilingual text in its entirety, without going through language detection and the use of monolingual classifier for each language detected in the text.

As for the Tunisian Dialect SA which is our goal in this work, we can notice that there is very little literature that addresses this problem. Among the four surveyed works, three of them (Mdhaffar et al. [5], Sayadi et al. [15] and Mulki et al. [16]) have had as objective, to classify TD comments by sentiment. We however notice, that only, Mdhaffar et al. [5] and Mulki et al. [16] considered a code-switched corpus enclosing both Arabic and Latin scripts, while Sayadi et al. [15] have only dealt with the Arabic script, and haven't considered the Latin script which is massively used in the TD writings nor the phenomena of code-switching which is also very frequent on the social media. As for the adopted approaches, we can see that deep learning-based methods have been practically not explored with this language and TD SA has been approached, mainly by experiencing classical machine learning classifiers. For this reason, we propose in this work to study and evaluate some deep learning techniques applied to the sentiment analysis of code-switched Tunisian dialect textual productions. We focus in particular on using LSTM-based RNNs.

3   Proposed Approach

Based on the study of various works of the literature addressing the SA of code switched text in different languages, and which have shown the effectiveness of approaches considering a multilingual classification of this kind of texts over those using several monolingual classifiers and requiring language detection, we propose to experiment this type of approach on TD. For this purpose, we propose to implement and evaluate some deep learning techniques that have not yet been explored in the context of TD SA. Our approach is based on RNNs (Recurrent Neural Networks) and more precisely on LSTM [17] networks.

Indeed, and as explained in [18], RNNs are considered to be more suitable for the SA task than CNNs (Convolutional Neural Networks), since they consider the sequential aspect of an input, where the words order is important and since they are able to treat inputs having variable lengths. Considering the remarkable results achieved in various classification tasks using LSTM networks, which are enhanced variants of RNNs [18], we propose to explore a set of models, based on variants of LSTM networks for the TD SA. The global architecture of the proposed models is presented in Fig. 1:

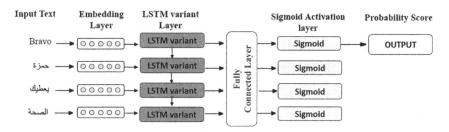

Fig. 1. Global architecture of the proposed models

In this architecture, each extracted review is mapped into vectors of real numbers, a very well-known technique when working with text called word embedding [19, 20]. In this technique, words are encoded as real-valued vectors in a high dimensional space, such as the similarity between the words in terms of close meaning, translates to closeness in the vector space. In our case, we used the **Keras**[2] Embedding Layer that is learned jointly within our examined LSTM models. Each word is taken as one input in a sequence. The first layer is initialized randomly, and the word embeddings are learned jointly on 13,655 reviews from the TSAC corpus.

In this work, we propose to explore the following LSTM-based models:

- **Long Short-Term Memory (LSTM).** LSTM is a type of artificial RNN, which was developed to address the issues of explosion and disappearance of gradients that can be experienced during the training of traditional RNNs [18]. A common LSTM unit consists of a cell, an input gate, an output gate and a forgetting gate. The cell stores values over arbitrary time intervals and the three gates control the flow of information into and out of the cell, controlling thus the information to forget or to pass on to the next time step.

- **Deep LSTM.** Also called stacked LSTM [21], it is an expansion of the original model that includes several hidden LSTM layers, each layer containing several memory cells. A stacked LSTM architecture can be indeed, defined as an LSTM model composed of several LSTM layers. An LSTM layer on the above provides a sequence output instead of a single value output to the LSTM layer below. The stacking of LSTM hidden layers allows the model to become deeper, by adding levels of abstraction of input observations over time and aims to give a more accurate description of the deep learning technique.

- **Bi-LSTM (Bidirectional LSTM).** A bidirectional LSTM consists of a forward LSTM, considering the input from the beginning to the end and backward LSTM, considering the input from the end to the beginning [18]. It interconnects two separate hidden layers that operate in opposite directions to a single output, which enables them to collect information from past and future states.

- **Deep (Stacked) Bi-LSTM.** This model is a combination of the two previous models. It is based on stacking two Bi-LSTM layers.

---

[2] https://keras.io/layers/embeddings/.

4   Experiments and Results

In this section we present the various performed experiments in order to evaluate the proposed models and discuss the obtained results. We first, start by describing the datasets we used in these experiments.

4.1   Used Datasets

For our experiments, we used the freely available annotated Tunisian dialect corpus, proposed by Mdhaffar et al. [5] and called TSAC (Tunisian Sentiment Analysis Corpus). TSAC is corpus of 17k comments that were extracted from Tunisian Facebook pages, mainly from official pages of Tunisian radios and TV channels during the period between January 2015 and June 2016. Extracted comments were cleaned and then manually labeled according to their polarity, into positive and negative comments. Some basic statistics describing the TSAC Corpus are given in Table 1.

Table 1. Statistics of the TSAC corpus [5]

	Positive	Negative
#Total words	63,874	49,322
#Unique words	24,508	17,621
#Comments	8,854	8,215
Avg. Sentence length	7.22	6.00

As shown, in Table 1, TSAC contains a total number of 17,069 TD comments in total of which, 8,854 are annotated as positive and 8,215 as negative comments. It contains both comments transcribed in the Arabic script and comments transcribed in the Latin script. Some comments mix the two scripts. As mentioned in [5], the collected corpus is composed of informal and non-standard vocabulary enclosing elongated words, abbreviations, emoticons, etc.

TSAC corpus was split into a training set and a test set as shown in Table 2.

Table 2. TSAC datasets

Data set	#Total comments
Total corpus	17,069
Training Set	13,655
Testing Set	1,707
Validation Set	1,707

We used the same datasets as in [5]; in order to be able to compare the performance of our proposed models with those experimented in [5].

4.2   Results and Discussion

All our experiments were performed using **Keras**[3], the Python Deep Learning library. The four proposed models were trained using the TSAC training set and tested using the TSAC test set (see Table 2).

Table 3 shows the obtained results while recalling the performance achieved by Mdhaffer et al. [5] models.

Table 3. Models' Evaluation Results on TSAC corpus

Mdhaffar et al. models [5]		Proposed models[a]	
Model	Accuracy	Model	Accuracy
SVM	0.77	LSTM	0.67
NB	0.58	Bi-LSTM	0.70
MLP	**0.78**	**Deep LSTM**	**0.90**
		Deep Bi-LSTM	0.88

[a]The models' parameters were tuned as follows: Epoch = 4 (all models); Batch size = 500 (LSTM model) and Batch size = 100 (the other models).

Let us first examine the evaluation results of the four proposed models which are based on various variants of LSTM networks. We can clearly see that, in our case the deep LSTM model leads to the best performance with 90% of correctly classified comments, while the simple LSTM model was the least performant with an accuracy of 67%.

We can also notice that using a bi-directional LSTM slightly improves the classification compared to the simple LSTM model. It seems that the Bi-LSTM model benefits only very little from exploring the preceding and following contexts in the case of the handled informal, multi-script and code-switched Tunisian dialect corpus. On the other hand, performance improved significantly with stacking layers within deep models. Deep LSTM and Deep Bi-LSTM had led indeed, to the best results with 0.9 and 0.88 accuracy values.

As the bi-LSTM model improves the simple LSTM classification and the deep-LSTM model significantly improves it, we were expecting the model combining layer stacking and bidirectional LSTM (the deep bi-LSTM model) to lead to the best results, but this was not the case since this model was outperformed by the deep LSTM model. Here again, the deep model doesn't seem to benefit from the double exploration of the preceding and following contexts (bi-LSTM). Even though predictions of complex deep neural networks are very difficult to interpret [22], we may explain this result by:

– The very particular nature of the handled data (composed of unformal vocabulary, mixing different scripts and enclosing code-switching that may lead to rather complex grammatical structures).

---

[3] https://keras.io/.

– The relatively limited size of the used corpus. We believe indeed, that the efficiency of the proposed models is likely to increase with a larger volume of training data.

When it comes to compare our results with those obtained by Mdhaffar et al. [5], the best results (90%) are obtained using the deep LSTM model, significantly outperforming the best results obtained by Mdhaffer et al. (78% and 77%, that were achieved by the MLP and the SVM classifiers).

5   Conclusion and Perspectives

In this paper, we tackled the issue of sentiment analysis of Tunisian dialect textual productions that are generated on social media. This type of data still presents number of challenges, due to its unformal, multi-scripted and code-switched nature.

We consider our work as a preliminary study that aimed to explore some deep learning techniques that were not yet applied to the case of the Tunisian dialect on the social media. We proposed indeed to experiment with various variants of RNNs, namely: LSTM, bi-LSTM, deep LSTM and deep Bi-LSTM. Our experiments performed on TSAC datasets [5] showed that we can reach a high performance with an accuracy of 90% using a deep (two-layer) LSTM model, outperforming the latest best proposed models on TSAC datasets in Mdhaffer et al. [5].

Furthermore, we intend to expand this work and enhance it, by working on generating a larger volume of annotated data on the one hand, and on the exploration of other approaches, such as introducing attention mechanism, using other types of RNNs such as GRUs, etc., on the other hand.

References

1. Poplack, S.: Code-switching (linguistic). Int. Encycl. Soc. Behav. Sci. **12**, 2062–4555 (2001)
2. Wang, Z., Zhang, Y., Lee, S., Li, S., Zhou, G.: A bilingual attention network for code-switched emotion prediction. In: Proceedings of COLING 2016, the 26th International Conference on Computational Linguistics: Technical Papers, Osaka, pp. 1624–1634 (2016)
3. Younes, J., Souissi, E., Achour, H., Ferchichi, A.: Un état de l'art du traitement automatique du dialecte tunisien. TAL Traitement Automatique des Langues **59**, 93–117 (2018)
4. Medhaffar, S., Bougares, F., Estève, Y., Hadrich-Belguith, L.: Sentiment analysis of tunisian dialects: Linguistic ressources and experiments. In: Proceedings of the Third Arabic Natural Language Processing Workshop, Spain, pp. 55–61 (2017)
5. Mataoui, M.H., Zelmati, O., Boumechache, M.: A proposed lexicon-based sentiment analysis approach for the vernacular Algerian Arabic. Res. Comput. Sci. **110**, 55–70 (2016)
6. Vilares, D., Alonso, MA., Gómez-Rodríguez, C.: Sentiment analysis on monolingual, multilingual and code-switching Twitter corpora. In: Proceedings of the 6th Workshop on Computational Approaches to Subjectivity, Sentiment and Social Media Analysis, Portugal, pp. 2–8 (2015)
7. Barman, U., Das, A., Wagner, J., Foster, J.: Code mixing: a challenge for language identification in the language of social media. In: Proceedings of the First Workshop on Computational Approaches to Code Switching, Qatar, pp. 13–23 (2014)

8. Supraja, C., Rao, V.M.: Emotion detection in code-switching text. Int. J. Eng. Technol. Sci. Res. **4**(12), 988–992 (2017)
9. Vilares, D., Alonso, MA., Gómez-Rodríguez, C. EN-ES-CS: an English-Spanish code-switching Twitter corpus for multilingual sentiment analysis. In: Proceedings of the Tenth International Conference on Language Resources and Evaluation (LREC 2016), Slovenia, pp. 4149–4153 (2016)
10. Prabhu, A., Joshi, A., Shrivastava, M., Varma, V.: Towards sub-word level compositions for sentiment analysis of Hindi-English code mixed text. In: Proceedings of COLING 2016, The 26th International Conference on Computational Linguistics: Technical Papers, Osaka, pp. 2482–2491 (2016)
11. Baly. R., et al.: A characterization study of Arabic twitter data with a benchmarking for state-of-the-art opinion mining models. In: Proceedings of the Third Arabic Natural Language Processing Workshop, Spain, pp. 110–118 (2017)
12. Nabil, M., Aly, M., Atiya, A.: ASTD: Arabic sentiment tweets dataset. In: Proceedings of the 2015 Conference on Empirical Methods in Natural Language Processing, Portugal, pp. 2515–2519 (2015)
13. Ameur, H., Jamoussi, S., Hamadou, A.B.: Exploiting emoticons to generate emotional dictionaries from Facebook pages. In: Czarnowski, I., Caballero, A., Howlett, R., Jain, L. (eds.) Intelligent Decision Technologies 2016, pp. 39–49. Springer, Cham (2016). https://doi.org/10.1007/978-3-319-39627-9_4
14. Sayadi, K., Liwicki, M., Ingold, R., Bui, M.: Tunisian dialect and modern standard Arabic dataset for sentiment analysis: Tunisian election context. In: Second International Conference on Arabic Computational Linguistics, ACLING, Turkey, pp. 35–53 (2016)
15. Mulki, H., Haddad, H., Bechikh Ali, C., Babaoglu, I.: Tunisian dialect sentiment analysis: a natural language processing-based approach. Computacion y Sistemas **22**(4), 1223–1232 (2018)
16. Hochreiter, S., Schmidhuber, J.: Long short-term memory. Neural Comput. **9**(8), 1735–1780 (1997)
17. Baziotis, C., Nikos, P., Christos D.: Datastories at SemEval-2017 task 4: Deep LSTM with attention for message-level and topic-based sentiment analysis. In: Proceedings of the 11th International Workshop on Semantic Evaluation, Vancouver, Canada, pp 747–754 (2017)
18. Collobert, R., Weston, J.: A unified architecture for natural language processing: deep neural networks with multitask learning. In: Proceedings of ICML, Helsinki, pp 160–167 (2008)
19. Mikolov, T., Sutskever, I., Chen, K., Corrado, G.S., Dean, J.: Distributed representations of words and phrases and their compositionality. In: Advances in Neural Information Processing Systems, pp. 3111–3119 (2013)
20. Graves, A., Mohamed, A.R., Hinton, G.: Speech recognition with deep recurrent neural networks. In: 2013 IEEE International Conference on Acoustics, Speech and Signal Processing, Vancouver, Canada, pp. 6645–6649 (2013)
21. Lundberg, S., Lee, S.: Advances in Neural Information Processing Systems 30, pp. 4768–4777. Curran Associates, Inc. (2017)

Modeling Modern Standard Arabic

Building an Extractive Arabic Text Summarization Using a Hybrid Approach

Said Moulay Lakhdar and Mohamed Amine Chéragui$^{(\boxtimes)}$ (ID)

Mathematics and Computer Science Department,
Ahmed Draia University, Adrar, Algeria
`moulaylakhdarsaid@yahoo.fr, m_cheragui@univ-adrar.dz`

Abstract. Nowadays, textual information in numerical format is hugely produced, which requires the development of tools such as Automatic Text Summarization to produce a condensed and relevant representation, thus helping the reader to decide whether the source document contains the information they are looking for or not. The Text Summarization has known these last decades an enormous progress, in particular works of Arabic language. The objective of this paper is to contribute more to these advances by proposing an Arabic text summarization tool (SumSAT), which adopts an extraction approach using hybridization between three techniques which are: Contextual exploration, indicative expression, and the graph method. Experimental results showed that the proposed approach achieved competitive and promising in the optic of generating a small and coherent summary.

Keywords: Arabic text summarization · Extractive based summarization · Contextual exploration method · Indicative expression method · Graph method

1 Introduction

Facing the exponential increase of textual resources, both on the various numerical supports and on the Internet (80% of the information that circulates on them is textual) [1], the development of tools that can manipulate this important volume such as automatic text summarization (ATS) has become crucial, since it can generate useful and relevant information by reducing the size of documents, thereby saving time and effort [2]. Radev et al. [3] defined a summary as "a text which is produced from one or more texts and conveys core information in the original texts; typically, it is no longer than half of the original text(s) and usually less than that.

In the literature, the automatic production of abstracts (or summary) is done using several methods and techniques that can be classified into two approaches, either by abstraction or extraction [4]. The first one (Abstraction approach) owes its origin to the work of van Dijk and Kintsch [5] from the fields of cognitive psycholinguistics and artificial intelligence, whose principle consists in producing the summary after comprehension, as humans do normally. This production process remains relatively difficult to compute, and text generation is still very imperfect. In the current situation, some methods use only very partial representations that reduce the original text, such as [6]: sentence reduction, sentence fusion, and sentence splitting.

© Springer Nature Switzerland AG 2019
K. Smaïli (Ed.): ICALP 2019, CCIS 1108, pp. 135–148, 2019.
https://doi.org/10.1007/978-3-030-32959-4_10

However, in the extraction-based approach was essentially inspired by the approaches resulting from the information retrieval and the work of Luhn [7] and Edmundson [8]. The main purpose is to extract the most important or significant sentences in the original text and combining them to make a summary. Its objective is to produce the summary without going through deeper analysis, so the main task is to determine the relevance of these sentences according to one or more criteria (generally a statistical features) [9, 10].

The purpose of this paper is to present our Arabic text summarization tool SumSat. We adopt an extraction approach, where the originality of the work lies in making twofold contribution, the first in the pre-processing phase which consists in preparing the text for the summarization process, and the second in the processing phase where we have chosen a hybrid approach that combines three techniques: Contextual Exploration method, Indicative expression method, and Graph method.

The rest of this paper is organized as follows: Sect. 2 briefly describes related work on text summarization, especially in the Arabic language. In Sect. 3 we cover the general architecture and the methodology of SumSAT. In Sect. 4 we introduce the SumSat tool. The results of experiments on Arabic dataset are discussed in Sect. 5. The last section concludes the paper with pointers to future works.

2   Related Work

As a research topic, the text summarization is not recent; it dates back to the fifties (1950's) with Luhn's work [7], giving rise to a wide range of works and methods that can be classified into three categories: statistical (features extraction: TF/IDF, upper-case words, sentence length, similarity with the title, and sentence position in the document, etc.), linguistic (Rhetorical Structure Theory, Lexical chain, etc.) and Machine learning (Neural Network, VSM, etc.). If these works have a positive impact on the Text summarization for some languages such as English or French by out-standing achievements, works on the Arabic language are very few due mainly to its morphological and syntactic complexity. In this section, we give an overview of some works concerning the Arabic text summarization.

One of the earlier Arabic text summarization adopting an extractive methodology was LAKHAS. It was developed by Douzidia and Lapalme [11]. This system works on the journalistic text and uses several statistical features (sentence position, terms frequency, title words, and cue words). To evaluate its performance LAKHAs participated in the DUC 2004 (Document Understanding Conferences) where the result is translated into English and then evaluated using the ROUGE measure.

AlSanie et al. [12] proposed one of the first Arabic text summarization system adopting Rhetorical Structure Theory (RST) where the idea is to create all Rhetorical Structure trees (RST-trees) that describe the structural organization of the source text, based on the relationships between the text segments. For this purpose, a set of eleven Arabic rhetorical relations and twenty-five cue sentences have been used. Finally, the system produces the summary by selecting the best tree. To evaluate the performance of their system, the authors have created their own corpus (from different Sources: technical article, newspaper articles, and books, on different fields: accounting, technology, society … etc.) with the corresponding summaries. The System gives good results in the case of small and medium-sized documents.

Sobh et al. [13] described a classification method to generate Arabic summaries. Based on two phases: first phase: extraction of the features, 11 features were defined: Sentence Weight, Sentence Length, Sentence Absolute Position, Sentence Paragraph Position, Sentence Paragraph Length, Sentence Similarity, Number of Infinitives, Number of Verbs, umber of Identified, Number of "Marfoa'at" and Is Digit. (some of these features require the use of a POS tag) all these features will be standardized. The second phase is the classification where the authors have combined two classifiers (Bayesian classifier and Genetic Programming classifier) to extract the summary sentences. For training and evaluation, a corpus was collected from the Ahram site. To measure performance, three measures were used, precision, recall and F-measure.

El-Haj and Hammo [14] developed two Arabic text summarization systems: Arabic Query-Based Text Summarization System and Arabic Concept-Based Text Summarization System. The first one AQBTSS takes a text and a query (In the Arabic language), and generates a summary for the document following the query. The second ACBTSS system takes a set of keywords representing a certain concept as input to the system. Both systems adopt two methods: Vector Space Model (VSM) and the cosine similarity measure to find the most relevant passages extracted from the Arabic document to produce a text summary.

Azmi and Al-Thanyyan [15] presented a system called Ikhtasir which combined between two techniques: the first one is RST (Rhetorical Structure Theory) to build the Rhetorical Structure tree for the text and then extracts the primary summary. The second was the Sentence scoring, which is applied to determine the importance of each sentence in the text by using a score and generate the final summary whose size is set by the user based on several words, percentage of original or the number of sentences. To evaluate Ikhtasir the authors used a set of Arabic texts (Ten different sample texts collected from the Saudi's Ar-Riyadh daily newspaper web site) and three measures were used: precision, recall and F-measure.

Belkebir and Guessoum [16] proposed a Machine Learning-based approach to Arabic text summarization based on two steps. The first one aims to build a learning model by using adaptive boosting (AdaBoost) based on a set of statistical features (the number of common words between the sentence and the title, the first or the last sentence, The number of keywords in the sentence, the number of words in a sentence). In the second step, the model which was produced was tested by identifying whether a sentence is to be included in the summary. For training, the authors created their parallel corpus (<source, summary>) composed of 20 Arabic technology news articles with the summary that corresponds to them (The summaries were manually produced). For the evaluation, they used the F1-measure metric.

Al-Radaideh and Bataineh [17] developed a hybrid text summarization approach (extraction methodology). The approach combines domain knowledge, statistical features, semantic similarity, and genetic algorithms. In this approach, genetic algorithms are used to identify the optimal sentence combination for a summary based on maximizing informative scores and cohesion between sentences. The approach was tested on two corpora: KALIMAT corpus and Essex Arabic Summaries Corpus (EASC). To evaluate the performance the authors used ROUGE and F-measure.

Recently, Al-Abdallah and Al-Taani [18] described Arabic text summarization system using three techniques which are: Informative Scores, where it calculates a score for each sentence based on Title similarity, sentence length, and Sentence location. The second method, Calculate Semantic Scores, indicates the degree of similarity between two sentences by using the cosine similarity after that a similarity matrix for a document was building to know which sentences are useful to be picked based on semantic, finally, the matrix was converted to a DAG weighted graph. The third method was a meta-heuristic search algorithm called Firefly. The algorithm starts with a random set of candidate summaries, to evaluate the quality of each candidate summary, a fitness function is defined by multiplying Semantic Scores and Informative Scores, or each sentence in the summary candidate. After several iterations when the value of the fitness function does not change. the evolution stops and the summary with the highest score will generate. For the evaluation, the EASC corpus was used and to calculate the performance the choice was the ROUGE metric to determine the accuracy.

3   The General Architecture of Our ATS SumSAT

This section introduces the general architecture of our extractive Arabic text summarization system (SumSAT), based on a hybrid approach combining three techniques which are: Contextual exploration, Indicative expression, and the graph method. Figure 1 presents the various steps to generate a small and coherent summary.

Fig. 1. The main process of our Arabic Summarization system SumSAT.

3.1 Step 1: Pre-processing

This step involves performing several basic operations to prepare the document or text for processing, including segmentation, elimination of stop words and stemming.

Segmentation is a fundamental step in automatic text processing. Its purpose is to divide a text into units of a specific type that we have previously defined and identified, in our case is the sentence. The method used to divide a text is based on the contextual exploration method, where the input is a plain text in the form of a single text segment. The segmentation starts with detecting the presence of indicators, which are punctuation marks («.», «;», «:», «!», «?»). If there is an indicator, segmentation rules will be applied to explore the contexts (before and after) to ensure that additional indicators are present and that certain conditions are met. In the case of an end of a sentence, this decision is converted into the action of segmentation of the text into two textual segments. By repeating this operation on the resultant segments, we obtain a set of textual segments which placed next to each other, which form the input plain text.

It is important to mention that in our segmentation the dot «.» cannot be always considered as an indicator of a sentence end; i.e., cases like abbreviation, acronym or a number in decimal, where particular rules can be added.

Stemming. This operation consists of transforming, eventually agglutinated or inflected word into its canonical form (stem or root) [19] (Table 1).

Table 1. Example of extracting a root from Arabic words.

Word	English Translation	Root
"مدرسة"	School	
"درس"	Lesson	درس
"مدرس"	Teacher	(D+R+Q)
"دارس"	Student	

In our case, we need the results of the stemming in the graph method to define the most important sentences. To generate these roots, we use the Full-Text Search technique, which allows us to generate the roots of words composing the sentences and eliminate the stop words. This technique also generates other features such as ranking (rank value) to classify the found sentences in order to filter the relevant ones according to their scores.

3.2 Step 2: Processing

Since we adopt an extractive methodology, the main task is to evaluate each sentence in the document to determine the importance of each them (sentence) and select the most relevant ones, to generate the most coherent and meaningful summary at the end. For this purpose, we have set up a hybrid approach combining three methods: the contextual exploration (main method), the indicative expression and graph method (secondary methods). The secondary methods will scramble on the result of the principal method to give better results or provide a solution in the case that contextual exploration is not efficient.

Contextual Exploration Method. Allows access to the semantic content of a text, without the need for deep syntactic analyses [20]. Sentences are classified into hierarchical semantic categories (Hypothesis, Objective, Definition, etc.). This method has been chosen to produce a consistent summary and to offer users the possibility to choose the summary by point of view, where the information to be summarized is classified into discursive categories. The contextual exploration (CE) module receives a segmented text as input (the result of the segmentation module). The first task is to detect the presence of some linguistic indicators in each sentence. Once an indicator is found, all contextual exploration rules related to that indicator will be set to find additional clues and to verify the conditions required by that rule. If all conditions are verified, an annotation action, determined by the exploration rule, is performed on the sentence exactly where the linguistic indicator is placed.

For our approach, we have defined 13 discursive categories; each category has its complementary clues (See Fig. 2).

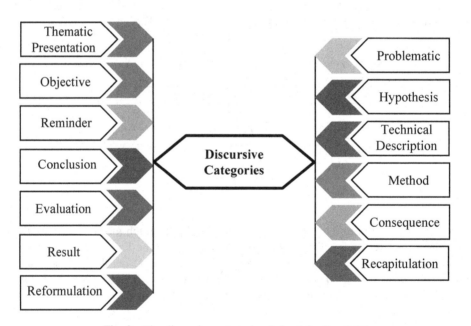

Fig. 2. The discursive categories defined for SumSAT.

Example: The following example illustrates an application of our method to select sentences that contains information about the discursive category "conclusions and results". One of the rules associated with this category is as follows (Fig. 3):

```
<Rule   NameRule= "RConclusion"   Task="Summary"   Point_of_View = "conclu-
sion">

<Conditions>

<Indicator Search_Space="sentence" Value = "form_conclusion"/>

<clue Search_Space="." Value = "ClueConclusion"  Context = "After"/>

</Conditions>

<Actions>

<Annotation   Annotation="Conclusion"/ >

</Actions>
```

Fig. 3. Example of a rule describing a discursive category.

The rule, delimited by the tag (<Rule> and </Rule>), consists of two parts:

- Condition part: delimited by (<Conditions> and </Conditions>): It groups information about the indicator (delimited by <Indicator and />) associated with an information category, and information about the additional clues (<clue and/>) that are associated with it.
- Actions part: delimited by (<Actions> and </Actions>): Action to be done, after verifying the existence of additional clues and the required conditions.

Where:

- NameRule: the name that identifies the rule.
- Task: The task this rule performs since contextual exploration can be used for annotation and summary generation, as it can be used for segmentation.
- Point of View: Represents the category name of the information retrieved.
- Search_space: Space or context, where the additional clue is located; whether the search is done in the phrase itself or the paragraph.
- Value: It is the name of the file where the indicators are stored, or the name of the file where the clues are stored, associated with this category of information.
- Context: Specifies whether the search for additional clues should be done before or after the indicator.

Consider the following sentence to be annotated (applying the above-mentioned rule) (Fig. 4):

> فعلى سبيل المثال، أظهرت الدراسات الحيوانية أن نبتة "روزماري" تقي من سرطان
> الثدي، وأن الكركم يحمي من بعض أنواع الأورام.
>
> For Example, animal studies have shown that rosemary protects against breast cancer and that turmeric proctects against some types of tumours.

Fig. 4. Example of a contextual exploration rule.

In this sentence, it can be said that the complementary clue (أن) is present after the indicator (أظهرت الدراسات). Therefore, the action to be taken is indicated in the actions part (delimited by <Actions> and </Action>); so, this sentence assigned the value 'Conclusion' to indicate that it contains information concerning a result or conclusion.

In some cases, the information in the form of a discursive category cannot be detected or not present in the document for summarizing. In this case the performance of the contextual exploration method will be compromised. To reduce the deficiencies of our Arabic text summarization system, we have associated with the method mentioned above (CE) two statistical methods, which are: the indicative expression and the graph method, in order to give the user the possibility to choose a default summary (general or specific field).

Indicative Expression Method. In this method, the weight of each sentence depends on some specific indicators or expressions used by the author. These indicators differ according to the field covered because the choice of text units depends on the subject matter [11]. For example, the following expressions: 'this present paper', 'in this paper we propose', 'in conclusion', can be considered relevant to a scientific topic. This method is selected to offer the possibility of generating a summary of a general order, or a specific field; sport, culture, economy, etc., by identifying sentences that contain indicators. These indicators are determined according to the field of the text to be analyzed using the following formula:

$$\text{Score}_{cue}(S) = \begin{cases} 1 & \text{if S corresponds to an Indicator} \\ 0 & \text{else} \end{cases} \tag{1}$$

Graph Method. The generation of the summary, using the graph method, consists of selecting the most representative phrases of the source text, since it attributes to the sentences a relevance score or similarity measure by calculating the number of intersection terms [21, 22]. These terms are the result of the stemming process performed in the pre-processing process.

Suppose that we have a Document composed of six sentences (P1, P2, P2,..., P6). After applying stemming for each sentence, the total number of terms shared with all the others is given in the table below (Table 2):

Table 2. Sentences weights.

Phrases	P1	P2	P3	P4	P5	P6
Total number of Stems (Roots) shared with all other Sentences	9	8	7	3	6	5

Modelling this problem for the summary is like considering: The document as an undirected graph "G = (N, E)", the sentences as nodes (Ni) of this graph, the intersections of the sentences as edges (Ej) of this graph, the total number of intersecting terms (stems or roots), of a sentence with all the others, as a weight of the node representing this sentence. Finally, to generate the summary we use the Greedy algorithm (Table 3 and Fig. 5).

Table 3. Matrix for representing sentence intersections.

	P1	P2	P3	P4	P5	P6
P1	0	0	1	1	1	1
P2	0	0	1	1	0	1
P3	1	1	0	0	1	0
P4	1	1	0	0	0	1
P5	1	0	1	0	0	1
P6	1	1	0	1	1	0

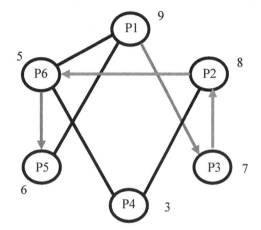

Fig. 5. Pathway followed using the Greedy algorithm.

The followed path is represented by brown arrows on the graph, and the final summary will be composed of the sentences that correspond to the visited nodes. If the final summary is limited to only four sentences: the list of selected sentences is P1, P3, P2, and P6. This list of sentences appears in the summary in the same order as the sentences appear in the source document: P1, P2, P3, and P6.

3.3   Step 3: Filtering and Selection

The generation of the summary must take into consideration the user's requirements, and the compression ratio to determine the relevant phrases to be selected. The final summary is made up of all phrases that fulfill the following conditions:

- Sentences that belong to the discursive categories, or the selected domains (chosen by the user);
- And/or the Sentences that appear in the list of nodes visited by the graph method (the case of the default summary);
- The number of sentences is limited by the summary rate, introduced by the user;
- The appearance order of the sentences in the summary must respect the order of these sentences in the source text.

To generate a dynamic summary, a link is established between the summary sentences and their corresponding phrases in the source text.

4 Presentation of SumSat

SumSAT (Acronym of Summarization System for Arabic Text) is a web application system that runs on web browsers. Its execution is local to the IIS server (Internet Information Server), of Windows. The interaction between our system and Microsoft SQL Server is done by queries (T-SQL transactions). SumSAT is introduced to the user through a GUI, based on HTML5, ASP, C#, and Silverlight (Figs. 6 and 7).

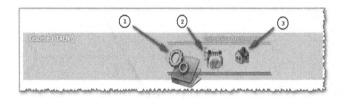

Fig. 6. GUI main menu.

Fig. 7. GUI generation of summary.

5 Evaluation and Results

SumSAT's summary generation is based on a hybrid approach where the discursive annotation constitutes its main task. The generated summary is based on the concept of point of view. Therefore, the relevance of a sentence depends on the presence of surface linguistic markers referring to a discursive category. The evaluation of the summary generation process consists of the evaluation of the discursive annotation task made by SumSAT.

The objective of this evaluation is to know the percentage of sentences correctly annotated by the system, compared to the total number of annotated sentences, and compared to the total number of manually annotated sentences (reference summaries). This can be expressed by measuring:

The Precision Rate: The number of correct discursive categories, detected by the system, compared to the total number of discursive categories detected by the system.

The Recall Rate: The number of correct discursive categories, detected by the system, compared to the total number of discursive categories presented in the reference summary.

The precision and recall rates are calculated as follows:

$$\text{Precision}(\%) = (a/b) * 100 \tag{2}$$

$$\text{Recall}(\%) = (a/c) * 100 \tag{3}$$

Where:

- a: Number of automatically assigned correct annotations.
- b: Number of automatically assigned annotations.
- c: Number of manually assigned correct annotations.

For this purpose, we have constructed corpora composed of twenty-five documents, and their corresponding summaries (The reference summaries are manually compiled by two experts). For each of the selected documents, we have proceeded to the generation of summaries, by discursive categories. The evaluation consists of applying the metrics, to criticize and conclude based on the results obtained.

The results of the calculated rates, as well as the precision and recall results, are illustrated in Tables 4, 5 and 6 and by representative graphs (Figs. 8, 9 and 10). These results are calculated for all the selected documents in the corpora, and each of the discursive categories adopted by SumSAT. For all categories, the precision rate is higher than 66%, except for four of them (hypothesis, Recapitulation, Reminder, Prediction), which have a precision rate between 40% and 50%. Similarly, the recall rate is higher than 66%, except for the three categories that have a recall rate between 30% and 50% (Prediction, Definition, and Reminder). This shows that SumSAT has promising results which can be improved, despite the difficulties of generating coherent summaries.

Precision rate: These results show that much more work needs to be done on refining surface markers to maximize this rate. In technical terms, it is necessary to work on two parameters. The first parameter, related to regular expressions, detects discursive markers (indicators and additional clues). The second parameter is linguistic (the good choice of these discursive markers).

Recall rate: The results show that the work which can contribute to improving these results will be linguistic, especially the collection of discursive markers to enrich linguistic resources.

It is important to mention that the obtained results are influenced by the divergence of the texts from the point of view of style, discursive and argumentative strategies, and the covered topic. This means that the surface markers, for some categories, are rarely the same from one text to another. Similarly, the indicators are sometimes weak and cannot refer to a discursive category. Moreover, the additional clues are sometimes equivocal.

Table 4. SumSat evaluation (01)

Category	Precision (%)	Recall (%)
Objective	73,68	82,35
hypothesis	42,03	70
Conclusion	77,78	70
Explanation	88,57	95,38
Consequence	77,27	70,83

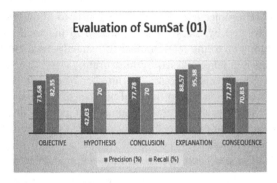

Fig. 8. Graphical representation of SumSat's evaluation results (01).

Table 5. SumSat evaluation (02)

Category	Precision (%)	Recall (%)
Definition	66,67	32,67
Confirmation	97,5	82,98
Problematic	66,67	66,67
Reminder	50	44,02
Recapitulation	50	88,24

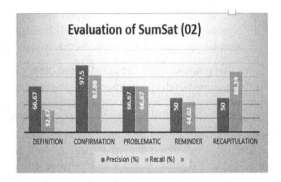

Fig. 9. Graphical representation of SumSat's evaluation results (02).

Table 6. SumSat evaluation (03)

Category	Precision (%)	Recall (%)
Author, Title & Subtitle	91,94	91,94
Thematic	85,71	66,67
Prediction	50	50
Finding & opinion	90	69,26
Enunciation	94,94	91,85

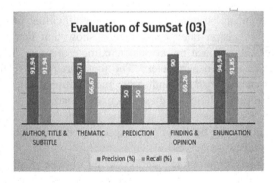

Fig. 10. Graphical representation of SumSat's evaluation results (03).

6 Conclusion and Future Work

In this paper we have developed a hybrid Arabic text summarization system, combining two approaches: symbolic (by Contextual Exploration) and numerical (by the indicative expression method and the graph method). During the different steps of the development process, we were confronted with several problems related mainly to the nature of the Arabic language itself. In pre-processing, the incorrect use of punctuation marks (author's style) induces segmentation errors, and as a result, the relevance of phrases is incorrect, which gives an incoherent summary. The second problem is the quality of the stemming, the tool we used for this operation presented some limitations, hence the importance of choosing a performing Arabic stemmer, to ensure that the graph method gives better results.

In the processing step, one of the difficulties met, and which influences the performance of the system, is the manual search for linguistic indicators, to enrich the list of discursive categories. This task costs time and resources, which has reduced the list of the information offered by SumSAT. Also, we found that the representative sentences with a high weight may not be selected because of the restrictions on incrementing the list of visited nodes when the transition is made only between the adjacent ones (Graph model method).

As future work, we can improve the quality of the summary generated by our SumSAT system, especially in the processing step, as well as for graph method we use to generate the summary by making a modification, such that the greedy algorithm gives the advantage to the representative nodes, without being limited by the transitions between the adjacent summits. Also, the integration of a tool for identifying surface linguistic markers in documents is a good way to enrich the system's linguistic resources.

References

1. Lamsiyah, S., El Alaoui, S.O., Espinasse, B.: Résumé automatique guidé de textes: État de l'art et perspectives. In: Proceedings of the 15th Conférence en Recherche d'Information et Applications, France (2018)
2. Modaresi, P., Gross, P., Sefidrodi, S., Eckholf, M., Conrad, S.: On (commercial) benefits of automatic text summarization systems in the news domain: a case of media monitoring and media response analysis. CoRR, arXiv:1701.00728 (2017)
3. Radev, D., Hovy, D., McKeown, K.: Introduction to the special issue on summarization. Comput. Linguist. **28**(4), 399–408 (2002)
4. Dalaland, V., Malik, L.: A survey of extractive and abstractive text summarization techniques. In: Proceedings 6th International Conference on Emerging Trends in Engineering and Technology, pp. 109–110 (2013)
5. Kintsch, W., Van Dijk, T.A.: Toward a model of text comprehension and production. Psychol. Rev. **85**(5), 363–394 (1978)
6. Genest, P.E., Lapalme, G.: Fully abstractive approach to guided summarization. In: Proceedings of the 50th Annual Meeting of the Association for Computational Linguistics, Korea, pp. 354–358 (2012)

7. Luhn, H.P.: The automatic creation of literature abstracts. IBM J. Res. Dev. **2**(2), 159–165 (1958)
8. Edmundson, H.P.: New methods in automatic extracting. J. Assoc. Comput. Mach. **16**(2), 264–285 (1969)
9. Mohamed, A.A.: Automatic summarization of the Arabic documents using NMF: a preliminary study. In: Proceedings of the 11th International Conference on Computer Engineering and Systems (ICCES), Egypt, pp. 235–240 (2016)
10. Oufaida, H., Noualib, O., Blache, P.: Minimum redundancy and maximum relevance for single and multi-document Arabic text summarization. J. King Saud Univ. Comput. Inf. Sci. **26**(4), 450–461 (2014)
11. Douzidia, F.S., Lapalme, G.: Lakhas, an Arabic summarization system. In: Proceedings of 2004 Document Understanding Conference (DUC 2004), Boston, pp. 128–135 (2004)
12. AlSanie, W., Kotsis, G., Taniar, D., Bressan, S., Ibrahim, I.K., Mokhtar, S.: Towards a suitable rhetorical representation for Arabic text summarization. In: iiWAS, vol. 196, pp. 535–542. Austrian Computer Society (2005)
13. Sobh, I., Darwish, N., Fayek, M.: An optimized dual classification system for Arabic extractive generic text summarization. In: Proceedings of the 7th Conference on Language Engineering, pp. 149–154 (2006)
14. El-Haj, M., Hammo, B.: Evaluation of query-based Arabic text summarization system. In: Proceeding of the IEEE International Conference on Natural Language Processing and Knowledge Engineering, pp. 1–7 (2008)
15. Azmi, A., Al-thanyyan, S.: Ikhtasir a user selected compression ratio Arabic text summarization system. In: Proceeding of International Conference of Natural Language Processing and Knowledge Engineering (NLP-KE 2009), pp. 1–7 (2009)
16. Belkebir, R., Guessoum, A.: A supervised approach to Arabic text summarization using AdaBoost. In: Rocha, A., Correia, A.M., Costanzo, S., Reis, L.P. (eds.) New Contributions in Information Systems and Technologies. AISC, vol. 353, pp. 227–236. Springer, Cham (2015). https://doi.org/10.1007/978-3-319-16486-1_23
17. Al-Abdallah, R.Z., Al-Taani, A.T.: Arabic text summarization using firefly algorithm. In: Proceedings of the IEEE Amity International Conference on Artificial Intelligence, Dubai, pp. 61–65 (2019)
18. Al-Radaideh, Q.A., Bataineh, D.Q.: A hybrid approach for Arabic text summarization using domain knowledge and genetic algorithms. Cogn. Comput. **10**, 651–669 (2018)
19. Rouibia, R., Belhadj, I., Cheragui, M.A.: JIDR: towards building hybrid Arabic stemmer. In: Proceeding of the 1st IEEE International Conference on Mathematics and Information Technology (ICMIT), Algeria, pp. 183–190 (2017)
20. Alrahabi, M., Ibrahim A.H., Desclés, J.P.: Semantic annotation of reported information in Arabic. In: Proceedings of the Nineteenth International Florida Artificial Intelligence Research Society Conference, Florida, pp. 263–268 (2006)
21. Al-Taani, A.T., Al-Omour, M.M.: An extractive graph-based Arabic text summarization approach. In: Proceedings of the International Arab Conference on Information Technology, Oman, pp. 158–163 (2014)
22. Alami, N., Meknassi, M., Ouatik, S.A., Ennahnahi, N.: Arabic text summarization based on graph theory. In: Proceedings of the 12th International Conference of Computer Systems and Applications (AICCSA), Marrakech, pp. 1–8 (2015)

On Arabic Stop-Words: A Comprehensive List and a Dedicated Morphological Analyzer

Driss Namly[1(✉)], Karim Bouzoubaa[1], Rachida Tajmout[1], and Ali Laadimi[2]

[1] Mohammadia School of Engineers,
Mohammed V University in Rabat, Rabat, Morocco
namly_driss@yahoo.fr, tajmoutrachida@yahoo.fr,
karim.bouzoubaa@emi.ac.ma
[2] Faculty of Arts and Humanities,
Mohammed V University in Rabat, Rabat, Morocco
alilaadimi95@gmail.com

Abstract. Stop-words detection is a key preprocessing step and an important component for many Natural Language Processing applications. For Arabic language, stop-words detection is a complex task due to Arabic morphology richness and to the nonexistence of a commonly accepted list. In this paper, we compile a new comprehensive Arabic stop-words list along a stop-words analyzer that combines that list with a machine-learning-based approach to get the most probable stop-word. The first step in our approach provides a context-free analysis and the most appropriate stop-word according to the sentence context is detected in the second step using the Hidden Markov Model. The developed analyzer evaluation yields to over than 97% of accuracy. This achievement outperforms the state of the art analyzers.

Keywords: Natural Language Processing · Arabic language · Information retrieval · Stop-words · Hidden Markov Model · Viterbi algorithm

1 Introduction

Called common words, noise words or negative dictionary, stop-words are very common words that frequently appear in the text [1], carrying no information when isolated. Stop-words never form a full sentence when used alone but have a very important grammatical and syntactic function when used in a sentence [2]. Stop-words have been studied for many languages such as Chinese [3], French [4], Mongolian [5], Arabic [6] or Farsi [7].

Generally, stop-words are filtered from the other words in the pre-processing stage of text processing applications, such as spell checking [8], text summarization [9] or automatic translation [10]. Indeed, this pre-processing has a great impact and plays a major role in those applications. For example, in the information retrieval field, these stop-words removal reduces the corpus size typically by 20 to 40% [11], leading to higher efficiency without affecting retrieval effectiveness. Also, almost all search engines [12] clean out stop words from both search queries and search indexing entries.

© Springer Nature Switzerland AG 2019
K. Smaïli (Ed.): ICALP 2019, CCIS 1108, pp. 149–163, 2019.
https://doi.org/10.1007/978-3-030-32959-4_11

To remove stop-words, it is necessary to identify them first. Knowing that every Arabic word belongs to one of the three categories noun, verb or particle, and that there is no category entitled "stop-word", their identification becomes a challenging task. For that, text processing applications rely on two main identification techniques. The first one consists in using a static stop-words list while the second one involves the use of morphological analysis.

In the case of the Arabic language, stop-words have been the subject of a number of studies and an amount of lists have been published [1, 2, 13]. However, most of these lists are corpus-dependent because they were compiled for a particular context using a specific corpus relying on the frequency feature of that particular corpus. Within these conditions, the gathered stop-words lists cannot have a general usage because they do not contain all stop-words. For instance, the information retrieval system Apache Lucene[1] includes in its list the stop-words "زيارة" (visit) and "لوكالة" (to the agency) even if they are not Arabic stop-words and are specific to the corpus they were extracted from. In addition, these lists don't consider all clitized forms of the stop-word. For example, if the list contains the stop-word "هو" (he is), generally it excludes its clitized forms such as "وهو، فهو،..." (and he is, ...) that are also stop-words.

The second stop-words identification method involves the use of morphological analysis. A large number of the aforesaid Arabic text processing applications uses morphological analysis as a preprocessing step instead of a simple search in a stop-words list. Doing so, usually stop-words are identified when the given word is analyzed as a "particle". However, stop-words definition in the Information Retrieval context applies on words of different grammatical categories not only the particle one. Therefore, stop-words of the noun or verb grammatical categories are not considered as stop-words. For example, "مَنْ" (who) and "كَانَ" (it was) are not recognized as stop-words because their analysis provides respectively noun and verb grammatical categories. This is what we call "the grammatical category default". In addition, the clitized form omission, as introduced above, applies also in the context of morphological analysis, i.e. even if a morphological analyzer recognizes some words as particles, it does not recognize many of its clitized forms. Thus, Arabic morphological analyzers fail to recognize a number of stop-words. For example, the analysis of a sample 1,000 stop-words from the state of the art lists (detailed in the next section) fail to identify more than 73% of the stop-words.

To overcome these problems, the first objective in this work is to offer a comprehensive Arabic rule-based stop-words list including not only all grammatical categories of stop-words but also all stop-words clitized forms. Indeed, the adopted rule-based approach to compile the stop-words list is fundamentally inspired from Arabic word structure. The second objective is to take advantage of the collected rule-based stop-words list to design a contextual stop-words analyzer recognizing all stop-words grammatical categories and all clitized forms that could be plugged to existing morphological analyzers.

In the rest of the paper, related works are reviewed in Sect. 2. In Sect. 3, we explain the proposed approach. Section 4 exposes the evaluation and the comparison with existing works. Conclusion is presented in Sect. 5.

---

[1] https://lucene.apache.org/.

2   State of the Art

Since there are two stop-words identification techniques, related works cover both stop-words lists compilation and morphological analyzers.

2.1   Stop-Word Lists

Arabic stop-words review reveals quite a few stop-words lists. We survey the most useful ones.

- Khoja [14] use a stop-words list in the pre-processing step of the APT application. Developed using a combination of both statistical and rule-based techniques, APT is an Arabic POS Tagger including a stop-words list containing 168 stop-words
- El-Khair [2] created three stop-word lists. The first one is a general stop-words list based on the Arabic language syntactic classes. The general stop-words consists of 1,377 stop-words. The second stop-words list is a corpus-based one. Words occurring more than 25,000 times were selected to create this list. After the manual checking of the words verifying this condition, 124 words were discarded and the final list contains 235 words. The third stop-words list is the result of the merging of the general and the corpus-based lists leading to 1,529 stop-words
- Medhat et al. [6] proposed a different methodology for generating stop-word lists from a corpus. Their methodology consists to establish a list of the most frequent 200 words, to check the validity of a word to be a stop-word and to add all possible prefixes and suffixes to the obtained list of words. The final corpus-based list contains 1,061 words
- Alajmi et al. [15] present a statistical approach to extract Arabic stop-words list. They generated three lists, the first one is constructed by determining Word Frequency, the second one is based on Mean and Variance and the third list is established by calculating the Entropy. The three generated lists were aggregated using Borda's Rule to obtain the final list. The extracted list was compared to a general list. The resulting list contains 200 words but authors show only an extract of twenty words
- Stop words project[2] (List 1) is a stop-words collection in 29 languages created under the GNU GPL v3 license. The Arabic list consists of 162 stop-words. The author doesn't give details about the methodology followed to design these lists. But, as it contains stop-words such as "مليار، قوة، اعلنت" (billion, force, announced) we guess this list is generated applying the frequency on a corpus
- Ranks NL[3] is a project managed by the 'Ranks' Dutch company. The project makes Keyword Analyzer Tools for search engine optimization and other purposes. The project offers an Arabic stop-words list containing 102 stop-words without providing details about the acquiring technique, although it seems to be a corpus-dependent one since it contains stop-words like "واوضح، واضاف، مقابل" (he explained, he added, opposite).

---

[2] http://code.google.com/p/stop-words. Retrieved May 02, 2019.

[3] http://www.ranks.nl/stopwords/arabic. Retrieved May 02, 2019.

Except Abu El-Khair's who tried to add a rule-based stop-words list (but not diacritized and not comprehensive), all cited lists are corpus-dependent and do not contain all clitized forms of every stop-word.

2.2 Morphological Analyzers

There are few morphological analyzers for Arabic, some of them are available while others are either commercial applications or published but not-available. Among those known in the literature we find out Xerox Arabic Morphological Analysis [16], Buckwalter Arabic Morphological Analyzer [17], ElixirFM [18], Qutuf [19], SALMA [20], Alkhalil morpho sys [21, 22], MADAMIRA [23] and CALIMA-star [24]. We limit this morphological analyzers review to the well-known and freely available ones.

- Buckwalter Arabic Morphological Analyzer version 1.0 [17] (BAMA) relies on three lexicon files (prefixes, suffixes and stems), regulated by the morphological compatibility tables devoted to control prefix-stem, stem-suffix and prefix-suffix combinations. In BAMA there are 41 stop-words in the stems lexicon with the POS "FUNC_WORD". However, when BAMA is given one of these stop-words as part of a sentence, it is analyzed with an empty POS
- Alkhalil morpho sys [22] (ALKHALIL v1 and v2) is a Java Arabic morphological analyzer. Alkhalil identifies all possible solutions of a word based on set of Arabic morphological rules and linguistic resources. For every possible solution, Alkhalil establishes a list of morphological features (vowelized form of the word, the root, the stem, the stem pattern, the clitics, the POS tag, the lemma, the lemma pattern and the syntactic state, proclitic, enclitic, etc.) in HTML or CSV formats. Stop-words in Alkhalil are stored in an XML file named "toolwords" containing 418 stop-words with their possible clitics associations. These toolwords are used in the analyzer processing but not displayed as stop-words in the analysis output
- MADAMIRA [23] is a freely available morphological analyzer resulting of the mix of two tools MADA [25] and AMIRA [26]. MADAMIRA makes use of SAMA (the second version of BAMA) analyzer to get a free of context words analysis, then apply the Support Vector Machine and N-gram language models techniques on an annotated corpus to rank the analyses. The output (can be supplied as plain text or in XML format) is a contextually ranked list of morphological analyses containing several tags such as word form, lemma, stem, part-of-speech, clitics. MADAMIRA does not carry information about stop-words
- CALIMA-star [24] is an out-of-context morphological analyzer and generator implemented in Python, providing morphological features as tokenization, phonological representation, root, pattern, POS, lemma, gender, number, state, case or lexical rationality. This analyzer does not deliver any stop-words knowledge.

Thus, the use of traditional analyzers as a stop-words detection tool in the pre-processing stage exhibits unsatisfying results because of the different reasons explained above.

3   Proposed Approach

Our approach consists firstly to build a rule-based stop-words list that includes all stop-words grammatical categories and its inflected forms. Secondly, we use this list to conceive a contextual stop-words analyzer.

3.1   Stop-Words List Design

Despite the availability of a number of Arabic stop-word lists and as previously mentioned, most of them are corpus-dependent relying on the frequency feature of this particular corpus. Thus, in order to offer a comprehensive Arabic rule-based stop-words list including not only all grammatical categories of stop-words but also all their clitized forms, we design a new stop-words list.

Our stop-words list structure is inspired from the Arabic language itself and designed into three classes: native particles, special nouns and special verbs. Consequently, stop-words belonging to the particles grammatical category are classified as native particles, those of nouns category in the special nouns and verbs in special verbs. This classification is motivated from one side by the fact that every grammatical category holds its own morpho-syntactic features, and from another side by the fact that every grammatical category agglutinates to its own specific clitics. For example, stop-words that belong to the noun category, don't agglutinate with the "س" (will) proclitic that expresses the future ("س" is specific for verbs)

For instance, as shown in Fig. 1, since relative pronouns in Arabic belongs to the noun grammatical category, they are classified in our list in the special nouns class, while conjunction particles are classified in the native particles class.

The developed list is designed in a two-stage process. In the first step, we inventory words having stop-words features according to the adopted classification to obtain the simple stop-words list. In the second step, we add all possible clitics to the simple stop-words list to get the complex one. Likewise, simple stop-words list encloses single stop-words of all grammatical categories, while complex stop-words list covers stop-words clitized forms.

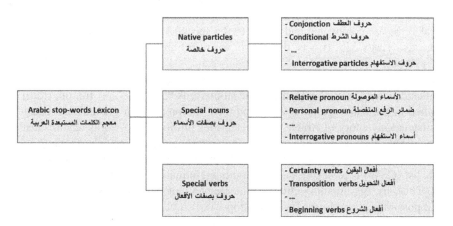

Fig. 1. Adopted Arabic stop-words classification.

The Simple stop-words list (SSW) list elaboration was done manually by a linguist relying on the Arabic literature [27]. It is inventoried as follows. The Native particles (NP) class contains the well-known Arabic particles which are conjunction, preposition, conditional particles, negative particles, vocative particles, accusative particles, amendment particles, supplemental particles and inceptive particles, enriched by some rarely used classes such as answer particles, exceptive particles and exhortation particles. The Special nouns (SN) category clusters Arabic nouns possessing stop-words characteristics such as relative pronouns, personal pronouns, demonstrative pronouns and interrogative pronouns.

Table 1. Simple stop-words list examples.

Simple stop-words		Class	Grammatical category
but, did, for	...،حَتَّى ، هَلْ ، لَكِنْ	NP	inceptive particle
to, on, from, of, ...	...،عَنْ ، مِنْ ، عَلَى ، إِلَى	NP	Preposition
If there's, only, As for, ...	...،أَمَّا ، إِلاَّ ، إِذْمَا	NP	conditional particle
except for, when, only, ...	...،إِلاَّ ، لَمَّا ، خَلاَ	NP	exceptive particle
if not, for what, not to, ...	...،ألاَ ، هَلاَّ ، لَوْمَا	NP	exhortation particle
who, which, whom, ...	...،اللاَّئِي ، الَّذِي ، الَّتِي	SN	relative pronoun
me, he, you, ...	...،أَنْتُنَّ ، هُوَ ، أَنَا	SN	personal pronoun
this, that, ...	...،ذَاكَ ، هَذَا	SN	demonstrative pronoun
who, what, ...	...،مَا ، مَنْ	SN	interrogative pronoun
find, discover, know, ...	...،دَرَى ، أَلْفَى ، وَجَدَ	SV	certitude verb
take, restore, change, ...	...،صَيَّرَ ، رَدَّ ، تَخِذَ	SV	transposition verb
claim , pretend, count, ...	...،عَدَّ ، حَجَا ، زَعَمَ	SV	hopefulness verb
start, abrade, start, ...	...،قَامَ ، انْبَرَى ، ابْتَدَأَ	SV	starting verb

The Special verbs (SV) category groups Arabic verbs holding stop-words features such as certitude verbs, transposition verbs, hopefulness verbs and starting verbs. These special verbs are conjugated and added to the special verb list. For instance, the stop-words "كُنَّا ؛ كَانُوا ؛ كُنْتُ" (I was, they were, we were) are conjugated forms of the verb "كَانَ" (To be).

Table 1 above shows examples of the stop-words of our list with their classes and grammatical categories. For example, the stop-words "مِنْ ، عَلَى ، إِلَى" (to, on, from) are classified in the native particles class and have the preposition grammatical category. This manual inventory of Arabic word categories fulfilling stop-words features insured the inclusion of all stop-words and avoids the corpus-dependency shortcoming.

After this comprehensiveness step, the next one for designing the complex stop-words list (CSW) is to ensure the maximum agglutination respecting Arabic language rules. Thus, by agglutinating clitics to the elements of our simple stop-words list, we get all possible clitized forms for every stop-word. A clitic is a proclitic-enclitic couple knowing that a proclitic and an enclitic concatenates respectively before and after the stop-word. Placed before the stop-word or another proclitic, the *Proclitic* modifies the stop-word's meaning, as by making the causality (السببية), by signaling conjunction (العطف), confirmation (التأكيد), giving the reason (التعليل) or by indicating accompanying (المصاحبة). Placed after the stop-word or another enclitic, the Enclitic has a metaphoric function for the speaker (المتكلم), the addressee (المخاطب), or absent (الغائب). Depending on its category, a simple stop-word concatenates to some clitics to yield the complex stop-words. For example, preposition can't be agglutinated to the proclitic "ال" ("the") but can be agglutinated to the proclitic "ف".

The design of the diacritized stop-words list named ASL (Arabic Stop-words List) was done in two phases, the simple list development and the complex one. Proceeding in such way, guarantees the inclusion in our list of all clitized forms of all stop-words grammatical categories without relying on any corpus. Table 2 shows an extract of our Arabic stop-words list. For instance, the complex stop-word "أَوَإلَيْهِم" (and for them?) of the category native particle is the combination of the simple stop-word "إلَى" (for) with the proclitic "أَوَ" (and?) and the enclitic "هُم" (them).

Table 2. ASL extract.

Enclitic	Simple stop-word		Proclitic	Complex stop-word		Category
-	maybe	عَلَّ	And وَ	And maybe	وَلَعَلَّ	NP
-	that	ذَلِكَ	like كَ	like that	كَذَلِكَ	SN
-	you are	تَكُونِينَ	will سَ	we will be	سَتَكُونِينَ	SV
them هُنَّ	without	لَوْلاَ	-	without them	لَوْلاَهُنَّ	NP
you كِ	no more than	غَيْرُ	-	no more than you	غَيْرُكِ	SN
you كَ	maybe	عَسَى	-	Maybe you	عَسَاكَ	SV
they هُم	to	إلَى	And is أَوَ	And is to they	أَوَإلَيْهِم	NP
they هِمْ	another	غَيْرُ	and with فَبِ	and with Otherwise	فَبِغَيْرِهِمْ	SN
them هُنَّ	They find	يَجِدُونَ	and فَ	And They find them	فَيَجِدُونَهُنَّ	SV

Table 3 below shows statistics about the number of words contained in ASL. The simple one contains 3,931 stop-words while the complex one encloses 67,153 stop-words.

Table 3. ASL statistics.

	Native particles	Special nouns	Special verbs	Total
Simple list	84	263	3,584	3,931
Complex list	1,590	9,627	55,936	67,153

3.2   Stop-Words Analyzer Design

Given that stop-words identification using a morphological analyzer fail to recognize a number of stop-words due to the clitized forms omission and grammatical category default, we take advantage of the collected rule-based stop-words list to design a contextual stop-words analyzer. Indeed, this specific stop-word analyzer would be useful to be used alone but most importantly would be useful to be integrated in existing morphological analyzers that are exploited in the context of IR applications where the detection of stop-words has a great impact on the accuracy of the whole system.

In the context of Arabic language, let us remind that morphological analysis should take into account the challenge of having the input text (such as a stop-word) without diacritics. In addition, when the stop-word is isolated and without the context of a sentence, many solutions are possible. For instance, the word "ومن" (transliterated as "wmn") admits a set of solutions such as "مِن" (from), "مَنْ" (who), "مَنّ" (grace) whereas in the sentence "ومن جفاك فصد عنه" (who is rough with you repel him), the word "ومن" (wmn) admits a single solution which is "مَنْ" (who). Thereby, our stop-words analyzer design is done in two steps. Firstly, we get all possible solutions of every input word using the ASL list. Secondly, we get the most appropriate one according to sentence context using a supervised learning technique.

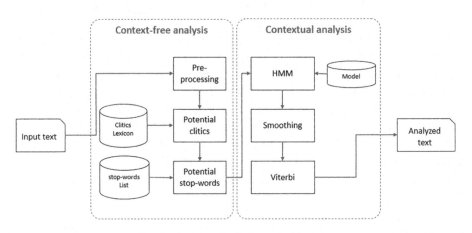

Fig. 2. Stop-words analyzer architecture.

As shown in Fig. 2, in the out of context analysis, we get all potential stop-words from the input text using a clitics lexicon [28] and ASL. After that, the contextual analysis involves the use of a supervised learning technique to detect the most appropriate solution according to sentence context.

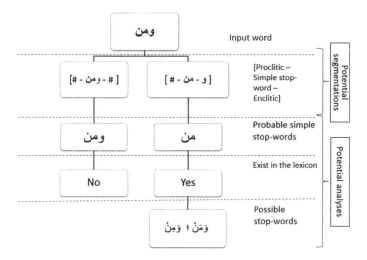

Fig. 3. Stop-words analyzer context-free analysis.

The context-free analysis step is divided into two sub processes. As illustrated in Fig. 3, the first sub process is the segmentation of the input using the clitics lexicon. The word "ومن" (transliterated as wmn) provides two potential segmentations {# - ومن - #} and {# - من - و}. The first potential segmentation corresponds to the simple stop-word "ومن" associated with an empty proclitic and enclitic. While, the second potential segmentation matches to the simple stop-word "من" (mn) associated with the proclitic "و" (w) and an empty enclitic. Then, comes the role of the stop-words list in the second sub process to check the existence of the probable simple stop-words. If it exists, we get all possible corresponding diacritized stop-words. In the case of multiple possible stop-words like in the example in Fig. 3 "وَمَنْ، وَمِنْ" (and who, and from), a disambiguation phase becomes necessary. It's the context detection step.

The contextual analysis step serves to remove the ambiguity related to the most appropriate stop-word within the possible ones. This disambiguation task is achieved through a supervised learning technique. Specifically, Hidden Markov Model (HMM) [29], a smoothing technique [30] and the Viterbi algorithm [31].

The bi-grams HMM associated with the Absolute Discounting smoothing method [32] is used in the contextual analysis to build a model trained using Al-Mus'haf corpus [33] and Nemlar [34].

As illustrated in Fig. 4, the input words represent the observed states in our HMM, and the list of potential stop-words provided by the context-free analysis step for the input word represents the hidden states. The contextual analysis consists firstly in the estimation of the HMM parameters by applying the smoothing technique, secondly, we apply the Viterbi algorithm to identify the most probable sequence representing the best solution according to the input sentence context. In the example in the Fig. 4 below, two paths are possible but the best one is the path starting with "وَمَنْ" (and who).

To check the effectiveness of the designed stop-words analyzer, we evaluate our stop words list and compare our analyzer with available ones.

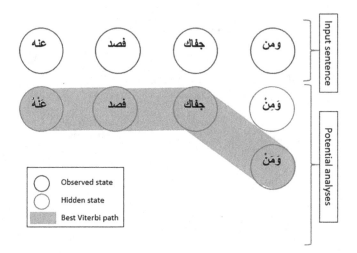

Fig. 4. Stop-words analyzer context-free analysis.

4   Evaluation and Comparison

On one hand, the evaluation consists to detect stop-words in a corpus using different lists. On the other hand, the comparison involves the comparison of our analyzer for both context-free and the contextual analysis.

4.1   Stop-Words List Evaluation

To test the comprehensiveness of the ASL list, we evaluate it with four other available ones:

- Khoja stop-words list [14], extracted from the Arabic Part-of-speech Tagger tool that contains 168 stop-words
- Abu El-Khair's [2] general stop-words list containing 1,377 stop-words
- List 1: a stop-words collection consisting of 162 stop-words
- Ranks NL list: it enumerates 102 stop-words

The best way to evaluate the lists lies to use a large evaluation corpus tagged with the "stop-word" tag and compute the accuracy measure of the corpus analysis using the evaluated lists. However, the absence of a such corpus leads us to do otherwise. Thus, using the five stop-word lists (ASL and the four above), we check the existence of the stop-words of every list in the Quran text (diacritized and undiacritized). This evaluation assesses the stop-words list coverage.

The used Quran text corpus is composed of 78,477 tokens, 19,251 unique diacritized tokens and 15,684 unique undiacritized tokens. Table 4 displays the number of stop-words detected in the corpus using the four evaluation lists and ASL.

Table 4. Stop-word lists evaluation.

Quran text	Khoja	Abu El-Khair	List 1	Ranks NL	ASL
Undiacritized	144	552	98	68	1,247
Diacritized	–	–	–	–	916

This quantitative evaluation reveals that in terms of coverage, ASL outperforms the four other lists. In addition, the four lists are undiacritized. And the absence of diacritics increases the ambiguity in Arabic language. That explains the difference between the number of diacritized and undiacritized stop-words of ASL list. For example, the verb "مَنّ" (grace) is confused with the native particle "مِنْ" (from) or with the special noun "مَنْ" (who), because without diacritics they have a similar spelling "من" (mn).

As long as ASL is a rule-based manually gathered stop-words list and the quantitative evaluation affirms its supremacy, we can conclude that from both qualitative and quantitative point of view, ASL outstrips the other lists. This list will be soon freely available from our team[4] website.

4.2   Context-Free Evaluation

To test the efficiency of the context-free analysis, we compare our analyzer context-free analysis with known analyzers offering an out of context analysis. The evaluation consists to analyze a manually tagged corpus with the five analyzers to get their accuracy. The accuracy formula is as follow: Accuracy $= \frac{TP + TN}{nbw}$

Where

TP: The number of stop-words correctly identified (the solution exists in the analysis list) without considering the grammatical category of the solution.

TN: The number of the non-stop-words correctly identified

nbW: The number of words in the corpus

As the morphological analyzers does not carry information about stop-words, the number of correctly identified ones (TP) is computed by comparing the analysis output to the correct solution in the evaluation corpus without taking into account the POS of the analysis.

For example, if the analysis of the sentence "تنفرد المدينة العتيقة بمؤهلات متنوعة ولا محدودة، انصهرت فيها روافد ثقافية متباينة ميزتها عن غيرها من المدن" (The Old City is distinguished by a variety and non-limited qualifications, and there are many cultural tributaries that are different from other cities) gives the following output "تنفرد المدينة العتيقة بمؤهلات متنوعة [وَلَا] محدودة، انصهرت [فيها] روافد ثقافية متباينة ميزتها [عَنّ، عُنْ، عَنْ] [غِيَرَها، غَيَّرَها] [مَنَّ، مُنْ، مِنْ، مَنّْ، مَنْ] المدن", the accuracy is 94.11% ($\frac{4+12}{17} = 0.94114$) because the correct stop-word exists in the analysis list of the words "فيها ، من ، عن ، ولا" (in itself, from, of, nor), while for the word "غيرها" (another one) the correct stop-word which is "غَيْرُها" does not exist in the analysis output.

---

[4] http://arabic.emi.ac.ma/.

The used evaluation corpus is a set of articles from an electronic newspaper[5] containing 419 stop-words manually annotated with their correct analysis. The corpus contains 1,628 words which can appear relatively small. However, due to the lack of a corpus annotated with the stop-word tag (including nouns and verbs grammatical categories), we were strained to do the arduous manual task of annotation to build the evaluation corpus.

Figure 5 presents an extract of this corpus where all stop-words of that list are annotated with an "s" type.

```
<w unv="إنسانِيّ" type="-" />
<w unv="عالـمِيّ" type="-" />
<w unv="سنة" type="-" />
<w unv="ومع" type="s" vow="مَعَ" />
<w unv="ذلك" type="s" vow="ذَلِك" />
<w unv="لم" type="s" vow="لَمَ" />
<w unv="تشبع" type="-" />
<w unv="لها" type="s" vow="لَهَا" />
<w unv="هذه" type="s" vow="هَذِه" />
<w unv="الخصوصيّات" type="-" />
<w unv="للتنال" type="-" />
<w unv="نصيبها" type="-" />
<w unv="من" type="s" vow="مِنْ" />
```

Fig. 5. Evaluation corpus extract.

From results exposed in Table 5, we observe that our analyzer outperforms the others by achieving 99.94% of accuracy. This non detection by the other analyzers is due to the clitized forms omission drawback like the stop-words "أَفَكَغَيْر ، أَفَبِتِلْك، فَكَتِلْكُما، أَفَإِلَيْه" (and is like another one, and is with that, and like that two, and is for him) that are not recognized by other analyzers.

Table 5. Context-free evaluation.

	BAMA	Alkhalil 1	Alkhalil 2	CALIMA-star	Our analyzer
Accuracy (%)	91.09	88.70	93.98	93.12	99.94

4.3   Stop-Words Analyzer Comparison

Adopting the same corpus used in the context-free evaluation, we compare in this stage the performance of the developed stop-words analyzer with MADAMIRA since it is the only analyzer offering a contextual analysis. The objective is to get the accuracy of the first analysis solution. In this case, the accuracy of the previous example (in the context-free evaluation section "تنفرد المدينة العتيقة...") will be 82.35% instead of 94.11%

---

[5] https://www.hespress.com/.

because even if the correct stop-word exists in the analysis list of the words "من، عن" it is not the first solution.

Table 6 shows that our analyzer provides better results than MADAMIRA with 97.85% of accuracy versus 90.17%.

Table 6. Analyzers comparison.

	MADAMIRA	Our analyzer
Accuracy (%)	90.17	97.85

5   Conclusion

In this paper, we study stop-words identification issue relying on both static lists and morphological analysis techniques. The state of the art study demonstrates the absence of a comprehensive Arabic rule-based stop-words list including all grammatical categories and all their clitized forms and that the use of traditional analyzers as a stop-words detection tool gives poor results due to clitized forms omission and grammatical category default.

To address these problems, we designed firstly a comprehensive Arabic rule-based stop-words list including all grammatical categories and all clitized forms and secondly a stop-words analyzer that detects stop-words by getting in the first step all acceptable analyses for every input word using the static stop-words list, and by getting the most appropriate one according to the sentence context based on the hidden Markov model in the second step.

The context-free evaluation has led to 99.94% of accuracy and the contextual steps using HMM has led to 97.85% of accuracy. The conducted comparison with the state of the art analyzers provides our own with a leading position.

References

1. AL-Shalabi, R., Kanaan, G., Jaam, J.M., et al.: Stop-word removal algorithm for Arabic language. In: Proceedings of 1st International Conference on Information and Communication Technologies: From Theory to Applications, CTTA 2004, pp. 545–550 (2004)
2. Abu El-Khair, I.: Effects of stop words elimination for Arabic information retrieval: a comparative study. Int. J. Comput. Inf. Sci. 4(3), 119–133 (2006)
3. Zou, F., Wang, F.L., Deng, X., et al. Automatic construction of Chinese stop word list. In: Proceedings of the 5th WSEAS international conference on Applied computer science, pp. 1010–1015
4. Savoy, J.: A stemming procedure and stopword list for general French corpora. JASIS **50** (10), 944–952 (1999)
5. Zheng, G., Gaowa, G.: The selection of Mongolian stop words. In: 2010 IEEE International Conference on. IEEE Intelligent Computing and Intelligent Systems (ICIS), pp. 71–74 (2010)

6. Medhat, W., Yousef, A.H., Korashy, H.: Corpora preparation and stopword list generation for Arabic data in social network. arXiv preprint arXiv:1410.1135 (2014)
7. Davarpanah, M.R., Sanji, M., Aramideh, M.: Farsi lexical analysis and stop word list. Libr. Hi Tech **27**(3), 435–449 (2009)
8. Al-Jefri, M.M., Mohammed, S.A.: Arabic spell checking technique. U.S. Patent No. 9,037,967, 19 May 2015
9. Hanane, F., Lachkar, A., Ouatik, S.A.: Arabic text summarization based on latent semantic analysis to enhance arabic documents clustering. arXiv preprint arXiv:1302.1612 (2013)
10. Habash, N., Sadat, F.: Arabic preprocessing schemes for statistical machine translation. In: Proceedings of the Human Language Technology Conference of the NAACL, Companion Volume: Short Papers, June 2006, pp. 49–52. Association for Computational Linguistics (2006)
11. Yang, Y.: Noise reduction in a statistical approach to text categorization. In: Proceedings of the 18th Annual International ACM SIGIR Conference on Research and Development in Information Retrieval, pp. 256–263. ACM (1995)
12. Glossbrenner, A., Glossbrenner, E.: Search Engines for the World Wide Web. Peachpit Press, Berkeley (2001)
13. Medhat, W., Yousef, A., Korashy, H.: Corpora preparation and stopword list generation for arabic data in social network. arXiv preprint arXiv:1410.1135 (2014)
14. Khoja, S.: APT: Arabic part-of-speech tagger. In: Proceedings of the Student Workshop at NAACL, pp. 20–25 (2001)
15. Alajmi, A., Saad, E.M., Darwish, R.R.: Toward an ARABIC stop-words list generation. Int. J. Comput. Appl. **46**(8), 8–13 (2012)
16. Beesley, K.: Finite-state morphological analysis and generation of Arabic at Xerox Research: Status and plans in 2001. In: ACL Workshop on Arabic Language Processing: Status and Perspective, vol. 1 (2001)
17. Buckwalter T.: Issues in Arabic orthography and morphology analysis. In: Proceedings of the Workshop on Computational Approaches to Arabic Script-Based Languages. Association for Computational Linguistics (2004)
18. Smrž O.: ElixirFM: implementation of functional arabic morphology. In: Proceedings of the 2007 Workshop on Computational Approaches to Semitic Languages: Common Issues and Resources. Association for Computational Linguistics, (2007)
19. Altabba, M., Al-Zaraee, A. and Shukairy, M.A.: An Arabic morphological analyzer and part-of-speech tagger. Actes de JADT (2010)
20. Sawalha, M., Atwell, E., Abushariah, M.A.: SALMA: standard Arabic language morphological analysis. In: 2013 1st International Conference on Communications, Signal Processing, and Their Applications (ICCSPA). IEEE (2013)
21. Boudlal, A., Lakhouaja, A., Mazroui, A., et al.: Alkhalil morpho sys1: A morphosyntactic analysis system for Arabic texts. In: International Arab Conference on Information Technology, Benghazi Libya (2010)
22. Boudchiche, M., Mazroui, A., Bebah, M.O.A.O.: AlKhalil Morpho 2: Sys a robust Arabic morpho-syntactic analyzer. J. King Saud Univ. Comput. Inf. Sci. **29**(2), 141–146 (2017)
23. Pasha, A., Al-Badrashiny, M., Diab, M., et al.: MADAMIRA: a fast, comprehensive tool for morphological analysis and disambiguation of arabic. In: LREC, vol. 14 (2014)
24. Taji, D., Khalifa, S., Obeid, O., Eryani, F., Habash, N.: An Arabic morphological analyzer and generator with copious features. In: Workshop on Computational Research in Phonetics, Phonology, and Morphology. The Confernece on Empirical Methods in Natural Language Processing (EMNLP 2018), Brussels, Belgium (2018)

25. Nizar, H., Rambow, O., Roth, R.: MADA+ TOKAN: a toolkit for Arabic tokenization, diacritization, morphological disambiguation, POS tagging, stemming and lemmatization. In: Proceedings of the 2nd international conference on Arabic language resources and tools (MEDAR), Cairo, Egypt, vol. 41 (2009)
26. Mona, D.: Second generation AMIRA tools for Arabic processing: fast and robust tokenization, POS tagging, and base phrase chunking. In: 2nd International Conference on Arabic Language Resources and Tools, vol. 110 (2009)
27. المرادي، الحسن بن قاسم، فخر الدين قباوة ومحمد نديم فاضل. الجنى الداني في حروف المعاني، دار الكتب العلمية الطبعة 1، 1992م
28. Driss, N., Regragui, Y., Bouzoubaa, K.: Interoperable Arabic language resources building and exploitation in SAFAR platform. In: 2016 IEEE/ACS 13th International Conference of Computer Systems and Applications (AICCSA). IEEE (2016)
29. Oliver, I.: Markov Processes for Stochastic Modeling, 2nd edn. Elsevier Insights, Elsevier Science (2013)
30. Ney, H., Essen, U.: On smoothing techniques for bigram-based natural language modelling. In: Proceedings of ICASSP 1991: 1991 International Conference on Acoustics, Speech, and Signal Processing, Toronto, Ontario, Canada, vol. 2, pp. 825–828 (1991)
31. Forney, D.: The viterbi algorithm. Proc. IEEE **61**(3), 268–278 (1973)
32. Ney, H., Essen, U.: On smoothing techniques for bigram-based natural language modelling. In: Proceedings of ICASSP 1991: 1991 International Conference on Acoustics, Speech, and Signal Processing, Toronto, Ontario, Canada, vol. 2, pp. 825–828 (1991)
33. Zeroual, I., Lakhouaja, A.: A new Quranic Corpus rich in morphosyntactical information. Int. J. Speech Technol. (IJST) **19**, 339–346 (2016)
34. Mohamed, B., Azzeddine, M.: Enrichment of the Nemlar corpus by the lemma tag. In: Workshop Language Resources of Arabic NLP: Construction, Standardization, Management and Exploitation. Rabat, Morocco, 26 November 2015 (2015)

Negation in Standard Arabic Revisited: A Corpus-Based Metaoperational Approach

Mohamed-Habib Kahlaoui[(✉)] [iD]

Sultan Qaboos University, Muscat, Oman
mhabibkahlaoui@yahoo.fr

Abstract. The standard assumption of the present study is that the speaker's processing strategy in discourse is the key to understanding the logic of negating in Standard Arabic (SA). Paradoxically, the metalinguistic richness of negation in SA, compared with English and French for instance, has not triggered any significant research that attaches due importance to the context of production and reception of utterances and accounts for the working of negators from a contrastive perspective. Rather, traditional approaches to Arabic syntax still dominate the grammatical landscape and continue to exercise unquestioned authority in pedagogical grammar. The paper shows that these approaches are inadequate, unsystematic and heavily handicapped by direct assignment of chronological meaning to formal negators. By offering a framework for systematic analysis of negation in relation to affirmative utterances on one hand, and to the binary micro-system Phase 1/Phase 2 on another, the study suggests a redefinition of the status, scope and values of six negators – *lam, leisa, maa, laa, lan* and *lammaa* – as well as their counterparts in the affirmative pole.

Keywords: Phase-1/phase-2 negators · Metalinguistic status · Modal negator · Aspectual · Negator · Processing strategy · Intervenient/detached strategy

1 Introduction

This paper claims that the metalinguistic richness of negation in Standard Arabic (abbreviated SA) has not triggered any significant research that distances itself from the traditional account of negation. Rather, traditional approaches to Arabic syntax still dominate the grammatical landscape and continue to exercise absolute authority in pedagogical grammar. Whether approached from a prescriptive, descriptive, explicative or typological perspective, pre-verbal and pre-nominal negators have been treated essentially as conveying a temporal value that accounts for their working in discourse: negation in the past, in the present, and in the future.

Based on a corpus of utterances collected from different sources, such as the International Arabic Corpus, the Quran, and literary texts, this study questions the chronological treatment of negation in the dominant theoretical and pedagogical grammar. It also shows that negators in SA do not function as time locators of the predicative relation (R) or work in free variation. Rather, they constitute a micro-system of interrelated units governed by an enunciative logic and contextual factors.

© Springer Nature Switzerland AG 2019
K. Smaïli (Ed.): ICALP 2019, CCIS 1108, pp. 164–180, 2019.
https://doi.org/10.1007/978-3-030-32959-4_12

2   The Traditional Approach to Negators

The Arabic grammatical tradition should not be understood as a homogeneous school but as an episteme indicative of an autonomous stage in human linguistic thought. It shares with western traditional grammars their prescriptive, semantic, atomistic, tax-onomic, context-insensitive, and writing-oriented approach that envisages not language at work but language as an end-product. These epistemic features are detectable in the treatment of negation and other grammatical operations in SA. In spite of its hetero-geneity, the traditional approach to negation reflects a consensus on several premises and theoretical presuppositions:

   i. The main linguistic corpus used by all traditional grammarians is collected either from authentic Quranic and poetic texts or made of intuition-based sentences generally constructed with Zeid and 'amr as hypothetical subjects.

  ii. Negation was not researched as an autonomous linguistic category but as a "linguistic style" associated with affirmation, its opposite. Compared with other grammatical operations, negation received scant mentions, often taxonomic and semantic, in the context of non-affirmation and reference to time. The most influential grammarians, such as Sibaweihi [54], Al Mubarrad [12], Al Zamakhshari [23], Ibn Hisham [42], Ibn Al Sarraj [41], Ibn Ya'iish [45], and Ibn Jinni [43], to name a few, touched on "particles of negation" but never elaborated on negation.

 iii. All grammarians, except Al Jurjani [10, p. 417-418], a prominent rhetorician, considered affirmation to be the origin of speech, and negation extrinsic to the sentence's basic structure, always affirmative.

 iv. Although some grammarians, Sibaweihi [54, vol. 2, p. 116] and Al Khaliil, [11, vol. 8, p. 350] assigned a corroborative 'meaning' to some negators, such as *lam*, and *lan,* Al Zamakhshari, [24, p. 407] and Al Suyuti, [14, vol.2, p.287], negators were always associated with extralinguistic temporal (present, past, future) values.

  v. The traditional approach was focused on the all-pervading theory of governance. Negators were described and classified according to their declensional potential or operative force (Versteegh, [57, p. 6]. A typical traditional definition of a negator, such as *lan,* generally includes three functional properties: it negates, puts the verb in the accusative, and locates the event in the future.

 vi. Some grammarians, namely Ibn Jinni [43], adopted a morpho-semantic approach exploring forms of verbal and nominal negation other than negative particles. The case of morphological patterns, like /'af'ala/ and /fa''ala/, which, by interlocking with a root, assign negative properties to the new lexical unit. This phenomenon is studied in Al-Sajustaanii [24], Ibn Saiyidih [44], and Al Zajjaaj [22].

Often based on Quranic, poetic, and contextless sentences, negators are associated with temporal "meanings". Thus, the negator *laa* (لا) is said to "negate the event in the future" (Ibn Hisham, [42, vol. 1, p. 6]). Other grammarians argue that *laa* may negate present states, as well (Al Muraadii, [13, p. 296]; *leisa*يس / negates "future and sometimes present events or states" (Al Istiraabaadii, [9, p. 197]; *lammaa* (لمّا) is used "to negate past events related to the present time" (Sibaweihi, [54, vol. 4, p. 223]; *lam /*

لم affects verbs in the imperfective and puts them in the past and the jussive mood Ibn Al Sarraaj, [41, vol. 2, p. 157]; and *lan* /لن is defined as "a particle of negation, futurity and the accusative [mood]" (Ibn Hisham, [42, vol. 1, p. 464]. It is noteworthy that Ibn Hisham [42] and other grammarians, like Ibn 'usfuur (in Al Muraadii, [13, p.274], disagrees with Al- Zamakhshari's [24, p.407] claim that *lan* conveys corroboration and perpetuity of negation; *maa* / ما is used to negate present states [53, vol. 5, p. 24]. When it collocates with the so-called expletive *min* / من, it is said to corroborate negation [41, p. 374]. Finally, the archaic negator *'in* (إن) works in nominal and verbal past and imperfective sentences to denote a present temporal value. It is defined as *synonymous* to and interchangeable with the negator *maa* / 12] ! ما, vol. 1, p. 188].

This temporal approach is approximated by Al Mabkhout [18, p. 119] in the following visualization (Fig. 1):

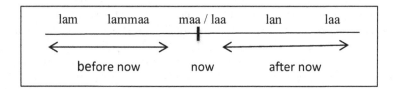

Fig. 1. Temporal values assigned to negators

3   Contemporary Research on Negation in SA

The unchallenged prevalence of traditional grammatical views in current pedagogical grammar is indicative of the severe limitations of contemporary linguistic research on SA. The direct assignment of a chronological 'meaning' to formal categories without any referential value in the extralinguistic, such as *lam, lan, maa*, etc., is largely detectable in contemporary views, from different theoretical frameworks, on negation. Al-Makhzumi [19], though he defined negation as "a linguistic style governed by the contexts of speech" [19, p. 244], did not seem to take the context factors into consideration by adhering to the traditional temporality of negators. Amaira's definition pertinently associates negation with the speaker's intentions [25, p. 154] but his analysis of negators reiterates the same chronological treatment. Hamasa [38] approaches negation as a category "extrinsic to the structure of the sentence. It denotes the non-validity of the predicative relation in verbal and nominal sentences" [38, p.280]. His approach does not break with the predominant views on negation; it reduces the working of negators to distinctions of tense [38, p. 285-301]. By adopting a pragmatic approach, Al-Mabkhout [18] distances himself from the predominant grammatical orientation. First, he starts from negation not from negators and considers that the non-referentiality – literally " the referential emptiness" [18, p. 485] - which specifies negation relates it to the categories of expressive language acts ('al 'if- saahiyaat 18] (الافصاحيات, p. 485]; thus, a negative sentence does not necessarily presuppose an affirmative one [18, p. 451]. Second, he assumes that the non-referentiality of negation presupposes a complex structure made of two components;

the first expressing negation and the second conveying its specification [18, p. 421], as exemplified in:

لم يسافر زيد بعد فحقيبته لاتزال في غرفة النوم.

[*lam yusaafir zeidun ba'du*] [*fa haqiibatuhu laa tazaalu fii ghorfati-n-nawmi*]
Zeid has **not** gone yet; his bag is still in the bedroom.

According to Al Mabkhout, this binary structure, reminiscent of the structures of the conditional, oath, and the vocative in SA, is based on a semantic link [18, p. 421]. The second clause "is understandable only in the context of the negative one" [18, p. 423]. It assumes different context-dependent functions, such as resumption, corroboration, justification, specification, or restriction. However, this line of demarcation from predominant grammatical orientations, does not seem sharply drawn when it comes to the working of negators. "The differences between negators are basically temporal" [18, p. 484].

Negation in Standard and Dialectal Arabic has also received considerable theoretical attention in the different stages of generative linguistics, notably the Minimalist approach to Universal Grammar, Shlonsky [53]), Benmamoun [26], Ouhalla [51]. This theoretical framework has been associated with a formalist and typological approach which has long stressed the primacy of thought over its external realization in languages. Negation is therefore investigated within a parametric approach to the linguistic differences permitted by the human language faculty. Attention is mainly devoted to the underlying representations of negation, not to how negators work in real contexts of communication. The traditional Past/non-Past temporal distinction has resurfaced in Minimalist literature to account for the differences between negators in Arabic. Fassi-Fehri [37, p. 163] proposes that the negators *laa*, *lam*, *lamma* and *lan* should be treated as modal negatives. Section 6 demonstrates that the validity of this claim is restricted to two negators only.

4 The Metaoperational Framework: From Enunciation to Metaoperation

Negation in SA has not to date received any systematic analysis from a Metaoperational perspective that takes into consideration the utterance's context of production and reception. The conceptual framework used in this study is based on the findings of the applications of the Metaoperational theory on different natural languages, such as in Adamczewski [2–6], and [8], Delmas [31], Delmas & Girard [32], Delechelle [30], Delmas, Adams, Deléchelle, Girard, Lancri & Naudé [33]. Santin-Guettier & Toupin [52], and Toupin [55]. Adamczewski's theory has developed in the wake of the major anti-mentalist shift in linguistics from "langue" (collective intelligence) to "parole" (individual act of language) which dethroned the study of "langue" as a self-contained system. The shift is initiated essentially by Benveniste [27] and [28], a student of Saussure, who formulated the Enunciation theory. Benveniste claims that the Saussurean Structuralist paradigm, by reducing language study to an over-emphasis on language as a code, eliminated the speaking subject (utterer) and the relationship he/she maintains with his/her interlocutor (co-utterer); two parameters without which utterances cannot be properly decoded. The theory holds that "before enunciation, language is but the possibility of language. After enunciation language is realized in an instance of discourse which has its origins in the speaker" [28, p.80]. Benviniste maintains that every utterance bears on its surface permanent and variable formal traces of its utterer and his/her co-utterer. Such traces are the confirmation that subjectivity and intersubjectivity are interdependent properties of language and language use [27]. The status of the speaking subject in discourse will later constitute the basis of Culioli's Enunciative Operations theory [29] and Adamczewski's Metaoperational grammar [4].

In his groundbreaking work on "Be + ing" in English, Adamczewski [3] asserts that the direct assignment of meaning to meaningless categories, such as the so-called progressive form, is the main reason for the failure of the descriptive approach to account for the working of language. For him, the linear utterance is the final product of a complex and multi-faceted phonological, lexical and syntactic process [7]. Utterances exhibit on their surface observable traces of an invisible activity and codify the mental operations whose main object is not to enable the speaker to refer to the world, but to indicate how the utterance was processed in a given context, as well as the speaker's position relative to both the propositional content and the co-utterer (co-U).

The significance of surface binary operators, such as (Ø/ Be + ing), (V-s/do), (nearly/almost), (shall/will), (may/can), (this/ that), (too/ also), etc., to cite just a few English oppositions, is that they constitute a *natural* metalanguage indicative of the working of language itself, hence their metalinguistic status. Adamczewski [8] refers to them as real "portholes" to the underlying language activity. For him, these operation tracers constitute the real subject of languages study. Most, perhaps all, grammatical phenomena are organized in pairs based on the Rhematic (phase 1 / open paradigm) Thematic –> (phase 2 / closed paradigm) vector. According to Adamczewski [7], "[this] basic principle is repeated cyclically to create different grammatical tools that are necessary to the working of languages". Contrastivity as a systematic intra- and inter-lingual analysis of authentic data collected from languages is a methodological prerequisite.

The following section is restricted to six formal Arabic negators working in verbal and/or nominal utterances: *lam, maa, lammaa, leisa, laa,* and *lan*.

5   A Metaoperational Analysis of Negation in SA

Lam, maa, leisa, lammaa, laa, and *lan* constitute the nucleus of the Arabic negation system and behave as a micro-system governed by inter-related binary oppositions. These oppositions are not only intra-operational, i.e. within negation, but also inter-operational, i.e. in symmetry with their functional correspondents in affirmation. Consequently, intra- and inter-contrastivity is the approach adopted to investigate the working of the following pairs: (*lam* vs. *maa*), (*lam* vs. *lammaa*), (*leisa* vs. *maa,*) and (*laa* vs. *lan*).

5.1   *Lam* vs. *Maa* : Intra- and Inter-Operation Analysis

5.1.1   Corpus

(1)   حين وصلت الى بيتنا ، أحسست شيئا غير عادي ، فخشيت قليلا عندما لم أر أمّي تسرع لتفتح لي الباب.

Hiina wasaltu 'ilaa beitina, 'aḥsastu shei'an gheira `aadiyyin, fa-khashiitu qaliilan `indamaa lam 'ara 'ummii tusri`u lifatḥi-l-baabi.

When I arrived home, a feeling of apprehension came over me. Thus, I was slightly worried when I did not see my mother rushing to open me the door.

(2)   لا ! لم يغيّر موقفه، ولكنه بدأ الآن يفتح أذنيه.

Laa! lam yugheiyyir mawqifahu, wa laakinnahu bada'a -l-'aana yaftaḥu 'udhuneihi.

No! he did not change his attitude, but he now started to lend attentive ears.

(3)   لم يكذب وما كان كاذبا عليها. / lam yakdhib wa maa kaana kaadhiban `aleihaa.

He did not lie and he would not.

(4)   لكن من هو الجاني الحقيقي الذي حول حياة رانيا إلي جحيم وهي طفلة لم تتعدّ السنوات الأربع ؟!

Laakin man huwwa-l-jaani-l-ḥaqiiqii -l-ladhii ḥawwala ḥayaata raaniya '1aa jaḥiimin wa hiya ṭiflatun lam tata`addaa-s-sanawaati-l-'araba`a?

But, who is the real criminal who made the life of Raniya, a child who did not exceeded four years, a living hell?!

(5)   هي تدّعي بأنها تغيّرت وما تغيّرت بل ازدادت تعصّبا.

Hiyya tadda`ii bi'annahaa tagheiyarat wa maa tagheiyarat bal izdaadat ta`aṣṣuban

She claims she has changed; she did not! She has just become more intolerant.

(6)   ألم تر اسمك على قائمة الانتظار ؟ / 'a lam tara-s-maka `alaa qaa'imati-l-intiḍhaari ?

Didn't you see your name on the waiting list?

(7)   أ ما رأيت الضوء الأحمر ؟ / 'amaa ra'eita-ḍaw'a -l-'aḥmara ?

Haven't you seen the red light on?

(8)   ما كان عليه أن يصدّق مثل تلك الترّهات. / *He should not have believed such nonsense.*

5.1.2   Intra-Operation Analysis

(1)   حين وصلت الى بيتنا ، أحسست شيئا غير عادي ، فخشيت قليلا عندما لم أر أمّي تسرع لتفتح لي الباب.

Hiina wasaltu 'ilaa beitina, 'aḥsastu shei'an gheira `aadiyyin, fa-khashiitu qaliilan `indamaa **lam** 'ara

'ummii tusri`u lifatḥi-l-baabi.

When I arrived home, a feeling of apprehension came over me. Thus, I was slightly worried when I did not see my mother rushing to open me the door.

As seen in sections two and three above, grammarians agree that *lam* is a verbal negator; though it affects an imperfective verb, it conveys negation in the past. This means that the verb is morphologically in the present (muḍhaari`) and grammatically in the past. However, negation in the context of the past is also conveyed by *maa*.

The affirmative sentence (*ra'eitu 'ummii* / I + see + past + my mother) has two possible negative realizations in Arabic:

  i. *lam 'ara 'ummii* / *I did not see my mother.*
  ii. **maa** ra'eitu 'ummii / I did/have not see(n) my mother.

Lam and *maa* share two grammatical features: they negate and both are used in the context of the past. Yet, they are not interchangeable as they are produced in two different contexts. In (1) for instance, the use of *maa* would be ungrammatical. The temporal adverb *'indamaa / when* announces an open paradigm "*when I did not see [my father/ sister/ mother (√), etc.]*", i.e. a new piece of information selected by the linguistic subject from a set of choices in a specific context. The fact that the predicative relation (R) is posed and not presupposed invalidates the possibility of *maa* due to its presupposing properties. In Adamczewski's terms [4], compared with *maa*, *lam* is a phase 1 negator. It has a rhematic status, encodes the non-validity of the predicative relation in the context of the past, and is governed by a speaker's informative strategy. A possible context for *maa* in (ii) is when the utterer does not negate to address an informational deficit but to deny a claim or refute a wrong view held by the co-utterer.

(2), (3), (4) and (6) also include negation with *lam* and provide further clarifications about its working in discourse. The context of (2) لا! لم يغير موقفه، ولكنه بدأ الآن يفتح أذنيه / (*No! he did not change his attitude, but he now started to lend attentive ears.*) includes a questioner seeking information. The answer therefore is reducible into a negative short form.

- وهل غيّر موقفه من زملائه من بعد ذلك؟
And did he change his attitude towards his colleagues after that?

– لا !/ laa / **No!** (He did not).

The non-validation of the predicative relation in the past reflects a detached strategy of the linguistic subject. Whereas the use of *maa*, generally triggered by an intervenient strategy of the speaker, would convey a judgment, not a piece of information. (3) is an interesting utterance as it includes both *lam* and *maa* in the context of the past. The first clause introduces a neutral negative statement where the linguistic encodes the extralinguistic, while in the *maa*-clause the linguistic takes the lead over the extralinguistic; the linguistic subject (the speaker), in the light of his previous knowledge of (*He*), the grammatical subject, categorically excludes the possibility of the predicative relation (*X lying to Z in the past*). The filter of the speaker's judgement obstructs the utterance's direct reference to the extralinguistic event; hence the metalinguistic function of *maa* which works not to inform about the non-validity of R, but to codify a processing strategy of the speaker. The shift from *did* to *the* modal *would* in the English translation provides a revealing insight into the working of both negators in Arabic. In (4), the phase-one negator *lam* is associated with an additional information about the grammatical subject (هي / hiyya / she). *Maa* is possible only in a context of denial including a speaker rejecting and rectifying the claim that the girl is over the age of four. (6) includes a neutral interro-negation with *lam* (*Did you not see your name on the waiting list?*) awaiting a yes/no response from the co-utterer. The same sentence with *maa* would presuppose a different presumptive context, such as when the utterer does not understand how that can be, and therefore awaits explanation, not information.

(5), (7) and (8) shed more light on the working of the phase-two negator *maa*. (5) is an interesting compound sentence. The negative clause (ما تغيّرت / *She did not!*) is preceded and governed by the affirmative clause (هي تدّعي بأنها تغيّرت / *She claims she has changed.*) which conveys the utterer's judgment that 'her change is just pretense'. The verb (ادّعى / 'idda'aa / claim) is the trigger of the Arabic modal operator أنّ / 'anna / which has a corroborative value comparable to the emphatic *do* in English. The speaker's conviction that *change* is a mere *claim* is the co-textual factor which justifies the use of *maa* instead of *lam*. (7) is an interro-negative utterance that introduces a doubtful speaker who finds it hard to believe the co-utterer's claim. An interro-negation with *lam* would be possible only if the questioner was seeking information, such as in (6) above. Therefore, what is negated in (7) and (5) is not the extralinguistic event itself, but the co-utterer's claim that R did not take place. In both cases, *maa* functions as a meta-negator codifying a metalinguistic activity. The translation of (8) into a sentence with a negated modal past sheds more light on the status of the grammatical subject هو) /He) as an object of discourse, not an autonomous agent. The utterer considers that it was wrong for X to believe such nonsense. The direct object (*such nonsense*) serves as a justification of the judgement passed by the major player in the utterance, i.e. the linguistic subject. It is noteworthy that the triggers of any phase-two meta-negator differ from one utterance to another according to the enunciative strategy at work in the context of production and reception alone.

5.1.3   Inter-Operation Analysis

In the previous section, the approach to *lam* and *maa* is intra-operational, i.e. the two negators are contrasted as different realizations of the same operation. The present section explores negation (NEG) in relation to affirmation (AFF), the polar opposite of negation. Such extension is expected to provide further elucidation on the status and the working of the two negators in Arabic. However, this inter-operational contrastivity should on no account lead to considering *lam* and *maa*, or any other negators, as the negative duplicates of the affirmative markers they are contrasted with. In fact, each linguistic utterance is governed and justified by its unique context of production and reception. In the present case, the NEG-AFF opposition is rooted in the assumption that the symmetry detected is not between affirmative and negative markers, but between the two phases in both poles.

What is said about the strategies and the role of the linguistic subject in negation is valid for affirmative utterances too. Consider (9) and (10) below:

(9)   هي تشتري ملابسها من محلات هارودز.

hiyya tashtarii malaabisahaa min maḥallaati Harrods
She buys her clothes at Harrods.

(10)   إنّها تشتري ملابسها من محلّات هارودز.

'innahaa tashtarii malaabisahaa min maḥallaati Harrods
She's buying her clothes at Harrods.

If the difference between the two utterances is particularly noticeable in the absence of *'inna* (Ø) in (9) and its presence in (10), what really distinguishes this grammatical pair is their context of *production* and their structures. A possible context of (9) is the co-utterer's question (*Where does she buy her clothes from?*). A short answer (*From Harrods*) is expected given the most important piece of information it includes. The marker (Ø) encodes the non-intervenient speaker strategy where the linguistic subject acts just as information provider, whereas in (10) the utterer endorses the predicative relation {S-P}:{*hiyya* – tashtarii malaabisahaa min maḥallaati Harrods}

{she – buys her clothes at Harrods}

In fact, the context of (10) includes not an information seeker, but a co-utterer expressing 'amazement at the great elegance of the lady'. Therefore, if (9) informs about the place where (*she*) buys her clothes, the purpose of (10) is completely different: the speaker talks about the grammatical subject (*she*) and assigns her the property (*buying-clothes-at-Harrod's*), a phrase nominalized by the operator (-*ing*) and in which (*at Harrods*) is not a new piece of information. A phase-two metaoperator encoding a justification strategy of the utterer, *'inna* has a metalinguistic status, works outside the predicative relation, obstructs reference to the extralinguistic, puts the grammatical subject in the accusative and announces that the strategy engaged by the utterer is the key to understand and therefore to translate the utterance. As shown in a previous work [46, p. 181] and [48, p. 224], the working of *'inna* in Arabic offers a comfortable validation of this analysis; in fact, its emergence in discourse automatically puts the grammatical subject in the accusative.

The grammatical subject is stripped of its original mark of agentivity (the nominative) to bear the accusative case which marks grammatical objects in Arabic. In English, the metaoperator (Be + ing) is the effective solution to render (10). Thus, the major difference between (9) and (10) is related neither to tense nor to aspect, but to the two phases at work in discourse. This leads to the provisional conclusion that the two phases define the line of symmetry between affirmation and negation markers in SA.

5.2   *Lam* Vs. *Lammaa* : Intra- and Inter-Operation Analysis

5.2.1   Corpus

(11)   استوفيت الكتاب ولمّا يتنفّس الفجر . / Istawfeitu-l-kitaaba wa lammaa yatanaffasi-l-fajru
Dawn had not come up yet when I finished the book.

(12)   لا يزال يذكر حينما انتزعوه من أمّه ولمّا يبلغ الخامسة من عمره .
Laa yazaalu uḏkuru ḥiinamaa intaza'uuhu min 'ummihi
He can still recall when they snatched him away from his mother, he not yet having reached five years old.

5.2.2   Analysis

Lam and *lammaa* are approached in opposition because they share the following properties: they are verbal negators, they affect a verb morphologically in the mudhaari' and grammatically denoting the past, they work to fill an information deficit, and both have a phase-one status. However, if *lam*, as seen above, encodes the non-validity of the predicative relation in the context of the past and introduces a closed relation {R}, i.e. a finished act; *lamma*, often an inter-verbal negator, as in (13):

(13) احلّ الضيف ولمّا يصل المضيّف / ! halla-ḍ-ḍaifu wa lammaa yaṣil almuḍhayyifu
The guest was here but the host had not arrived yet!

emerges in contexts always implying a probable prospective validation of the predicative relation. An aspectual negator, *lammaa* denotes a verbal event which has not occurred up to the time of speech but is likely to happen in the future. The predicative relation is therefore awaiting realization {R} and this is what explains why *lamma*, unlike *lam,* is incompatible with conditional markers, such as إن / *'in* and إذا / *'iḏaa*. The aspectual behavior of *lammaa* is detectable in (11) and (12) which include an implied aspectual adverb (*baʻdu/yet*). Whether explicit or not, this adverb is inherent in any utterance with *lammaa*. In the English translation, a negated present perfect is often the most viable solution. In fact, the adverb (*baʻdu/yet*) belongs to a class of negative polarity items conveyors of an aspectual value and associated with the past, present and future times:

- *lam ... qaṭṭu (lam* +past time-oriented never)
- lammaa... baʻdu (lammaa + not yet)
- *lan...'abadan (lan* +future time-oriented never)

Qaṭṭu and *'abadan* convey maximization values in the past and the future, respectively.

5.2.3   Inter-Operation Analysis

Traditional grammarians, such as [52, vol. 3 p. 117] and [41, vol. 1, p. 458], have already detected a bilateral symmetry between the negator *lammaa* and the affirmative verbal marker *qad* when it affects a verb in the past. Yet, the opposition should include *lammaa* and the aspectual *laqad,* instead of the epistemic modal *qad.* The latter always affects either verbs in the past to encode a high degree of speaker certainty, or with verbs in the mudhaariʻ (imperfective) to encode uncertainty or doubt. Therefore, like the affirmative *'inna,* *qad* is a speaker visibility marker in discourse and assumes a modal not an aspectual function. *Laqad,* however, indicates completeness of the verbal event in the past and that is why an English perfective, often with *already,* emerges in translation, like in (13), (14), and (15):

(13) سيّدي، لقد وصل ضابط الشرطة وهو الآن في المختبر.
Sayidii, laqad waṣala ḍhaabiṭu-sh-shurṭati wahwa-l-'aana fi-l-mukhtabari
Sir, the police officer has (already) arrived. He is now in the lab.

(14) عفوا ! لقد نفد رصيدكم ./ 'afwaa laqa nafada raṣiidukum
Sorry, you have exhausted your balance.

(15) لقد أذاعوا البيان العسكري للتّو. / Laqad 'adhaaʻu-l-bayaana li-t-tawwi
They have just broadcast the military communiqué.

Intralingually, the aspectual behavior of *lammaa* is in symmetry with that of the affirmative *laqad.* It is noteworthy that *aspect* and *modality* in Arabic have been under-researched in traditional and contemporary research, and are entirely absent from pedagogical grammar. Viable Arabic equivalents for the terms *aspect* and *modality* and their derivatives are still to be coined [47]. Didactically, this has not been without adverse implications on translation students who encounter difficulties in negotiating effective translation to the English aspectual and modal markers [1, 16, 20, 35, 36, 50, and 58].

5.3   *Leisa* vs. *Ma* : Intra- and Inter-Operational Analysis

5.3.1   Corpus

(13)   ليس كل ما تقرأه في كتب التاريخ صحيحا .
Not everything you read in history books is true.

(14)   ا تنتظره منها ليس بالأمر الهيّن. / maa tantaḍhiruhu minhaa leisa bi-l'amri-lhaiyyini
What you expect from her is not a trivial matter.

(15)   ما كل ما يتمنى المرء يدركه. / maa kullu ma yatamanna-l-mar'u yudrikuhu
Nothing ever happens exactly as one would wish.

(16)   ما هذا بشرا. / maa haḍaa basharan/
This is not a human being! (This is not other than a noble angel!)

(17)   ما أنا بمهمل لواجباتي. / maa 'anaa bi-muhmilin li-waajibaatii
I am not careless about my duties.

5.3.2   Analysis

Traditional grammarians disagreed about *leisa* as a grammatical category. Some, like Ibn Al-Sarraj (in [15, vol. 2, p. 73], argue that it is a particle, while for Sibaweihi and his followers it is a verb. In Al-Horais [17], *leisa* is categorized as a verb, a particle and an adverb. Using a corpus of artificial sentences, Al-Horais incorrectly considers that *leisa* "can be replaced by *maa kaana*" [17, p. 10]. *Leisa* and *maa*, as explained below, have different statuses and are opposable, but not interchangeable.

   Leisa is a partly conjugable negator that works in three different structural contexts: as an auxiliary verb in verbal sentences, like in (18) below, a lexical verb in nominal sentences, such as in (19), and as an operator in stripping constructions (20).

(18)   ليس يعلم ما تخبّئه له الأيّام. / leisa ya'lamu maa tukhabbi'uhu lahu-l-'ayyaamu.
He doesn't know what the future holds for him.

(19)   هذه معضلة أخرى ليس لها تفسير. / haaḍihi mu'ḍilatun 'ukhraa laisa lahaa tafseerun.
This is another inexplicable dilemma.

(20)   هي تنتظر منك اعتذارا وليس تبريرا. / Hiyya tantaḍhiru i'tiḍaaran wa leisa tabriiran
She is expecting an apology, not a justification.

Compared with the negator *maa* approached in 6.1 above, *leisa* is not associated with an intervenient speaker strategy. Whenever used, it denotes the non-occurrence of the predicative relation, hence its referential or world-oriented, not metalinguistic, value. In (13) and (14), *leisa* is a phase-one inherently negative copula (be + not) associated with the time of discourse in (14), and with a timeless event in (13). The examples (15–17), which include negation with *maa*, are also possible with *leisa*, but with different contextual triggers and meanings. As seen above, *maa* is an anaphoric negator that presupposes an antecedent contextual element, whereas *leisa* poses and negates a new relationship anchored in the time of discourse. (16) is an interesting example as it is possible with the two negators, *maa* and *leisa*. Embarrassed by the structural similarities between the two sentences, Sibaweihi claims that *maa* in (16) and *leisa* are interchangeable [21]. (16) is in fact a case of what Ducrot [34] and Horn [39] and [40] call metalinguistic negation, i.e. when negation is not a truth-functional statement. In this case we have "a formally negative utterance which is used to object to a previous utterance on any grounds whatever, including the way it was pronounced" [40, p. 374]. This is confirmed by the context of the Quranic narrative about prophet Joseph; when he was introduced to the Egyptian women - who are the linguistic subject in (16) - they were too mesmerized by his unearthly beauty to believe he was an ordinary man. *Leisa*, a world-oriented negator, would require a totally different context:

(20) أنظري إلى عينيه الغائرتين وجبهته النّاتئة. لا لا! **ليس** هذا بشرا. لابدّ أنّه مخلوق فضائي.

'unḍurii 'ilaa 'ainaihi-l-ghaa'irataini wa jabhatihi-n- naati'ati. Laa laa! leisa haḍaa basharan; Laa budda 'annahu makhluuqun faḍaa'iyyun.

Look at his receding eyes and swollen forehead! No, no! this is not a human being. This must be an extraterrestrial!

The importance of (17) is that the negator *maa* works with the preposition *bi-*:

maa 'anaa **bi**-muhmilin li-waajibaatii / *I am not careless about my duties.*

This discontinuous phase-two negator [*maa ...bi...*] has its correlative discontinuous marker in affirmation, ['*inna ...la...*], such as in:

(21) إنّني لمهمل لواجباتي! / '*inna*-nii **la**-muhmilun li-waajibaatii
Definitely, I am careless about my duties.

In traditional grammar, *bi-* in negation with *maa* or *leisa* is treated as a redundant preposition, and *la-* a corroborative particle. In fact, these two operators, which have no clear equivalents in English, constitute the predicative node and the scope of the phase-two markers *maa* and '*inna* respectively.

5.4 *Laa* vs. *Lan* : Intra- and Inter-Operation Analysis

5.4.1 Corpus

(22) **لا** تدور الشمس حول الأرض / Laa taduuru-sh-shamsu ḥawla-l-'arḍi
The sun does not revolve around the earth.

(23) أراك **لا** تبالي حتى بما يجري من حولك
I see that you don't even care what's going on around you.

(24) لم يستهينوا بك يا سيّدي، انّهم فقط **لا** يفهمون شيئا ممّا تقول.
They are not disrespectful sir, they just haven't understood anything of what you are saying.

(25) **لا** يدخل الجنة قاطع رحم. / laa yadkhulu-l-jannata qaaṭi'u raḥimin
He who severs family bonds will not go into paradise.

(26) **فلن** أكلّم اليوم إنسيا. / Fa-*lan* 'ukallima-l-yawma 'insiyyan
Therefore, I shall not speak this day to any human being.

(27) ولا تمش في الأرض مرحا إنّك لن تخرق الأرض **ولن** تبلغ الجبال طولا.
And walk not in the land exultant, for you cannot cut through the earth nor stretch to the height of the mountains.

(28) **إن** أدع ما حصل يفسد طموحي وآمالي... **لن** أفعل. **لن** أستسلم، سأقاوم!
I won't let what happened ruin my hopes... I shall not. I shall not surrender. I shall resist!

5.4.2 Analysis

If in verbal negation *lan* works always with a muḍaari' commonly associated with reference to futurity - 'al 'istiqbaalu / الاستقبال - *laa* is possible in four temporal contexts: in timeless events (22), in the present - 'al-ḥaalu / 23) - الحال and 24), in the future (25), and not often in the past (30) when it joins alternatives:

(30) فلا صدّق ولا صلّى. / fa-laa ṣaddaqa wa laa ṣallaa
For he neither believed, nor prayed.

In nominal negation, the use of *laa* is associated with the time of speech:

(31) لا حاجة لي بكل هذه الأدوات لأفكّ برغيا!
laa ḥaajata lii bi-kulli heḍihi-l-'adawaati li 'afukka burghiyyan
I don't need all these tools to unscrew a screw.

Whatever its context of use, *laa* conveys a core grammatical value: it signals that the non-validity of R is a new piece of information not endorsed by the linguistic subject. A comparison with *lan* is expected to elucidate the working of both negators.

A yes/no question is a possible context for *laa* in (22); the questioner seeks information that is provided by the questioned. An answer with *lan* would be ungrammatical, even though well-formed. *Lan* is a modalizing negator typical of contexts conveying a guarantee of the linguistic subject that R will not take place. In (28), where *it* is used three times, *lan* is a phase-two negator which encodes the speaker's sheer determination 'to achieve her goals', thus conveying a deontic modality. *laa* is not compatible with such a context. In English, the negator *not* and the modal marker are always discrete even when they are in a contracted form (*mustn't*), but in Arabic the distinction is between modalizing and non-modalizing negators. This may induce translation students into confusion, especially in comparison with English. (32), (33) and (34) are pertinent examples of the interplay between negation and modality (M):

(32) يجب أن **لا** يتخلّف عن الموعد. / yajibu 'an **laa** ytakhallafa 'ani-l-maw'idi
/ Must - not – he – miss the appointment /

(33) **لا** يجب أن يتخلّف عن الموعد. / **laa** yajibu 'an ytakhallafa 'ani-l-maw'idi
/ Not – must – he – miss the appointment /

(34) أعرفه جيّدا، إنّه **لن** يتخلّف عن الموعد مهما كانت العواقب.
'a'rifuhu jaiyyidan, 'innahu **lan** ytakhallafa 'ani-l-maw'idi
I know him very well, he won't be missing the appointment, no matter what happens.

The following configurations visualize the difference between (32) and (33) (Fig. 2):

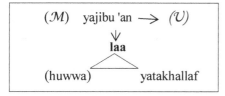
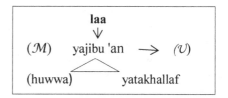

Fig. 2. Interaction of negation and modality

Even though the figure clearly shows the scope of the negator, R in (32) and M in (33), it does not totally eliminate semantic ambiguity resulting from the mobility of the negator and the modal; in fact 24 out of 25 translation students surveyed for this article provided the same English translation for both sentences (*He must not miss this meeting.*). Only one trainee suggested *mustn't* for (32) and *must not* for (33).

Lan in (34) is possible with the same predicative relation (*He / miss the meeting*), but it is neither triggered by the same context of (32) and (33) nor does it convey the same grammatical value or translation. The presence of the epistemic modal marker *'inna*, which encodes certainty of U, in the context of *lan*, itself a modal negator, over-modalizes the utterance and complicates the task of the translator. 19 students out of 25 (76%) provided the same English translation to (34), an utterance with *inna + lan*, and (35) an utterance without *'inna* (Ø).

(35)   أعرفه جيّدا، Ø هو لن يتخلّف عن الموعد مهما كانت العواقب.

> *I know him very well, he will not be missing the appointment, no matter what happens.*

The utterances were given separately for translation in two different tasks. The respondents who suggested different translations used a modal adverb, such as *definitely*, to render *'inna*. In (23), (24) and (25), *Laa* has the same phase-1 status and conveys the same referential value. The modal *'inna* in (24) takes scope over a predicative relation negated by *laa*. The context of (23), (24) and (25) are not permeable to *lan*. (26) is a very interesting example as it refutes the claim of temporality associated with negators. The time locator of R is the adverb *'al-yawma / today*, *lan* is there to convey a deontic modality, like in (28). (27) is slightly different as *lan* is an epistemic modal negator conveying certainty, not determination. A phase-1 negator, *laa* would be ungrammatical in the contexts of (26), (27) and (28).

6   Conclusion

The paper has proposed a metaoperational analysis of the major verbal and nominal negators in SA and has demonstrated that the metalinguistic richness of negation in SA, compared with the single formal negator (*not*) in English, is governed by an underlying binary microsystem (phase 1 phase 2 vector) that accounts for this diversity. *Lam, maa, leisa, lammaa, laa, lan,* and *kallaa* are in fact more effectively understood, taught, learned, and translated when they are approached from the perspective of the language user and the processing strategy at work in discourse. The dominant approach in theoretical and pedagogical grammar is too reductionist to account for the working of negators in SA. By direct assigning of meaning to formal markers, it simply confounds the linguistic with the extralinguistic and induces learners and translators into error and mistranslation. Yet, the diversity of negation markers in Arabic provides a highly significant case of operators which convey referential, metalinguistic, modal, and aspectual values. The interaction of operations, such as reference to time, aspect, and modality with negation is still to be investigated from a corpus-based explicative perspective. This is expected to provide valuable assistance especially to language learners, translation trainees and computational linguistics.

Tables 1 and 2 recapitulate the key findings related to the application of the binary *microsystem underlying discourse:*

Table 1. Intra-operation Contrastivity

Negation		
Phase 1	vs.	Phase 2
lam	vs.	maa
lamma	vs.	no equivalent
leisa	vs.	maa
laa	vs.	lan
laa	vs.	kallaa
leisa...bi...	vs.	maa...bi...

Table 2. Inter-operation Contrastivity

Negation	vs.	Affirmation
lam	vs.	$\emptyset + v_{+ \text{past}}$
maa	vs.	'inna
lamma	vs.	laqad
laa	vs.	$\emptyset + v_{+ \text{imperf.}}$
lan	vs.	sa-/sawfa
maa...bi...	vs.	'inna...la...
laa	vs.	na'am
'ajal	vs.	kallaa

References

1. Abu-Judeh, M., Asassfeh, S.M., Al-Shaboul, Y., Alshboul, S.: Translating arabic perfect verbs into english by jordanian undergraduates. J. Lang. Lit. **4**(2), 44–53 (2013)
2. Adamczewski, H.: Be + ing Revisited. New Insights in Applied Linguistics. 45–75 (1974)
3. Adamczewski, H.: Be + -ing dans la Grammaire de l'Anglais. Atelier de reproduction des thèses, Lille (1976)
4. Adamczewski, H., Delmas, C.: Grammaire Linguistique de L'Anglais. Armand Colin, Paris (1982)
5. Adamczewski, H.: Le Français déchiffré, Clé du langage et des langues. Armand Colin, Paris (1991)
6. Adamczewski, H.: Genèse et développement d'une théorie linguistique. La TILV éditeur, Paris (1996)
7. Adamczewski, H.:. http://henriadamczewski.perso.libertysurf.fr/index.html. Last accessed on 22 Feb 2019
8. Adamczewski, H.: The Secret Architecture of English Grammar. EMA, Précy-sur-Oise (2002)

9. Al Istiraabaaḏi, R.E.: Sharḥu Kaafiyati Ibn Al ḥaajib. Daar Al kutubi Al'ilmiyyati, Beirut (1998)
10. Al Jurjani, A.: Dalaa'ilu-l-'i'jaaz. Ed. Mohamed Abdah and Rachid Ridha. Daar Mofem Publications, Algiers (1991)
11. Al Khaliil, A.: Al 'ain. Mu'assasatu Al 'A'lamii li-l-Maṭbuu'aati, Beirut (1988)
12. Al Mubarrad, M.Y.: Al Muqtadhab. vol. 1, Aalamu Al kutubi, Beirut (1963)
13. Al Muraadii, H.Q.: Al Janaa al Daanii fii Ḥuruufi-l-Ma'aanii. Dar Al 'Aafaaq, Beirut (1983)
14. Al Suyuti, J.E.: Ham'u Al Hawaami' fii Sharḥi Jam'i-l-Jawaami'. Dar Al kutubi Al 'ilmiyyati, Beirut (1998)
15. Al Suyuti, J.E.: Al Ashbaahu Wa Al Nadhaair fi Al Nahwi. vol. 1, Part 3. Mu'assasatu Al Risaalati. Beirut (1985)
16. Al-Fallay, I.: English tenses and aspects: are they too difficult for Arab learners to master? Abhath Al-Yarmouk 15 (4), (1999)
17. Al-Horais, N.: On negation and focus in standard arabic: interface-based approach. J. Univ. Lang. **18**(1), 1–34 (2017)
18. Al-Mabkhout, Ch.: 'Inshaa'u-n-Nafyi. Markazu Al Nashri al Jaami'ii, Tunis (2006)
19. Al-Makhzumi, M.: Fi-n-Naḥwi-l-'arabii: Naqdun wa Tawjiihun. Daar Al Raa'id Al 'Arabii. (1986)
20. AI-Qinai, J.: On Translating Modals. Translation and Interpreting Studies, 3(1&2), 30–67 (2008)
21. Al Qortubi, M.A.: 'aljaami' li 'aḥkaami-l-Qur'aani, Mu'assasati Al Risaalati, Beirut (2006)
22. Al Zajjaaj, A.I.: Kitaabu Fa'alat wa 'af'alat.. Al Sharikatu-l-Muttaḥidatu li Al Attawzii' (1984)
23. Al Zamakhshari, M.O.: Asaasu Al Balaaghati. Daar Al Kutubi, Beirut (1973)
24. Al Zamakhshari, M.O.: Al Mufaṣṣal fii 'ilmi-l-Lughati. Daar 'Iḥyaa'i-l- 'uluumi, Beirut (1990)
25. Amaira, K.A.: Fi-t-Taḥliili-l-lughawii: Manhajun Wasfii Taḥliilii. Al Zarqaa', Maktabatu-lManaari (1987)
26. Benmamoun, E.: The Feature Structuire of Functional Categories: A Comparative Study of Arabic Dialects. OUP, Oxford & New York (2000)
27. Benveniste, E.: Problèmes de linguistique générale I. Gallimard, Paris (1966)
28. Benveniste, E.: Problèmes de linguistique générale II. Gallimard, Paris (1974)
29. Culioli, A.: Pour une Linguistique de L'énonciation. Ophrys, Paris (1990)
30. Delechelle, G.: L'expression de la cause en anglais contemporain: étude de quelques connecteurs et operations. A.N.R.T, Lille (1989)
31. Delmas, C.: Quelques éléments de la métalangue naturelle. Unpublished doctoral dissertation. Université de Paris III (1980)
32. Delmas, C., Girard, G.: Grammaire métaopérationnelle et théorie des phases. Pierre Cotte, et al., Les Théories de la grammaire anglaise en France, 97–124. Hachette, Paris (1993)
33. Delmas, Adams: Deléchelle, Girard, Lancri & Naudé: Faits de langue, faits de discours en anglais. Editions de l'Espace Européen, La Garenne-Colombes (1992)
34. Ducrot, O.: Dire et ne pas dire: principes de la semantique linguistique. Hermann, Paris (1972)
35. El-Hassan, S.: Expressing modality in english and standard Arabic. J. King Saudi Univ. **2**(2), 149–166 (1990)
36. Farghal, M., Shunnaq, A.: Translation with reference to english and arabic: a practical guide. Dar Al-Hilal for Translation, Irbid (1999)
37. Fassi-Fehri, A.: Issues in the Structure of Arabic Clauses and Words. Kluwer, Dordrecht (1993)
38. Hamasa, A.M.: Bunyatu-l-jumlati-l'arabiyya. Daar Ghariib li-n-nashri, Cairo (2003)

39. Horn, L.R.: Metalinguistic negation and pragmatic ambiguity. Language **61**(1), 121–174 (1985)
40. Horn, Laurence R.: A Natural History of Negation. University of Chicago Press, Chicago (1989)
41. Ibn Al Sarraaj, A.B.: Al 'Uṣuul fi –n-Naḥwi. Mu'assasata al Risaalati. Beirut (1999)
42. Ibn Hisham, J.: Mughni-l-labiib 'an kutubi-l-'a'aariib, vol. 1. Daar Al Fikr, Beirut (1979)
43. Ibn Jinni, O.: Al Khasaa'is. Dar Al Kitab, Beirut (1952)
44. Ibn Saiyidih, A.H.: Al Mukhaṣṣiṣ. Daar 'iḥyaa'I 'atturaathi-l-'arabii, Beirut (1996)
45. Ibn Ya'iish, A.B.: Sharḥu-lMufassal. Daar al kutub Al 'ilmiyyati, Beirut (2001)
46. Jespersen, O.: Negation in English and other languages. A.F. Høst, Copenhagen (1917)
47. Kahlaoui, M.H.: Theoretical linguistics in the service of translation. building bridges: integrating language, linguistics, literature, and translation in english studies. In: Al Zidjali, N. (ed.) 183-200. Cambridge Scholars Publishing, UK (2009)
48. Kahlaoui, M.H.: A framework for the description and analysis of modality in standard Arabic. Arab World Eng. J. **4**, 214–233 (2015)
49. Leech, G.: Meaning and the English Verb. Longman, London (1971)
50. Mansour, A.S.: Difficulties in Translation of the English Present Perfect Simple and the Past Perfect Simple into Arabic and Some Suggested Solutions. Al 'ustaadh. Anbaar University, 200 (2012). https://www.iasj.net/iasj?func=fulltext&aId=30087. Last accessed on 2 Feb 2019
51. Ouhalla, J.: The Structure and Logical Form of Negative Sentences in Arabic
52. Shlonsky, U. (ed.) Themes in Arabic and Hebrew Syntax, 299–320. Kluwer, Dordrecht (2002)
53. Santin-Guettier, A-M., Toupin, F.: Adamczewski, Henri. In: Brown, K. (ed.). Encyclopedia of Language & Linguistics. pp. 48–9, (2006). https://doi.org/10.1016/b0-08-044854-2/02414-7. ISBN 978-0-08-044854-1. Last accessed on 15 Feb 2019
54. Shlonsky, U.: Clause Structure and Word Order in Hebrew and Arabic: An Essay in Comparative Semitic Syntax. Oxford University Press, New York (1997)
55. Sibaweihi, A.O.: Al Kitaab. Khanji Library, Cairo (1992)
56. Toupin, F.: La philosophie spontannee d'un savant. Anglophonia, 20. (2015)
57. Versteegh, K.: Landmarks in Linguistic Thought III: the Arabic linguistic tradition. Routledge, London (1997)
58. Zhiri, Y.: The translation of tense and aspect from english into arabic by moroccan undergraduates: difficulties and solutions. Arab World Eng. J. **5**(4), 288–296 (2014)
59. Al-Sajustaanii, A.H.: Kitaabu Fa'alat wa 'af'alat. Daar Saadir, Beirut (1979)

Skew Correction and Text Line Extraction of Arabic Historical Documents

Abdelhay Zoizou$^{(\boxtimes)}$, Arsalane Zarghili, and Ilham Chaker

Faculty of Sciences and Technologies, USMBA-Fez, Fes, Morocco
{abdelhay.zoizou,arsalane.zarghili,
Ilham.chaker}@usmba.ac.ma

Abstract. The field of optical character recognition for the Arabic text is not getting much attention by researchers comparing to Latin text. It is only in the last two decades that this field was being exploited, due to the complexity of Arabic writing and the fact that it demands a critical step which is segmentation; first from text to lines, then from lines to words and finally from words to characters. In case of historical documents, the segmentation is more complicated because of the absence of writing rules and the poor quality of documents. In this paper we present a projection-based technique for the segmentation of text into lines of ancient Arabic documents. To override the problem of overlapping and touching lines which is the most challenging problem facing the segmentation systems, firstly, pre-processing operations are applied for binarization and noise reduction. Secondly a skew correction technique is proposed beside a space following algorithm which is performed to separate lines from each other. The segmentation method is applied on four representations of the text image, including an original binary image and other three representations obtained by transforming the input image into: (1) smeared image with RLSA algorithm, (2) up-to-down transitions, (3) smoothed image by gaussian filter. The obtained results are promising and they are compared in term of accuracy and time cost. These methods are evaluated on a private set of 129 historical documents images provided by Al-Qaraouiyine Library.

Keywords: Arabic text line segmentation · Historical documents · Projection · Skew correction

1 Introduction

Since the beginning of research on optically captured text recognition of Arabic printed and handwritten text, the work on historical documents is still poor and not much researches could be found in literature, although there is a huge number of ancient documents in libraries and archives. These ancient documents contain important records either artistic, scientific, or referring to historical events. These files have not been digitally exploited yet, because the processing of ancient text is much different and harder than the processing of modern printed or handwritten text, especially for the Arabic text. The tasks of segmentation and recognition are more complicated due to the nature of Arabic writing and variety of shapes, where in most of Arabic ancient text there is a lot of additional signs and diacritics as shown in Fig. 1. The Arabic writing is

© Springer Nature Switzerland AG 2019
K. Smaïli (Ed.): ICALP 2019, CCIS 1108, pp. 181–193, 2019.
https://doi.org/10.1007/978-3-030-32959-4_13

done from right to left and each character can have different shapes depending on its position in the word Fig. 2.

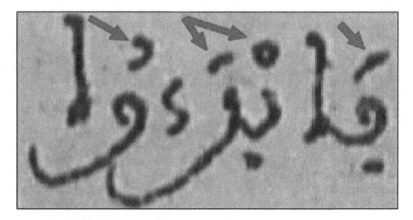

Fig. 1. Additional diacritic signs

Following the analytical approach, the recognition of an Arabic text must include a major step which is the segmentation of text into small classifiable units. To do this, the text must be decomposed first into lines and then into words and finally into characters [1]. One of the most challenging tasks for all text line extraction systems is the segmentation of overlapping and touching lines especially when dealing with skewed text. In this paper, we describe first, the pre-processing operations to be applied to the text image. Then, we propose a projection-based process to correct the skew of the text and to extract text lines by finding the path separating overlapping and touching lines.

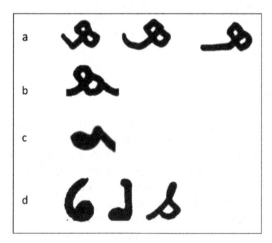

Fig. 2. Shapes of the same letter (ھ). a: in the beginning, b: in the middle, c: in the end, d: isolated

Historical documents have always presented a challenge to the segmentation systems, not only on the first level of text to line segmentation but also for line to words and word to characters. As handwritten, ancient text is often skewed and many additional signs could be found (Fig. 1), and it is written randomly with the pen thickness that changes frequently from one word to another.

OCR systems had always the challenge to find the right segmentation path between handwritten lines, either for Arabic or other languages. Multiple approaches have been adopted to deal with line segmentation problem; in [2], an overview of works on segmentation of Handwritten Document was presented. Authors of [3] proposed a language independent method for text line extraction. The Partial projection method was adopted in [4–6]. It is based on calculating the projection profile in multiple columns of the document. The clustering approach was adopted in many works on segmentation [7–9]. In [10], An algorithm based on adaptive local connectivity map was proposed for line extraction from historical documents. Authors in [11] developed a new cost function that considers the interactions between text lines and the curvilinearity of each text line. Recently, the problem of text line extraction starts having attention by deep learning researches, where in [12], deep convolutional network has been used for the segmentation of text lines of historical Latin documents.

The lines of text in Arabic historical documents are very close to each other and the distance between lines may also change many times in the same document. All these facts give the effect of overlapping and touching lines as indicated in Fig. 3. Lines overlapping effect occurs when ascenders and descenders of two successive lines share the same horizontal position. While touching line effect occurs when a descender of the first line meets an ascender of the second line. Another common challenge between Arabic Optical processing systems dealing with ancient documents is the absence of standard databases, although there is a huge number of historical documents in libraries.

This paper is structured as follows: some previous works are presented in Sects. 2, and 3 describes the contributions of this work; First the algorithm of skew correction is presented. Then, the four presentations of the text image are described and the process of line extraction is explained. Finally, the experimental setup and discussion of the results are presented in Sect. 4 and the conclusions and future work in Sect. 5.

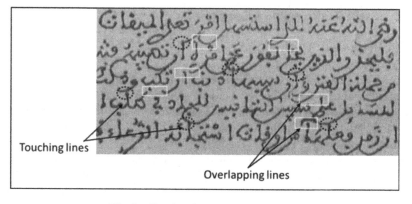

Fig. 3. Overlapping and touching lines

2   Previous Works

The task of text line extraction has been discussed since the very beginning of the OCR systems. The text line extraction is an important task in the process of segmentation which is the second step of a character-based recognition system. The text line extraction process depends on the nature of text, we found several methods applied for printed text as well as for the handwritten text. In 2001, authors in [4] proposed a method for text line segmentation, it is applied on modern handwritten text. The method is based on a combination of partial projection technique and partial contour. Authors claimed having a segmentation success rate of 82%, but the method fails in case of touching lines and the presence of diacritics signs.

Since then many approaches have been developed to deal with the special case of historical documents either for Latin [2, 3, 7, 8, 10], Chinese [9, 11], or Bangla [5]. Although, the work on the Arabic documents is still not getting much attention. In order to segment Arabic text lines, authors in [6] segment a page into columns, and they separate each column into blocks by using partial projection. Then, they use a KNN algorithm to classify each block into three classes depending on its dimensions: a class of big blocks representing overlapping components, a class for diacritic signs, and a class for words. The method has been tested for both printed and handwritten Latin text and only printed Arabic text, but no final success rate was given. In [13], a method for text line extraction from historical Arabic was developed. Its process goes first by detecting multi-skewed zones using an automatic paving and the Winger-Ville Distribution. Then the orientation of each zone and the baseline are analyzed to extract lines. Authors claim having a segmentation rate of 98.6%. This method is still weak in case of false inclinations and false maxima which is due to diacritics appearing in the beginning of the line.

Recently, machine learning techniques have been adopted to line extraction. In [12] authors used a method based on Convolutional Neural Network for Latin text line extraction from historical documents. Firstly, a patch size is identified on the basis of an overall text line distance. The CNN is fed for training with several patches. Then the CNN model is used for line segmentation. This method has been evaluated by using two sets of Latin databases and no results have been revealed. The use of CNNs is still unavailable in case of Arabic historical text because of the absence of a standard database of Arabic historical documents.

3   The Proposed Method

Text line segmentation is the operation of extraction of a text line separately with all its words and characters. In this work, the segmentation is done by using a projection profile-based method. The projection profile of a text image in a particular direction refers to the running count of the black pixels in that direction [14]. In our case, we use a horizontal projection.

The text in historical documents is often skewed because it is written by hand and the tools used did not help to write straightly on the line. For Arabic, writing was more difficult because lines were being written too close to each other with many ascenders, descenders and additional signs. This produce often the problem of more overlapping and touching between lines. The problem that was always the main challenge facing segmentation systems either for Latin or Arabic text. Even the most accurate systems haven't found a complete solution for the problem of overlapping and touching lines.

To address the line segmentation problem of historical Arabic documents, we propose a method based on projection first to correct skew angle of the whole page text at once, and then to separate lines. Before applying the segmentation and skew correction process, the text image is first being subject to some pre-processing operations including: Binarization and noise reduction. The method is tested on four different representations of the text image (Fig. 4). These representations were obtained by applying three transformations: smearing with RLSA algorithm, conversion into up-to-down transitions, and finally a gaussian smoothing.

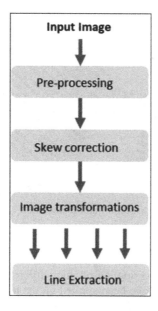

Fig. 4. The process of segmentation

3.1 Skew Correction

Skew correction problem has been discussed since decades. Many techniques have been used since then. But Hough Transform [15] and projection [14] are still the most used and efficient. Our skew correction process is based on horizontal projection which has been chosen to provide simplicity and efficiency and also for its rapidity. The algorithm is based on the calculating of the maximum peak of the projection profile of the text image in multiple rotations. But the weakness of this method is known face to overlapping and condensed lines; When applying the algorithm of skew correction on the original binary image, a false angle may be found, because often the orthogonal of a condensed text image has more pixels than lines, so that when rotating the image and calculating the projection profile, the maximum peak corresponds to this angle (Fig. 5).

Therefore, the original binary text image is first transformed into its up-to-down transitions (Fig. 6b). For each column of the binary image, only the black-to-white transitions are kept. The main goals of this transformation are first, to override the problem of condensed lines, and then to reduce the processed information to speed up the process because of the fact that the up-to-down transitions represent the baseline position and consequently the skew angle could be obtained by processing only the transitions.

The transition image is rotated in a range of angles [-a, a], with "a" is the fixed angle value. In each rotation, projection profile is calculated and its maximum value is saved as shown in Fig. 7. The principle is that the highest peak will be obtained by best rotation angle which gives straight lines since horizontal projection is used.

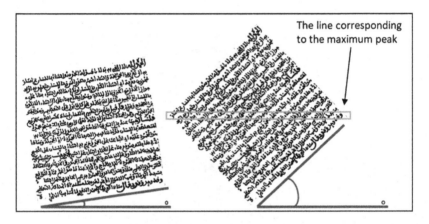

Fig. 5. False skew correction due to condensed and overlapped lines

3.2   Image Transformations

The process of segmentation is applied on four different representations of the text image. Three transformations have been applied on the text image (Fig. 8). The results of segmentation using each representation are compared to the original binary image (Fig. 8a). The first transformation is obtained by using Run length Smoothing Algorithm (RLSA) [16]. The algorithm is a smoothing technique that blacken the space between two black pixels in a single row or column. The white space is blacked if its size is less than a predefined threshold. It can be applied either on horizontal or vertical directions (Fig. 8b). The second transformation consists in converting the original binary image into its left-to-right and up-to-down black-white transitions. (Fig. 8c). The choice of keeping right transitions came from the fact that both Arabic writing and segmentation are done from right to left. While bottom transitions are chosen because they represent the baseline of the words and consequently the position of the line. The third and final transformation is done by using a binary gaussian filter. Similar to RLSA, the BGF transformation consists in applying a gaussian blur filter to add gray pixels between black pixels. Gaussian blur is a blurring technique based on a gaussian function which calculates the transformations to apply on a pixel. Then we apply a thresholding to convert the added gray pixel into black. (Fig. 8d).

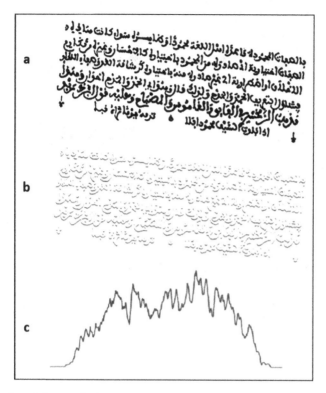

Fig. 6. Example of input of skew correction. a: original text image. b: its transitions transformation. c: its horizontal projection profile

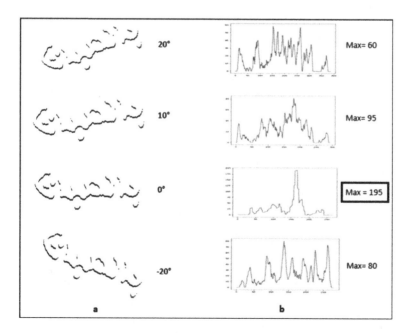

Fig. 7. Detection of the best angle for skew correction

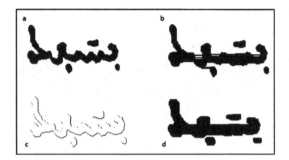

Fig. 8. Transformations applied to the text image. a: original image, b: transitions image, c: RLSA image, d: Binary gaussian transformation.

3.3 Text Line Segmentation

Text lines in historical documents are written too close to each other. Therefore, the obtained horizontal profile is noisy and lines' positions can't be found easily. To address this obstacle, we smooth the projection data vector using the SavGol filter [17]. Then local maxima representing the global line positions are detected and the segmentation area for each two consecutive lines is extracted, it is the area between the two

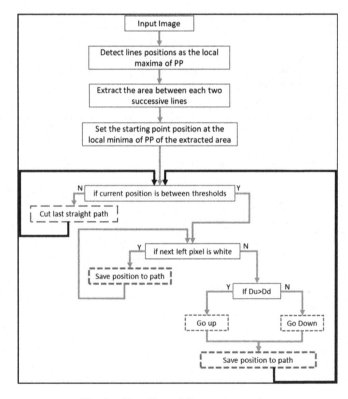

Fig. 9. Algorithm of lines segmentation

global baselines. Starting from the right index of local minima of the segmentation area, the algorithm of Fig. 9 is followed to find the segmentation path and separate lines from right to left. Let us mention that up and down thresholds are set to 20% of the segmentation area size, and Du (Dd) is the distance between the current pixel and its closest up (down) black pixel and PP is the projection profile. Figure 10 shows a segmentation area with the thresholds and the segmentation path obtained by using the Binary gaussian transformation.

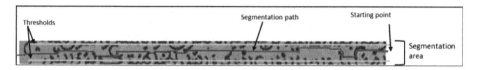

Fig. 10. Lines segmentation result

4   Experimental Results

Because of the absence of a public and standard database of Arabic historical documents, and in order to evaluate the present segmentation method, we have used a private set of Arabic historical documents. The documents were provided by Al-Qaraouiyine library[1], scanned with a 300 dpi optical scanner. The set contains a total of 129 pages with a total of 3068 text lines images. They were prepared manually to remove borders and to remove big black spots and the other effects that were caused by users during manual use. The tests were performed using Python-OpenCV on windows-10 of a PC with a Quadcore 2.8 Gz Processor and an 8 Gb of random-access memory.

4.1   Rules

The segmentation method described in this paper consists in finding a path through the white space between lines. In literature, we noticed the absence of standard scheme to decide if a line is well segmented or not. That's why we define the following strict rule to consider a successful segmentation: A line segmentation is checked manually and considered failed if the segmentation path crosses (cuts) one or more characters of the line in condition that a crossed character loses its global shape. Figure 11 shows some successful and failed segmentations.

---

[1] Al-Qaraouiyine Library: Founded in 860 in Fez, Morocco. Al-Qaraouiyine is believed to be the oldest working library in the world. It is part of Al-Qaraouiyine University which, according to the UN, is the oldest operating educational institute in the world.

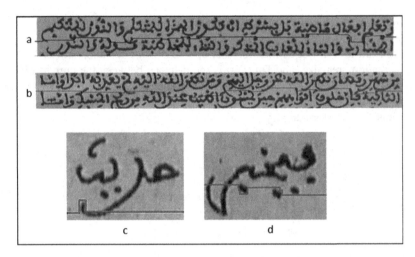

Fig. 11. a, c: Successful segmentations. b, d: failed segmentations

4.2   Skew Correction

In the skew correction step, the angle range is chosen experimentally as [−40°:40°] to cover all rotation variations that may exist in historical documents. The step angle of rotation is determined after several tests summarized in Fig. 12. We have chosen several divisions of the angle range, and calculated the error rate "r" using formula (1) and the time cost. We noticed that time increases whenever the number of steps increases since there are always new iterations to process, while the error rate of skew correction is stabilized at r = 1.8% at the number of steps of 70. Therefore, the range angle is divided by 70 which means the step angle is set to 80°/70 = 1.14°.

$$r = \frac{|ca - ea|}{ea} * 100 \tag{1}$$

Where 'ca' is the calculated angle, and 'ea' is the exact angle calculated manually.

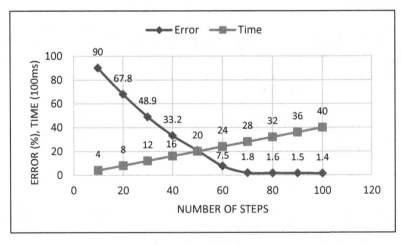

Fig. 12. Summary of skew correction tests

4.3   Text Line Segmentation

We present in Fig. 13 a comparison between the 4 previous tests in term of error rate and time consuming. The error rate is calculated using the formula (2). For the first representation in which the image is only binarized and got noise reduced, a global binarization algorithm is applied and a 2×2 kernel is used for a morphological 3-iterations opening to reduce noise. In the horizonal-RLSA representation, the threshold is experimentally fixed after many experiments in 15 pixels, the same as the kernel used for the gaussian filter.

$$e = \frac{|m - n|}{n} * 100 \qquad (2)$$

Where 'm' is the number of lines well segmented, and 'n' is the total of lines in database.

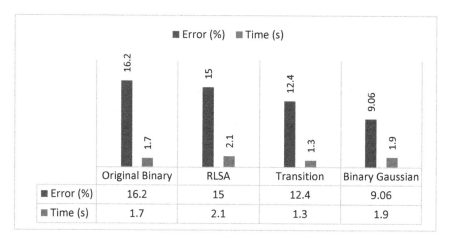

	Original Binary	RLSA	Transition	Binary Gaussian
■ Error (%)	16.2	15	12.4	9.06
■ Time (s)	1.7	2.1	1.3	1.9

Fig. 13. Segmentation rates and time cost

In term of speed, processing the transitions image gives the best results since the transitions image have less data compared to the others. But the binary gaussian transformation gives the best results in term of accuracy nevertheless it takes more time than the original binary image and the transitions images. This is due to the fact that the binary gaussian transformation reduces noise, smooths the borders and converts the words into a smeared form, which is more compacted than the result of RLSA transformation. This last, smears the text image without reducing noise which can cause the loss of the segmentation path. While the transitions transformation creates more space and options for the segmentation path. Table 1 summarizes the obtained results.

Table 1. Results of segmentation using the four image representations

Representation	Segmentation rate
Original binary	83.8%
RLSA	85%
Transitions	87.6
Binary gaussian	**90.94%**

5 Conclusion

In this paper, we have presented a projection-based method for text line segmentation of historical documents preceded by skew correction. Since skew and noise are major weaknesses of projection-based approaches of text line segmentation, we first perform a preprocessing step including binarization and noise removing. Then, a skew correction method is proposed to provide straight lines to the segmentation process. It is based on the horizontal projection, which is applied on the transformation of the text image into transitions. The segmentation algorithm is applied on multiple versions of the text image to see the effect of each transformation. We have found that adding a gaussian blur followed by thresholding to a binary text image may be the best option and can increase the segmentation rate up to 90.94%. As perspective of this work, we aim to study the robustness of our method on bigger databases and other Latin and Chinese scripts. Also, we aim to create a standard database for Arabic historical text, to allow the application of new machine learning techniques in this field.

References

1. Zoizou, A., Zarghili, A., Chaker, I.: A new hybrid method for Arabic multi-font text segmentation, and a reference corpus construction. J. King. Saud. Univ. – Comput. Inf. Sci. (2018). https://doi.org/10.1016/j.jksuci.2018.07.003
2. Katsouros, V., Papavassiliou, V.: Segmentation of handwritten document images into text lines. Image Segmentation (2012). https://doi.org/10.5772/15923
3. Saabni, R., Asi, A., El-Sana, J.: Text line extraction for historical document images. Pattern Recognit. Lett. **35**, 23–33 (2014). https://doi.org/10.1016/j.patrec.2013.07.007
4. Zahour, A., Taconet, B., Mercy, P., Ramdane, S.: Arabic hand-written text-line extraction. In: Proceedings International Conference Document Analysis Recognition, ICDAR 2001-January, pp. 281–285 (2001). https://doi.org/10.1109/ICDAR.2001.953799
5. Pal, U., Datta, S.: Segmentation of Bangla unconstrained handwritten text. In: Proceedings International Conference Document Analysis Recognition, ICDAR 2003-January, pp. 1128–1132 (2003). https://doi.org/10.1109/ICDAR.2003.1227832
6. Boussellaa, W., Zahour, A., Elabed, H., et al.: Unsupervised block covering analysis for text-line segmentation of Arabic ancient handwritten document images. In: Proceedings - International Conference Pattern Recognition, pp. 1929–1932 (2010). https://doi.org/10.1109/ICPR.2010.475

7. Garz, A., Fischer, A., Bunke, H., Ingold, R.: A binarization-free clustering approach to segment curved text lines in historical manuscripts. In: Proceedings International Conference Document Analysis Recognition, ICDAR 1290–1294 (2013). https://doi.org/10.1109/ICDAR.2013.261

8. Garz, A., Fischer, A., Sablatnig, R., Bunke, H.: Binarization-free text line segmentation for historical documents based on interest point clustering. In: Proceedings- 10th IAPR International Work Document Analysis System DAS 2012, pp. 95–99 (2012). https://doi.org/10.1109/DAS.2012.23

9. Yin, F., Liu, C.L.: Handwritten text line extraction based on minimum spanning tree clustering. In: Proceedings 2007 International Conference Wavelet Analysis Pattern Recognition, ICWAPR 2007 3, pp. 1123–1128 (2008). https://doi.org/10.1109/ICWAPR.2007.4421601

10. Shi, Z., Setlur, S., Govindaraju, V.: Text extraction from gray scale historical document images using adaptive local connectivity map. In: Proceedings International Conference Document Analysis Recognition, ICDAR 2005, pp. 794–798 (2005). https://doi.org/10.1109/ICDAR.2005.229

11. Koo, H.L., Cho, N.I.: Text-line extraction in handwritten Chinese documents based on an energy minimization framework. IEEE Trans. Image Process. 21, 1169–1175 (2012). https://doi.org/10.1109/TIP.2011.2166972

12. Capobianco, S., Marinai, S.: Text line extraction in handwritten historical documents. In: Grana, C., Baraldi, L. (eds.) IRCDL 2017. CCIS, vol. 733, pp. 68–79. Springer, Cham (2017). https://doi.org/10.1007/978-3-319-68130-6_6

13. Ouwayed, N., Belaïd, A., Auger, F.: General text line extraction approach based on locally orientation estimation. Doc. Recognit. Retr. XVII 7534, 75340B (2009). https://doi.org/10.1117/12.839518

14. Casey, R.G., Lecolinet, E.: Survey of methods and STR in character segmentation. IEEE Anal. 18, 690–706 (1996). https://doi.org/10.1109/34.506792

15. Likforman-Sulem, L., Hanimyan, A., Faure, C.: A hough based algorithm for extracting text lines in handwritten documents. In: Proceedings International Conference Document Analysis Recognition, ICDAR 2, pp. 774–777 (1995). https://doi.org/10.1109/ICDAR.1995.602017

16. Wong, K.Y., Casey, R.G., Wahl, F.M.: Document analysis system. IBM J. Res. Dev. 26, 647–656 (2010). https://doi.org/10.1147/rd.266.0647

17. Savitzky, A., Golay, M.J.E.: Smoothing and differentiation of data by simplified least squares procedures. Anal. Chem. 2, 1627–1639 (1964). https://doi.org/10.1021/ac60214a047

Authorship Attribution of Arabic Articles

Maha Hajja[✉], Ahmad Yahya, and Adnan Yahya[✉]

Department of Electrical and Computer Engineering,
Birzeit University, Birzeit, Palestine
maha.durgham19977@gmail.com, ahmad007yahya@gmail.com,
yahya@birzeit.edu

Abstract. With the huge size and large diversity of web content and the appearance of more social media platforms and blog websites, more people are contributing content of varying quality. Many users prefer to keep themselves anonymous when posting material to the web, which resulted in more pieces of text: articles, blogs, essays and emails being published under assumed identities or have no known author. This may result in copyright and other legal issues and thus the need for good authorship attribution systems. The problem may be more acute for Arabic texts due to restrictions, actual and perceived, on electronic content publication and the prevailing social norms. In this paper we study the issue of Arabic author attribution (AAA) concerned with designating a particular author of an Arabic (MSA) article from among a given set of potential authors. Many features were taken into consideration for training and testing our models for AAA. We studied the effects of features like part of speech (PoS) tags, stylistic issues like punctuation marks usage and sentence characteristics, word types and word diversity. In general, PoS features, word n-grams features and rare words proved to be the most informative for our task. We also investigated the effect of factors like number of potential authors, number of articles per author, and the size of text chunks used and we report on the results.

Keywords: Arabic authorship attribution · Arabic plagiarism detection · Writing style recognition · Arabic special features · Arabic text author identification

1 Introduction

Authorship attribution (AA) is the process of identifying the author of a document, given a number of documents with known authors. When performed on text, AA can rely heavily on using NLP resources. Authorship attribution is important to deal with older texts that may not have their authors clearly identified, also for cases when texts may be incorrectly attributed to people other than their real authors for one reason or another. Authorship attribution gained in importance with the fast growth of the Internet and Internet usage worldwide, which lead to a vast increase in web content in the form of articles, news items, emails, papers and social media posts. The degree of control can be minimal, and as a result, it is easy to post web material without proper author attribution. Authorship attribution is mostly a type of a classification problem; what differentiates this from text categorization and classification is that it doesn't only

© Springer Nature Switzerland AG 2019
K. Smaïli (Ed.): ICALP 2019, CCIS 1108, pp. 194–208, 2019.
https://doi.org/10.1007/978-3-030-32959-4_14

depend on the text content alone. The type of text or its topic are rarely enough to identify the text author because the style of writing can be a crucial factor in authorship attribution.

For AA we need to find a way to determine the author of a document that has unclear source. For example, it is useful in case of two or more people claiming to be the author of a text or when no one is willing to acknowledge being the author of a text piece. Authorship attribution has applications including plagiarism detection (for example: college essays), identifying writers for inappropriate documents and texts that were sent anonymously (for example: dangerous or slanderous e-mails), for solving copyright issues, determining the source of anonymous posts in blogs and resolving problems of unclear authorship for important historical documents.

General AA has been a big topic of interest for many years now [2–7, 10, 15]. But Arabic authorship attribution (AAA) has received limited, though lately growing, attention [8, 9, 11, 12]. AAA is the topic we sought to address in this paper.

In most cases, the common approach is to use machine learning to build AA models. The success of authorship attribution as a machine learning task depends on what features are chosen to be used for the training process. Lots of features can be extracted from the text, but which feature will help improve the result and which ones will do the opposite is a question that should be answered. In search for an answer, various syntactic features (e.g. average sentence length), part of speech (PoS) features (e.g. PoS percentages) and content features (e.g. percentage of so-called positive words) were calculated and considered for the training process. Other factors that may be considered are the number of authors to choose from, the number of articles per author as well as the length of the training texts. To make sure the most informative features are taken, many feature selection methods were implemented and many combinations of features were tested to determine their effect on the AAA results.

The rest of the paper is organized as follows: in the next section we review related work and how the work on authorship attribution developed. In Sect. 3 we talk about the dataset: its sources and characteristics. After that, in Sect. 4, the candidate features for extraction are introduced and explained. In Sect. 5, we discuss the feature selection process used to improve the AAA results. Finally, in Sect. 6 we draw some conclusions and point to possible directions for future research.

2 Related Work

There are hundreds of researches done on authorship attribution. This is probably because of the huge increase of web content and the ability of users to post content anonymously making authorship attribution an important issue. The researchers studied different properties of texts, different features of articles and lots of studies and experiments have been done. However, our focus here is authorship attribution for Arabic web documents. The research done on Arabic texts is much less than that for English and other languages, both in number and in depth and in that not a lot of features and language specific aspects were considered.

Kjell [2] did lots of experiments using Bayesian classifiers and neural networks for authorship attribution and obtained a success rate of 80–90%.

Stamatatos et al. [3] divided authorship attribution features into five groups: character, lexical, semantic, syntactic and application-specific features. It was noticed that lexical and character features have rich information about the author's writing style and topical preferences. Moreover, it is observed that the latter types of features can be extracted for many languages and datasets easily.

In Diederich et al. [4], support vector classifiers were studied through a series of experiments and managed to identify authors with 60% to 80% success rates and using various parameters.

In Argamon et al. [5], the usefulness of function words in Authorship attribution is examined. The authors used support vector machine classifiers to examine 20 novels and they got a success rate above 90%. At the end they concluded that functional words is an acceptable and good approach for authorship attribution.

Grieve et al. [6] performed experiments using the Chi-squared test on "The Telegraph Columnist" corpus, which involved 39 types of textual measurements commonly used in attribution studies. The conclusion was that effective features for representing authors are the combination of word and punctuation marks.

In Stamatatos [7], Discriminant Analysis and Multiple Regression were done. A success rate of %65 and %72 was obtained in their study for authorship recognition.

Variation in documents sizes also got the researchers to more approaches depending on the size. For example, Altakrori et al. [8], focused on small context and tiny texts, specifically on tweets. Their approach was mainly using n-grams on both word and character levels, PoS features, textual features, syntactic features along with function words and showed that the n-grams and the user-profile models can give comparative results to the state-of-the-art techniques. Similarly, Rabab'ah et al. [9], focused on small sized documents which are tweets, they used two main approaches: Bag-of-Words (BoW) and Stylometric Features (SF). The highest accuracy achieved was 68.67% and obtained by running the SVM classifier on the combined feature sets.

Ding et al. [10], introduced the problem of stylometric representation learning into the AA. The authors presented three learning models for vectorized stylometric representations, they found that this works well for prolific authors but not as good for small sized texts.

From the reviewed work, and many others, it is clear that various features and methods were tested with varying degrees of success. This paper will focus on in depth study of authorship attribution for Arabic documents and the effect of different features on the system evaluation metrics. For that, many experiments were conducted to see how various combinations of features affect the performance of the AAA process. We studied the effect of textual features plus features like: number of authors, number of articles per author, article readability score and article size. Many feature combinations and learning algorithms were tested using the 10-fold cross validation method for calculating the accuracy, recall, precision and F-measure.

3   Dataset

A proper dataset for Arabic articles authorship attribution was not found, most likely because this subject wasn't studied in depth. Therefore, a suitable dataset was manually collected. It consisted of 7 authors, with 10 articles each for a total of 70 articles. To make the data as fair as possible, almost all the articles were collected from the website blogs.aljazeera.net except for one author.

The articles used are homogenous, which means they are close to each other topic-wise, which makes the judgment more challenging since writing style features will be addressed and emphasized, given that the overall topic is almost the same.

The number of authors and articles was based on the authors with sufficient numbers of articles suitable for building machine learning models. All texts are MSA.

For each article we created a metadata file to contain items such as author name, class index for author, title of article, article link, size, date of publication and language. These metadata files would make a source of data about the articles and thus make the training process easier. The dataset and its expansions and metadata are being made available for other researchers.

4   Feature Extraction

Extracting features that can represent both the structure and style of the author's writing leads to robust detection of the author's identity. Hence, several feature types were investigated, with each set of features targets a specific area of one's writing style. The feature extraction framework was split into several stages starting from preprocessing the raw articles, to applying several NLP related tasks to the text like Part of Speech (PoS) tagging, Tokenization, Stemming, Spell Checking, etc.., that can help in the later stages of feature extraction. This section is divided as follows: the first subsection discusses the preprocessing steps used, the second section is about the feature sets and types and the last section discusses the methodology of extracting those features and how the NLP related tasks were applied.

4.1   Preprocessing

Due to variations in writing methods, preprocessing is a common step in most of Arabic NLP tasks. However, we believe that keeping the preprocessing to the minimum can lead to better results of identifying the author in the Authorship Attribution problem, because many author identifying details can be removed if heavy preprocessing is applied. On the other hand, many features depend on the preprocessed text like unigram frequencies whereas there are features that depend on the original text, like the percentage of diacritics used and punctuation marks. This diversity resulted in us extracting features before and after the preprocessing stage.

The first step for preprocessing is taking the top word unigrams and bigrams in all the articles, to later represent the frequencies of top unigrams and bigrams as a set of features. Then for each article, the percentage of diacritics will be taken before splitting the article into paragraphs and then removing the diacritics from them. For each resulting paragraph tokenization and stemming are performed, and a spell correction is done for the same paragraph and then tokenization is done for the spell corrected paragraph separately, to find the richness with respect to a standard term distribution of unigrams collected from Al Jazeera documents corpus. Figure 1 illustrates the pre-processing steps.

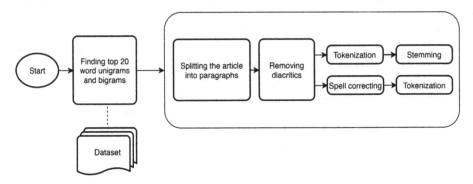

Fig. 1. The preprocessing workflow

4.2   Feature Types

Many features were studied for ability to distinguish an author's writing style. They are split into Style features, POS features and Content features. All the features proposed are summarized in Table 1.

Table 1. Feature types

Feature type	Feature
Style features	Average word length
	Average sentence length
	Percentage of punctuation
	Percentage of short words
	Percentage of hapax-legomena
	Percentage of numbers
	Percentage of typos
	Percentage of diacritics
	Type to token ratio
	Nuraihan readability score
	Percentage of function words
PoS features	PoS percentages for top PoS tags
Content features	Frequency of top 20 unigrams
	Frequency of top 20 bigrams
	Percentage of positive words
	Percentage of negative words
	Percentage of neutral words

Style Features. Style features are categorized into Lexical and Syntactic features. Lexical features are the features that represent the statistics about the text from the average sentence length in words to the percentage of hapax-legomena, whereas in the syntactic features of interest were the frequency of function words and the punctuation used. More details are given in the following subsections.

Lexical Features. Averages/percentages were computed for the following features: average length of words and sentences, percentage of words of length not greater than 3, percentage of words that are almost hapax-legomena (also dis-legomena and so on) until a frequency of 3, percentage of numbers used in the text, percentage of typos the author made, percentage of diacritics on the letters, type to token ratio (TTR) and the Arabic readability test score that measures the complexity of the text in terms of the rare words used. The readability test score used was as in [16] (Eq. (1)) which returns the rank of the given token depending on its word frequencies and number of tokens.

$$ReadabilityScore = \frac{\sum_i rank(token(i))}{N} \tag{1}$$

The readability score measures the complexity of a text by knowing the "global" rank of each word. The rank of a word was taken by sorting out all the words found in Al Jazeera documents by their frequencies in descending order then the index of each word would represent its rank. Table 2 shows the top 10 unigrams in Al Jazeera documents with their frequencies.

Table 2. Top 10 type in Al-Jazeera corpus and their frequencies

Word Rank	Word	Frequency
1	في	3671564
2	من	2330186
3	أن	1534168
4	على	1520368
5	إلى	1103242
6	عن	641711
7	التي	597724
8	إن	463476
9	مع	460636
10	ما	442644

The words from Table 2 are all correctly spelled, hence, to map a word from an article to a global corpus rank, one needs to spell correct the words and sentences, and for that the FARASA spell corrector was used [14].

The list of words has 824,179 types and 211,311,782 tokens, and proved to have a Zipfian distribution such that the percentage of types with frequency 1 is about 42.7% of all the types and the percentage of types with frequency 2 took 13.8% percentage. Figure 2 shows the distribution of the fraction of words with that frequency.

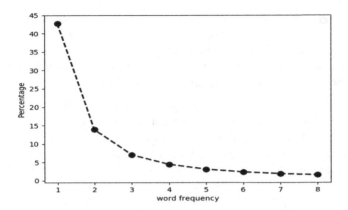

Fig. 2. Frequency of corpus word types

Syntactic Features. The syntactic features used were the percentage of function words used and the percentage of the punctuations in the text. The function words are the words used to connect two parts of a sentence. Arabic is rich in function words and function words are categorized into different categories, Table 3 illustrates some of the function word types and the particular instances that were used in this paper.

Table 3. Function types and words

Function type	Function words used
Conditional function words (أدوات الشرط)	ان، من، ما، متى، اين، أينما، لو، لولا، ما
Accusative function words (أدوات النصب)	لن، حتى، ان، كي، اللام، لام الجحود، الفاء
Questioning function words (أدوات الاستفهام)	من، ما، متى، اين، كيف، كم، لماذا، هل
Simile function words (أدوات التشبيه)	الكاف، كأن
Preposition and postposition function words (أدوات الجر)	من، الى، على، في، عن، حتى، رب، الباء، الكاف، اللام، الواو، التاء، مذ، منذ

One needs to note that a lot of the function words may not exist in all the languages. For example, the accusative function words do not exist in English but one can find them in German.

Part of Speech (PoS) Features. Writing behavior can be strongly determined by the different PoS elements used in the text. Therefore, the FARASA PoS tagger [15] was used to extract the PoS tags for each article tokens, then the frequencies of the used PoS tags were taken to serve as features. The number PoS tags used was 13, as illustrated in Table 4.

Table 4. Parts of Speech Used

PoS code	PoS description
NSUFF	Noun Suffix
PRON	Pronoun
ADJ	Adjective
NUM	Number
PREP	Preposition
CASE	alef of tanween fatha
DET	determiner
ADV	Adverb
PART	Particles
V	Verb
CONJ	Conjunction
NOUN	Noun
PUNC	Punctuation

Content Features. Authors tend to use some words or phrases more often than others. Based on this fact, knowing the author top unigrams and bigrams from all his/her training articles can help in identifying the author. Therefore, the top 20 unigrams and top 20 bigrams from all the articles were taken as a preprocessing step, then for each article, the unigrams and bigrams that are in the top 20 unigrams and top 20 bigrams from all the articles are represented with their percentage (normalized frequency) in the article.

Another content feature is how the author tends to use positive (good), negative (bad) or neutral words in the article, hence the percentages of positive, negative and neutral words were taken as content features. The positiveness of a word was measured by using a sentiment analyzer from [13], which employs a set of labeled Arabic online reviews.

4.3   Extracting Methodology

All the features mentioned previously need robust tools and methods to find and extract them. For the lexical features, both the readability test and the TTR require prior knowledge of the rank and frequency of a given word in a large set of documents. For this the pre-collected set of unigrams frequencies on Al Jazeera documents from FARASA was used [1, 18].

The PoS tagger used was also the FARASA PoS tagger for its accurate representation of each word. For the sentiment analyzer the ArabicTools from Ali Salhi were used to determine the word positiveness [13].

5   Features Selection

Lots of features were calculated as described previously, some of which may not be as informative as others. Irrelevant features can decrease the model accuracy. Therefore, feature selection was used to ensure having a precise and well-made model. This can be done by either automatically generating the possible subsets and evaluating them separately, or by finding the subset of features greedily or by a statistical measure.

5.1   Statistical Approach

The first naive approach is to find the information gain (IG) of all the features and cancelling out the ones that have IG less than some threshold. We did that and the features selected from the strongest to the least strong (based on IG) after cancelling the features with the lowest information gain are illustrated in Table 5.

From that table, it is easily seen that the PoS percentages features have relatively large IG compared to the other features. Other high IG features include TTR, punctuation percentage and word length.

Table 5. Selected features and their information gain

Feature	Information gain
Determiner (PoS, ال التعريف)	1.000582
Type to token ratio (TTR)	0.990532
Percentage of punctuation	0.937544
Average word length	0.886882
Adverb (PoS)	0.847305
Percentage of short words	0.75187
Adjective (PoS)	0.728352
Pronoun (PoS)	0.707754
Average sentence length	0.654821
NOUN (PoS)	0.631447
Unigrams (average IG value)	0.6155228
VERB (PoS)	0.583294
Nuraihan readability score	0.583221
Particles (PoS)	0.569106
Noun suffix (PoS)	0.480477
Neutral words percentage	0.467596
Percentage of Hepax-Legomena	0.463519
Conjunction (PoS)	0.42083
Bigrams (average IG value)	0.319848

5.2   Search Approach

The second feature selection process is by using a search-based method that finds the best subset of features that are most representative. Unfortunately, this problem is NP-hard and the computations for the number of features proposed would be very large. Hence, a greedy algorithm was used, and the results of the subset selection problem are shown in Table 6.

Table 6. Selected features for feature type

Feature type	Feature
Style Features	Average word length
	Average sentence length
	Percentage of punctuation
	Percentage of short words
	Percentage of hapax-legomena
	Percentage of typos
	Type to token ratio
	Nuraihan readability score
PoS features	PoS percentages for top PoS
Content features	Frequency of top 20 unigrams
	Frequency of top 20 bigrams
	Percentage of neutral words

These results are computed when assuming that all the 7 authors are in the training set, hence, many important features like the function words frequencies and percentage of diacritics were discarded because of the large number of authors to choose from. However, we believe that if the evaluation was limited to the case of two authors at a time where one author uses diacritics or function words more frequently, those features would have a larger IG value and may have been selected.

6   Experiments and Results

To assess the effectiveness of the features extracted and selected, a complete evaluation needs to be done on different classifiers. We tested SVM (SMO), Decision Tree and Naive Bayes, since the SVM is a binary classifier, the OneVsOne approach was chosen.

The evaluation across those classifiers was done using 10-fold cross validation for all the pairs of 2 authors (the combinations of 2 authors were taken and trained and then the average value over the combinations was calculated), the results after 10-fold validation are given in Table 7.

The SVM proved to have the best results under all evaluation metrics, hence the next experiments are done using the SVM.

Table 7. Evaluation metrics with different algorithms

Classifier	Macro precision	Macro recall	Macro F-score
SVM	98.24%	98.10%	98.17%
Decision tree	84.97%	84.52%	84.75%
Naive bayes	97.97%	97.61%	97.79%

6.1   Testing How the Results Change with the Number of Authors

As discussed, the SVM used OneVsOne approach to deal with the multiple classes. However, the increase of the number authors to choose from can make the classifier misjudge and select the wrong author. Therefore, the relation between the number of authors in the SVM and the evaluation results is studied where for the 7 authors: we started with k = 2, i.e. for all the pairs of authors, then for subsets of k authors where k = 3, 4 …until the original problem where k = 7. For each 2<= k<=7 we trained then evaluated all possible combinations using 10-fold cross validation, then the average Precision, Recall and Accuracy for each k were computed and the results are depicted in Fig. 3.

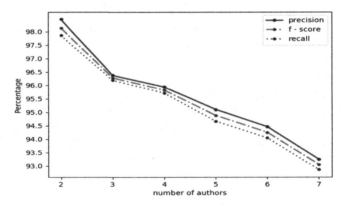

Fig. 3. AAA evaluation metrics vs number of authors

As seen, increasing the number of authors increases the options that the classifier needs to choose from and hence reduces the Precision, Recall and Accuracy, but not by much as the results are still in the 90% range even for 7 authors. The experiment was extended with an additional dataset [18] to have a total of 16 authors. The preliminary evaluation shows that the metrics are still going down as the number of authors increases, but the results are still encouraging.

6.2 Testing the Effect of the Number of Training Articles for Each Author

The original dataset collected contains 7 authors and 10 articles for each author, but for many circumstances in AA, it happens that an author does not have enough articles for training. Hence, the relation between the number of training articles that an author has and the accuracy of the model was studied, for each of the values n = 3, 4, ..., 10 articles. To make the choice of the articles fair, all the article combinations from a given n were evaluated and averaged. The results are shown in Fig. 4.

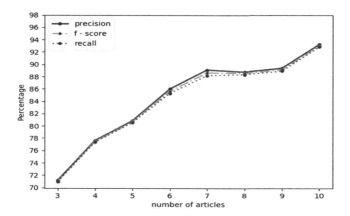

Fig. 4. AAA evaluation metrics vs number of articles per author

From Fig. 4, it is easily seen that increasing the number of articles produced better results because the information taken from an author is increased. Given the high results we have (about 97%) for 10 articles, it may be of interest to see the effect of adding additional articles on the performance and if things stabilize at a certain article count.

An additional experiment was done to further test the effect of article numbers for each author. A subset of 6 authors with 30 articles each was selected from the datasets in [17] and [18]. The experiment showed a convergence when the number of articles reached 12–14. Our preliminary conclusion is that increasing the number of articles for an author beyond a certain threshold doesn't necessarily imply an improvement in the results.

6.3 Testing How the Results Change with the Size of Context Taken

We wanted to test if we can redesign our model using less than the full article for elements of the training set for each author. To test the results for parts of the article in the training set vs the full article, several approaches where proposed and used.

Cutting Continuous Chunks from the Article. The first approach was working with continuous chunks of the articles and training on them only. For this purpose, the first and second halves of each article were taken separately and used as the training set then evaluated and averaged, then the four quarters were used for training then evaluated and averaged and finally the procedure is repeated for the eight eighths of each article[1]. This was done by using 21 combinations for all possible subsets of authors pairs (k = 2) and then averaging the results of each combination. Figure 5 illustrates the results.

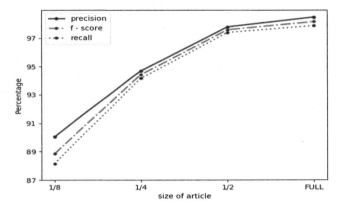

Fig. 5. AAA evaluation metrics vs article size (continuous chunks)

Choosing Random Bag of Words from the Article. The second approach was selecting random words from the articles (random bag of words) and compute the results as done previously, of course, the bigrams frequencies are not available for this case and thus are not used for this approach as a feature set. To demonstrate the effect of the text context features, the PoS features were pre-calculated then the experiment was done with and without PoS features for the pairs of 2 authors (k = 2), for a different number of randomly selected words. The results are given in Fig. 6.

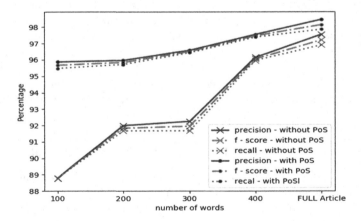

Fig. 6. AAA evaluation metrics vs article size (Random bag of words) with and without POS tags

---

[1] To avoid problematic splits, the split was always aligned with section boundaries.

It is noticeable that reducing the context has negative effect on the results. However, in the case of continuous chunks (Fig. 5), the results were not as negative as choosing random words (Fig. 6). That is mainly because the continuity of the text kept some features (like word bigrams and POS tags) alive and meaningful, something that is lost in random sampling, even for larger sample sizes. The significant improvement on the results when the context-driven features such as POS tags were included as can be seen in the upper part of Fig. 6.

7 Conclusions and Future Work

In this paper, the problem of Arabic Authorship Attribution (AAA) was studied and assessed. The AAA is not a trivial task for the variety of writing styles and different structures people have. Many feature types were proposed and evaluated to know what features determine the authorship the most. To account for the diversity of the dataset size and the rarity of articles or posts an author may have, the relation between the number of articles and the evaluation metrics was studied, and it showed how reducing the number of articles can affect the results negatively. Moreover, the relation between the number of authors a classifier needs to select from and the evaluation metrics was tested. The results showed that reducing the number of authors for a classifier to choose from resulted in better results. The last parameter tested was the size of context, through reducing the article size to half, to quarter then to one eighth of the original. We also studied the effect of choosing random tokens from the article on the evaluation metrics. We concluded that the continuity of the text preserves a lot of useful features that is lost in randomized word selection and the performance was much better for continuous text chunks and random tokens with in context features like POS tags. For the random tokens case, the more words selected, the better, with remarkable improvements when the random tokens had their POS tags as additional features.

For better evaluation, we need to test on larger datasets, say in terms of the number of authors and the number of articles per author as well as more topic diverse texts. Another interesting experiment would be evaluating the features proposed for a real-life application scenario like plagiarism detection in Arabic, or identifying authors for posts with hidden identity like the spammers on social media. Another possible extension is to test on smaller context posts like tweets.

References

1. Abdelali, A., Darwish, K., Durrani, N., Mubarak, H.: Farasa: a fast and furious segmenter for Arabic. In: NAACL-2016 (2016)
2. Kjell, B.: Authorship attribution of text samples using neural networks and bayesian classifiers. In: IEEE International Conference on Systems, Man and Cybernetics. San Antonio, TX, USA (1994)
3. Stamatatos, E., Fakotakis, N., Kokkinakis, G.: Computer- based authorship attribution without lexical measures. In: Computers and Humanities, pp. 193–214 (2001)

4. Diederich, J., Kindermenn, J., Leopold, E., Pass, G.: Authorship attribution with support vector machines. Appl. Intel. **19**, 109–123 (2003)
5. Argamon, S., Shlomo, L.: Measuring the usefulness of function words for authorship attribution. In: Proceedings of ACH/ALLC Conference 2005. Victoria, BC, Canada, June 2000
6. Grieve, J.: Quantitative authorship attribution: an evaluation of techniques. Literary and Linguist. Comput. **22**(3), 251–270 (2007)
7. Stamatatos, E.: A survey of modern authorship attribution methods. J. Am. Soc. Inf. Sci. Technol. **60**, 538–556 (2009)
8. Altakrori, M., et al.: Arabic authorship attribution: an extensive study on Twitter posts. ACM Trans. Asian and Low-Resource Lang. Inf. Process. (TALLIP) **18**(1), 5 (2019)
9. Rabab'ah, A., Al-Ayyoub, M., Jararweh, Y., Aldwairi, M.: Authorship attribution of arabic Tweets. In: AICCSA (2016)
10. Ding, S., Fung, B., Iqbal, F., Cheung, W.: Learning stylometric representations for authorship analysis. IEEE Trans. Cybern. **49**(1), 107–121 (2019)
11. Al-Ayyoub, M., Alwajeeh, A., Hmeidi, I.: An extensive study of authorship authentication of arabic articles. Int. J. Web Inf. Syst. **13**, 85–104 (2017)
12. Shaker, K.: Investigating features and techniques for arabic authorship attribution. PhD Thesis Proposal. Heriot-Watt University March 2012
13. Al-Salhi, A.: ArabiTools website. https://www.arabitools.com
14. Darwish, K., Mubarak, H.: Farasa: a new fast and accurate arabic word segmenter. In: LREC-2016 (2016)
15. Yuan, Z., Li, C., Barzilay, R., Darwish, K.: Randomized greedy inference for joint segmentation, pos tagging and dependency parsing. In: 2015 Conference of the North American Chapter of the Association for Computational Linguistics (2015)
16. Mat Daud, N., Hassan, H., Abdul Aziz, N.: A corpus-based readability formula for estimate of arabic texts reading difficulty. World Appl. Sci. J. (Special Issue of Stud. Lang. Teach. Learn.) **21**, 168–173 (2013)
17. Hajja, M., Yahya, A., Yahya, A.: An arabic author attribution datatset. Fada: Birzeit University repository, June 2019. https://fada.birzeit.edu/
18. Anini, B., Anini, Y., Yahya, A.: A dataset for arabic author identification. Fada: Birzeit University Repository, June 2019. https://fada.birzeit.edu/

Keyphrase Extraction from Modern Standard Arabic Texts Based on Association Rules

Mourad Loukam[1,2(✉)], Djamila Hammouche[1,2], Freha Mezzoudj[2], and Fatma Zohra Belkredim[1,2]

[1] LMA Laboratory, Faculty of Exact Sciences and Informatics,
Hassiba Benbouali University of Chlef, Chlef, Algeria
m.loukam@univ-chlef.dz
[2] Department of Computer Science,
Hassiba Benbouali University of Chlef, Chlef, Algeria

Abstract. Keywords or Keyphrases constitute a very important kind of concepts which can be extracted from texts. They reflect the semantic contained in these texts and are useful in many tasks of Information Retrieval, Text mining and Natural Language Processing. Their extraction is a challenging problem to which researchers have an active interest. In this paper, an approach based on the Association Rules model is described for extracting keyphrases from modern standard Arabic texts. The experiments done and the results obtained are promising: the performance values of the proposed system (in terms of precision, recall and f-score) are higher than 60% and can exceed 70%.

Keywords: Keyphrases Extraction · Keywords extraction · Association Rules · Arabic texts · Modern standard Arabic language

1 Introduction

Keyphrase extraction (KE) aims to identify a set of terms that best describe the content of a text. For example, one may ask what can be the most relevant terms which can represent the text of Fig. 1?

In the literature, depending on the granularity adopted, two different units have been used to represent the most relevant information contained in a text: keyphrases or keywords [1–4]. A keyphrase is a multi-word expression. For example, for the text of Fig. 1 we can suggest the following keyphrases: أسعار النفط (oil prices), الخام الأميركي (american crude), أسواق النفط (oil markets), whereas a keyword is a single word (e.g. الدولار (dollar), برنت (brent), الأسهم (stock exchange)). Using single words, as keyterms, can sometimes be misleading. For example, in a phrase like "وقف اطلاق النار" (ceasefire), the single words constituting the expression do not have their usual meanings and we have a misunderstanding if these words are taken separately. This is why in this field of Research, it is more relevant to talk about keyphrase extraction rather than keyword extraction.

KE is a challenging problem, because assigning manually keyphrases/keywords to documents is a tedious and very costly task, especially when it is remembered that the number of digital available documents is in growing.

© Springer Nature Switzerland AG 2019
K. Smaïli (Ed.): ICALP 2019, CCIS 1108, pp. 209–220, 2019.
https://doi.org/10.1007/978-3-030-32959-4_15

تواصلت الضغوط على أسعار النفط العلمية صباح
اليوم الأربعاء بسبب المخاوف من الكميات الفائضة في
السوق رغم انخفاض الدولار الأميركي الذي يشجع
المتعاملين عادة على الشراء.

وانخفض سعر العقود الآجلة لمزيج برنت في التعاملات
المبكرة اليوم بنحو 0.20% ليصل إلى نحو 41.70
دولارا للبرميل، كما تراجع سعر الخام الأميركي بنسبة
مماثلة ليصل إلى نحو 39.40 دولارا للبرميل.

وكانت أسعار النفط قد أنهت جلسة أمس الثلاثاء على
انخفاض بنحو 1%، متأثرة بتراجع الأسهم الأميركية
إلى أدنى مستوياتها منذ ثلاثة أسابيع، ولم ينقذها
انخفاض الدولار الذي سجل أدنى مستوياته منذ ستة
أسابيع.

Fig. 1. What keyphrases for this text?

Keywords/Keyphrases are widely used in Information Retrieval (IR), Text Mining (TM) and Natural Language Processing (NLP).

Since they represent in a condensed form the main content of a document, Keyphrases/Keywords are very important for IR systems [4–6]. They are used to build an automatic index for a collection of documents. This index is considered as the core of the IR system: when a user query is introduced, the IR engine refers to this index, using the keywords/keyphrases, to retrieve the most relevant elements satisfying the query. In addition to this, Keywords/Keyphrases are used in many other tasks, including: automatic summarization, high-level semantic description, text or website classification or clustering, constructing domain-specific dictionaries, name entity recognition, topic detection, tracking, etc. [7, 8].

In this paper, we propose an approach based on the Association Rules (AR) model to extract keyphrases from texts written in modern standard Arabic (MSA) language. The idea is that keyphrases are composed by words between which exists a high level co-occurrence, and AR are well suitable to detect such relationships.

The paper is organized as follows: after the introduction, Sect. 2 describes related works done in the KE field in general and in MSA in particular. In Sect. 3 we give a brief overview of the Association Rules model. Our approach is described in Sect. 4. An experiment of the proposed KE system is illustrated in Sect. 5. Section 6 gives details on the system assessment. Finally, we conclude and give a brief guideline for future research.

2 Related Works

Different approaches for automatic keyphrase extraction have been proposed, they can be grouped in five major classes:

1. Rule based linguistic approaches: These approaches use the features of the linguistic elements (words and sentences) present in the documents. They include the lexical, syntactic and discourse analysis. They require important domain knowledge in addition to a high language expertise. The advantage of rule based linguistic approaches is that they are generally more accurate than the other approaches, but the disadvantage is that they are not easily adaptable to a new domain [1, 2].

2. Statistical approaches: These approaches are generally based on statistical features derived from linguistic corpus. The most important advantage of them is that they are independent of the language on which they are applied and hence the same technique can be used on multiple languages [1–4]. These methods may be less accurate than the rule based approaches.

3. Machine learning approaches: These approaches generally employ supervised learning methods. The objective is to build, through a learning process, from a collection of training documents, a satisfactory model. This model is then used to predict the results (keyphrases) from new documents. Among the supervised methods, we can cite: Support Vector Machine, Maxent, etc. However, to yield good results, supervised learning methods require large annotated corpus which are difficult to build. In the absence of such resources, unsupervised and semi-supervised learning methods are used [1–4].

4. Graph-based approaches: A graph is a mathematical model, which enables the exploration of the relationships and structural information very effectively. Within this approach, a document is modeled as a graph where terms are represented by nodes and relations between terms are represented by edges. Edge relation between two terms can be established on many principles, including [9, 10]:

   - words co-occurring together in a sentence, paragraph or section;
   - intersecting words from a sentence, paragraph, section or document;
   - semantic relations–connecting words that have similar meaning, words spelled the same way but have different meaning, synonyms, antonyms, heteronyms, etc.

5. Hybrid approaches: Various approaches including different methods of the above classes can be applied to a specific domain.

In the field of MSA language KE, many works have been conducted, among them we can cite:

Awajan [11] has proposed a method for extracting keywords from Arabic documents which includes linguistics and statistical analysis of the text without using any prior knowledge. The text is preprocessed to extract the main linguistic information, such as the roots and morphological patterns of derivative words. A cleaning phase is then applied to eliminate the meaningless words from the text. The most frequent terms are clustered into equivalence classes in which the derivative words generated from the same root and the non-derivative words generated from the same stem are placed together, and their count is accumulated. A vector space model is then used to capture the most frequent N-gram in the text. The author revealed that his method achieves good results with an average precision of 31% and average recall of 53%.

Duwairi and Hedaya [12] have proposed a framework, based on KEA system, for extracting keyphrases from Arabic news documents. Its objective is to extract the most relevant keyphrases, on the basis of Naïve Bayes method.

In Amer and Foad [13], AKEA, a keyphrase extraction algorithm for single Arabic documents is presented. AKEA is an unsupervised algorithm. The authors relied on heuristics that include linguistic patterns based on Part-Of-Speech (POS) tags, statistical knowledge, and the internal structural pattern of terms. The authors used Arabic Wikipedia to improve the ranking of candidate keyphrases by adding a confidence score if the candidate exists as an indexed Wikipedia concept. The authors attested that on average, AKEA is more accurate than the other compared algorithms.

Omoush and Samawi [14] have proposed an automatic Arabic keyword extraction (AAKE) technique from single document using full-text based indexing. A proper feature-set that improves AAKE performance is specified. Self-organizing map (SOM) neural network is used as an unsupervised learning method. The authors revealed that their method gives encouraging results compared to Sakhr keyword extractor.

Sahmoudi and Lachkar [15] have proposed a new improvement of their previous Arabic keyphrase extraction system based on Suffix Tree Data Structure (KpST system). They added linguistic patterns specialized in extracting Arabic noun phrases, and using adapted C-value multi-terms extraction method to calculate the keyphrase relevance and solve the sub-keyphrases problem.

Helmy et al. [16] have proposed a deep learning based approach for Arabic keyphrase extraction. The authors attested that their method achieves better performance compared to the related competitive approaches.

Suleiman et al. [17] have proposed a keyword extraction method based on bag-of-concepts. The proposed algorithm uses semantic vector space model instead of traditional vector space model to group words into classes. The method generates a word-context matrix where the synonym words were grouped into the same class.

Rammal et al. [18] have proposed to apply a local grammar (LG) to develop an indexing system which automatically extracts keywords from titles of Lebanese official journals. To build this LG, the first word that plays the determinant role in understanding the meaning of a title is analyzed and grouped as the initial state. These steps are repeated recursively for the whole words. When a new title is introduced, the first word determines which LG should be applied to suggest or generate further potential keywords, based on a set of features calculated for each node of a title. The authors attested that the performance of their system is 67%. The proposed system has two limitations. First, it is applied to a sample of 5,747 titles and it should be developed to generate all finite state automata for all titles. The other limitation is that named entities are not processed due to their varieties that require specific ontology.

Najadat et al. [19] have proposed an algorithm for Automatic Keyphrases Extraction from Arabic (AKEA). The authors revealed that the evaluation show that the system achieves 83% precision value in identifying 2-word and 3-word keyphrases from agricultural domains.

3 Mining Association Rules

Association rules are employed to identify important relationships within a group of variables in a large dataset. Mining association rules is useful for a wide range of applications [20, 21], such as:

- Business data analysis: One application of this category is the popular "market basket" problem which aims to find in a dataset of transactions representing purchases done by customers what are the articles which are often bought together.
- Medical data analysis: in this field, it is interesting to know if there is any relationship between data present in a database of patients monitoring (age, gender, social class, disease, treatment, etc.).
- Text-mining: One purpose of this field is to detect in texts linguistic units linked by a pattern (e.g. the words which often appear together in a sentence, like a keyphrase).

In the following, we give an overview of the basic concepts of Association Rules [21, 22]:

Let $I = \{i_1, i_2, ..., i_n\}$ be a set of items and $D = \{d_1, d_2, ..., d_m\}$ a database of transactions where each $d_i \subseteq I$. Given two itemsets: $A \subset I$, $B \subset I$, and $A \cap B = \emptyset$; an association rule of the form $A \rightarrow B$ holds if it has a strong support ($\geq$ minsup) and a strong confidence ($\geq$ minconf) where support($A \rightarrow B$) equals to the probability of P(A union B) and confidence($A \rightarrow B$) equals to P($A|B$) with respect to the transactions in D.

To generate association rules, we normally need to identify all frequent itemsets (i.e., those with support values $\geq$ minsup). One popular solution is Apriori algorithm proposed by Agrawal and Srikant [22], which first identifies frequent 1-itemsets in a database and extends them with a single item to get 2-itemsets. After that, it prunes those 2-itemsets that do not satisfy the *minsup* value. Such a process is repeated level-by-level until no frequent k-itemsets can be found. The algorithm is costly in both memory and time in that it needs to generate and maintain a large number of candidate itemsets and repeatedly scan the database for counting their frequencies [21].

Once the frequent itemsets are generated, we can generate the rules out of them. Rules are formed by binary partition of each itemset. If $\{i_1, i_2, i_3\}$ is the frequent itemset, candidate rules will look like: $(i_1 \rightarrow i_2, i_3)$, $(i_2 \rightarrow i_1, i_3)$, $(i_3 \rightarrow i_1, i_2)$, $(i_1, i_2 \rightarrow i_3)$, $(i_1, i_3 \rightarrow i_2)$, $(i_2, i_3 \rightarrow i_1)$. From a list of all possible candidate rules, we aim to identify rules that fall above a minimum confidence level ($\geq$ minconf).

4 The Proposed System

In this section, we describe our proposed system for keyphrase extraction from MSA texts using Association Rules.

The global architecture is shown in Fig. 2. We can see that the extraction system is composed by two main modules: Preprocessing and Association Rules. Each of them is developed as a cascade of tasks. For the Preprocessing module, three tasks are necessary: Stopwords removal, normalization and vectorization. The Association rules module is composed by two parts: Frequent itemsets construction and candidate rules generation.

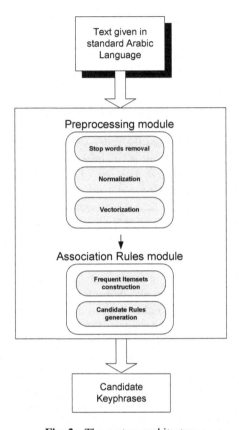

Fig. 2. The system architecture

The process can be described as follows:

1. **Preprocessing Module**: This module performs three main tasks: stop-words removal, normalization and vectorization.
   - Stop-words removal: The text given in input is processed for removing stop-words; i.e. words which are considered as irrelevant for indexing purposes because they occur frequently in the language (like pronouns هم، هي، هو, language particles في، لن، عن ,..., numbers, adverbs, etc.). The result of this step is a reduced text.
   - Normalization: A normalization (more general than the stemming) is made in order to reduce each item of the text to its canonical form. Verbs are reduced to their masdars (e.g. in the text given in Fig. 1, the verb "انخفض" will be replaced by its normal form "انخفاض"). Nouns are replaced by their undetermined and singular form (e.g. the noun "الضغوط" will be replaced by its normal form "ضغط"). Adjectives are reduced to their undetermined, singular and masculine gender form (e.g. the adjective "العالمية" will be replaced by its normal form "عالمي"). If the text contains proper names (e.g. "سوناطراك", the Algerian national oil company), these items are left as they appear in their original form.

– Vectorization: The text obtained at the precedent step is transformed in an appropriate data structure: a matrix. Each line in the matrix represents a sentence of the text, and in the columns we put the normalized words. In this way, the obtained matrix has binary values (0 or 1). A cell M[i, j] of this matrix is equal to 1 if the sentence i in the text (corresponding to line i in the matrix) contains the normalized word of column j, otherwise it is equal to 0.

To perform properly all the above mentioned tasks, the pre-processing module uses several linguistic resources present as tables in an internal database: stop-words, verbs, nouns, adjectives and named entities (locations, organizations, personalities). For the verbs, nouns and adjectives, each item is registered with its canonical form.

6. **Association Rules Module**: This module achieves the association rules extraction and mining in two complementary tasks: frequent itemsets construction and candidate rules generation.

– Frequent itemsets construction: The binary matrix obtained at the precedent step is exploited by Apriori algorithm to construct frequent itemsets (verifying support >= *minsup*).
– Candidate rules generation: The candidate rules verifying confidence >= *minconf*) are generated from the frequent itemsets. These rules represent the most relevant candidate keyphrases.

Technically, the preprocessing module has been developed with Java, and the "Association Rules module" has been implemented with the integration of R System libraries.

5   Experiment Description

In this section, we describe an experiment of our solution by using the example of the text presented in Fig. 1. We note that the text contains 3 sentences.

After the stop-words removal step, the obtained result is the following reduced text (see Fig. 3). On average, the size of the reduced text is about 75% of the original text (25% are stop-words).

Figure 4 shows the normalized text obtained after the normalization step.

Since the original text contains 3 sentences, the matrix constructed at the vectorization step has 3 lines. The number of columns depends on the number of normalized words obtained (35 in this case). Table 1 shows a fragment of this matrix.

After performing the whole preprocessing process, we can finally apply the Association Rules module by specifying the min value for the support and the confidence (generally upper than 70% for both of them). For this example, among the best candidate rules we have (see Table 2):

The 5-top rules concern the same words (انخفاض/سعر/دولار) and have a support and a confidence of 100%. These results suggest adopting as keyphrase: انخفاض سعر دولار (decline of the US dollar) which seems logical regarding to the content of the text. All the other candidate rules have a support or a confidence less than 100%.

تواصلت الضغوط أسعار النفط العالمية
المخاوف الكميات الفائضة السوق انخفاض
الدولار الأميركي يشجع المتعاملين الشراء.

انخفض سعر العقود الآجلة مزيج برنت
التعاملات المبكرة يصل دولارا البرميل،
تراجع سعر الخام الأميركي نسبة مماثلة يصل
دولار البرميل.

أسعار النفط نهاية جلسة انخفاض متأثرة
تراجع الأسهم الأميركية أدنى مستويات انقاذ
انخفاض الدولار تسجيل أدنى مستويات

Fig. 3. The experimental text after Stopwords removal.

تواصل ضغط سعر نفط علمي مخاوف كمية
فائض سوق انخفاض دولار أميركي تشجيع
متعامل شراء.

انخفاض سعر عقد تأجيل مزيج برنت تعامل
مبكر وصول دولار برميل، تراجع سعر خلم
أميركي نسبة مماثل وصول دولار برميل.

سعر نفط نهاية جلسة انخفاض تأثر تراجع
سهم أميركي تدني مستوى انقاذ انخفاض
دولار تسجيل تدني مستوى

Fig. 4. The experimental text after the Normalization step.

Table 1. Fragment of the matrix representing the text

	أمريكي	انخفاض	إنقاذ	برميل	برنت	تأثر	تأجيل	تدني	تراجع	...
Line 1	1	1	0	0	0	0	0	0	0	...
Line 2	1	1	0	1	1	0	1	0	1	...
Line 3	1	1	1	0	0	1	0	1	1	...

Table 2. A part of the best candidate rules.

Id	Candidate Association rule	% Support	% Confidence
1	سعر ← انخفاض، دولار	100	100
2	دولار ← سعر، انخفاض	100	100
3	انخفاض ← سعر ، دولار	100	100
4	سعر ، دولار ← انخفاض	100	100
5	دولار ، انخفاض ← سعر	100	100
6	سعر ← نفط	66	100
...	...	...	...

6 Evaluation

6.1 Corpus

For the evaluation purposes, we have collected a corpus of 100 press articles extracted from 5 medias: Arabic Skynews, Al Jazeera net, Al Qudsu Al Arabi journal, Al Chourouq Journal (Algeria), Al Hayat. Each document contains in average 319 words. Each document has its own keyphrases composed by its authors. The total number of keyphrases in the corpus is 360. That is, each document contains in average about 3.6 keyphrases. Table 3 gives an overview on this corpus.

Table 3. Description of the corpus used in the evaluation

Media	#Articles	#Keyphrase
Arabic Skynews	20	100
Al Jazeera net	20	140
Al Qudsu Alarabi	20	20
Al Chourouq	20	60
Al Hayat	20	40

6.2 Performance Measures

In order to evaluate the performance of our system we have used the popular measures of: recall, precision and f-score. These measures are defined briefly below, using Table 4 (inspired by [23]).

Precision is equal to: a/(a + b). Precision is defined as the number of correct keyphrases generated by the KE system divided by the total number of keyphrases extracted by the system.

Recall is equal to: a/(a + c). Recall is defined as the number of correct keyphrases generated by the KE system divided by the total number of correct keyphrases present in the evaluation corpus.

F-score is equal to 2 × (Precision × Recall)/(Precision + Recall). F-score is the common weighed average of the above two measures (precision and recall).

Table 4. Original and extracted keyphrases

		Original keyphrases (given with the articles themselves)	
		True	False
Keyphrases extracted	True	a	b
by our system	False	c	d

6.3   Results and Discussion

The keyphrases obtained by our KE system for all the texts of the corpus can be classified in 3 categories:

- Keyphrases that fully match the original keyphrases given with the articles of the evaluation corpus,
- Keyphrases that match, even partially, the original keyphrases,
- Keyphrases that are completely different from the original keyphrases.

Table 5 below gives the results of the evaluation. We can see that for the first class (full matching) we have obtained 68.53% of precision, 57.66% of recall and 62.62% of f-score. For the second class (partial matching), the results are slightly better: 72.41% of precision, 63.14% of recall and 67.45% of f-score.

Table 5. Results of the KE system applied to the corpus of 100 texts

Matching	% of Precision	% of Recall	% of F-score
Full	68.53	57.66	62.62
Partial	72.41	63.14	67.45

The failure cases of our KE system may be explained by several reasons:

- In nearly 30% of the documents, keyphrases never appear in the body of the texts they are supposed to represent. This observation confirms the idea that typically only 70% to 80% of the authors' keyphrases appear somewhere in the body of their documents [24]. This kind of keyphrases is obviously difficult to detect.

- About 25% of the keyphrases composed by their authors exist in their papers only in a partial form.
- The normalization algorithm, in the preprocessing module of our KE system, needs to be improved, because its performance has a great impact on the final results. For example, if we had a synonyms thesaurus of arabic words (which attests that خام (crude) is a synonym of نفط (oil)) we could have a better score for the candidate rule نفط → سعر (which has only 66% as support).
- Even if we have the exact words (given by good candidate rules) composing a keyphrase, it is not always easy to order them to make the correct keyphrase. This part of the system should be improved too.

7 Conclusion

Keyphrases are very important for several applications of Information Retrieval, Text-Mining, and Natural Language Processing. Their automatic extraction is a challenging problem.

In this paper we have presented an approach based on the Associations Rules model to extract keyphrases from modern standard Arabic texts. The proposed system is articulated around two main modules: Text pre-processing and Association Rules mining.

The experiments done and the results obtained are promising: the performance values of the proposed system (in terms of precision, recall and f-score) are higher than 60% and can exceed 70%. But a larger evaluation is necessary, with the comparison with other approaches in a benchmarking context.

Furthermore, many other extensions have been noted. Among them, we can cite: improving the preprocessing module, including synonyms of keywords/keyphrases, treating keyphrases in partial forms, enhancing the keyphrases construction from their components (keywords) obtained after the Association Rules mining, etc.

References

1. Beliga, S.: Keyword extraction: a review of methods and approaches. University of Rijeka, Department of Informatics, pp. 1–9 (2014)
2. Bougouin, A.: Etat de l'art des méthodes d'extraction automatique de termes-clés. In: Proceedings of Rencontre des Etudiants Chercheurs en Informatique pour le Traitement Automatique des Langues (RECITAL), Sables d'Olonne-France, pp. 96–109 (2013)
3. Hasan, K.S. Ng, V.: Automatic keyphrase extraction: a survey of the state of the art. In: Proceedings of the 52nd Annual Meeting of the Association for Computational Linguistics, vol. 1, pp. 1262–1273 (2014)
4. Siddiqi, S., Sharan, A.: Keyword and keyphrase extraction techniques: a literature review. Int. J. Comput. Appl. **109**(2), 18–23 (2015)
5. Berry, M.W., Kogan, J.: Text Mining: Applications and Theory. Wiley, Chichester (2010)

6. Palshikar, G.K.: Keyword extraction from a single document using centrality measures. In: Ghosh, A., De, R.K., Pal, S.K. (eds.) PReMI 2007. LNCS, vol. 4815, pp. 503–510. Springer, Heidelberg (2007). https://doi.org/10.1007/978-3-540-77046-6_62

7. Habibi, M., Popescu-Belis, A.: Keyword extraction and clustering for document recommendation in conversations. IEEE/ACM Trans. Audio Speech Lang. Process. **23**(4), 746–759 (2015)

8. Onan, A., Korukoğlu, S., Bulut, H.: Ensemble of keyword extraction methods and classifiers in text classification. Expert Syst. Appl. **57**, 232–247 (2016)

9. Beliga, S., Meštrović, A., Martinčić-Ipšić, S.: An overview of graph-based keyword extraction methods and approaches. J. Inf. Organ. Sci. **39**(1), 1–20 (2015)

10. Zhang, Q., Wang, Y., Gong, Y., Huang, X.: Keyphrase extraction using deep recurrent neural networks on Twitter. In: Proceedings of the 2016 Conference on Empirical Methods in Natural Language Processing, pp. 836–845 (2016)

11. Awajan, A.: Keyword extraction from arabic documents using term equivalence classes. ACM Trans. Asian Low-Resour. Lang. Inf. Process. **14**(2), 7:1–7:18 (2015)

12. Duwairi, R., Hedaya, M.: Automatic keyphrase extraction for Arabic news documents based on KEA system. J. Intell. Fuzzy Syst. **30**(4), 2101–2110 (2016)

13. Amer, E., Foad, K.: AKEA: an Arabic keyphrase extraction algorithm. In: Hassanien, A., Shaalan, K., Gaber, T., Azar, A., Tolba, M. (eds.) AISI 2016. AISC, vol. 533, pp. 137–146. Springer, Cham (2016). https://doi.org/10.1007/978-3-319-48308-5_14

14. Omoush, E.H., Samawi, V.W.: Arabic keyword extraction using SOM neural network. Int. J. Adv. Stud. Comput. Sci. Eng. **5**(11), 7–12 (2016)

15. Sahmoudi, I., Lachkar, A.: Towards a linguistic patterns for arabic keyphrases extraction. In: 2016 International Conference on Information Technology for Organizations Development (IT4OD), pp. 1–6. IEEE (2016)

16. Helmy, M., Vigneshram, R.M., Serra, G., Tasso, C.: Applying deep learning for arabic keyphrase extraction. Procedia Comput. Sci. **142**, 254–261 (2018)

17. Suleiman, D., Awajan, A.: Bag-of-concept based keyword extraction from Arabic documents. In: 2017 8th International Conference on Information Technology (ICIT), pp. 863–869. IEEE (2017)

18. Rammal, M., Bahsoun, Z., Al Achkar Jabbour, M.: Keyword extraction from Arabic legal texts. Interact. Technol. Smart Educ. **12**(1), 62–71 (2015)

19. Najadat, H.M., Hmeidi, I.I., Al-Kabi, M.N., Issa, M.M.B.: Automatic keyphrase extractor from arabic documents. Int. J. Adv. Comput. Sci. Appl. **7**(2), 192–199 (2016)

20. Salloum, S.A., Al-Emran, M., Monem, A.A., Shaalan, K.: Using text mining techniques for extracting information from research articles. In: Shaalan, K., Hassanien, A., Tolba, F. (eds.) Intelligent Natural Language Processing: Trends and Applications. SCI, vol. 740, pp. 373–397. Springer, Cham (2018). https://doi.org/10.1007/978-3-319-67056-0_18

21. Li, X., Song, F.: Keyphrase extraction and grouping based on association rules. In: The Twenty-Eighth International Flairs Conference, pp. 181–186 (2015)

22. Agrawal, R., Srikant, R.: Fast algorithms for mining association rules. In: Proceedings of 20th International Conference on Very Large Data Bases VLDB, vol. 1215, pp. 487–499 (1994)

23. HaCohen-Kerner, Y., Gross, Z., Masa, A.: Automatic extraction and learning of keyphrases from scientific articles. In: Gelbukh, A. (ed.) CICLing 2005. LNCS, pp. 657–669. Springer, Heidelberg (2005). https://doi.org/10.1007/978-3-540-30586-6_74

24. Turney, P.: Learning algorithms for keyphrase extraction. Inf. Retr. J. **2**(4), 303–336 (2000)

HPSG Grammar Supporting Arabic Preference Nouns and Its TDL Specification

Samia Ben Ismail[1(✉)], Sirine Boukédi[2(✉)], and Kais Haddar[3(✉)]

[1] Miracl Laboratory, ISITCom Hammam Sousse,
Sousse University, Sousse, Tunisia
Samia_benismail@yahoo.fr
[2] Miracl Laboratory, National Engineering School,
Gabes University, Gabes, Tunisia
sirine.boukedi@gmail.com
[3] Miracl Laboratory, Faculty of Science of Sfax, Sfax University, Sfax, Tunisia
kais.haddar@yahoo.fr

Abstract. An Arabic preference noun (i.e. comparative and superlative) is among the nominal forms derived from a verb that we have treated. Our work is pure morphological processing to generate automatically the derivatives of nouns and verbs from canonical forms. This treatment is an important step in Natural Language Processing (NLP). It represents a pretreatment for syntactic analyses and contributes in the construction of extensional lexicon. In this paper, we present a part of our work, the Head Driven Phrase Structure Grammar (HPSG) representation of preference nouns for Arabic language. The choice of this formalism is justified. In fact, HPSG is a unification grammar based on a set of principles, essentially inheritance. This principle allows treating several phenomena with a minimum number of rules.. For this reason, we start by classifying different patterns of preference nouns and representing them with HPSG. After that, each pattern was specified with Type Description Language (TDL). Then, it was validated on Linguistic Knowledge Building (LKB) system. The obtained results are encouraging which proves the effectiveness of our system.

Keywords: Arabic preference noun · Head-driven Phrase Structure Grammar (HPSG) · Type Description Language (TDL) · Linguistic Knowledge Building (LKB) system

1 Introduction

Arabic language is very rich by morphological phenomena. In fact, it marks its diversity of morphological structure. Indeed, for one lexeme, we can generate several form types (i.e. inflectional and derivational). Thus, the automatic generation of Arabic morphological forms is a primordial task in NLP domain. It allows the construction of extensional lexicon with large coverage and guarantees the reusability and the interoperability of resources, essentially by using a unification grammar such as HPSG. Certainly, this type of formalism offers a complete representation with a minimum number of rules. Among the most delicate derivational forms, we identify the preference nouns for Arabic. However, works treating Arabic preference noun especially

© Springer Nature Switzerland AG 2019
K. Smaïli (Ed.): ICALP 2019, CCIS 1108, pp. 221–234, 2019.
https://doi.org/10.1007/978-3-030-32959-4_16

with HPSG are very limited or almost non-existent. Indeed, preference noun has several forms and its treatment isn't evident. It is based on several criteria (i.e., the radical, the verb scheme, the semantic aspect and the preference notion).

Among the forms that we have treated, we were interested on preference noun (i.e. comparative and superlative) within LKB. To do this, we begin by studying the Arabic preference noun to identify its different specificities. Based on this study, we identified the various constraints characterizing each pattern. These constraints were described using HPSG formalism. To validate the elaborated HPSG grammar, each pattern is specified in TDL. The originality of our work appears in the use of such formalism like HPSG to model NLP resources. Moreover, the lack of researchers treating the Arabic morphology especially preference forms with the LKB platform represents another novelty.

In the present paper, we begin by describing and discuss some previous works treating Arabic morphological aspect. After that, we present a detailed linguistic study about the Arabic preference nouns. According to this study, we present, in the next section, the elaborated HPSG grammar for Arabic preferences noun and its TDL specification. Then, we experiment and evaluate the different preference forms with the LKB system. Finally, we conclude our work and we give some perspectives.

2   Previous Works

In NLP domain, there exist two main approaches used: statistical and linguistic ones. Moreover, we conclude two methods for the generation of linguistic resources. The first method consists in the development of morphological parsers. The second method consists in the use of generator systems like LKB (Linguistic Knowledge Building) and TRALE, an extension of ALE (Attribute Save Engine). All these generators are very performing and they are based on normalized representation.

For the first method, AlKhalil Morph Sys2 [3] is an Arabic morphological analyzer based on linguistic method. It detects all the possible morphological features for each word. Based on the root of a word, this analyzer can search and find all the derivational and flexional forms in the text. Moreover, it identifies its location in the text, its occurrence and its context. The obtained results can be in HTML (HyperText Markup Language), CSV (Comma-separated values) or XML format. In fact, Alkalil Morph Sys2 is developed in five steps. The first step is "Preprocessing" that segments the text into words and eliminates khashida and diacritic marks. Besides, it stores in memory a copy of diacritic marks of input words. The second step illustrates the "Segmentation" phase. It identifies the obtained word from the first step as a series of constituents (Proclitic+Stem+Enclitic). The third one, the "Analysis of the stem" step, is divided into four sub-steps analysis to detect the type of stem (i.e. exceptional word, non-derived word, derived word or verb). The fourth step: "Validation of results", checks the validity of morphological constraints. The final step "Display of the mophosyntactic analyzer's results", identifies for each word the possible solutions and its morpho-syntactic features. After the implementation phase, [3] evaluates the performance of Alkhalil Morph Sys2 by comparing it to three other analyzers: the first version of the analyzer Alkhalil Morpho Sys, BAMA and SAMA. Based on this comparison, the authors obtained great results with AlKhalil Morph Sys2.

YAMAMA [11] a multi-dialect Arabic morphological analyzer motivated by the FARASA approach. The main goal of YAMAMA is to combine the output of MADAMIRA with FARASA's approach. Besides, it conserves the same architecture and uses the same dataset of MADAMIRA system while making some modification. Indeed, they were interested essentially in the generation of the maximum likelihood model selecting for each word the highest frequent analysis. The selected analyses are stored in a dictionary used when the system is running. They contain all the morphological and lexical features. For Analysis and Disambiguation step YAMAMA ranks for each words all of the analyses using the multiplication of their lemma probability and their Buckwalter tag probability. With the same way, both probabilities are compared using the training data and the highest score analysis is selected. After that, the word and analysis are added to the analysis dictionary. For the output generation, YAMAMA uses the same format as MADAMIRA's. Moreover, concerning its evaluation, the authors choose to make two types of tests. The first test aims to fix the targets accuracy and speed while the second test allows fixing the targets machine translation quality. Besides, they compare YAMAMA with two systems MADAMIRA and FARASA. As result, YAMAMA is five times faster than MADAMIRA while FARASA is four times faster than YAMAMA. Therefore, as conclusion for the first method, all output formats are not normalized such as HPSG formalism. Although this task is the base for interoperability and interchangeability of linguistic resources between NLP applications.

For second method based on existed parser, we find some works such as [1, 8–10] for Arabic language. All these works treat some specificities of Arabic grammar with HPSG formalism.

[10] proposes an HPSG representation for verb-derived nouns. This representation is treated on several steps. The first step for this work is to construct a type hierarchy for Arabic verbal noun. In fact, in this step, they classify all types of verbal noun and its properties. Then, based on this type hierarchy, they propose an AVM for Arabic noun adopted from AVM for English. After that, [10] extends from AVM for Arabic noun an AVM for a verbal noun. Finally, they propose construction rules of a verbal noun from root verb by expanding the MORPH, SYN and SEM features. This work treats verbal noun from trilateral non-sound Form I and quadrilateral verbs. Additionally, [2] treats all types of gerund forms for Arabic with HPSG grammar. This work used a linguistic approach to develop its derivational rules. Moreover, to validate this work, the authors use LKB to generate their HPSG grammars.

[9] generates an HPSG representation with TRALE platform for Arabic nominal declension including all feature's type (i.e. morphological, syntactic and semantic). This generation is treated according to some steps. First, the type hierarchy designation of Arabic declension is the initial and the base step of this work. Then, based on this hierarchy, they represent HPSG rules. After that, they implement all these steps with TRALE platform to validate its grammar.

As [1, 9] proposes an HPSG analysis for simple and construct-state noun phrases in Modern Standard Arabic (MSA). In fact, they treat the definite and indefinite affixes within HPSG. They try to propose three cases of analyses. However, after these tries, they deduce that nouns appear in head-adjunct complement structures in which they treat it as the third case.

Despite works are evolved, Arabic language is still among languages that have less linguistic resources. The lack appears during the grammar generation with such formalism especially for the morphological analyzer. In fact, the inflectional/derivational and lexical rules of these grammars are limited.

3 Arabic Preference Noun HPSG Representation

According to [5], the preference noun (PN) is a derived noun obtained from an Arabic verb. PN denotes two nouns related by a characteristic comparative tool. In fact, to obtain this type of noun, the verb must accept the notion of preference. Moreover, it must have a tense and trilateral. In fact, Table 1 illustrates the construction conditions of the preference noun.

Table 1. Construction conditions of preference noun

Verb example	Construction Condition of preference noun	Preference noun
فَضُلَ (فَعُلَ) faḍula	Have a tense: yes Trilateral: yes Preference notion: yes	أفضل āfóḍalu
نعم n'óma	Have a tense: no Trilateral: yes Preference notion: yes	no
زاحم zāḥama	Have a tense: yes Trilateral: no Preference notion: yes	helped element + the gerund of verb
مات māta	Have a tense: yes Trilateral: yes Preference notion: no	no

As shown in Table 1, if one among the conditions is absent, we cannot construct the preference noun from this verb. For example, the preference noun from the verb "māta /مات" doesn't exist because this verb not contains the condition "preference notion". Thus, this condition is important in the construction of preference noun to eliminate the ambiguity and the incorrect forms. Furthermore, it is necessary to consider these conditions as HPSG features to represent an Arabic verb. Besides, the construction of preference noun from a verb is based on the schemes "āf'ala/أفعل" for the male gender and the scheme "fu'lai /فعلى" for the female gender.

However, it exists some exception for some type of verb. Indeed, if the Resembling participle of this verb is obtained according to the scheme "āf'ala" or if this verb is not triliteral verb, the preference noun cannot be generated as a sample form. Thus, the preference noun is constructed as a composed form (helped element + gerund of verb). In fact, a helped element is a noun based on the scheme "āf'ala" and generated from a triliteral verb such as "ākṭaru /أكثر", "āqalwu /أقل" and "āšadwu /أشد". For example, the preference noun for the verb "aḥtarama /احترم" is a composed form "ākṭaru aḥtaramā /أكثر احتراما". In fact, this compound is treated just syntactically. While, for this paper, we just focus on the preference noun construction with morphological aspect (i.e. derivational forms).

After this linguistic study, we conclude all necessary features adding to HPSG rules representation to construct the preference noun.

First, HPSG [7] is based on a typed feature structure called AVM (Attribute Value Matrix) and sets of schemata based on a set of constraints and inheritance principle modeling the different grammatical phenomena. Besides, it represents the different linguistic structures (i.e. types, lexicon and morphological/syntactical rules). We give in Fig. 1 the sign of HPSG formalism.

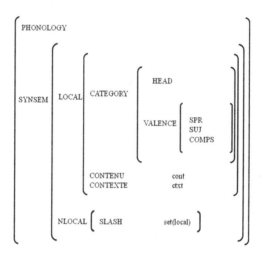

Fig. 1. HPSG sign.

According to [7], the PHONOLOGY contains the phonological information of the sign. The feature SYNSEM describes the sign at the morphological, syntactic and semantic level. The first one is representing in the feature HEAD. Then, the second one is describing in the feature VALENCE. Finally, the semantic aspect can be represented in features CONTENU and CONTEXTE. In fact, inspired by some previous works such as [2] and based on our linguistic study [5], we adapted the HPSG representation of Arabic preference noun. Besides, we add the feature "PREFERENCE" to the HPSG representation of Arabic Verb. In fact, an example of HPSG representation of this type of derived forms illustrates in Fig. 2.

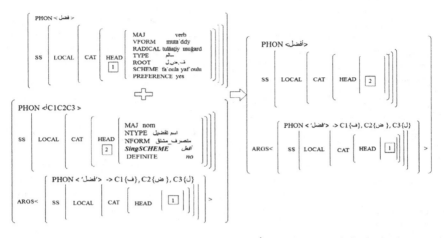

Fig. 2. AVM of preference noun "āfḍalu /أفضل" applying morphological rule.

Figure 2 shows the used lexical rule that transforms the verb "faḍula /فضل" to the derived noun "āfḍalu /أفضل". Besides, it adds entire specific features of this derived noun. In fact, this derived noun is a preference noun "NTYPE اسم تفضيل" and its singular schema is "SingSCHEME أفعل". Indeed, this rule adds the AVM "ARGS" to describe original verb that allows constructing this type of form. Moreover, according to our example, this preference noun is a singular noun and its genre is male. However, for the female genre, we need to apply another morphological rule based on the scheme "fu'lai /فضلى".

On all preferences nouns, as common nouns, we can apply inflectional rules (dual and plural). Indeed, HPSG representation of this transformation is illustrated in Fig. 3.

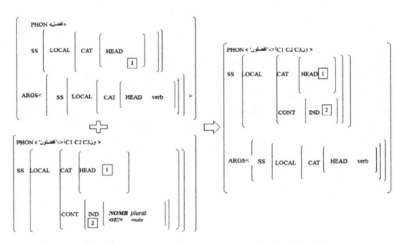

Fig. 3. AVM of preference noun "أفضلون/ afḍlūn".

As represented in Fig. 3, the used lexical rule transform a noun in plural with the male gender. In fact, this rule specifies two essential features. The first one NOMB describes the number of noun. The second one GEN describes its gender. These two features are added at the level of the CONT.IND feature. Moreover, this type of noun can applied the definiteness notion. In fact, we add to the feature DEFINITE the Boolean value 'yes'. After the HPSG representation, to validate this elaborated grammar, we should specified it with a description language. In the next section, we present the TDL specification of the elaborated Arabic HPSG of preference noun.

4   TDL Specification of Preference Noun

To implement the proposed HPSG preference nouns within LKB system, it is necessary to specify it in TDL. It is recommended to support some formalism such as HPSG. Indeed, TDL [6] syntax is very similar to HPSG and based on typed features connected by a set of principles, especially inheritance.

Table 2. TDL syntax.

Operator	Function
&	The constraints addition allows on type
# [a..z]	For structures indexation and labeling
#|...|#	For comments addition of several lines
:=	Element on the left is defined like constraints by element on the right
[ ]	To define a feature structure: attribute value Matrix
< >	To define a list
,	To separate attribute-value couples in an AVM
;	For comments addition on the same line
.	To indicate the end of type description. Also equivalent to [ ]

The specification of the elaborated HPSG grammar is based on these operators describing in Table 2. Based on these operators, we specify the type hierarchy of our grammar, the lexicon and different morphological rules. In fact, this specification is based on general syntax: ***type: = body {,} * option***, where *type* is the type name to be set. In the same way, the syntax definition of a sub-type is: ***subtype: = supertype &*** ***constraints***, which *subtype* is a sub-type inherits from the type root (*supertype*) after checking constraints. In addition, the *AVM* type has as a subtype: *cons*. Indeed, the definition of this subtype in TDL is: ***cons: = avm & [FIRST, REST]***. So the concept of inheritance is expressed in TDL by ": =" and the expression which lies between "[ ]" is a constraint to check. For more explanation, Fig. 4 illustrates the type hierarchy of the Arabic preference noun with TDL description.

```
nom := tete&[MAJ "nom",
            NTYPE ntype,
            NFORM nform].
nom_variable:= nom &
            [NFORM متصرف,
            NGENRE ngenre,
            NRADICAL nradical,
            NAT nat,
            SingSCHEME nscheme,
            ADJ boolean,
            ROOT string,
            DEFINI boolean].
nom_variable_derive:= nom_variable & [NFORM
متصرف_مشتق].
nom_preference:= nom_variable_derive & [NTYPE
اسم_تفضيل].
```

Fig. 4. Type hierarchy of preference noun with TDL description.

In Fig. 4, the Arabic preference noun is inherited from the variable derived noun that is inherited itself from the variable noun type and the noun that is a general type. As well as the Arabic noun is inherited from the base sign "tete". Since the preference noun is a derived form from an Arabic verb, it is necessary also to specify the type hierarchy of the Arabic verb. So, each type (verb, noun) has its own specifications developed in the type files (i.e. type.tdl and lex-type.tdl). Figure 5 shows the type specification for an Arabic verb.

```
lex-verb := lexeme & [SS [LOC [CAT [TETE verbe,
            VAL [ SUJ < [LOC [CAT [TETE nom,
                                VAL[COMPS< >]],
                  CONT.IND #indice ],
                  NONLOC.REL <! !>] > ],
            MARQUE non-marque],
      CONT [IND referentiel,
            RELS <! [ARG1 #indice,
                        RELN rel-sem-verb] !>]],
      NONLOC.REL <! !>]].
verbe := tete &

            [MAJ "verbe",
            TYPE type,
            RADICAL radical,
            SCHEME scheme,
            VFORM vform,
            ROOT string,
            PREFERENCE boolean].
```

Fig. 5. Type specification of Arabic verb.

As we mentioned in our linguistic study, the construction of Arabic preference noun need a complete description of the verb as we are illustrated in Fig. 5. In fact, the semantic description is representing in the feature "RELN". Moreover, the morphological description is representing in following the features: "TYPE", "RADICAL", and "SCHEME", "VFORM", "ROOT and "PREFERENCE".

After the type specification of each type of word (i.e. noun and verb), we specify all entries with its features and values in the file "lexicon.tdl". Figure 6 shows the entry specification of an Arabic verb.

```
فضل := lex-verb-complet-sain-intact &
[PHON <! "فضل" !>,
 SS.LOC [CAT[TETE[ RACINE "ل،ض،ف",
            SCHEME فَعُلَ يَفْعُلُ,
            RADICAL ثلاثي_مجرّد,
            VFORM غير_متعدي,
            PREFERENCE نعم]]]].
```

Fig. 6. Verb "فضل" with TDL syntax.

As shown in Fig. 6, the verb "فضل" is an instance from "lex-verb-complet-sain-intact". This class contains all the verb of type intact "سالم". Each verb is specified by phonetic "PHON" and morphological features. In fact, this verb is a triliteral "ثلاثي_مجرّد" and transitive "متعدي" verb. Besides, it accept the transformation to a preference noun according the feature "PREFERENCE". This constraint is necessary to generate the morphological rules. In fact, for more explanation, Fig. 7 illustrates TDL specification of morphological rules to construct Arabic preference noun.

```
%(letter-set (!p ش ص ن ح ق ي د ك ك ع ج ر ف ب س م ز ل))

(1) prefnoun-trileteral-nu-mal :=
%prefix(!p ﺃ!p)!!!
  l2m-flex &
  [SS
    [LOC.CAT [TETE [NFORM متصرف_مشتق, NTYPE اسم_التفضيل, SingSCHEME أفْعَل,
    DEFINI لا,NAT اسم_صحيح, RACINE #string,NGENRE اسم_مذكر, ADJ لا]]],
    ARGS < [SS.LOC.CAT.TETE[TYPE type, RACINE #string , RADICAL ثلاثي_مجرّد,
    PREFERENCE نعم]] >].


(2) prefnoun-trileteral-nu-fem :=
%suffix(* ى)!!!
  l2m-flex &
  [SS
    [LOC.CAT [TETE [NFORM متصرف_مشتق, NTYPE اسم_التفضيل, SingSCHEME فُعْلى,
    DEFINI لا,NAT مقصور,RACINE #string,NGENRE اسم_مؤنث, ADJ لا]]],
    ARGS < [SS.LOC.CAT.TETE[TYPE type, RACINE #string , RADICAL ثلاثي_مجرّد,
    PREFERENCE نعم]] >].
```

Fig. 7. Preference noun TDL rules

As shown in Fig. 7, in the first rule (1), we added the letters "أ" before the first letter of the verb. All the possible first letter of the verb are regrouped in the set "letter-set" called "!p". This rule is applied to a set type of verbs combined in the type "TYPE" such as intact verb. Moreover, these types of verb must belong to a set of properties "*RADICAL* مجرّد ثلاثي *PREFERENCE* نعم". This rule construct all preference nouns for male gender. While the second rule (2) construct all preference noun for female gender. After this transformation from one lexeme to word (l2m-flex), the obtained preference nouns can be applied to inflectional rule (i.e dual or plural). In fact, in the following figure (Fig. 8), we give an example of inflectional rule transforming the obtained singular preference noun to plural preference noun.

```
    (1)  nom-pluriel-regulier_sain :=
%suffix (* ونَ)
  m2m-flex &
  [SS #synsem &
    [LOC[CAT [TETE nom & [NAT nat1,NFORM متصرف,DEC مرفوع]],
        CONT. IND[ NOMB سالم_مذكر_جمع,
            GEN مذكر]]],
  ARGS < [SS #synsem] >].


    (2)  nom-pluriel-fem-reduit_subjectif_maksour :=
%suffix (ى يَاتٍ)
  m2m-flex &
  [SS #synsem &
    [LOC[CAT [TETE nom & [NAT مقصور,NFORM متصرف,DEC dec5]],
        CONT. IND[ NOMB سالم_مؤنث_جمع,
            GEN مؤنث]]],
  ARGS < [SS #synsem] >].
```

Fig. 8. Example of inflectional rule transforming singular noun to plural.

Figure 8 illustrates the transformation of some type of Arabic nouns, from singular to plural. The first rule (1) shows the transformation to regular male plural. In fact, it is made by adding the suffix (ون / wn), to the obtained derived form and by inheriting the rule "m2m-flex". Indeed, this last rule enables to transform a word to another word. With the same manner, the second rule (2) transforms the female preference noun to regular female plural noun with replacing the last letter "ى" by "يَاتٍ". All these rules add its two specific features values: NOMB and GEN.

After the TDL specification, the proposed type hierarchy and the different developed derivational and inflectional rules were validated within the LKB platform. In the following section, we give the validation of the elaborated HPSG grammar supporting the preference nouns. Then, we evaluate the obtained results.

5 Experimentation with LKB and Evaluation

To experiment and evaluate the elaborated grammar generate preference nouns, we used LKB (Linguistic Knowledge Building). This system uses its own algorithms and generates a reliable analyzer [4]. It is used to validate unification grammars based on constraints and feature structures. In fact, this platform is composed from two types of files: lisp files (i.e. files system configuration) and TDL files representing the established grammar.

In our work, we developed 5 TDL files describing the prference Arabic grammar such as the lexicon file "lexicon.tdl". This file contains all canonical verbs as lexemes. Besides, as we already mentioned, our morphological rules are specified in the file "rlex.tdl". In fact, since to constraint principle that is based in HPSG formalization, we specified our rules. Therefore, based on this principle, we can eliminate all wrong forms.

After application of the added rules, LKB platform adds automatically, ten morphological features describing this preference noun such as NTYPE, SingSCHEME, NGENRE and NAT. Moreover, this platform generates an adequate derivation tree that proves the effectiveness of our system. Thus, Fig. 9 illustrates an example of our result obtained with LKB. It shows the generation of the preference noun "أفضل" from the canonical form of verb "فضل". We can note also in this figure all the adding morphological features. Moreover, the description of the preference noun's origin verb is added in the feature "ARGS". In fact, for this example, it is an intact verb defining in the lexical rule called "lex-verb-complet-sain-intact".

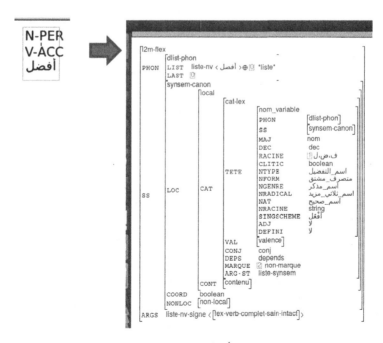

Fig. 9. HPSG Preference noun "أفضل" generated with LKB

As shown in Fig. 9, the HPSG generation of this preference noun define that it is derived variable noun. Thus, this type of noun can be applied with inflectional rules (dual and plural). Therefore, Fig. 10 illustrates examples the HPSG representation of regular plural (male and female) for preference nouns. Indeed, this generation can have two steps with adding the two features NOMB and GEN. In fact, Fig. 10 describes the HPSG representation for the two plural preference nouns "أفضلون" and "فضليات" male and female respectively. Moreover, it describe the full process of generation representing in the feature ARGS.

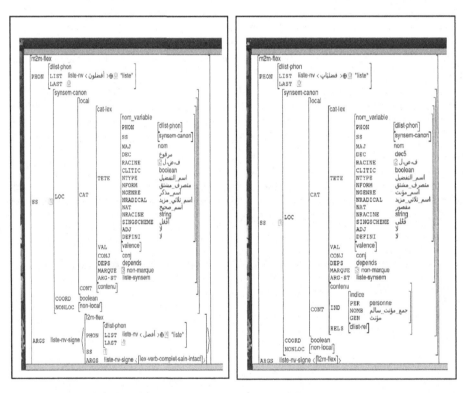

Fig. 10. HPSG Preference nouns "أفضلون" and "فضليات" generated with LKB

As we indicate in figures above, HPSG morphological representation of all forms of preference noun is generally complete. For evaluation, we calculate the performance average (P) of the correct features automatically added. This average is defined by the Eq. (1):

$$P = \text{(total number of correct features automatically added)}/\text{(total number of features automatically added)} \tag{1}$$

Our system generates all preference nouns of Arabic verb that respect the condition of construction. However, for HPSG representation, the feature NRACINE for the obtained preference noun is not defined. So, according to average of performance, we obtain 90% percent (i.e correct features: 9 and total number of features: 10) for each preference noun specified with HPSG representation. In fact, the obtained values (90%) prove the effectiveness of our proposed transformation system. However, the percent of failure is because of the ambiguous information during the transformation process (verb to noun).

6 Conclusion

In this paper, we have developed a system allowing the generation of all forms of preference nouns within LKB. Based on linguistic approach, this system is based on an Arabic HPSG grammar specified in TDL. In fact, for this step, we have adapted some exist features elaborated in other previews works. Besides, we have added another feature called "PREFERENCE" that can eliminate wrong forms. For the experimentation and the evaluation phases, we have tested the generation of this type of derived noun. Therefore, as shown in the evaluation phase, our system can represent all the morphological features of preference nouns. These obtained results prove its effectiveness.

As perspectives, we aim to treat other irregular morphological phenomena such as Arabic agglutination and exaggeration noun. This treatment requires the extension of the established Arabic HPSG grammar to treat all types of morphological phenomena. Moreover, we aim to integrate, in our system, syntactic rules to test our established grammar on an Arabic corpus.

References

1. AlQurashi, I.S.: An analysis of simple and construct-state noun phrases in modern standard Arabic. In: Muller, S. (eds.) 22nd International Conference on Head-Driven Phrase Structure Grammar Proceedings, pp. 6–26. CSLI Publications, Nanyang Technological University (NTU), Singapore Stanford (2015)
2. Ben Ismail, S., Boukédi, S., Haddar, K.: The treatment of gerund forms for Arabic nouns with LKB system. In: The 10th International Conference on Knowledge Engineering and Ontology Development (KEOD 2018), Seville, Spain, 18–20 September 2018 (2018)
3. Boudchiche, M., Mazroui A., Ould Bebah, M., Lakhouaja, A., Boudlal, A.: AlKhalil Morpho Sys 2: a robust Arabic morpho-syntactic analyzer. J. King Saud Univ. Comput. Inf. Sci. 29, 141–146 (2016)
4. Copestake, A.: Implementing Typed Feature Structure Grammars. Cambridge University Press, Cambridge (2002)
5. Dahdah, A.: معجم قواعد اللغة العربية في جداول و لوحات„, 5th edn. Lebenon library, Lebanon (1992
6. Krieger, H., Schäfer, U.: TDL: A Type Description Language for HPSG. Part 2: User guide. Technical reports, Deutsches Forschungszentrum für Künstliche Intelligenz, Saarbrücken, Germany (1994)

7. Pollard, C., Sag, I.: Head-Driven Phrase Structure Grammars. Chicago University Press, Chicago (1994)
8. Mammeri, M.F., Bouhacein, N.: Le syntagme nominal défini en arabe standard contemporain. Prague Bull. Math. Linguist. **97**, 55–82 (2012)
9. Masum, M.H., Sadiqul Islam, M., Rahman, M.S., Ahmed, R.: HPSG analysis of type-based Arabic nominal declension. In: 13th International Conference on Arab Conference on Information Technology (ACIT 2012), Jordan, pp. 10–13 (2012)
10. Sadiqul Sadiqul, M., Masum, M.H., Shariful Islam Bhuyan, M., Reaz, A.: Arabic nominals in HPSG: a verbal noun perspective. In: 17th International Conference on Head-driven Phrase Structure Grammar, France, pp 158–178 (2010)
11. Khalifa, S., Zalmout, N., Habash, N.: YAMAMA: yet another multi-dialect Arabic morphological analyzer. In: 26th International Conference on Computational Linguistics: System Demonstrations, Osaka, Japan, 11–17 December 2016, pp 223–227 (2016)

Resources: Analysis, Disambiguation and Evaluation

"AlkhalilDWS": An Arabic Dictionary Writing System Rich in Lexical Resources

Mohammed Reqqass[1](✉), Abdelhak Lakhouaja[1],
and Mohamad Bebah[2]

[1] Faculty of Sciences, Mohamed First University,
Av Med VI BP 717, 60000 Oujda, Morocco
reqqass.mohammed@gmail.com, abdel.lakh@gmail.com
[2] Arab Center for Research and Policy Studies, Doha, Qatar
mohamad.bebah@dohainstitute.org

Abstract. In the classical lexicography, making dictionary was accomplished with pen and paper which increases the effort and the time spent by editors. To avoid this challenge, the modern lexicography resort to computer linguistics technologies. As a consequence, many software programs called Dictionary Writing Systems (DWS) were developed to simplify the work of editors, to guarantee the compilation of dictionaries in a structured data allowing the publication of interactive versions of produced dictionaries and to allow the exchange of lexical data in other natural language processing applications like automatic translation and semantic web.

The purpose of this paper is to describe the Arabic Dictionary Writing System "AlkhalilDWS", a new web application used to edit and publish monolingual Arabic dictionaries. It provides many functionalities that minimize the time and the efforts spent to make an Arabic dictionary. Also, using "AlkhalilDWS" guarantees the exportation of the dictionary in the standard format Lexical Markup Framework (LMF) which is recognized by the International Standards Organization (ISO).

Keywords: Dictionary writing system · Making arabic dictionaries · Lexical Markup Framework

1 Introduction

Using computer technology in lexicography is inevitable [1]. The computer technology changes the way in which dictionaries are written, edited [2] and published.

In the present paper, we describe "AlkhalilDWS" system. This system designed to assist the editors to make their Arabic dictionaries more efficiently from the beginning to the end. It supports editors during the process of building their dictionaries from the identification of the lexical entries to the edition of these entries and their publication:

- Identification of lexical entries: different options are available for the collection and identification of lexical entries,

© Springer Nature Switzerland AG 2019
K. Smaïli (Ed.): ICALP 2019, CCIS 1108, pp. 237–250, 2019.
https://doi.org/10.1007/978-3-030-32959-4_17

- Editing lexical entries: the system allows editors to edit lexical entries collaboratively from different places; indeed, an editor can create a group of editors to
elaborate his dictionary. Also, it offers many features and lexical resources that
make the entry edition easier,
- Publication of lexical entries: the system allows editors to publish their dictionaries
in different formats such as XML. It offers also a web interface to publish an
interactive version of the produced dictionaries.

The rest of this paper is organized as follows. In Sect. 2, we describe the characteristics of a typical Dictionary Writing System, then we present some of the most
known DWS. In Sect. 3, we present our system "AlkhalilDWS" used to produce
Arabic dictionaries respecting the LMF standard (Lexical Markup Framework).

2 Characteristic of a DWS

The lexicography is a discipline that is interested in producing dictionaries. We can
summarize the process of production in two essentials steps:

- The collection of lexical entries in the dictionary: in this step lexicographer searches
and collects the terms used in a specific language or discipline,
- Editing the lexical entries of the dictionary: in this step, lexicographer edits the
terms and organizes them according to a specific macrostructure and microstructure
already defined.

To accomplish these steps lexicographer spends a lot of time and effort especially
for rich and modern languages such Arabic. For that, lexicographers need to find and
use a writing system that allows them to:

- Write and edit dictionary entries,
- Control the quality of entries and ensure their consistency,
- Exploit available linguistic resources (documents, web, electronic dictionaries, etc.),
- Produce the dictionary in several forms: paper, electronic...,
- Exchange with other applications,
- Make collaborative group work to produce the dictionary.

To meet fully or partly these needs, several dictionary writing systems have been
developed [3]. Among the most advanced systems on the market, we mention:

- TshwaneLex: a commercial writing system of monolingual dictionaries, bilingual
dictionaries and multilingual dictionaries [4].
- Matapuna: an open source dictionary writing system developed as part of the
"Matapuna" project. It was used to build a dictionary of Maori language [5].
- Glossword: is a system for writing and publishing multi-language dictionaries. It is
a web application, open source, allowing to designate several profiles of users,
which offers the possibility of distributing the production of a dictionary on several
people [6].

The dictionary writing systems are undergoing continuous improvement. They respond to most editors' requirements. But we believe that making Arabic dictionaries by using these systems is still less efficiently. Below we mention some restrictions of these systems for making Arabic dictionaries:

- The editor can't enter the morphological information of lexical entries in the specific field (root, lemma, type),
- Lemmas are not searchable by their inflected forms in the dictionary entries,
- Errors caused by editors are not detected. For example, the same entry can be entered multiple times without any control of redundancy.

These findings have brought us to build a new dictionary writing system that meets the needs of Arabic lexicography while ensuring consistency of data control and management of making dictionary process.

A dictionary writing system must allow the construction of a dictionary in an interactive environment. It must facilitate the collection of lexical dictionary entries and ensure their consistency. It must also guarantee the management of human resources and the quality control of their work.

2.1 Nature of DWS

The DWS must be based on a server-client architecture [7] to allow many lexicographers working collaboratively and from a different place to produce their dictionaries. Also, this architecture allows the storage of shared data centrally.

2.2 Data Base of DWS

Nowadays, making a dictionary requires processing and storage of an important data. The data is coming from the corpus used to collect lexical entries and their edition, from the lexical resources that the DWS offers and from the informations used to manage the process of making dictionary (user's account, task plan, date of each action...).

This data must be stored in a structured and extensible database. To guarantee an efficient and an easier storage, retrieval, update and delete of data records, is required to use a database management system [8].

2.3 Morphological Analyzer

Morphological analysis plays an important role in dictionary making [9]. The morphological analyzer breaks down a given word form into its morphological constituents, assigning suitable labels or tags to these constituents [10]. Using the morphological analyzer in DWS allows to:

- Find new lexical entries: automatically extract the new lemmas that appeared in the corpus and not contained in the dictionary.
- Add grammatical information to each lexical entry of the dictionary,
- Improve the search for a lexical entry in the dictionary.

2.4 The Spell Checker

The spell checker is a program that detects spelling errors in a text. It is used in a DWS to indicate spelling mistakes that the lexicographer may do while editing the lexical entries. These errors can be grouped into five categories [11]:

- Reading errors: errors occurring when the user tries to write a word from a written source;
- Hearing errors: errors occurring when the user does not have a good knowledge of phonological variations;
- Touch-typing errors: errors occurring when the user types an adjacent letter with another in its keyboard;
- Morphological errors: errors occurring when the user does not have a good knowledge of morphological words;
- Editing errors: errors committed when the user adds, forgets a character in the edit operations.

In "AlkhalilDWS" we have used the Arabic spellchecker dictionary hunspell-ar [12], an open source application based on Hunspell the spellchecker's OpenOffice.org project.

2.5 Lexical Markup Framework

In addition to the usual formats of the dictionaries produced for human use like the paper format or web format, the DWS must guarantee the production of dictionaries in a standard format recognized by the International Standards Organization (ISO). The most common standard is the LMF standard. It is used in the normalization of lexical resources in most languages [13].

LMF is a model that provides a common standardized framework for the construction of natural language processing lexicons. It provides a common model for the creation and the use of the lexical resource, which ensures the exchange of data between these resources [14].

This model has been adopted in many lexical works in NLP for several languages, including Arabic. Indeed, it was adopted in the construction of a lexical database for the Modern Standard Arabic [15], as well as in the modelling of editorial electronic dictionaries [16].

Adopting LMF in a DWS avoids the publication of dictionaries containing some anomalies such as [16]:

- Inconsistency anomalies: the existence of invalid lexical entry knowledge.
- Incoherence anomalies: harmony between the component of the lexical entry.
- Incompleteness anomalies: overlook some of the important information about a lexical entry.
- Redundancy anomalies: the same information occurs more than once.

3 Making Dictionary Using "AlkhalilDWS"

"AlkhalilDWS" is a web application developed with Java language, the data is stored and managed by the database management system MySQL.

3.1 Dictionary Structure

To build the dictionary, the chief editor should define the macrostructure and the microstructure of the dictionary:

- macrostructure: editor defines the global order of the lexical entries in the dictionary;
- microstructure: editor defines the internal structure of the lexical entry and the information it contains.

In "AlkhalilDWS" the definition of macrostructure is not necessary to build the dictionary. However, we define the following microstructure of the dictionary:

- each lexical entry is characterized by the morphological information: root, lemma, type;
- each lexical entry has one or more definitions;
- each definition may have a specific semantic field;
- each definition may have one or more examples.

We note that this microstructure respects the standard LMF.

3.2 Lexical Resources in "AlkhalilDWS"

The main task of the editor is to give a definition for each entry. That takes an important time and effort especially when the editor doesn't have greater familiarity with the various meanings of the lexical entry. For that reason, we have added some Arabic dictionaries to the database of "AlkhalilDWS". The four Arabic dictionaries added to our database are:

- "Almaany dictionary" (معجم المعاني): an electronic dictionary based on several classical dictionaries such as: "... الغني", "الرائد", "لسان العرب" see [17].
- "The interactive dictionary of the Arabic language" (معجم اللغة العربية التفاعلي): an interactive open source web application based on "Alwassyt" dictionary [18].
- "Almustakshif dictionary" (معجم المستكشف): presented in [19] as the first Arabic lexical encyclopedia of the dictionary "المحيط". The numerical version used in this work was published in [20].
- "The Dictionary of the Modern Arabic Language" (معجم اللغة العربية المعاصرة): dictionary targeting to cover classical Arabic words still in usage, as well the new words used in different Arab countries [21].

The first three dictionaries were available in a numerical version able to be integrated into our database. However, the numerical version available for the fourth dictionary was MS Word format. We explain our methodology to build a new structured version of this dictionary in Sect. 3.3. In the following table (Table 1) we summarize the obtained results:

Table 1. The statistic about the lexical resources in "AlkhalilDWS"

Dictionary	Root	Lemma	Meaning	Example	Semantic field
Almaany dictionary	5607	44093	198653	0	0
The interactive dictionary of the Arabic language	7081	133591	133594	11643	247
The modern Arabic dictionary	5739	32258	91874	30909	35
Almustakshif dictionary	5386	20112	26561	0	37

3.3 Operating "The Dictionary of the Modern Arabic Language"

To organize and use the data of "The Dictionary of the Modern Arabic Language", we generated a structured file from the Word version of this dictionary.

We structured the MS Word version of the "The Dictionary of the Modern Arabic Language" by defining entities, fields and their relations as follows:

- Root: a set of consonants. The root regroups all derived lemmas.
- Lemma: the head of the lexical entry. The lemma can have one or more meaning.
- Meaning: the definition of the lexical entry. The meaning can have a semantic field, also it can have one or more example.
- Example: the sentence used to clarify the meaning or to show some usage cases of the lemma.
- Semantic: the semantic field to which the meaning belongs.

To extract data from Word file and to integrate it in the new structure, we proceeded as follows:

- convert the document format of the dictionary to a text file,
- keep only the lexical entries;
- identify and build a mapping root, headword of lexical entries and the content of lexical entries;
- The root is extracted from the line that start with a number followed by the character "-" and isolated Arabic characters. We keep the isolated Arabic characters only.
  - The headword is extracted from the line that does not start with a number or that start with the character "•". We keep the word that appears before the character ":" and the character "[".

- The content of lexical entries is extracted from the line that does not contain root and from the line that contains a headword. If the line contains a headword, we keep only the words appearing before the first occurrence of the character ":";

• extract meaning, semantic field and example from the content of lexical entry;

- the semantic is the word that appears between the first occurrence of the character ")" and the first occurrence of the character "(";

- the examples appear between the character "ıı", each example is separated by the character "-" or the character "○";

- the meaning is the set of words that do not represent the semantics or the examples.

• normalize the writing of the root by removing the space with the isolate Arabic character and replace the characters "آ", "إ", "أ" by the character "ء";

• normalize the writing of the lemma by analyzing them with the morphological analyzer Alkhalil2 [22] and keeping only the result that corresponds to the lexical entries.

We note that the fifth and sixth step are essentials to allow the search in the dictionary by the flexional forms of the lemma. For example, the lexical entry "أَسَد" (lion) in the Word version in "The Dictionary of Modern Arabic Language" was (see Fig. 1):

149 - أ س د

أَسَد [مفرد]: ج آساد وأُسْد وأُسُد وأُسُود، مؤ أَسَدة:

1 - (حن) حيوان مفترس شديد الضراوة من فصيلة السِّنَّوريّات ورُتْبة اللَّواحم، يشمل الذكر والأنثى ويطلق على الأنثى أسدة ولَبُؤَة، وله في العربيّة أسماء كثيرة أشهرها الليث والضيغم والغضنفر والضرغام "رأيت أسدًا- هذا الشِّبل من ذاك الأسد: يشبه الابن أباه في صفاته- *أَسَد عليّ وفي الحروب نعامةٌ*" ○ أسد الله: حمزة بن عبد المطلب رضي الله عنه- بين فكَّيّ الأسد: في خطر، في مأزق- حِصَّة الأسد: الجزء الأكبر.

Fig. 1. Example of lexical entries in The Dictionary of Modern Arabic Language

This lexical entry in the new version becomes (Table 2):

Table 2. Example of the lexical entry

Element	Translation	Content
Root	**A s d**	أ س د
normalized root	a s d	ءسد
Lemma	Lion (assad)	أَسَد
normalized lemma	lion	أَسَد
Meaning	Very predatory animal. wild member of the felidae family. It includes males and females. The female is called lioness. it has many names in Arabic, including "leith", "Ghadanfar", "Dirgham" etc..	حيوان مفترس شديد الضراوة من فصيلة السِّنَّوريّات ورُتْبة اللّواحم، يشمل الذكر والأنثى ويطلق على الأنثى أسدة ولَبُؤَة، وله في العربيّة أسماء كثيرة أشهرها الليث والضيغم والغضنفر والضرغام
Semantic	Animal	حيوان
Examples	• I saw a lion • This cub is from that lion • A lion against me and soft in the war (proverb) • Lion of Allah: Hamza ibn Abdul-Muttalib (person) • Between lion's jaws: in danger, in trouble • The lion's share: the major share of something	• رأيت أسدًا • هذا الشِّبل من ذاك الأسد: يشبه الابن أباه في صفاته • *أسَد عليّ وفي الحروب نعامةٌ* • أسد الله: حمزة بن عبد المطلب رضي الله عنه • بين فكّيْ الأسد: في خطر، في مأزق • حِصّة الأسد: الجزء الأكبر

3.4 Profiles in "AlkhalilDWS"

As "AlkhalilDWS" is based on a server-client architecture, it allows editors to make their dictionaries collaboratively. In "AlkhalilDWS" we have defined three types of profiles:

- Administrator: this profile was created to manage the accounts of chief editors.
- Chief Editor: This profile is designated to the chief editor of the dictionary. It allows the user to create his own working group, to identify lexical entries, to assign lexical entries to the members of his group, to approve the works submitted by editors, to export the dictionary in XML.
- Editor: This profile is designated to the editor of the dictionary. It allows the user to edit entries affected to him.

3.5 Identification of Lexical Entries

The identification of lexical entries is the first step in the process of making the dictionary. In this step, the chief editor is led to select the list of words to be included as dictionary entries. "AlkhalilDWS" offers three options for that (see Fig. 2). It allows:

- Manual entering: the editor enters the words one by one. This is done by filling in the following information: lemma, type, and root.
- Importation of lemmas: the editor imports a list of words from a text file. Each line in the file contains the morphological information of word: lemma; type; root.
- Automatic extraction of lemmas: the editor can download a text file. "AlkhalilDWS" analyzes the words of the text and extract the new lemmas. Every lemma is linked with its morphological information.

We note that "AlkhalilDWS" controls the existence of a lemma in the dictionary. This avoids the redundancy of the lemmas in the dictionary.

Fig. 2. Identification of lexical entries

3.6 Edition of Lexical Entries

Edition of a lexical entry in "AlkhalilDWS" is done by following these steps (see Fig. 3):

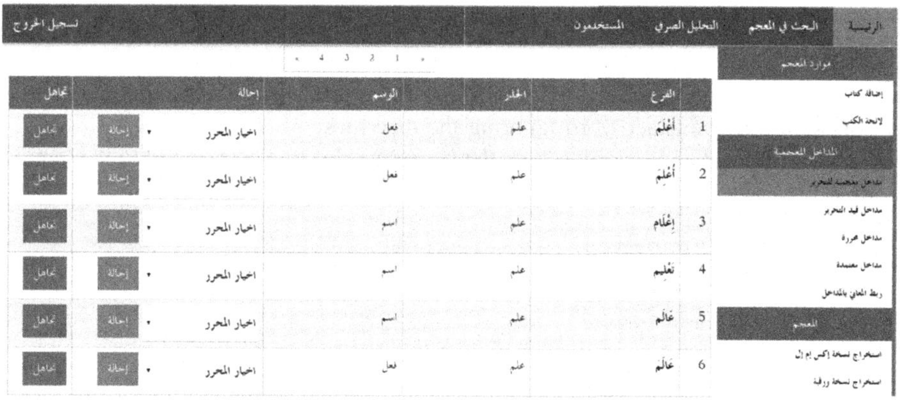

Fig. 3. Assignment of the lexical entries

- Assignment of the lexical entry: the chief editor assigns the lexical entry to an editor
- The edition of the lexical entry: the editor enters the definitions; if necessary, he specifies the semantic field of each definition. Also, he can add illustrative examples to each definition (see Fig. 4).

Fig. 4. Edition of the lexical entry

- Approval of the lexical entry: after finishing the edition of lexical entry, the editor sends it to the chief editor. In this step, the chief editor corrects the work, if it is necessary, and approves each entry to be published.

3.7   Publishing of Lexical Entries

Every approved lexical entry will be searchable in "AlkhalilDWS", and it will be exportable in XML format (following the LMF standard).

The Interactive Version

"AlkhalilDWS" offers an interactive version of the dictionary. It allows the chief editor to search in his produced dictionary with the following options (see Fig. 5):

- Search with exact matching: search the exact word in the lexical entries;
- Search with exact matching and ignore the diacritics: search the lexical entries that correspond to the exact word ignoring the diacritics;
- Search after analyzing word: search the lexical entries that correspond to the lemma of the search entry [20].

Fig. 5. Search in the interactive version

We note that the search is also allowed in 'Almustakshif dictionary' and 'the Dictionary of the Modern Arabic Language'. Moreover, these dictionaries can be browsed by the semantic field (see Fig. 6). This option allows the user to browse the lexical entries which have the same semantic field.

Fig. 6. Browse the dictionary by the semantic field

XML Format

The chief editor can export his produced dictionary in XML format. This format respects the standard LMF. Bellow an example of some entries edited with "AlkhalilDWS" (see Fig. 7):

```xml
<?xml version="1.0" encoding="UTF-8" standalone="no"?>
<Dictionary>
<entry id="1887">
<feat att="partOfSpeach" val="اسم"/>
<root>
<feat att="writtenForm" val="خير"/>
</root>
<lemme>
<feat att="writtenForm" val="آخر"/>
</lemme>
<meaning>
<definition>
<feat att="text" val="غيره بمعى أو مغاير ،مختلف"/>
</definition>
</meaning>
<meaning>
<definition>
<feat att="text" val="واحد جنس من يكونان شيئين أحد"/>
</definition>
</meaning>
</entry>
<entry id="2276">
<feat att="partOfSpeach" val="فعل"/>
<root>
<feat att="writtenForm" val="دون"/>
</root>
<lemme>
<feat att="writtenForm" val="آن"/>
</lemme>
<meaning>
<definition>
<feat att="text" val="أن المال :ء  مِنْه."/>
</definition>
</meaning>
<meaning>
<definition>
<feat att="text" val="صاحبها :الغرس هذا خال أنا."/>
</definition>
</meaning>
</entry>
</Dictionary>
```

Fig. 7. Example of XML version

4 Conclusion

In this article, we present the contribution of DWS in the Arabic lexicography. We have defined the different components that these systems must contain. Our proposed system "AlkhalilDWS" meets the requirements of Arabic lexicography. It offers many features and lexical resources that make the construction and updating of Arabic dictionaries easier. We have adopted the LMF standard to ensure the exchange and communication between produced dictionaries and any tool that complies with this standard.

In the future, we plan to enrich "AlkhalilDWS" with new features as well as extracting good examples from the corpus, allowing the chief editor to define the structure of the lexical entry.

References

1. Suhardijanto, T., Dinakaramani, A.: Building a collaborative workspace for lexicography works in Indonesia. In: Electronic Lexicography in the 21st Century: Proceedings of eLex 2017 Conference, pp. 299–308, Lexical Computing (2017)
2. Durkin, P. (ed.): The Oxford Handbook of Lexicography. Oxford University Press, Oxford (2016)
3. Abel, A.: Dictionary writing systems and beyond. In: Granger, S., Paquot, M. (eds.) Electronic Lexicography. Oxford University Press, Oxford (2011)
4. Joffe, D., de Schryver, G.M.: TshwaneLex Suite (2008)
5. Matapuna. http://sourceforge.net/projects/matapuna/. Accessed 13 Mar 2018
6. Glossword. http://glossword.biz/. Accessed 13 Mar 2018
7. Rambousek, A., Horák, A.: DEBWrite: free customizable web-based dictionary writing system. In: Electronic Lexicography in the 21st Century: Linking Lexical Data in the Digital Age. Proceedings of the eLex 2015 Conference, pp. 443–451. Lexical Computing (2015)
8. Coronel, C., Morris, S.: Database Systems: Design, Implementation, & Management. Cengage Learning, New York (2016)
9. Sarkar, P., Purkayastha, B.S.: Morphological analyzer in the development of bilingual dictionary (Kokborok-English): an analysis for appropriate method and approach. Int. J. Eng. Innov. Technol. **10**, 98–103 (2015)
10. Zaghouani, W., et al.: Correction annotation for non-native arabic texts: guidelines and corpus. In: Proceedings of the 9th Linguistic Annotation Workshop, Denver, pp. 129–139 (2015)
11. Shaalan, K., Allam, A., Gomah, A.: Towards automatic spell checking for Arabic. In: Proceedings of the 4th Conference on Language Engineering, Egyptian Society of Language Engineering (ELSE), Cairo, pp. 240–247 (2003)
12. Zerrouki, T., Kebdani, M.: The project Ayaspell an open source Arabic spell checker dictionary. In: Proceedings of the Expert Meeting on the Arabic Interactive Dictionary Project, Damascus (2009). (in Arabic)
13. Francopoulo, G., et al.: Lexical markup framework (LMF). In: International Conference on Language Resources and Evaluation-LREC, Genoa (2006)
14. Namly, D., Bouzoubaa, K., Tahir, Y., Khamar, H.: Development of Arabic particles lexicon using the LMF framework. Colloque pour les Etudiants Chercheurs en Traitement Automatique du Langage Naturel et ses applications (CEC-TAL 2015), Sousse Tunisia (2015)
15. Attia, M., Pecina, P., Toral, A., Tounsi, L., van Genabith, J.: A lexical database for modern standard Arabic interoperable with a finite state morphological transducer. In: Mahlow, C., Piotrowski, M. (eds.) SFCM 2011. CCIS, vol. 100, pp. 98–118. Springer, Heidelberg (2011). https://doi.org/10.1007/978-3-642-23138-4_7
16. Wali, W., Gargouri, B., Hamadou, A.B.: Evaluating the content of LMF standardized dictionaries: a practical experiment on arabic language. ACM Trans. Asian Low Resour. Lang. Inf. Process. (TALLIP) **16**(4), 22 (2017)
17. Almaany Homepage. https://www.almaany.com/. Accessed 13 Mar 2018
18. Rebdawi, G., Ghneim, N., Desouki, M.S., Sonbol, R.: An interactive Arabic dictionary. In: International Conference on innovations in Information Technology (IIT), pp. 83–86. IEEE (2011)
19. Attih, I.: Almustakshif (an Arabic dictionary). Islamic Educational, Scientific and Cultural Organization (ISESCO) (2011)

20. Reqqass, M., Lakhouaja, A., Mazroui, A., Atih, I.: Amelioration of the interactive dictionary of Arabic language. IJCSA **12**(1), 94–107 (2015)
21. Omar, A.M.: Dictionary of the Modern Arabic Language. Alam Al-Kutub (208)
22. Boudchiche, M., Mazroui, A., Bebah, M.O.A.O., Lakhouaja, A., Boudlal, A.: AlKhalil Morpho Sys 2: a robust Arabic morpho-syntactic analyzer. J. King Saud Univ. Comput. Inf. Sci. **29**(2), 141–146 (2017)

T-HSAB: A Tunisian Hate Speech and Abusive Dataset

Hatem Haddad[1,3](✉), Hala Mulki[2,3], and Asma Oueslati[1]

[1] RIADI Laboratory, National School of Computer Sciences,
Manouba University, Manouba, Tunisia
haddad.hatem@gmail.com, asmaoueslati67@gmail.com
[2] Department of Computer Engineering, Konya Technical University,
Konya, Turkey
hallamulki@gmail.com
[3] iCompass Consulting, Tunis, Tunisia

Abstract. Since the "Jasmine Revolution" at 2011, Tunisia has entered a new era of ultimate freedom of expression with a full access into social media. This has been associated with an unrestricted spread of toxic contents such as Abusive and Hate speech. Considering the psychological harm, let alone the potential hate crimes that might be caused by these toxic contents, automatic Abusive and Hate speech detection systems become a mandatory. This evokes the need for Tunisian benchmark datasets required to evaluate Abusive and Hate speech detection models. Being an underrepresented dialect, no previous Abusive or Hate speech datasets were provided for the Tunisian dialect. In this paper, we introduce the first publicly-available Tunisian Hate and Abusive speech (T-HSAB) dataset with the objective to be a benchmark dataset for automatic detection of online Tunisian toxic contents. We provide a detailed review of the data collection steps and how we design the annotation guidelines such that a reliable dataset annotation is guaranteed. This was later emphasized through the comprehensive evaluation of the annotations as the annotation agreement metrics of Cohen's Kappa (k) and Krippendorff's alpha (α) indicated the consistency of the annotations.

Keywords: Tunisian dialect · Abusive speech · Hate speech

1 Introduction

Tunisia is recognized as a high contact culture with dense social networks and strong social ties; where online social networks play a key role in facilitating social communications [1]. With the freedom of expression privilege granted after the Tunisian revolution, sensitive "taboo" topics such as the religion have become popular and widely discussed by Tunisians across social media platforms. However, on the down side, it became easy to spread abusive/hate propaganda against individuals or groups. Indeed, recent events like the legalization of gender equality in inheritance, the appointment of a Jewish as the Tourism Minister

© Springer Nature Switzerland AG 2019
K. Smaïli (Ed.): ICALP 2019, CCIS 1108, pp. 251–263, 2019.
https://doi.org/10.1007/978-3-030-32959-4_18

of Tunisia and the murder of a Sub-Saharan African student caused intensive debates between Tunisians, most of which took place on social media networks leading to a high emergence of abusive/hate speech. This evoked the need for tools to detect such online abusive/hate speech contents.

In the literature, there has been no clear distinction between Abusive speech (AS) and Hate speech (HS). [2] defined HS as *"any communication that disparages a person or a group on the basis of some characteristic such as race, color, ethnicity, gender, sexual orientation, nationality, religion, or other characteristic"*. Although HS can be conducted as a subtask of the abusive language detection [3], it remains challenging since it requires to consider the correlation between the abusive language and the potential groups that are usually targeted by HS. Further challenges could be met when HS detection is investigated with complex, rich and ambiguous languages/dialects such as the Arabic language and its relevant dialects.

Compared to the increasing studies of AS/HS detection in Indo-European languages, similar research for Arabic dialects is still very limited. This is mainly attributed to the lack of the needed publicly-available AS/HS resources. Building such resources involves several difficulties in terms of data collection and annotation especially for underrepresented Arabic dialects such as the Tunisian dialect.

Tunisian dialect, also known as "Tounsi" or "Derja", is different from Modern Standard Arabic; where the Tunisian dialect features Arabic vocabulary spiced with words and phrases from Amazigh, French, Turkish, Italian and other languages [4]. In this study, we introduce the first **Tunisian Hate Speech and ABusive (T-HSAB)** dataset. The dataset combines 6,039 comments labeled as Abusive, Hate or Normal[1]. With the objective of building a reliable, high quality benchmark dataset, we provide a comprehensive qualitative evaluation of the annotation process of T-HSAB. To achieve this goal, agreement without chance correction and Inter-annotator agreement (IAA) reliability measures are employed. In addition, our dataset was examined as a benchmark AS/HS dataset through subjecting it to supervised machine learning experiments conducted by SVM and NB classifiers.

To the best of our knowledge, this is the first study on Tunisian Abusive and Hate speech. This could be deduced in the next section where we will present the state-of-the-art of the Arabic AS and HS detection.

2 Arabic Abusive/Hate Speech Detection

As seeking to propose a new dialectal Arabic dataset for AS and HS, we opted to review the Arabic AS and HS datasets proposed in the State-Of-The-Art focusing on their characteristics in terms of: source, the tackled toxic categories, size, annotation strategy, metrics, the used machine learning models, etc. Recently, [5] presented a preliminary study of the Arabic AS and HS detection domain,

---

[1] Will be made publicly available on github.

where they aimed to classify the online toxic content on social media into: Abusive, Obscene, Offensive, Violent, Adult content, Terrorism and Religious Hate Speech.

The first attempt to detect Arabic abusive language was performed by [6]. A dataset of 25 K Arabic tweets was manually annotated as abusive or not abusive. However, annotation evaluation measures were not provided.

To detect offensive speech in Youtube, the authors in [7] created a data set of 16 K Egyptian, Iraqi and Libyan comments. The comments were annotated as offensive, inoffensive and neutral by three annotators from Egypt, Iraq and Libya. The annotation evaluation measurements of the Egyptian and Libyan annotators were 71% and 69.8% for inter-annotator agreement and Kappa metric, respectively. The best achieved F-measure was 82% with Support Vector Machines (SVM) algorithm used for classification. Similarly, to detect offensive speech, [8] proposed two datasets:a dataset of 1,100 dialectal tweets and a 32 K inappropriate comments dataset collected from a popular Arabic news site. To support the detection of the offensive content, the authors relied on common patterns used in offensive and rude communications to construct a list of obscene words and hashtags. The tweets and comments were annotated as obscene, offensive, and cleaned by three annotators. With only obscene instances considered, the average inter-annotator agreement was 85% for the Twitter dataset and 87% for the comments dataset.

[9] focused on religious HS detection to identify religious groups targeted by HS such as Muslims, Jews, Christians, Sunnis, Shia and so forth. For this purpose, a multi-dialectal Arabic dataset of 6.6 K tweets was introduced and annotated by 234 different annotators. As a result, three Arabic lexicons were constructed. Each lexicon combined the terms commonly used in religious discussions accompanied with scores representing their polarity and strength. The inter-rater agreement regarding differentiating religious HS tweets from non-religious ones was 81% while this value decreased to 55% when it comes to specify which religious groups are targeted by the religious HS. The proposed dataset was evaluated as a reference dataset using three classification models: Lexicon-based, SVM and GRU-based RNN. The results revealed that the GRU-based RNN model with pre-trained word embedding was the best-performing model where it achieved an F-measure of 77%.

In order to detect bullying in social media texts, [10] presented a Twitter dataset of 20K multi-dialectal Arabic tweets annotated manually with bullying and non-bullying labels. In their study, neither inter-rater agreement measures nor classification performances were provided.

More recently, a Twitter dataset, called L-HSAB, about AS and HS was introduced in [11] as a benchmark dataset for automatic detection of online Levantine AS and HS contents. The dataset composed of 6K tweets, manually annotated as Normal, Abusive and Hate. The high obtained values of agreement without chance correction and inter-annotator agreement indicated the reliability of the dataset. The inter-rater agreement metric denoted by Krippendorff's alpha (α) was 76.5% and indicated the consistency of the annotations. Given that their study is the first attempt to measure the reliability and the consistency of a

Levantine Abusive/Hate speech dataset, we followed the same approach, in our paper. Therefore, to verify reliability and the consistency of our T-HSAB dataset, we adopted agreement without chance correction, inter-annotator agreement and inter-rater agreement metrics within the annotation evaluation task.

3   T-HSAB

T-HSAB can be described as a sociopolitical dataset since the comments are mainly related to politics, social causes, religion, women rights and immigration. In the following subsections, we provide the annotation guideline, the annotation process and the annotation quantitative/qualitative results.

3.1   Data Collection and Processing

The proposed dataset was constructed out of Tunisian comments harvested from different social media platforms. We collected the dataset comments based on multiple queries, each of which represents a potential entity that is usually attacked by abusive/hate speech. Among the used queries, we can mention: "اليهود" (*Jews*), "الأفارقة" (*Africans*) and "المساواة في الميراث" (*gender equality in inheritance*). To harvest the query-related comments, the collection process focused on the comments posted within the time period: October 2018-March 2019. Initially, we retrieved 12,990 comments; after filtering out the non-Arabic, non-textual, AD-containing and duplicated instances, we ended up with 6,075 comments, written in the Tunisian dialect.

In order to prepare the collected comments for annotation, they were normalized through eliminating platform-inherited symbols such as Rt, @ and #, Emoji icons, digits, in addition to non-Arabic characters found in URLs and user mentions.

3.2   Annotation Guidelines

The annotation task requires labeling the comments of T-HSAB dataset as Hate, Abusive or Normal. Based on the definition of Abusive and Hate speech stated in the introduction, differentiating HS from AS is quite difficult and is usually prone to personal biases; which, in turn, yields low inter-rater agreement scores [3]. However, since HS tends to attack specific groups of people, we believe that, defining the potential groups to be targeted by HS, within the scope of the domain, time period and the context of the collected dataset, can resolve the ambiguity between HS and AS resulting in better inter-rater agreement scores. Hence, we designed the annotation guidelines such that all the annotators would have the same perspective about HS. Our annotation instructions defined the 3 label categories as:

- Normal comments are those instances which have no offensive, aggressive, insulting and profanity content.
- Abusive comments are those instances which combine offensive, aggressive, insulting or profanity content.

- Hate comments are those instances that: (a) contain an abusive language, (b) dedicate the offensive, insulting, aggressive speech towards a person or a specific group of people and (c) demean or dehumanize that person or that group of people based on their descriptive identity (race, gender, religion, disability, skin color, belief).

Table 1 lists the relevant examples to each class.

Table 1. Comment examples of the annotation labels

Label	Example
Normal	انا ما فهمت شي الا تتحدثون ألعربيه I couldn't understand anything, don't you speak Arabic?
Abusive	انسانة ساقطة مريضة نفسيا What a despicable psychopath woman
Hate	اللاسف رجال تونس اصبحو نسوان Unfortunately, Tunisian men have become women

3.3 Annotation Process

The annotation task was assigned to three annotators, two males and one female. All of them are Tunisian native speakers and at a higher education level (Master/PhD).

Besides the previous annotation guidelines, and based on the domain and context of the proposed dataset, we provided the annotators with the nicknames usually used to refer to certain minorities and ethnic groups. For instance, within an insulting context, Sub-Saharan African ethnic groups are usually referred to using these nicknames: "عبيد" (*slaves*), "أوصيف" (*black*), "نيغرو" (*nig**a*) and "كحلوش" (*of a dark skin*).

Having all the annotation rules setup, we asked the three annotators to label the 6,075 comments as Normal, Abusive or Hate. For the whole dataset, we received a total of 18,225 judgments. When exploring these annotations, we faced three cases:

1. Unanimous agreement: the three annotators annotated a comment with the same label. This was encountered in 4,941 comments.
2. Majority agreement: two out of three annotators agreed on a label of a comment. This was encountered in 1,098 comments.
3. Conflicts: each rater annotated a comment differently. They were found in 36 comments.

After excluding the comments having 3 different judgments, the final released version of T-HSAB is composed of 6,039 comments. A summary of the annotation statistics is presented in Table 2.

Table 2. Summary of annotation statistics

Annotation case	#Comments
Unanimous agreement	4,941
Majority agreement (2 out of 3)	1,098
Conflicts	36

4   Annotation Results

Having all the annotations gathered in one data file, we decided the final label of
each comment in the dataset according to the annotation cases in Sect. 3.3. For
comments falling under the first annotation case, the final labels were directly
deduced, while for those falling under the second annotation case, we selected
the label that has been agreed upon by two annotators out of three. Thus, we
got 3,834 Normal, 1,127 Abusive and 1,078 Hate comments. Bearing in mind
that HS is naturally a limited phenomenon [3], we kept the data unbalanced in
order to have a dataset that reflects the actual distribution of HS in an Arabic
dataset. A detailed review of the statistics of T-HSAB final version is provided in
Table 3, where Avg-S-L denotes the average length of comments in the dataset,
calculated based on the number of words in each comment.

Table 3. Comments distribution across 3 classes.

	Normal	Abusive	Hate
# Comments	3,834	1,127	1,078
Avg-S-L	11	8	12
Word Count	43,254	9,320	13,219
Vocabulary	19,162	6,358	7,789
Ratio	63.49%	18.66%	17.85%

As seeking to identify the words commonly used within AS and HS contexts, we investigated the lexical distribution of the dataset words across both
Abusive and Hate classes. Therefore, we subjected T-HSAB to further normalization, where we removed stopwords based on our own manually-built Tunisian
stopwords list. Later, we constructed a visualization map for the most frequent
occurring words/terms under the Hate category (Fig. 1. The ten most frequent
words and their frequencies in each class are reviewed in Table 4, where Dist.
denotes the word's distribution under a specific class.

As it can be seen from Table 4 and Fig. 1, both Abusive and Hate classes
can have terms in common such as "تونس" (*Tunisia*). These terms are not
only limited to the offensive/insulting words but also combine entity names
representing ethnic groups. This on one hand, explains the difficulty faced by

Table 4. Distribution of ten most frequent terms

Hate	Dist.	Abusive	Dist.
تونس (*Tunisia*)	2.01%	تونس (*Tunisia*)	1.39%
شعب (*people*)	0.74%	ع**ة (*Fu*k you!*)	0.40%
الاسلام (*Islam*)	0.43%	مي*ون (*faggot*)	0.32%
اليهود (*Jews*)	0.39%	لعنة (*curse*)	0.31%
التونسي (*Tunisian*)	0.26%	كلب (*dog*)	0.30%
عورة (*private parts*)	0.24%	تفوه (≪*t'fu*≫[a])	0.26%
لعنة (*curse*)	0.23%	جبري (*a boor*)	0.24%
العرب (*Arabs*)	0.23%	عاه*ة (*bi*ch*)	0.17%
مرأة (*woman*)	0.23%	تافه (*silly*)	0.17%
كافر (*pagan*)	0.22%	كلاب (*dogs*)	0.15%

[a]transliteration of an angry act of spitting on someone

annotators while recognizing HS comments. On the other hand, it justifies our annotation guidelines for hate comments identification, where we stressed that the joint existence of abusive language and an entity cannot indicate a HS, unless the abusive language is targeting that entity.

Fig. 1. Most frequent terms in hate comments.

To evaluate how distinctive are the vocabulary of our dataset with respect to each class category, we conducted word-class correlation calculations. First, we calculated the Pointwise Mutual Information (PMI) for each word towards its relevant category such that, for a word w and a class c, PMI is calculated as in Eq. 1.

$$PMI(w, c) = log(P_c(w)/P_c) \tag{1}$$

Where $P_c(w)$ denotes the appearance of the word w in the comments of the class c, while P_c refers to the number of comments of the class c.

$$HtS(w) = PMI(w, hate) - PMI(w, normal) \tag{2}$$

$$AbS(w) = PMI(w, abusive) - PMI(w, normal) \tag{3}$$

Then, to decide whether the words under the Abusive/Hate classes are discriminating, their correlation with the Normal class should be identified as well [12]. This is done by assigning a hate score (HtS) and an abusive score (AbS) for each of the most/least words under Hate and Abusive classes. Both scores indicate the difference of the PMI value of a word w under a Abusive/Hate category and its PMI value with the Normal category. The formula to calculate HtS and AbS is given in Eqs. 2 and 3.

Table 5. HtS score for most/least hateful words

Most Hate	HtS	Least Hate	HtS
كافر (*pagan*)	3.53	عجبني (*liked it*)	-1.13
اليهود (*Jews*)	2.08	الدولة (*the state*)	-1.04
لعنة (*curse*)	2.06	قانون (*law*)	-0.99
عورة (*private parts*)	1.51	الميراث (*inheritance*)	-0.38
شعب (*people*)	1.49	صادق (*honest*)	-0.35
الاسلام (*Islam*)	0.89	طفلة (*girl*)	-0.35
العرب (*Arabs*)	0.88	باهية (*nice*)	-0.35
تونس (*Tunisia*)	0.67	حاب (*I'd like*)	-0.35
التونسي (*Tunisian*)	0.36	عقبة (*obstacle*)	-0.35
المرأة (*woman*)	-0.08	احترام (*respect*)	-0.12

Table 6. AbS score for most/least abusive words

Most Abusive	AbS	Least Abusive	AbS
عاه*ة (*bi*ch*)	4.01	الرجل (*man*)	-3.43
مي*ون (*faggot*)	3.60	الدولة (*the state*)	-2.16
ع**ة (*Fu*k you!*)	3.36	نحبو (*we like*)	-1.16
كلب (*dog*)	2.78	فهمتش (*understand*)	-0.96
جبري (*a boor*)	2.54	سيناريو (*scenario*)	-0.70
تفوه (*«t'fu»*)	2.47	قلبك (*your heart*)	-0.70
لعنة (*curse*)	1.97	بالكلام (*by words*)	-0.70
تافه (*silly*)	1.53	الرئيس (*president*)	-0.70
كلاب (*dogs*)	1.32	الرجولية (*braveness*)	-0.37
تونس (*Tunisia*)	-0.07	مخو (*his mind*)	-0.15

It could be observed from Tables 5 and 6 that HtS and AbS scores for the most hateful and abusive words are positive indicating that they appear significantly under Hate and Abusive categories. In contrast, HtS and AbS scores for the least abusive/hate words are negative which emphasizes their appearance within Normal comments more than abusive/hate ones. On the other hand, given the specificity of the AS and HS used in Arabic, it is common to involve named entities such as locations, persons or organizations while disgracing, dehumanizing certain individuals or groups; this justifies why the country name "تونس" (*Tunisia*) has a small HtS and negative AbS scores as this word can be among the most abusive/hate words, yet, it is naturally used in normal contexts. Similarly, the word "المرأة" (*woman*) was found among the most hateful words but it had a negative hate score HtS. This is because this word is usually used when attacking women within hate contexts, whilst it can be mentioned in normal comments as well.

5   Annotation Evaluation

The annotation evaluation is based on the study of [14]. We used observed agreement A_0, all categories are equally likely S and Cohen's kappa as agreement without chance correction. For agreement with chance correction we used Krippendorff's α.

5.1   Agreement Without Chance Correction

Observed agreement A_0 is defined as the proportion of the agreed annotations out of the total number of annotations [14]. For our three annotators, the A_0 value was found of 81.82%. On the other hand, Pairwise Percent Agreement values between each pair of the three annotators are 97.963%, 83.11% and 82.563% (Table 7). Nevertheless, as observed agreement and Pairwise Percent Agreements are usually criticized for their inability to account for chance agreement [16]. Therefore, to take into account the chance agreement described by [14], we considered that all the categories are equally likely and computed the S coefficient which measures if the random annotations follow a uniform distribution in the different categories, in our case: three. With S having a high value of 72.73%, it could be said that, for an agreement constant observation, the coefficient S is not sensitive to the distribution of the elements in the categories.

Table 7. Pairwise Percent Agreement (PRAM) and pairwise Cohen's K results

Annotators	PRAM	Cohen's K
1 & 2	97.963%	0.961
1 & 3	83.11%	0.638
2 & 3	82.563%	0.624

Cohen's kappa (Cohen's K) [13] is another metric that also considers the chance agreement. It represents a correlation coefficient ranged from -1 to $+1$, where 0 refers to the amount of agreement that can be expected from random chance, while 1 represents the perfect agreement between the annotators. As it can be seen from Table 7, the agreement values between annotators 1 & 2 and 2 & 3 are moderate while the agreement between annotators 1 & 3 is substantial. It could be noted that, A_0, S and Cohen's K values obtained based on the annotations of our dataset, are high and show a little bias. Nevertheless, they put, on the same level, very heterogeneous categories: two minority but significant which are Abusive and Hate categories, and a non significant majority which is the Normal category.

Indeed, the categories were found unbalanced (Table 3). Here, we can observe that, despite the strong agreement on the prevailing category, the coefficients seem to be very sensitive to the disagreements over the minority categories. Thus, to make sure that the calculated coefficients for the three categories, reflect a significant agreement on the two minority categories: Abusive and Hate, we used a weighted coefficient (Inter-annotator agreement) which gives more importance to certain disagreements rather than treating all disagreements equally, as it is the case in A_0, S and Cohen's K [14].

5.2   Inter-Annotator Agreement (IAA)

According to [14], weighted coefficients make it possible to give more importance to certain disagreements. Thus, Inter-Annotator Agreement (IAA) measures can estimate the annotation reliability to a certain extent, on the assigned category. The kind of extent is determined by the method chosen to measure the agreement. For annotation reliability, Krippendorff's α has been used in the vast majority of the studies. Krippendorff's α is based on the assumption that expected agreement is calculated by looking at the overall distribution of judgments regardless of the annotator who produced those judgments. Based on Krippendorff's α, the annotation is considered: (a) Good: for any data annotation with an agreement in the interval [0.8, 1], (b) Tentative: for any data annotation with an agreement in the interval [0.67, 0.8] or (c) Discarded: for any data annotation where agreement is below 0.67. For T-HSAB dataset, the obtained Krippendorff's α was 75% which indicates the agreement on the minority categories without considering the majority category.

5.3   Discussion

The agreement measures with/without chance correlation have shown a clear agreement about the categories Normal and Abusive (Table 7). This was emphasized through our detailed study of the annotation results as the three annotators annotated abusive comments in the same way. Indeed, with the annotators following the annotation guidelines, they decided that a comment is abusive if it contains an abusive word of the Tunisian dialect. Hence, only few conflict comments (36 comments) where observed. These conflicts are mainly encountered in comments having no explicit abusive words where the annotator has to analyze the whole meaning to associate the comment with an abusive judgment.

On the other hand, more disagreement is observed when it comes to the Hate category (Table 7) and it is mainly related to the annotators' background knowledge, their personal taste and personal assumptions. The comments related to the religion topic, for instance, can be judged as Hate or not Hate according to the annotator believes. As it is seen from the examples in Table 8, where M and F denote Male and Female, respectively, the conflicts are occurred with

Table 8. Examples of annotators conflicts over the Hate category

Comment	A.#1(M)	A.#2(F)	A.#3(M)
حقيرة نحنو مسلمين يا بهلوانية (Hey scummy girl we are Muslims you clown)	Abusive	Abusive	Hate
قبح الله وجه كل من أيد هذا القانون الوسخ المقزم لبلاد الإسلام بلاد الزيتونة والقروان (God cursed all those who supported this nasty law which demeans our Muslim country, the country of Al-Zaytoonah and Kairouan)	Hate	Hate	Abusive

regard to the legalization of gender equality in inheritance. This indicates the sensitivity of this subject and reflects the divergence of opinions on social media towards such hot debates within the Tunisian community.

Another observation, is that the conflicts are not related to the annotator's gender. Indeed, despite that annotator 1 & 2 are from different genders, they achieved the highest Pairwise Percent Agreement) and pairwise Cohen's K results. Finally, based on the deduced value of Krippendorff's α, we can conclude that T-HSAB is a reliable dataset [14].

6 Classification Performance

T-HSAB dataset was used for the AS/HS detection within two experiments:

1. Binary classification: comments are classified into Abusive or Normal. This requires merging the Hate class instances with the Abusive ones.
2. Multi-class classification: comments are classified as Abusive, Hate or Normal.

For experiments setup, we first randomized the order of the comments in the dataset, then, we filtered out the Tunisian stopwords, then split the dataset into a training and a test set where 80% of the comments formed the training set. The comments distribution among the three categories in Training and Test sets is shown in Table 9, where Exp. denotes the experiment's number.

Table 9. Training and Test sets of T-HSAB

Exp.	Training			Test		
	Abusive	Normal	Hate	Abusive	Normal	Hate
1	1,770	3,061	–	434	774	–
2	889	3,061	881	237	774	197
Total	4,831			1,208		

We employed two supervised classifiers: SVM [15] and NB from NLTK [17]. Both classifiers are trained with several n-gram schemes: unigrams (uni), unigrams+bigrams (uni+bi) and unigrams+bigrams+trigrams (uni+bi+tri).

Term frequency (TF) weighting was employed to reduce the features size. Among several runs with various n-gram schemes and TF values, we selected the best results to be listed in Table 10, where the Precision, Recall, F-measure and Accuracy are referred to as P., R., F1 and Acc., respectively.

Table 10. Classification results over T-HSAB

Classes	Algorithm	Features	P.(%)	R.(%)	F1(%)	Acc.(%)
2	NB	uni+bi(TF≥2)	**93.5**	**91.5**	**92.3**	**92.9**
	SVM	uni	76.4	73.8	74.7	77.7
3	NB	uni+bi(TF≥2)	**89.5**	**79.8**	**83.6**	**87.9**
	SVM	uni	66.5	59.9	62.2	73.9

As it can be observed in Table 10, NB classifier performed, remarkably, better than SVM for both binary and multi-class classification experiments. This could be attributed to the fact that NB variant from NLTK is implemented as a multinomial NB decision rule together with binary-valued features [17]. This explains its effectiveness in dealing with our feature vectors that are formulated from binary values indicating the presence/absence of n-gram schemes.

7 Conclusion

This paper introduced a Tunisian dataset for Abusive speech and Hate speech known as T-HSAB. T-HSAB is the first public Tunisian dataset with the objective to be a benchmark dataset for automatic detection of online Tunisian toxic contents. To build our dataset, Tunisian comments were harvested from different social media platforms and 3 annotators conducted the manual annotation following an annotation guideline. The final version of the dataset combined 6,039 comments. While achieving high values of agreement without chance correction and inter-annotator agreement indicated the reliability of T-HSAB dataset, the agreement between annotators is still an issue when it comes to identify HS. This is attributed to the fact that, HS annotation does not only rely on rules but also is related to the annotators' background knowledge, their personal tastes and assumptions. The machine learning-based classification experiments conducted with NB and SVM classifiers to classify the AS/HS content in T-HSAB dataset, indicated the outperformance of NB over SVM for both binary and multi-class classification of AS and HS comments. T-HSAB was made publicly available to intensify the progress in this research field. In addition, a lexicon of Tunisian abusive words and a lexicon of hate words will be built based on the annotated comments. Both lexicons will be made publicly available. A natural future step would involve building further publicly-available Abusive speech and Hate Speech datasets for Algerian dialect and Moroccan dialect as Algeria and Morocco have an identical linguistic situation and share socio-historical similarities with Tunisia [18].

References

1. Skandrani, H., Triki, A.: Trust in supply chains, meanings, determinants and demonstrations: a qualitative study in an emerging market context. Qual. Res. Int. J. **14**(4), 391–409 (2011)
2. Nockleby, J.T.: Hate speech. In: Levy, L.W., Karst, K.L., et al. (eds.) Encyclopedia of the American Constitution, 2nd edn. Macmillan, Detroit (2000)
3. Waseem, Z., Davidson, T., Warmsley, D., Weber, I.: Understanding abuse: a typology of abusive language detection subtasks. In: Proceedings of the First Workshop on Abusive Language Online, pp. 78–84. Association for Computational Linguistics, Vancouver (2017)
4. Stevens, P.B.: Ambivalence, modernisation and language attitudes: French and Arabic in Tunisia. J. Multiling. Multicult. Dev. **4**(2–3), 101–114 (1983)
5. Al-Hassan, A., Al-Dossari, H.: Detection of hate speech in social networks: a survey on multilingual corpus. J. Comput. Sci. Inf. Technol. (CS IT) **9**(2), 83–100 (2019)
6. Abozinadah, E., Mbaziira, A., Jones, J.: Detection of abusive accounts with Arabic Tweets. Int. J. Knowl. Eng. **1**(2), 113–119 (2015)
7. Alakrota, A., Murray, L., Nikolov, N.: Dataset construction for the detection of anti-social behaviour in online communication in Arabic. J. Procedia Comput. Sci. **142**, 174–181 (2018)
8. Mubarak, H., Darwish, K., Magdy, W.: Abusive language detection on Arabic social media. In: Proceedings of the First Workshop on Abusive Language Online, pp. 52–56. Association for Computational Linguistics, Vancouver (2017)
9. Albadi, N., Kurdi, M., Mishra, S.: Are they our brothers? Analysis and detection of religious hate speech in the Arabic Twittersphere. In: International Conference on Advances in Social Networks Analysis and Mining (ASONAM), pp. 69–76. IEEE, Barcelona (2018)
10. Al-Ajlan, M., Ykhlef, M.: Optimized Twitter cyberbullying detection based on deep learning. In: Proceedings of the 21st Saudi Computer Society National Computer Conference (NCC), pp. 52–56. IEEE, Riyadh (2018)
11. Mulki, H., Haddad, H., Bechikh Ali, C., Alshabani, H.: L-HSAB: a Levantine Twitter corpus for hate speech and abusive language. In: Proceedings of the Third Workshop on Abusive Language Online. Association for Computational Linguistics, Florence (2019)
12. de Gibert, O., Perez, N., García-Pablos, A., Cuadros, M.: Hate speech dataset from a white supremacy forum. In: Proceedings of the 2nd Workshop on Abusive Language Online, pp. 11–20. Association for Computational Linguistics, Brussels (2018)
13. Cohen, J.: Weighted kappa: nominal scale agreement with provision for scaled disagreement or partial credit. Comput. Linguist. **34**(4), 555–591 (2008)
14. Artstein, R., Poesio, M.: Inter-coder agreement for computational linguistics. Psychol. Bull. **70**(4), 213–220 (1968)
15. Chang, C., Lin, C.: LIBSVM: a library for support vector machines. ACM Trans. Intell. Syst. Technol. **2**(3), 27 (2011)
16. McHugh, M.L.: Interrater reliability: the kappa statistic. Biochem. Med. **22**(3), 276–282 (2012)
17. Bird, S., Klein, E., Loper, E.: Natural Language Processing with Python: Analyzing Text With the Natural Language Toolkit. O'Reilly Media Inc., Sebastopol (2009)
18. Harrat, S., Meftouh, K., Smaili, K.: Maghrebi Arabic dialect processing: an overview. J. Int. Sci. Gen. Appl. **1**, (2018)

Towards Automatic Normalization of the Moroccan Dialectal Arabic User Generated Text

Ridouane Tachicart[(⊠)] and Karim Bouzoubaa[(⊠)]

Mohammadia School of Engineers, Mohammed V University in Rabat,
Rabat, Morocco
ridouane.tachicart@research.emi.ac.ma,
karim.bouzoubaa@emi.ac.ma

Abstract. Today social media is an important way of communication between people in the world. As the case of other countries, Moroccan people use several languages in their web communication leaving behind a considerable amount of user-generated text. The latter presents several opportunities for extracting useful information. However, processing this content is very challenging especially when facing the Moroccan Dialectal Arabic content in social media. This is to several factors such as scripts diversity (Arabic and Arabizi), orthographic errors and writing rules lack. In this context, the present work is a first attempt towards addressing the problem of Moroccan Dialectal Arabic spelling inconsistency in social media. We conduct a deep study that uses a systematic approach where we report on a series of experiments performed on Moroccan Dialectal social media text. The most interesting findings that have emerged is the orthographic inconsistency existing in written Moroccan Dialectal Arabic regarding both Arabic and Latin scripts. This phenomenon affects an important amount of texts in social media and proved the need of exploiting available Arabic tools in addition to building a customized spelling correction system.

Keywords: User-generated text · Social media · Moroccan Dialectal Arabic · Corpus · Lexicon · Natural language processing · Spelling correction · Standard Arabic · Code-switching

1 Introduction

With an increasingly important number of Moroccan social media users (15M active users on Facebook for example[1]), social media has become one of the major means of informal communication between Moroccan people today. As the case of other countries, social media in Morocco are always accessible and available whenever users want, allowing them expressing their opinions easily and instantly. It consists in sharing videos, images or texts with comments written mainly in MDA (Moroccan Dialectal Arabic), but also expressed in other languages such as MSA (Modern

---

[1] https://www.facebook.com/ads/audience-insights/people?act=270138063026911&age=18-&country=MA.

K. Smaïli (Ed.): ICALP 2019, CCIS 1108, pp. 264–275, 2019.
https://doi.org/10.1007/978-3-030-32959-4_19

Standard Arabic) and alternatively other European languages such as French. As a result, a huge amount of Moroccan User Generated Text (UGT) is produced continuously over social media pages.

MDA expressed in this UGT is a language spoken in Morocco and usually used in informal alternative such as daily conversation and social media. In [16], the authors showed that this dialect covers 73% of the UGT content. Therefore, in view of the importance of these stats, the processing of UGT in order to engage in advanced applications, such as sentiment analysis or machine translation, has become a necessity. However, it is currently not possible due to the lack of Moroccan NLP tools such as morphological analyzer. In addition, there is no clear idea currently about the spelling of the Moroccan UGT. Hence, it should be useful to analyze the MDA UGT at the orthographic level before engaging in the building of the MDA NLP applications.

This study uses a systematic approach where we report on a series of experiments in order to identify first different spelling variations of the MDA UGT and then focus on three main questions as follows:

- Are there any standards that social media users follow to write the MDA text? What is its impact on the automatic processing?
- How available Arabic NLP tools and resources can help the processing of this content?
- What measures need to be taken before engaging in the building of advanced NLP tools? How can these measures be applied?

For this purpose, we analyze the MDA UGT at the orthographic level in order to evaluate its writing rules regarding a reference vocabulary. To do so, we were forced to set up a new MDA reference vocabulary using available MDA resources [17] and following a set of linguistic rules that were adopted in the building of a bi-lingual lexicon. The analysis consists in comparing Moroccan UGT and this vocabulary at the orthographic level and then analyzing the differences. The remainder of this paper is organized as follows: Sect. 2 presents related works in the field of processing Arabic dialect (AD) user-generated text. Section 3 gives an overview of the Moroccan dialectal Arabic. Section 4 exposes the performed experiments in order to compare the MDA UGT and the standard MDA vocabulary at the orthographic level. In Sect. 4.3, we provide a discussion about results; finally, we conclude the paper in Sect. 5 with some observations.

2   Related Work

To the best of our knowledge, this paper is the first to deal with Moroccan dialectal UGT content at the orthographic level. In the following, we summarize related works regarding other Arabic dialects.

Habash et al. [8] proposed a unified framework called CODA to write all Arabic dialects with Arabic script based on the MSA-AD similarities. CODA is designed for NLP purposes and provide a set of guidelines to write all Arabic dialects. Using Arabic script, each AD word has a single orthographic rendering. CODA is adopted and extended to cover several ADs such as Egyptian, Levantine, Tunisian [22] and Algerian [15].

Eskander et al. [7] presented CODAFy, a pre-processing tool that converts Egyptian Arabic dialect text to CODA standards. To build their system, authors used a data consisting of an annotated Egyptian corpus [11] containing 160k words. In addition to the CODA equivalent form, each word is annotated with large morphological analysis. After dividing the data into training, development and test sets, they implemented two approaches: the first is non-contextual while the second is contextual. In the first one where it operates on the character level, they trained several classifiers on the transformation observed between colloquial form and CODA form using KNN algorithm [20]. In the second one which operates on word level, they built a unigram model that converts the colloquial word into its most likely CODA form as written in the training data. Evaluation results showed that the second approach slightly outperforms the first.

Boujelbane et al. [5] built an automatic normalization system that converts Tunisian dialect texts to CODA standards adopting a hybrid approach. Before engaging in experiments, they displayed a variety of spelling variations on a corpus of 7k words and then compared it with CODA. They trained several KNN classifiers on these spelling variations. Regarding words that contains orthographic errors, they defined a set of patterns to normalize these errors. To evaluate their system, they used 2640 words of STAC corpus [23] written in non-CODA standards. Results showed that their system achieves an accuracy of 86.6%.

Obeid, et al. [13] proposed MADARi, a tool for annotating and correcting the spelling of Gulf and Egyptian Arabic dialect social media texts. Human annotators can use a web interface to annotate texts with the spelling errors. Their task consists mainly in converting the orthography to CODA and then annotate each word's morphology (tokenization, POS, lemma, etc.). MADARi provides several morphological analyses as propositions using MADAMIRA analyzer [14], so that annotators can easily and quickly annotate the dialectal text following the CODA convention.

As a pre-processing step, Afli et al. [3] integrated an Automatic Error Correction system to an Arabic UGT machine translation in order to improve the quality of the translation. To this end, they trained and tested this system using a portion of QALB corpus [21] that contains 1.3M UGT words. After that, they aligned UGT sentences with their MSA equivalents using the MADA [9] morphological analyser. Authors implemented two different systems where the first is trained on data without tokenization and the second one is trained using MADA tokenization. Evaluation results on test data containing 66k words showed that the second system outputs with an accuracy of 68.68% while the first one outputs with 63.18% of accuracy. Hence, authors realized that including tokenized words in the training data is crucial for increasing error detection.

Abidi and Smaili [2] performed an empirical study of the Algerian dialect used in YouTube. They started by collecting a corpus containing 17M words from YouTube comments. The corpus contains different languages where an important amount of text is written in Latin script (LS) (47%). They noticed also that 82% of the collected sentences includes code-switching and that grammar was not respected when using either Arabic or Latin script. For this reason, they built a lexicon that contains, for each word its correlated words to deal with the problem of spelling inconsistency.

From the above surveyed works, it is clear that different solutions are proposed for the spelling inconsistency problem and that MDA has not been targeted yet. In the next sections, we present the conducted experiments in order to analyze the Moroccan UGT spelling.

3   Moroccan Dialectal Arabic

The Moroccan Dialectal Arabic is a primary language considered to be a variety of Arabic language that is used in informal venues. Moroccan people use in addition to Tamazight language the MDA in their daily life. However, MDA is the dominating language according to the official census[2] performed in 2014 where 90% of Moroccan people use MDA.

Table 1. MDA words origin

MCA word	Word origin	Language origin	English translation
فالصو	falso	Spanish	Scammed
بريكولاج	bricolage	French	DIY
مش	موش	Tamazight	cat
كتب	كتب	Arabic	write

Historically, MDA raised as a result of the interaction between Arabic and Tamazight in spreading Islam period and contained a mixture of these languages until the beginning of the 20th century. After the establishment of the French and Spanish protectorate, the MDA vocabulary integrated several words from these languages as illustrated in Table 1. For example, the word "بريكولاج" \Do It Yourself\ originates from French where the origin word is \bricolage\. Nevertheless, MDA is strongly influenced by Arabic (according to the work of authors in [18]) especially at the lexical level where 81% of the Moroccan vocabulary is borrowed from the Arabic language.

4   Methodology and Experiments

As cited in Sect. 1, this work consists in comparing the MDA UGT with a standard MDA vocabulary at the orthographic level. Results of this comparison help to build a clear idea about the measures that should be taken before processing the Moroccan UGT. For this purpose, it is necessary to prepare the elements to be compared before engaging in experiments. The following sections describe steps that have been taken in order to prepare these resources.

---

[2] http://rgph2014.hcp.ma.

4.1   Preparing Resources and Tools

MDA UGT
The first element to be prepared is the MDA UGT. It has been addressed in a previous work where we collected an amount containing 748,433 general comments following several rules and criterions. Since our final goal in this paper is to process the MDA language, we limit our investigation to the MDA content existing in the collected UGT. The MDA content is identified in the MDA UGT and then classified using a language identification system [19]. It is composed of 436k sentences written in two different scripts. The first is Arabic script that uses Arabic letters. While the second consists in mixing Romanized letters with numbers (Arabizi). Table 2 shows an example of MDA sentences written in the two scripts.

Table 2. MDA sentences

Script	Arabizi sentence	English equivalent
Arabizi	Lioma na7taflou b rass l3am	Today, we celebrate the new year
Arabic	شكوووون تفرج لبارح فالماتش ديال الريااااال	Who watched the "Real" match yesterday

On the other hand, the second element of this comparison consists in preparing an MDA reference vocabulary taking advantage from the availability of existing MDA resource (lexicon, morphemes list, generation rules and writing rules). In the following, we describe these resources.

MDA Reference Vocabulary Generation
To the best of our knowledge, there is currently no such resource. The MDA reference vocabulary is generated using the process described in Fig. 1 and follows the same writing rules that were adopted to build the Moroccan Lexicon MDED [17] where a word can be represented in only one form. The main purpose is to provide a resource that presents a good coverage of MDA words. It is generated by implementing an algorithm that combines an MDA lexicon and a morphemes list (affixes and clitics) with respect to generation rules.

First, as an MDA lexicon, we used the Moroccan Dialect Electronic Dictionary (MDED) previously built [17]. To the best of our knowledge, it is the most comprehensive Electronic lexicon for MDA that is updated periodically. It contains almost 12,000 MDA entries written in Arabic letters and translated to MSA. In addition, one major MDED feature is the annotation of its entries with useful metadata such as POS, origin and root as shown in Table 3.

Then, regarding the morphemes list, we generated and manually checked an exhaustive list of MDA affixes and clitics following linguistic rules. Since omitting the distinction between affixes and clitics will not affect the generation process, we do not make the difference between these morphemes. Table 4 presents a sample of the MDA affixes and clitics.

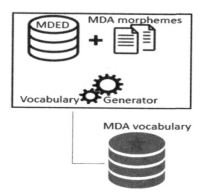

Fig. 1. MDA vocabulary generation

Table 3. Sample of MDED lexicon

MDA	MSA	Pos	Root	Origin	English[a]
ماكلة	طعام	Noun	كلا	MSA	Food
شحال	كم	Particle	شحال	MSA	How much
سطاسيونا	ركن	Verb	سطاسيون	French	Park

[a]This tag is not a part of the dictionary.

Table 4. Sample of the MDA affixes

Position	Affix	Pos
Prefix	وكان	Verb
Prefix	بال	Noun
Suffix	ين	Noun
Proclitic	وماب	Noun
Suffix	اتهمش	Verb
Enclitic	كش	Verb

Therefore, as an example of combination, the verb كتب taken from MDED can be combined with the prefix وكان (that can be plugged only with verbs) to form the word وكانكتب /and I write/.

Finally, we implemented a generation process using previous resources and taking into consideration linguistic constraints in order to produce possible MDA words. In fact, MDA is a variant of Arabic language. Thus, the MDA vocabulary can be generated following the used approaches in some MSA works [6, 4]. In our case, MDED entries and the morphemes list are used in order to generate possible MDA words with respect to morpho-syntactic rules. In addition, some orthographic adjustments are performed on the generated words in order to meet writing standard. As shown in Table 5, the result of this task outputs 4.590.000 words representing all the possible MDA vocabulary. By examining it, we notice an expected phenomenon where some words are duplicated given that they may refer to different syntactic features. As an example, with the same spelling, the verb ضربو have two analyses: ضربو /they hit/ and ضربو /he hit him/. For this reason, we reduced our vocabulary size by deleting redundant words (having the same spelling) to obtain 3,976,805 unique words. This reducing makes the processing fast and does not affect the process of comparing UGT and MDA vocabulary since we do not consider grammatical features in this work.

Table 5. MDA Vocabulary

	Raw	Unique
# words	4,590,000	3,991,949

4.2   UGT Analysis

Fig. 2. Google Translation tool

At this stage, the MDA UGT is composed of two elements according to scripts (Arabic script and Arabizi). On one hand, the UGT written in Arabic script (UGT_{Arabic}) which represents 40.86% of UGT is composed of 3,1M words. On the other hand, the UGT written in Arabizi ($UGT_{Arabizi}$) which represents 33.93% of the UGT contains almost 2,6M words. The remaining UGT contains other languages such as MSA and French that are outside the scope of this work.

To reach the goal of this work, we analyze the UGT "misspelled" words then we try to explain the reason why the UGT words are misspelled. In this work, we determine a misspelled word as an entry not found in the MDA reference vocabulary.

Experiments consist in comparing in several stages UGT_{Arabic} and $UGT_{Arabizi}$ to a vocabulary (MDA and MSA vocabulary). In fact, the generated MDA vocabulary is written in Arabic script. Thus, we started by converting $UGT_{Arabizi}$ to Arabic script. Given that few transliteration tools are available, we used Google translation tool[3] for

---

[3] https://translate.google.co.ma/?hl=en&tab=wT&authuser=0.

its good results compared to other tools such as LEXILOGOS[4]. The task consists in selecting Arabic as input text and typing Arabizi instead of Arabic text (as illustrated in Fig. 2). Then, we developed and implemented an algorithm that checks the existence of each UGT word in the compared vocabulary and returns the overlap between them. In each stage, we use different versions of UGT and the MDA vocabulary in order to observe the effect of this update and hence explain how far or close is the UGT to the MDA vocabulary. Figure 3 presents a global overview of the performed comparisons.

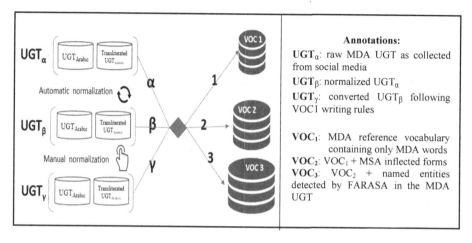

Fig. 3. Comparing UGT and the MDA reference vocabulary

In the first comparison ($C_\alpha 1$), where the UGT does not undergo any pre-processing after its collection from social media we compared this portion to the standard MDA vocabulary (VOC1). Results of this comparison, as reported in Tables 6 and 7, showed that only 28% of UGT_{Arabic} words and 2% of $UGT_{Arabizi}$ words are recognized (exist in VOC1). To explain the low observed score, we examined a sample of the UGT Out of Vocabulary (OOV) resulted from this comparison and noticed that these words are either written without standards, belong to other languages vocabulary (MSA, French, English, etc.), belong to named entities or written with keyboard errors. For example, the different UGT words كنشوفكم, كانشوفكوم, كانشوفكوم, كانشوفكم and كنشوفكم that refer to the same word كانشوفكم /I see you/ are identified as OOV given that they are written in the standard MDA vocabulary as كانشوفكم. Moreover, some UGT words are completely borrowed from MSA as المنازل /houses/ and الحواسيب /computers/ or belong to named entities such as the words الرباط /Rabat/ and سمير /Samir/ Regarding keyboard errors, users usually omit spaces between words or confuse similar and adjacent keys such as ح, خ, ج and ص, ض. In the second comparison ($C_\alpha 2$), we compared UGT to VOC2 which is composed of VOC1 and the MSA inflected forms that is introduced in the work of [12]. The overlap rate increased to 45% for UGT_{Arabic} and to 19% for

---

[4] https://www.lexilogos.com/keyboard/arabic.htm.

$UGT_{Arabizi}$. In $C_\alpha3$, we used FARASA NER [1] to enhance VOC2 by Arabic named entities that are detected in UGT. We observed that the overlap rate with the new compared vocabulary (VOC3) increased to 51% for UGT_{Arabic} and to 25% for $UGT_{Arabizi}$.

In order to improve the overlap rate between UGT and the compared vocabulary, we performed an automatic process that converts UGT_α to UGT_β using SAFAR normalization tool [10]. It consists in cleaning UGT by removing numbers, special characters, redundant letters, etc. For instance, the comment " 1 رااااني مشغ7ووووووول " is normalized to "راني مشغول". We noticed that, compared to $C_\alpha1$, the overlap rate increased to 39% for UGT_{Arabic} and to 18% for $UGT_{Arabizi}$ in $C_\beta1$. The same effect is observed in $C_\beta2$ and $C_\beta3$ (compared to $C_\alpha2$ and $C_\alpha3$) as shown in Tables 6 and 7.

Due to the large amount of the MDA UGT words, we decided to use, in the last comparison, a portion containing 3k words in each script (UGT_{Arabic} and the transliterated $UGT_{Arabizi}$). In this comparison, we converted UGT_β words and rewrite them regarding VOC1 writing rules in order to obtain $UGT\gamma$. For example, the word he knows me/ كيعرفني is manually converted to كايعرفني in order to meet $UGT\gamma$ writing standard. As a final overlap rates, we obtained 84% for UGT_{Arabic} and 54% for $UGT_{Arabizi}$ in $C_\gamma3$.

Table 6. The overlap existing between UGT and MDA vocabulary (Arabic script)

Arabic	VOC1	VOC2	VOC3
UGT_α	$C_{\alpha1} = 28\%$	$C_{\alpha2} = 45\%$	$C_{\alpha3} = 51\%$
UGT_β	$C_{\beta1} = 39\%$	$C_{\beta2} = 58\%$	$C_{\beta3} = 67\%$
UGT_γ	$C_{\gamma1} = 65\%$	$C_{\gamma2} = 81\%$	$C_{\gamma3} = 84\%$

Table 7. The overlap existing between UGT and MDA vocabulary (Arabizi)

Arabizi	VOC1	VOC2	VOC3
UGT_α	$C_{\alpha1} = 2\%$	$C_{\alpha2} = 19\%$	$C_{\alpha3} = 25\%$
UGT_β	$C_{\beta1} = 18\%$	$C_{\beta2} = 35\%$	$C_{\beta3} = 42\%$
UGT_γ	$C_{\gamma1} = 34\%$	$C_{\gamma2} = 51\%$	$C_{\gamma3} = 54\%$

4.3 Discussion

Going back to three questions raised in the beginning of this paper, the performed experiments allow us to response and discuss its results.

The first question is about MDA text standardization. In light of these results, it is clear that orthography presents a crucial feature that should be considered before engaging in any NLP task related to the processing of the Moroccan dialectal Arabic in social media. In fact, after identifying and analyzing the MDA UGT, we find that it is too noisy considering a reference standard vocabulary. The percentage of recognized words is 28% for the Arabic script and 2% for the Arabizi. In fact, users do not adopt any writing rules and feel free to use keyboard keys to write their MDA sentences since this dialect has no writing standards. Moreover, by using the Arabic script, the percentage of misspelled words (72% = 100% − 28%) is low compared to the percentage of misspelled words (98% = 100% − 2%) written in Arabizi. This result may be explained, on one hand, by the closeness existing between MDA and MSA (which has a writing standard) and on the other hand, by the accuracy of the used transliteration tool. As a result, the MDA content written in both Arabic and Arabizi scripts, is not useful for NLP purposes without performing necessary pre-processing tasks such as cleaning and normalization.

The second question seeks out answers about the usefulness of Arabic NLP tools in MDA processing purposes. In fact, we noticed that Moroccans use code-switching in both Arabic and Arabizi scripts. They usually include in their sentences some MSA words (including named entities) that don't belong to the MDA lexicon as cited previously. This can be noticed by enhancing the MDA vocabulary with the MSA one which increases the overlap rate. Hence, the recognition of Arabic words in dialectal texts can be performed using available Arabic NLP tools which improve the precision.

Finally, the third question concerns tasks before building advanced MDA tools. In our experiments, by performing a pre-processing task to the MDA UGT and enhancing the MDA reference vocabulary by the MSA one is not enough to reduce the OOV. After converting manually, the remaining UGT words to VOC writing rules, the percentage of misspelled words decreased from 33% = 100% − 67% to 16% = 100 − 84% for Arabic script and from 58% = 100% − 42% to 46% = 100% − 54% for Arabizi. This result showed clearly that processing MDA UGT directly without taking into consideration a writing standard yields to low accuracy. To remedy this problem, it is necessary to include in the pre-processing step a customized spelling correction tool that ensures cleaning and converting the dialectal words to a unique and standard writing form. In addition, it should detect MSA words and Named entities.

5   Conclusion

In this paper, we analyzed the Moroccan user generated text through a corpus collected from social media websites in Morocco. Results of the conducted experiments showed that MDA UGT is unsuitable for NLP tasks because of the noise existing in this content (35% of Moroccan UGT is noisy). Nevertheless, using a customized spelling correction tool, Arabic NLP tools and a customized transliteration tool for the Moroccan Colloquial Arabic will pave the way to engaging in more advanced processing such as morphological analysis and automatic translation. As a future work and taking into consideration the above constraints, we plan to build a spelling correction tool as a pre-processing step towards analyzing the MDA text in social media.

References

1. Abdelali, A., Darwish, K., Durrani, N., Mubarak, H.: Farasa: a fast and furious segmenter for arabic. In: 15th Annual Conference of the North American Chapter of the Association for Computational Linguistics, NAACL HLT 2016, San Diego, USA (2016)

2. Abidi, K., Smaïli, K.: An empirical study of the Algerian dialect of Social network. In: International Conference on Natural Language, Signal and Speech Processing, ICNSSP 2017, Casablanca, Morocco (2017)
3. Afli, H., Aransa, W., Lohar, P., Way, A.: From Arabic user-generated content to machine translation: integrating automatic error correction. In: 17th International Conference on Intelligent Text Processing and Computational Linguistics, CICLING 2016, Konya, Turkey (2016)
4. Amid Neme, A.: A fully inflected Arabic verb resource constructed from a lexicon of lemmas by using finite-state transducers. Revue de l'Information Scientifique et Technique **20**(2), 1–13 (2013)
5. Boujelbane, R., Zribi, I., Kharroubi, S., Ellouze, M.: An automatic process for Tunisian Arabic orthography normalization. In: 10th International Conference on Natural Language Processing, HRTAL 2016, Dubrovnik, Croatia (2016)
6. El Jihad, A., Namly, D., Hamdani, f., Bouzoubaa, K.: The development of a standard morpho-syntactic lexicon for arabic NLP. In: International Conference on Learning and Optimization Algorithms: Theory and Applications, LOPAL 2018. ACM, Rabat (2018)
7. Eskander, R., Habash, N., Rambow, O., Tomeh, N.: Processing spontaneous orthography. In: The 2013 Conference of the North American Chapter of the Association for Computational Linguistics: Human Language Technologies, NAACL-HLT 2013. ACL, Atlanta (2013)
8. Habash, N., Diab, M., Rabmow, O.: Conventional orthography for dialectal Arabic. In: 8th International Conference on Language Resources and Evaluation, LREC 2012, Istanbul, Turkey (2012)
9. Habash, N., Rambow, O., Roth, R.: Mada+tokan: a toolkit for arabic tokenization, diacritization, morphological disambiguation, POS tagging, stemming and lemmatization. In: Second International Conference on Arabic Language Resources and Tools, MEDAR 2009, Cairo, Egypt (2009)
10. Jaafar, Y., Bouzoubaa, K.: Arabic natural language processing from software engineering to complex pipeline. In: First International Conference on Arabic Computational Linguistics, ACLING 2015, Cairo, Egypt, vol. 19 (2015)
11. Maamouri, M., Bies, A., Kulick, S., Krouna, S., Tabassi, D., Ciul, M.: Egyptian Arabic Treebank DF Parts 1–8 (2012)
12. Namli, D., Bouzoubaa, K., Tajmout, R., Tahir, Y., Khamar, H.: A Complex Arabic stop-words list design. Deuxième Journée Doctorale Nationale sur l'Ingénierie de la Langue Arabe, JDILA 2015, Fes, Morocco (2015)
13. Obeid, O., et al.: Large scale Arabic error annotation: guidelines and framework. In: The Ninth International Conference on Language Resources and Evaluation, LREC 2014, pp. 2362–2369, Reykjavik, Iceland (2014)
14. Pasha, A., et al.: MADAMIRA: a fast, comprehensive tool for morphological analysis and disambiguation of Arabic. In: 9th International Conference on Language Resources and Evaluation, LREC 2014, Reykjavik, Iceland, May 2014
15. Saadane, H., Habash, N.: A conventional orthography for Algerian Arabic. In: Second Workshop on Arabic Natural Language Processing, WANLP 2015, Beijing, China (2015)
16. Tachicart, R., Bouzoubaa, K.: An empirical analysis of Moroccan dialectal user-generated text. In: 11th International Conference Computational Collective Intelligence, ICCCI 2019, Hendaye, France (2019)
17. Tachicart, R., Bouzoubaa, K., Jaafar, H.: Building a Moroccan dialect electronic Dictionnary (MDED). In: 5th International Conference on Arabic Language Processing, CITALA 2014, Oujda, Morocco, November 2014

18. Tachicart, R., Bouzoubaa, K., Jaafar, H.: Lexical differences and similarities between Moroccan dialect and Arabic. In: 4th IEEE International Colloquium on Information Science and Technology, CIST 2016, Tanger, Morocco (2016)

19. Tachicart, R., Bouzoubaa, K., Aouragh, S.L., Jaafa, H.: Automatic identification of Moroccan Colloquial Arabic. In: Lachkar, A., Bouzoubaa, K., Mazroui, A., Hamdani, A., Lekhouaja, A. (eds.) Arabic Language Processing: From Theory to Practice. CCIS, vol. 782, pp. 201–214. Springer, Cham (2018). https://doi.org/10.1007/978-3-319-73500-9_15

20. Wang, J., Jean-Daniel, Z.: Solving the multiple-instance problem: a lazy learning approach. In: 17th International Conference on Machine Learning, ICML 2000, pp. 1119–1126. Morgan Kaufmann Publishers Inc., San Francisco (2000)

21. Zaghouani, W., et al.: Large scale Arabic error annotation: guidelines and framework. In: The Ninth International Conference on Language Resources and Evaluation, LREC 2014, pp. 2362–2369, Reykjavik, Iceland (2014)

22. Zribi, I., Boujelbane, R., Masmoudi, A., Ellouze, M., Belguith, L., Habash, N.: A conventional orthography for Tunisian Arabic. In: Ninth International Conference on Language Resources and Evaluation, LREC 2014, Reykjavik, Iceland (2014)

23. Zribi, I., Ellouze, M., Ellouze, M., Hadrich Belguith, L., Blache, P.: Spoken Tunisian Arabic Corpus "STAC": transcription and annotation. Res. Comput. Sci. **90**, 123–135 (2015)

Arabic Search Results Disambiguation:
A Set of Benchmarks

Haytham Salhi⬤, Radi Jarrar$^{(\boxtimes)}$⬤, and Adnan Yahya⬤

Faculty of Engineering and Technology, Birzeit University, Birzeit, Palestine
hsalhi89@gmail.com, {rjarrar,yahya}@birzeit.edu

Abstract. Web search engines aim at retrieving relevant results in response to a user information need. The query expressing the user information need can be ambiguous by potentially referring to different meanings or senses. Search results clustering (SRC) attempts to disambiguate query results by grouping them into groups of sense-relevant clusters. Little research was done on Arabic SRC, and one important reason may be the lack of quality benchmarks for SRC testing and evaluation.

The main contribution of this paper is to introduce a set of benchmarks for Arabic SRC, called AMBIGArabic to aid in performing SRC experiments. The benchmarks include manually labeled datasets and a dataset based on blind relevance feedback (BRF). The designed benchmarks were used in a series of SRC experiments we performed and the results were encouraging. The benchmarks are being made available for use by researchers working on Arabic SRC.

Keywords: Search results clustering · Ambiguous arabic queries · Search results disambiguation · Arabic SRC

1 Introduction

Search results clustering (SRC) is concerned with grouping search results retrieved for an ambiguous user query according to the senses of query words [1]. A query for "Python" will return documents pertaining to the programming language, the reptile, or the movie even though the user has only one of these meanings in mind. This makes it difficult for users to identify relevant results. SRC seeks to group search results for "Python" into 3 groups corresponding to the 3 meanings of the word. For SRC one needs to develop clustering algorithms, select features and feature representations, build clustering models, and evaluate these models on the relevant benchmarks, when available. Given the lack of Arabic SRC benchmarks, this work aims to address the benchmark aspect of SRC by providing a set of benchmarks for use in Arabic SRC.

We describe these benchmarks: the sources of data and disambiguation senses, the way they are collected and annotated, and provide some results on their quality based on our initial tests. We present three benchmarks: 2 with human annotation and one exclusively based on automatic blind relevance feedback (BRF). The benchmarks were constructed using results from Google and Bing search engines. The benchmarks and their characterization are available online for possible use by interested researchers.

© Springer Nature Switzerland AG 2019
K. Smaïli (Ed.): ICALP 2019, CCIS 1108, pp. 276–291, 2019.
https://doi.org/10.1007/978-3-030-32959-4_20

1.1 Motivation

Over the recent years, Web search engines have become an important part of our everyday lives. When a user poses a query, traditional search engines return a list of results ordered by relevance to the query according to some metric. The user scans the top results until the intended information is found. This is useful when the query conveying the user information need is *clear* and *precise*. However, it is less effective when dealing with *ambiguous* queries that have more than one meaning [2], which may be the case for the majority of queries. For ambiguous queries, results can be a mix on different meanings with some senses appearing on later result pages. Helping users find results satisfying their information need for ambiguous queries, or even making users aware of the diversity in search results, is of great importance. To this end, researchers have proposed many approaches to solve this problem for English and other languages [3–6]. Work on Arabic search results disambiguation (SRD) is limited and one of the major obstacles is the lack of datasets for Arabic SRC. Creating benchmarks for Arabic SRC is the main focus of this paper. The development of these benchmarks was done in a framework of more elaborate work on Arabic SRC [7].

1.2 The SRC Problem

SRC is one approach to search results disambiguation, which seeks to group search results according to the different query meanings. Other approaches exploit NLP tasks such as word sense induction and word sense disambiguation [5, 8, 9]. Another early approach was based on classifying web pages as in the case of DMOZ project[1]. Other researchers concentrated on having search results achieve maximum diversity in returned senses using so-called diversification techniques [2, 10]. Others still exploited query logs to resolve ambiguous queries by applying mining techniques [6, 11]. Each approach has its merits and drawbacks, but the latter works only if the query logs are accessible.

SRC is challenged by three core requirements [12, 13]:

1. Effectiveness: the clusters should be of good quality in terms of the degree to which search results in a cluster belong to same meaning (i.e., effectiveness of clustering).
2. Labeling: the cluster labels must be understandable.
3. Efficiency: the clustering process must be efficient in terms of processing time.

Each of these challenges is a self-contained research problem.

Important factors defining effectiveness are feature generation and representations [12, 13], something often done in the preprocessing stage of SRC.

Most of SRC work dealt with English language. Despite the increasing interest in Arabic [14–17], major gaps still exist and include:

1. In contrast to English, there are no published benchmarks for Arabic SRC work.
2. There is no clear evidence as to the best feature source and representation to achieve effective high quality Arabic SRC.

---

[1] https://dmoz-odp.org/.

This work aims at addressing the first gap: presenting benchmarks for the Arabic SRC.

2 Background

This section briefly explains the notion of query and information need and gives an overview of clustering and their evaluation methodology as well the role of benchmarks in that. Finally, we give a quick overview of our SRC benchmarks.

2.1 Queries and Information Needs

From a user perspective, a search engine is an interface for posing *queries* and viewing *results*. Information need is the information a user is looking for. The query is the word expression of information need [12]. Moreover, the query can *be a poor representation of information need* because the user might find it difficult to express the information need or due to the limited context, or even due to limited user knowledge, leaving the query *ambiguous* or *imprecise* [12].

2.2 Search Result Disambiguation and Clustering

Search results disambiguation has been widely studied and different solutions have been proposed. One of the popular solutions is search result clustering (SRC). The motivation behind using clustering is that search results with same meaning of the posed query are expected to be similar, whereas search results with different meanings are expected to belong to different clusters.

2.3 Arabic Search Results Clustering

Most research on SRC targeted the English language. Many algorithms developed for the English SRC perform poorly when applied to other languages like Arabic, which is highly inflectional and morphologically rich. However, limited research was done for Arabic as in [14–17].

Sahmoudi and Lachkar [14] applied suffix tree clustering algorithm (STC) to Arabic Web search snippets. They achieved promising results though the evaluation they performed was subjective due to the lack of standard labeled test collections for Arabic [14]. To the best of our knowledge, there is no standard test collection for evaluating SRC. This is the main motivation behind building our labeled data collection for evaluating Arabic SRC. In another work [15], Sahmoudi and Lachkar proposed an interactive system for Arabic Web search results clustering (ISAWSRC) for Arabic query reformulation. The system enables users to click on produced cluster label so that the system can then retrieve results that are more relevant. More recently, the same authors studied how to integrate and adapt formal concept analysis (FCA) for Arabic web search results clustering [18]. They performed an experimental study to show that FCA is better than suffix tree clustering and Lingo in terms of both clustering and label quality [19]. They used a dataset of Arabic documents from the Open Directory Project[2] as a benchmark.

3 Building an SRC Benchmark for Arabic Language

One of the important aspects of any experimental research is understanding and collecting data required for experiments. In order to perform and evaluate experiments on search results clustering, real data from web search engines must be collected. English has a number of benchmarks for this aim. The most popular ones are AMBIguous ENTries (AMBI-ENT) [20] and MORE Sense-tagged QUEries (MORESQUE) [21]. Queries and their corresponding meanings in both benchmarks were selected from Wikipedia disambiguation pages.

In contrast, we found no benchmark for Arabic SRC published and publicly available. This is the task we undertook and describe here. We call our benchmark AMBIGArabic.

To build an Arabic SRC benchmark, one typically needs:

- A set of Arabic ambiguous queries.
- A set of meanings for each ambiguous query. The source could be any word disambiguation source such as Wikipedia disambiguation pages.
- A set of search results for each ambiguous query.
- A meaning label for each search result.

The queries in the initial set of ambiguous queries were selected manually.

3.1 Data Design

We designed a relational model with several core relations. Four core entities are related to search results: query, meaning, search result, and search engine, and two core entities for user labeling: user and user labeling. The full document (the inner page) is also a property of search result.

Figure 1 abstracts the core entities combined with the main relationships. The *query* table is used to store queries. Since the query could be either ambiguous or clear (disambiguated by adding text designating a specific meaning), the *query* table has a flag *is_ambiguous* to indicate whether the query is ambiguous (i.e., has multiple meanings) or not. The *meaning* table is used to store the meanings. When posing a query to a search engine, search results are retrieved and stored in the *search result* table. The *user* table stores *annotators*: users who can label search results with different meanings.

---

[2] Now DMOZ: https://dmoz-odp.org/.

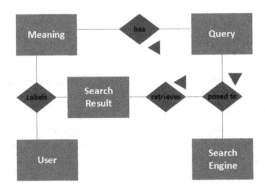

Fig. 1. A high-level entity relationship diagram of data.

3.2 Search Results Acquisition: The Fetcher System

We studied the feasibility and limits of fetching search results from the popular search engines: Google, Bing, and Yahoo. Based on a given query, the fetcher system is responsible for delivering search results, each of which contains the *title*, the *snippet* (a short summary), the *URL* pointing to the full document, and the *full document* itself.

The manually collected queries are loaded by the *data loader*. The *controller* gets the loaded queries from the *data loader* and passes them to the *crawler* to start fetching the search results. The *crawler* delivers the loaded queries into the *fetcher* components and then passes the search results to the *persistence* component for storage.

3.3 Characteristics of Search Results

Having collected the initial set of ambiguous queries, we looked into the search results returned by Google and Bing and the following issues were observed:

- A query can refer to different entities or even entity types. For example, the query آرمسترونج (Armstrong) can refer to different entities of person class and even different entities of location class.
- A search engine can return results belonging to a specific subset of the meanings (senses) and not necessarily for all of them. For example, if we query python on Google, most likely the first 100 results are about Python as a programming language. So covering multiple (or all) senses in the accessible (say top 100 or 200) search results is not guaranteed.
- The search engine may return documents that have the whole query words or a portion of them. As an example, the query الجامعة العربية (The Arab League) might return results that contain العربية (Arabic) only.
- Even if the query is disambiguated using Wikipedia disambiguation pages for persons only, the search engine may not return results for those persons only. The query سعود بن عبد العزيز (Saud bin Abdulaziz) for example, can refer to a person or a university, or even something we did not know about. New meanings or senses can show up over time.

3.4   Search Results Labeling

One important aspect of the benchmark is the data labeling with a specific meaning of the ambiguous query. This section outlines our labeling approach to generate the SRC dataset. First, we present two approaches for data labeling: *intersecting* and *mixing* approaches.

Intersecting Approach. For an ambiguous query q, with meanings/senses set S = {s_1, s_2, ..., s_n}, and for a search engine SE:

1. Fetch the results *Rq* for *q using SE*, so we have Rq = {r_1, r_2, ..., r_m}, where *m* is the number of search results that could be fetched and r_i is the ith search result $0 < i \leq m$.
2. For each clear query formed by combining *q* and s_i[3] where $1 \leq i \leq n$,
   a. Fetch the result set Rq(si) = {rs_{i1}, rs_{i2}, ..., rs_{ik} }, where k $\leq$ m.
   b. Annotate the search items as follows: $\forall$ item $\in$ (Rq $\cap$ Rq(si)), label item with s_i.

Table 1. The intersections between results of ambiguous and clear queries.

Query	Meaning (English)	Meaning	Formulated Query	Google Ret. Results	Google Intersections	Bing Ret. Results	Bing Intersections
المالكي (Almaliki)			المالكي	100	-	200	-
	Doctrine	المذهب	المذهب المالكي	100	2	200	24
	Nouri Almaliki	نوري المالكي	نوري المالكي	100	15	200	24
	Almaliki Murad	مراد المالكي	مراد المالكي	100	2	200	1
	Almaliki Fayez	فايز المالكي	فايز المالكي	100	3	200	6
عمان (A'man)			عمان	100	-	200	-
	Sultanate	سلطنة	سلطنة عمان	100	33	200	51
	City	مدينة	مدينة عمان	100	6	200	26
أمازون (Amazon)			أمازون	100	-	200	-
	River	نهر	نهر أمازون	100	4	200	5
	Company	شركة	شركة أمازون	100	23	200	49
البقرة (Albaqara)			البقرة	100	-	200	-
	Animal	حيوان	حيوان البقرة	100	4	200	6
	Quran Chapter	سورة	سورة البقرة	100	74	200	93

---

[3] For example, say we have q = أمازون (Amazon) and s1 = شركة (Company), then the resulting clear query is أمازون شركة (Amazon Company).

The above labeling steps were achieved through an online interface for Bing and Google[4]. Moreover, some statistics and charts were generated to show some insights of intersections between search results of meaning and search results for an ambiguous query. Table 1 shows sample statistics for 4 such queries. The full sheet is also available online[5].

A drawback of this approach is that not all search results will be labeled. Take the query المالكي (Almaliki) from Table 1 as an example; In Google, only 22 (i.e., 2 + 15 + 2 + 3) search results out of 100 were labeled. In Bing, only 55 (i.e., 24 + 24 + 1 + 6) search results out of 200 were labeled.

Mixing Approach The idea behind the mixing approach is slightly different. It is based on collecting the search results for the meanings (reformulated clear queries) first.

Formal Definition: For an ambiguous query q, with senses $S = \{s_1, s_2, ..., s_n\}$ and search engine SE:

- Using SE fetch the results for each clear query formed by combining of q and s_i to get $Rq(si)$ where
- $1 \leq i \leq n.$
- Label the top N results for each $Rq(si) = r_{si1}, r_{si2}, ..., r_{siN}$ with s_i where $1 \leq i \leq n$ and $Rq(si)$ is the list of search results of the clear query formed by q and s_i.
- Mix the labeled results for all meanings defined above together to get the balanced set of labeled results for the query q.

We make the following observations on the results of the two approaches:
Intersecting Approach: Some of the results for the ambiguous query may not be present in any of the clear queries and thus may not get labeled. Even though a search engine tries its best to retrieve relevant results as a response to a clear query, some items can still be non-relevant.

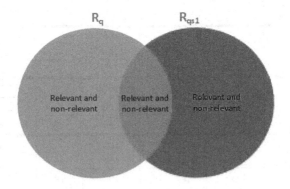

Fig. 2. A Venn diagram showing the two sets: R_q, R_{qs1}.

---

[4] https://goo.gl/DTEszH.

[5] https://goo.gl/8VW8eM.

As depicted in Fig. 2, given that both Rq with $Rq(s1)$ may have both relevant and non-relevant items to s1, the intersection may have non-relevant search results labeled relevant by our approach. Therefore, the intersecting approach cannot be adopted alone in the labeling process.

In the m*ixing approach* we get rid of the drawback of unlabeled results by ensuring that each query has all search results labeled[6]. Furthermore, the results are now more representative of the different meanings and we ensure that the search results of a query cover all available meanings and are balanced. However, as usual some of the results deemed relevant by the SE may not be so in reality and human annotation is necessary here as well. The controlled number of results for each sense and the ease of balancing the dataset gave an edge to the mixing approach.

3.5 Human Relevance Assessment

In order to build benchmarks with a gold standard judgment of relevance, a human relevance assessment interface was created to enable a group of users to label the collected search results manually. This interface supports two types of manual labeling: *Yes/No annotation* and *Choice-based annotation*.

Fig. 3. An example snapshot of yes/no interface.

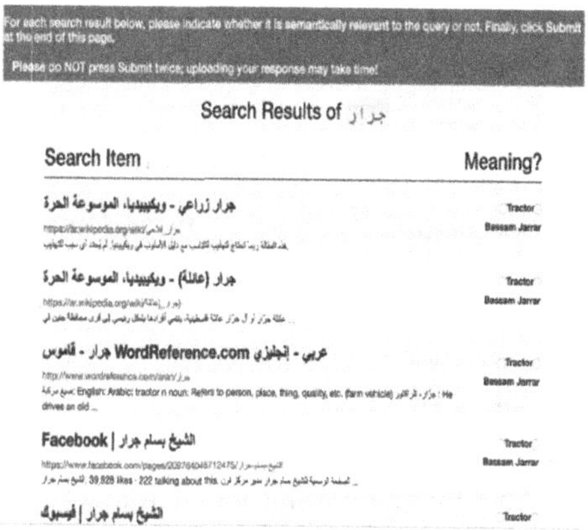

Fig. 4. An example snapshot of choice-based interface.

---

[6] To indicate the degree to which concatenating ambiguous query with its senses is successful, consider عمان (A'man) query (along with its meanings: "سلطنة" Sultanate and "مدينة" City). When using concatenation, the accuracy is 96% and 83% for both meanings, respectively. With the plain query alone, the accuracy is 19% and 11% for the two meanings, respectively. Detailed results are available online: https://goo.gl/jjcR2J for clear queries and http://bit.ly/2OMEcdI for ambiguous queries.

In the *yes/no annotation* strategy, an assessor indicates, for a specific information need expressed by a query, whether a search result is relevant to the information need. Figure 3 shows the yes/no annotation interface for a specific query, along with its search items and choices. Yes/no annotation was used to build a gold standard of the mixing-based benchmark using clear queries.

The second type of the labeling used is *choice-based annotation*. This strategy was used to label search results of a query with an element of a predefined set of meanings. For each search result, the user selects one meaning from the predefined set. If the item has a sense that is not in the predefined set, no selection is made. Figure 4 shows the choice-based annotation interface for a query along with its search result items and the available choices. Choice-based strategy was used to build a gold standard of the plain human-annotated (PHA) benchmark containing real search results of ambiguous queries (without resorting to clear queries).

4 AMBIGArabic Benchmarks

This section presents the three benchmarks we built, called AMBIGArabic (Ambiguous Arabic) Benchmarks. Two of these benchmarks: mixing-based and plain are gold standard with human annotation components while the third is based on the automatic blind relevance feedback (BRF) with no explicit human annotation.

4.1 Mixing-Based Human-Annotated (MBHA) Benchmark

This benchmark is based on the mixing and labeling approach discussed earlier. It leverages the search results of clear queries to build an SRC dataset. We aim to have balanced datasets in terms of available query meanings. All available meanings of the query are equally represented in the benchmark. The following steps were followed to build this benchmark:

1. 30 ambiguous queries were collected with their meanings to get 63 clear queries formed by combining ambiguous queries with meaning (disambiguation) text. So on average a query has 2.1 meanings. The full list of queries and meanings is available online[7].
2. Search results for each clear query were fetched for both engines, Google (100 results) and Bing (200 results). 100 and 200 are the max accessible results for Google and Bing, respectively.
3. Yes/No annotation labeling was performed by humans on the clear queries in order to produce balanced datasets. The final judged results are available online for Google[8] and Bing[9].

---

[7] https://goo.gl/UcSkkE.

[8] https://goo.gl/KRBvsB.

[9] https://goo.gl/epg2Ct.

4. After that, the top 30 human-judged relevant search results for each clear query along with their titles, snippets, and inner (full) pages were collected. Therefore, if an ambiguous query has two meanings, it would have 60 (30 + 30) search results. The lowest common value among the clear queries was 30 and that is the reason why 30 is selected.

Some statistics about human judgment giving information like number of judges and level of agreement were calculated. These are also available online for Google[10] and Bing[11].

4.2   Mixing-Based BRF-Annotated (BRFA) Benchmark

Blind Relevance Feedback (BRF), also referred to as pseudo relevance feedback, is used in information retrieval systems. The idea behind BRF is to assume that the top k ranked results are relevant to the query without user intervention [22]. There is an opportunity to check how useful the BRF could be for building a benchmark for SRC, by basing labeling of search results based on BRF with no human intervention.

To build this benchmark, we followed the same procedure as for the mixing-based benchmark above except for the third step, where the top 50 search results are assumed relevant to the clear query, to produce a balanced dataset in terms of different query meanings. The BRF-based benchmark contains the same number of queries and meanings as above but with a larger number of search results per meaning: 50 instead of 30.

4.3   Plain Human-Annotated (PHA) Benchmark

Search results disambiguation systems should work on real search results of an ambiguous query. Out of this need, benchmarks of search results of ambiguous queries were built with no reference to clear versions of the queries. To build this benchmark, the following procedure was followed:

1. Sets of ambiguous queries were manually selected for each search engine: 11 for Google and 15 for Bing[12]. The criterion for query selection was that each has a reasonable number of search results belonging to more than one meaning of the ambiguous query. Each selected query had two to three meanings represented within the viewable results of the respective search engine. This was based on manual inspection.
2. For each query, 100 search results for Google and 200 search results for Bing were fetched. Inner pages for most search results were also fetched. For Bing, the fetcher was able to crawl 2822 inner pages out of 3000 (15 times 200) search results. For Google, the fetcher was able to crawl 1033 out of 1100 (11 times 100).

---

[10] https://goo.gl/jjcR2J.

[11] https://goo.gl/v4xadq.

[12] They can be found here: https://goo.gl/SrBBWf.

3. After that, all search results were labeled manually using the developed assessment interface. The annotation process was choice-based selection. As an example, "sakhr" has three senses: "company" (شركة صخر), "sakhr bn amro", (صخر بن عمرو) or rock (صخر).

Therefore, the resulting plain benchmark consists of the following:

1. 11 ambiguous queries for Google and 15 queries for Bing along with their predefined meanings (between two and three for each query).
2. The top 100 ranked search results for Google and the top 200 ranked search results for Bing.
3. The human labels for each search result.

The results are available online for both Google[13] and Bing[14]. Some statistics about human judgment can be accessed online for Google[15] and Bing[16] as well.

Tables 2 and 3 summarize the three benchmarks in terms of number of queries, size of search results, and labeling method used. All benchmarks can be accessed through Fada[17] repository [23].

Table 2. Size of queries and labeling method for each benchmark.

Benchmark	Google queries	Bing queries	Google clear queries	Bing clear queries	Labeling method
Human-annotated mixing based	30	30	63	63	Mixing-based approach with human annotation
BRF-mixing approach	30	30	63	63	Mixing-based approach with relevance feedback
Plain	11	15	25	33	Human annotation

---

[13] https://goo.gl/VFebSk.

[14] https://goo.gl/dZm3jk.

[15] https://goo.gl/dsp4zh.

[16] https://goo.gl/658ftd.

[17] https://fada.birzeit.edu.

Table 3. Size of search results per query for each benchmark.

Benchmark	Search results per query/Google		Search results per query/Bing	
	Queries with 2 meanings	Queries with 3 meanings	Queries with 2 meanings	Queries with 3 meanings
Human-annotated mixing-based	60	90	60	90
BRF mixing-based	100	150	100	150
Plain	100		200	

5 Experimental Instantiation

Our aim here is to validate the presented data sets and to present preliminary tests using unsupervised learning to cluster search results. We confined ourselves in describing the dataset in this work. The extended experiments of the approaches on this dataset can be found in [7].

Several experiments were conducted on the presented benchmarks: the human-annotated, BRF-annotated, and plain benchmarks. Moreover, we tried to investigate how useful blind relevance feedback could be in search results clustering. The main goal of using BRF was to see whether it compares well with experiments results using human annotation, in which case one can utilize the automatic nature of BRF for future clustering model construction. The results are reported using the F-measure metric.

5.1 Data Pre-processing

Data pre-processing is an essential step to transform raw data into a form that is suitable for machine learning tasks. Data pre-processing is applied to the collected queries. The pipeline of data pre-processing is shown in Fig. 5. These are the standard preprocessing steps of Arabic text and will not be Features and Feature Space Representation.

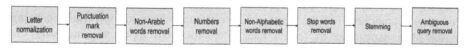

Fig. 5. The order of the preprocessing steps.

The following features were used to represent the collected dataset in order to perform clustering:

Word Frequency. It indicates how relevant a given document is to a specific word, which will affect the similarity computation between search results.

Words to Keep. This indicates the top most common words.

Inverse Document Frequency (IDF). This variable represents the informative words that occur frequently in a document but infrequently across documents.

Since preprocessing of search results aims at removing noise, all words with frequencies larger than 1 were kept. Moreover, all documents were normalized to a standard length before clustering. Furthermore, the following features were used as the input to the clustering algorithm: single words, single words with 2-grams, and single words with 2-grams and 3-grams.

5.2   Clustering Algorithm

The K-means clustering algorithm has been extensively used information retrieval tasks and text clustering [12]. In the context of this work, K-means clustering is used to cluster the returned search results.

The number of clusters (K) in K-Means depends on the experiment itself. Here, the natural choice is the number of predefined meanings of an ambiguous query. As for the experiments that are performed on the plain benchmark (i.e., the baseline), the value of K is set according to Calinski-Harabasz criterion [24]. Calinski-Harabasz index evaluates the clustering validity as a ratio of the between-cluster and the within-cluster sum of square. Another important factor in K-Means algorithm is the distance measure. Cosine similarity distance is the preferred similarity distance measure for text documents [25]. However, since all documents are normalized, we used the Euclidean distance as it gives the same results as the Cosine distance [26].

5.3   Evaluation Methodology

The external evaluation method we followed is the misclassification error of instances, which is also referred to as classes-to-clusters method [27]. Here, the class labels of the instances are ignored during the generation of clusters. During the test phase, instances are assigned classes based on the K-means generated centroids for the given ambiguous query. The classification error is then computed based on the assignment of instances.

The classes of each dataset within a benchmark (that includes an ambiguous query, predefined meanings, and search results) are represented by the predefined meanings. As an example, for the query Amazon (أمازون), the classes in this case are river (نهر) and company (شركة). We used the proposed benchmarks to validate and build different clustering approaches. The first approach involves traditional unsupervised clustering on the plain benchmark as testing data. The other two approaches are based on exploiting the search results of clear queries, as training data, to build supervised clustering models to test on the plain benchmark. Figure 6 shows the weighted averaged F-measure of mapping classes to clusters on the various datasets The MBHA-based approach outperforms the traditional one by 5% and 12% for the mean and 10% and 12% for the median, for Google and Bing, respectively. Moreover, the approach built on blind relevance feedback (BRF) datasets outperforms the traditional one by 2% and 10% in mean and 4% and 17% in median, for Google and Bing, respectively.

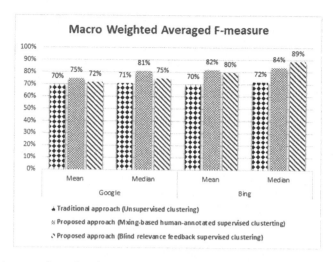

Fig. 6. A comparison chart between the three approaches based on macro F-measure.

6 Conclusions and Future Work

Using search results clustering as an approach to solve search results disambiguation problem is useful. To do experiments with Arabic SRC, there is an urgent need for publicly available datasets. There have been no publicly available benchmarks for Arabic SRC, thus we introduced such benchmarks (called AMBIGArabic) that can be used in other experiments involving search results clustering or even more generally search results disambiguation. This kind of benchmarks is very helpful for researchers who want, for example, to study and compare different methods or algorithms for search results clustering. Our use of these benchmarks attests to their utility. We also illustrated the data acquisition system, through which we collected our data. This can be used as a tool by other researches for similar tasks and for expanding this dataset in the future. Our hope is that the accessibility of these benchmarks will encourage SRC research especially to study other important factors such as increasing number of queries (i.e., the size of the dataset) and if the number of ambiguous concepts is higher.

References

1. Vannella, D., Flati, T., Navigli, R.: Wosit: a word sense induction toolkit for search result clustering and diversification. In: Proceedings of 52nd Annual Meeting of the Association for Computational Linguistics: System Demonstrations, pp. 67–72 (2014)
2. Song, R., Luo, Z., Wen, J.-R., Yu, Y., Hon, H.-W.: Identifying ambiguous queries in web search. In: Proceedings of the 16th International Conference on World Wide Web (WWW), pp. 1169–1170 (2007)
3. Zamir, O., Etzioni, O.: Web document clustering: a feasibility demonstration. ACM SIGIR **98**, 46–54 (1998)

4. Ma, H., Lyu, M.R., King, I.: Diversifying query suggestion results. In: Twenty-fourth AAAI Conference on Artificial Intelligence, pp. 1399–1404 (2010)
5. Di Marco, A., Navigli, R.: Clustering and diversifying web search results with graph-based word sense induction. Comput. Linguist. **39**, 709–754 (2013)
6. Xue, X., Yin, X.: Topic modeling for named entity queries. In: Proceedings of the 20th ACM International Conference on Information and Knowledge Management, pp. 2009–2012 (2011)
7. Salhi, H.: Arabic search results disambiguation: a supervised approach to unsupervised learning. Master's thesis, Faculty of Engineering and Technology, Birzeit University (2019)
8. Huang, Z., Niu, Z., Liu, D., Niu, W., Wang, W.: A novel method for clustering web search results with wikipedia disambiguation pages. In: International Conference on Database Systems for Advanced Applications, pp. 3–16 (2015)
9. Chen, J., Zaïane, O.R., Goebel, R.: An unsupervised approach to cluster web search results based on word sense communities. In: IEEE/WIC/ACM International Conference on Web Intelligence and Intelligent Agent Technology, pp. 725–729 (2008)
10. Swaminathan, A., Mathew, C., Kirovski, D.: Essential pages. In: IEEE/WIC/ACM International Joint Conference on Web Intelligence and Intelligent Agent Technology, pp. 173–182 (2009)
11. Wang, X., Zhai, C.: Learn from web search logs to organize search results. In: Proceedings of the 30th International ACM SIGIR Conference on Research and Development in Information Retrieval, pp. 87–94 (2007)
12. Croft, B., Metzler, D., Strohman, T.: Search Engines: Information Retrieval in Practice, vol. 520. Addison-Wesley, Reading (2010)
13. Carpineto, C., Osiński, S., Romano, G., Weiss, D.: A survey of web clustering engines. ACM Comput. Surv. (CSUR) **41**, 17 (2009)
14. Sahmoudi, I., Lachkar, A.: Clustering web search results for effective Arabic language browsing. arXiv preprint arXiv:1305.2755 (2013)
15. Sahmoudi, I., Lachkar, A.: Interactive system based on web search results clustering for arabic query reformulation. In: 3rd IEEE International Colloquium in Information Science and Technology (CIST), pp. 300–305 (2014)
16. Froud, H., Lachkar, A., Ouatik, S.: Arabic text summarization based on latent semantic analysis to enhance Arabic documents clustering. arXiv preprint (2013). arXiv:1302.1612
17. Abuaiadah, D.: Using bisect k-means clustering technique in the analysis of arabic documents. ACM Trans. Asian and Low-Resource Lang. Inf. Process. **15**, 17 (2016)
18. Sahmoudi, I., Lachkar, A.: Formal concept analysis for arabic web search results clustering. J. King Saud Univ.-Comput. Inf. Sci. **29**, 196–203 (2017)
19. Osiński, S., Stefanowski, J., Weiss, D.: Lingo: search results clustering algorithm based on singular value decomposition. In: Intelligent Information Processing and Web Mining, pp. 359–368, Springer (2004)
20. Carpineto, C., Mizzaro, S., Romano, G., Snidero, M.: Mobile information retrieval with search results clustering: prototypes and evaluations. J. Am. Soc. Inf. Sci. Technol. **60**, 877–895 (2009)
21. Navigli, R., Crisafulli, G.: Inducing word senses to improve web search result clustering. In: Proceedings of the 2010 Conference on Empirical Methods in Natural Language Processing, pp. 116–126 (2010)
22. Lv, Y., Zhai, C.: Positional relevance model for pseudo-relevance feedback. In: ACM SIGIR, pp. 579–586 (2010)
23. Salhi, H., Jarrar, R., Yahya, A.: Search Arabic Search Results Disambiguation Dataset. Fada: Birzeit University Repository, August 2019. https://fada.birzeit.edu/

24. Caliński, T., Harabasz, J.: A dendrite method for cluster analysis. Commun. Stat.-Theor. and Meth. **3**, 1–27 (1974)
25. Aggarwal, C., Zhai, C.: A survey of text clustering algorithms. In: Aggarwal, C., Zhai, C. (eds.) Mining text data, pp. 77–128. Springer, Boston (2012). https://doi.org/10.1007/978-1-4614-3223-4_4
26. Manning, C., Schütze, H.: Foundations of Statistical Natural Language Processing. MIT Press, Cambridge (1999)
27. Hall, M., Frank, E., Holmes, G., Pfahringer, B., Reutemann, P., Witten, I.: The WEKA data mining software: an update. SIGKDD Explorations **11**, 10–18 (2009)

An Arabic Corpus of Fake News: Collection, Analysis and Classification

Maysoon Alkhair[1]([⊠]), Karima Meftouh[2]([⊠]), Kamel Smaïli[3]([⊠]),
and Nouha Othman[4]([⊠])

[1] Sudan University of Science and Technology, Khartoum, Sudan
maysoonalkhier111@gmail.com
[2] University Badji Mokhtar, Annba, Algeria
k.meftouh@gmail.com
[3] LORIA, University of Lorraine, 54600 Nancy, France
smaili@loria.fr
[4] LARODEC, University of Tunis, Tunis, Tunisia
othmannouha@gmail.com

Abstract. Over the last years, with the explosive growth of social media, huge amounts of rumors have been rapidly spread on the internet. Indeed, the proliferation of malicious misinformation and nasty rumors in social media can have harmful effects on individuals and society. In this paper, we investigate the content of the fake news in the Arabic world through the information posted on YouTube. Our contribution is threefold. First, we introduce a novel Arab corpus for the task of fake news analysis, covering the topics most concerned by rumors. We describe the corpus and the data collection process in detail. Second, we present several exploratory analysis on the harvested data in order to retrieve some useful knowledge about the transmission of rumors for the studied topics. Third, we test the possibility of discrimination between rumor and no rumor comments using three machine learning classifiers namely, Support Vector Machine (SVM), Decision Tree (DT) and Multinomial Naïve Bayes (MNB).

Keywords: Rumors · Classifiers · Fake news corpus · Text analysis

1 Introduction

Social networks such as Facebook, Twitter, Google+ and YouTube have become popular channels of communication where people can express different attitudes and opinions [5]. Consequently, a vast volume of reviews and comments has been created in the last years in social networks. Obviously, anyone can express his opinion and related information, which leads to accumulation of a huge amount of unverified information [2]. This issue was widely studied by the NLP community with a view to differentiating between a rumor (or fake news) and a proven information.

K. Smaïli (Ed.): ICALP 2019, CCIS 1108, pp. 292–302, 2019.
https://doi.org/10.1007/978-3-030-32959-4_21

Researchers proposed automated or semi-automated approaches which can effectively help in handling and analyzing the tremendous amount of social network data. Recently, there has been much focus on the veracity of the information by studying and proposing algorithms in order to automatically detect rumors in social networks. However, most works analyze and measure the rumor only after its diffusion. The issue is that there is an important gap between its diffusion and its streaming detection. This can lead to a damaging effect on the social or political events of a country or even the world. The speed at which the breaking news is growing on the Internet does not allow enough time to check the information [8]. In order to analyse the rumors, the data are often extracted from Twitter, Facebook or YouTube [3, 18]. In fact, it is easier to spread a rumor in social networks since almost everything could be published.

Unlike most existing works which focus on identifying the rumors when they arise, in this paper, we investigate the content of the fake news in the Arabic world through the information posted on YouTube. The main objective of this work is to crawl Arabic rumors in order to build a corpus that we will share with the international community. We focused on three proven fake news concerning the death of personalities. We selected the death rumors of the following Arab celebrities: the dancer Fifi Abdou, the president Bouteflika and the comedian Adel Imam.

The remainder of this paper is structured as follows: in Sect. 2, we present related work on rumors analysis and rumors extraction. Then we give an overview of the rumors we collected and the way we categorize them. Thereafter, we give details about the collected corpus in Sect. 3. Several statistical analysis are described in Sect. 4. In Sect. 5, we present some results of machine learning classification algorithms and finally we conclude and outline some possible future works.

2   Related Work

In this section, we provide an overview of research into social media rumours with the focus on two crucial tasks namely, rumors extraction and analysis.

The comparability methods were widely used to identify similar data related to same rumors when the dataset is collected.

Authors in [11] investigated how rumors are arising, spreading in different ways and broadcasting quickly to a large number of audiences. In [9], the authors proposed a statistical approach that uses 3 features extracted from the microblogs, the Hashtags and URLs. They showed the effectiveness of these features in identifying disinformers and those who believe and spread the rumors. They annotated a dataset of 10K tweets collected on 5 different controversial topics.

The authors in [1] proposed methods for assessing the credibility of certain tweets. They analyzed microblog posts and classified them as credible or not credible, based on some features extracted from the tweets. An example of the used feature is the number of retweeting performed by a user. They evaluated their methods subjectively and remarked that credible news are propagated through authors that have previously written a large number of messages.

The authors in [4] suggested determining whether or not a given text is a rumor by using web mining algorithms and linguistic rules. They evaluated their approach on customer reviews which constitutes a good framework of possible disinformation.

In [6], an approach was proposed to capture the temporal evolution of the features of the microblogs based on the time series that model the social context information. The approach showed significant performance and has proven to be able to detect rumors at early stage after their initial broadcast.

Tolosi et al. [15] studied the challenges concerning the detection of the tweets that are likely to become rumors. In their work, the classifier used several features such as the user id, the user profile, the text style and the URL domains. The given classifier achieved an F1-score of 65%.

The authors in [17] introduced a novel approach to detect rumors that takes advantage of the sequential dynamics of publishing information during breakthroughs in social media. They employed Twitter datasets collected from five news stories. The classifier was based on Conditional Random Fields and exploited the context learned in a rumor detection event, which they compared to the rumor detection system at the same time.

3   Corpus

In the following, we will describe the methodology we followed to collect the necessary data for this research work. The Fig. 1 illustrates the overall steps. The details concerning each of them will be given in the next subsections.

3.1   Data Collection

To build the corpus, we harvested the data using the YouTube API which allows to search for all the videos that match certain criteria and retrieve all the related comments. In order to increase our chance to get data in which we get fake news, we selected the topic of *Personalities death*. In fact, a lot of rumors in Internet concern the death of singers, actors, presidents, etc. That is why, in this work we selected three famous people in the Arab world who are mostly concerned by rumors: Fifi Abdu (an Egyptian dancer), Abdelaziz Bouteflika (the former Algerian president) and Adel Imam (an Egyptian comedian). Obviously, retrieving comments from YouTube by using Hashtags related to these three personalities will capture comments corresponding to rumors and no rumors. Therefore, when these data were collected, we used a set of relevant keywords concerning rumors (Fifi died, Allah yarhemak, True news, Algerian president dies, Bouteflika death, yes death, adel imam dies, Allah yerhamo, Adel die). If any comment contains one of these keywords, it will be considered as a rumor comment and it is saved in a rumor dataset, otherwise, it will be saved in the no-rumor subset. Table 1 shows some statistics of the harvested data, where $|C|$ indicates the number of comments for each topic.

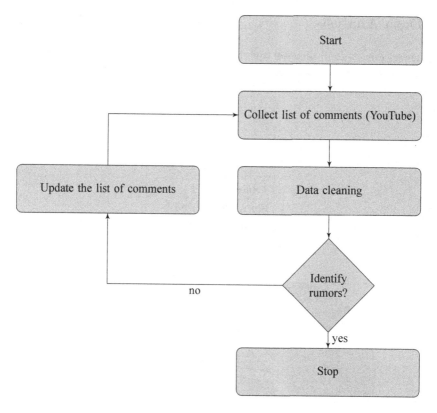

Fig. 1. Overview of the approach of collecting the rumors dataset

Table 1. The collected stories related to Fifi abdo, Bouteflika and Adel Imam.

Topics	$|c|$
Fifi Abdo	2,363
Bouteflika	1,216
Adel Imam	500

3.2 Data Cleaning

In order to have a relevant analysis and develop a robust classifier, we first need to clean the data. Data cleaning is an important step in major NLP tasks to improve the quality of text data and ensure the reliability of the statistical analysis. Our cleaning step aims to filter the rumors and extract the useful terms. To this end, we removed from the collected data the special characters such as: $\{*, @, \%, \&...\}$. We also removed URL links, words in foreign languages, duplicated comments, etc. Table 2 gives the updated statistics about the collected corpus. It shows that the total size of the dataset has been reduced by around 20% after the cleaning process.

4   Data Analysis

In this section, we will analyze our dataset in order to retrieve some knowledge about the transmission of rumors for the three studied topics. In Fig. 2, we give the distribution of the vocabulary of this dataset in accordance to the three topics.

Table 2. The collected stories related to Fifi abdo, Bouteflika and Adel Imam after the data cleaning step

Topics	$|c|$
Fifi Abdo	2,145
Bouteflika	964
Adel Imam	326

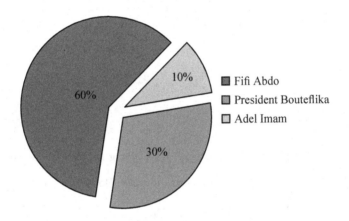

Fig. 2. Distribution of the vocabulary

We remark that, with this approach of collecting data related to rumors, we harvested more data concerning the death of Fifi Abdo than for the two others even, if the second personality was the President of a country. This is probably due to the fact that the dancer *Fifi Abdo* interests more people than the President Bouteflika and more than the famous actor *Adel Imam*.

Tables 3 and 4 show that the Internet users posted more comments on the topic of *Fifi Abdo* whether rumors or no rumors which confirms that people are more interested by this personality than the two others. In Table 4, we remark that the number of comments about *Fifi Abdo* which are not supposed to be rumors are twice as much as for the topic *President Bouteflika*.

Where $|c|$ represents the number of comments and $|W|$ the number of words.

In Fig. 3, we give the distribution of the rumors through the period of the data collection. Even if this corpus is small, we can mention that a rumor can subsist

Table 3. Statistics corresponding to the rumors dataset.

Topic	$|C|$	$|W|$
Fifi Abdo	187	1605
President Bouteflika	106	3507
Adel Imam	50	508

for several years such as for the one concerning *Fifi Abdo* or several months such as those concerning *Bouteflika* or *Adel Imam*. It would be interesting in a future work, to find the correlation between the spreading of the rumor and external events that induce the rumor.

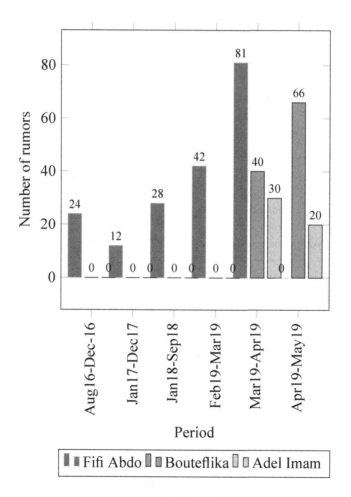

Fig. 3. Distribution of the rumors

Table 4. Statistics corresponding to the No rumors dataset

Topic	$|C|$	$|W|$
Fifi Abdo	1958	22708
President Bouteflika	858	11917
Adel Imam	276	3085

We analyze the collected data to learn and understand what characterizes the messages conveying rumors. In Table 5, we give some samples from the corpus we collected automatically. For each rumor or no rumor sentence, we give its translation. These samples show clearly that the collected data concern rumors. In Table 6, we listed the most significant words corresponding to the dataset of rumors. The most used word is الله (*God*). As these are rumors about death, Muslims come back to God and beg forgiveness for the deceased. This explains the existence of this word in a significant way. The words related to the death are in the top list (ماتت ,مات). As these rumors become truths for certain people, some people believe in them and even ask God to be merciful with the dead, which explains why we found the terms: يرحمو, يرحمها ,يرحمك.

Table 5. Some examples of the collected data

Topic	Examples	
	Rumor	**Non Rumor**
Fifi Abdo	فيفي عبدو ماتت (Fifi abdo is died)	خبر كاذب (Fake news)
	الله يرحمك يا فوفو (May God have mercy on you Fufu)	فيفي عبدو عايشة زي القردة (Fifi is alive as a monkey)
Bouteflika	بوتفليقة مات في 2015 وصرحوا بها في سويسرا (Bouteflika died since 2015 they announced it in Switzerland)	كذابين بوتفليقة ماماتش ناس تزرع في الفتنة (Bouteflika is not dead people want to spread sedition)
	الله يرحم رئسنا (May God have mercy on our President)	كذابة راهو حي (You are a liar he is alive)
Adel Imam	الله يرحمو مات عادل (May God have mercy on him Adel died)	عادل امام عايش كذاب انت (Adel Imam is alive you are a liar)
	صحيح مات بعملية بواسر (True he died after an operation of hemorrhoids)	الفنان عادل امام مامتش دول بيعملوا كذا عاشان يلمو ليكات (The artist Adel Imam is not dead they do this to get "like(s)")

If we analyze the corpus of no rumors (see Table 7), we also find the reference to the word God. Consequently, in the Arab world, this word could not be discriminating to identify rumor texts. However, we find numerous proper names corresponding to the studied topics: فيفي, عبدو and بوتفليقة. Negation terms alone

Table 6. Most frequent words in the rumor dataset

Word	الله	مات	ماتت	يرحمو	بوتفليقة	ربى	يرحمها	فيفي	يرحمك	ربنا	عادل
Trans	God	Died	she died	have mercy	Bouteflika	My God	mercy on her	Fifi	mercy on your soul	our God	Adel
Count	201	75	64	63	48	42	31	24	20	19	9

or agglutinated to verbs are present in the top list of words. They invalidate an event, namely the death of the personalities, this is the case of the words: مش and مامات. We also found the antonym of the word *death*: حي, which indicates that the person is alive. The corpus also contains the word *lie* that indicates that the message or the event we talked about is fake. The above mentioned words seem to be discriminating for these topics.

Table 7. Most frequent words in the non-rumor dataset

Word	الله	ربنا	فيفي	عبدو	بوتفليقة	مش	يشفيها	حي	مامات	عادل	كذب
Trans	God	Our God	Fifi	Abdo	Bouteflika	not	heals her	alive	he is not died	Adel	lie
Count	914	305	207	118	114	108	89	89	64	31	34

5 Classification

In order to test the possibility of discrimination between rumor and no rumor comments, three data classification methods have been conducted in this work: Decision Tree (DT), Multinomial Naïve Bayes (MNB) and Support Vector Machine (SVM).

The Decision Tree classifier is a supervised machine learning technique where the data is recursively split according to the different attributes of the dataset. The leaves constitute the decisions and the nodes correspond to the area where data are split [10].

The principle of SVM [16] consists in looking for the optimal linear separating hyperplane that separates the data of one class from the other. SVMs aim to define the optimal boundary separating classes in feature space. The best hyperplane is the one that maximizes the distance between classes. The classification of new data is based on which side of the boundary the data is placed. In our case, we picked out a linear kernel for the separation.

Naïve Bayes classifiers are widely used in different applications in natural language processing and particularly in text classification [7,12,14] due to their efficiency and their acceptable predictive performance. MNB estimates the conditional probability of a particular term given a class as the relative frequency of the term t in all documents belonging to the class C. To train the MNB classifier, we used 1-gram, 2-gram and 3-gram of words as features supported by a TFIDF vector scores [13].

We performed few experiments and evaluated the classifiers with the most widely used measures in Information retrieval namely, Recall, Precision and Accuracy. Their corresponding formulas are recalled respectively in 1, 2 and 3:

$$Recall = \frac{tp}{tp + fn} \qquad (1)$$

$$Precision = \frac{tp}{tp + fp} \qquad (2)$$

$$Accuracy = \frac{tp + tn}{tp + tn + fp + fn} \qquad (3)$$

where tp, tn, fp and fn are True Positive[1], True Negative[2], False Positive[3] and False Negative[4] respectively.

Table 8. Performance on detecting rumors

Topic	SVM			D. Tree			MNB		
	Acc	Prec	Rec	Acc	Prec	Rec	Acc	Prec	Rec
Fifi Abdo	**95.35**	**87.72**	82.16	93.59	79.94	**82.8**	92.63	78.01	73.42
Bouteflika	94.2	92.69	78.18	**95.56**	**94.09**	**83.9**	93.86	90.7	77.99
Adel Imam	**93.68**	**85.2**	78.82	89.47	73.15	**80.88**	90.53	74.87	72.65
Combi	**95.35**	**92.77**	83.12	93.47	84.07	**83.56**	92.38	82.76	76.94

In Table 8, we reported the results of the three classifiers. The training was done on 70% of the data and the test on the remaining subset of the corpus. We conducted two kinds of tests. The first one has been done on each rumor topic and the second one, on the mixture of all the topic rumors. We observed that the achieved performance varies depending on the rumor topic and the used classifier. The best accuracy and the best Precision for Fifi Abdo are obtained by the SVM classifier while the best recall is achieved by the decision tree. For the rumors concerning the president Bouteflika, the best results whatever the measure are produced by the decision Tree. For the third rumor topic, the best accuracy and the best precision are achieved by the SVM, while the best recall is the one of the decision tree. When all the rumor topics are mixed, the best results in terms of accuracy and precision are obtained by the SVM and the best recall is achieved by the decision tree. Overall, for this dataset, the best classifier is the SVM one, while the MNB has not succeeded to outperform the

---

[1] Case was positive and predicted positive.
[2] Case was negative and predicted negative.
[3] Case was negative but predicted positive.
[4] Case was positive but predicted negative.

other classifiers, in spite of its effectiveness in other classification applications, for any of the topics. This is probably due the fact that the MNB requires the use of more detailed features.

6   Conclusion

In this paper, we introduced a new Arabic corpus of fake news that we will make publicly available for research purposes. We detailed the collection process and gave important details about the harvested data on the subject of the death of three Arab celebrities. An exploratory analysis was carried out on the collected fake news to learn some features which characterize the messages conveying rumors such as, the frequent use of certain words. The classification task was performed using three classification methods namely Support Vector Machine (SVM) Decision Tree (DT) and Multinomial Naïve Bayes (MNB) to test the possibility of discrimination between rumor and no rumor comments. We witnessed that the achieved performance varies depending on the rumor topic and the used classifier. In the future, we look forward investigating the performance of other classification methods and also envisage enlarging our corpus by collecting more examples in various topics and performing a deep analysis on the data. One of our objective is to tackle the issue of detecting the rumors or the source of the rumors as soon as they arise.

References

1. Castillo, C., Mendoza, M., Poblete, B.: Information credibility on Twitter. In: Proceedings of the 20th International Conference on World Wide Web, pp. 675–684. ACM (2011)
2. Chomsky, N., Herman, E.: A Propaganda Model. Manufacturing Consent: the Political Economy of the Mass Media, 2nd edn, pp. 1–35. Pantheon Books, New York (2002)
3. Friggeri, A., Adamic, L.A., Eckles, D., Cheng, J.: Rumor cascades. In: ICWSM (2014)
4. Galitsky, B.: Detecting rumor and disinformation by web mining. In: 2015 AAAI Spring Symposium Series (2015)
5. Lazer, D., et al.: Life in the network: the coming age of computational social science. Science **323**(5915), 721 (2009). (New York, NY)
6. Ma, J., Gao, W., Wei, Z., Lu, Y., Wong, K.F.: Detect rumors using time series of social context information on microblogging websites. In: Proceedings of the 24th ACM International on Conference on Information and Knowledge Management, pp. 1751–1754. ACM (2015)
7. McCallum, A., Nigam, K., et al.: A comparison of event models for naive Bayes text classification. In: AAAI-98 Workshop on Learning for Text Categorization, vol. 752, pp. 41–48. Citeseer (1998)
8. Procter, R., Crump, J., Karstedt, S., Voss, A., Cantijoch, M.: Reading the riots: what were the police doing on twitter? Polic. Soc. **23**(4), 413–436 (2013)

9. Qazvinian, V., Rosengren, E., Radev, D.R., Mei, Q.: Rumor has it: Identifying misinformation in microblogs. In: Proceedings of the Conference on Empirical Methods in Natural Language Processing, pp. 1589–1599. Association for Computational Linguistics (2011)

10. Quinlan, J.R.: Learning decision tree classifiers. ACM Comput. Surv. **28**(1), 71–72 (1996)

11. Ratkiewicz, J., et al.: Detecting and tracking the spread of astroturf memes in microblog streams. arXiv preprint arXiv:1011.3768 (2010)

12. Rish, I., et al.: An empirical study of the naive Bayes classifier. In: IJCAI 2001 workshop on empirical methods in artificial intelligence, vol. 3, pp. 41–46 (2001)

13. Spärck Jones, K.: A statistical interpretation of term specificity and its application in retrieval. J. Doc. **28**, 11–21 (1972)

14. Su, J., Shirab, J.S., Matwin, S.: Large scale text classification using semi-supervised multinomial naive Bayes. In: Proceedings of the 28th International Conference on Machine Learning (ICML-11), pp. 97–104. Citeseer (2011)

15. Tolosi, L., Tagarev, A., Georgiev, G.: An analysis of event-agnostic features for rumour classification in Twitter. In: Tenth International AAAI Conference on Web and Social Media (2016)

16. Vapnik, V.: Statistical Learning Theory. Wiley, New York (1998)

17. Zubiaga, A., Liakata, M., Procter, R.: Learning reporting dynamics during breaking news for rumour detection in social media. arXiv preprint arXiv:1610.07363 (2016)

18. Zubiaga, A., Liakata, M., Procter, R., Hoi, G.W.S., Tolmie, P.: Analysing how people orient to and spread rumours in social media by looking at conversational threads. PLoS ONE **11**(3), e0150989 (2016)

Author Index